LOVE, SIN

&

SURVIVAL

THREE WOMEN IN
1930'S UTAH

BY
LAVON B. CARROLL

LOVE, SIN, & SURVIVAL: *Three Women in 1930s Utah*
By: LaVon B. Carroll

This is a work of fiction based on real life events. All names have been changed.

ISBN: 1-888106-94-8

LCCN: 99-60983

Cover Design: John Barnhill
Cover Drawings: Annette Trunnell

This novel won first place in fiction from the League of Utah Writers, 1989. The author expresses appreciation to the League of Utah Writers for their encouragement.

Printed in the United States of America by

Agreka™ Books

800 360-5284
www.agreka.com

Dedication

To the memory of my beloved grandmother
Ada Jane Mellor Adams
And all the loving family to whom I owe so much

Main Characters

Laurence Kent–Torn between what is expected of him as a Mormon man, and his deep desire for a promising musical career, Laurence marries Irene and enters the sheep business with his brother-in-law to make his fortune. As the Depression takes hold, he sees financial ruin is near.

Irene Kent–A woman of extraordinary beauty fits comfortably into the role of wife and mother, as defined by her culture. Suddenly widowed, Irene begins the painful journey of learning that her entire identify has been based on the love of a man. Struggling painfully with single life, Irene falls in love with Ed Barker and her entire belief system is challenged.

Ed Barker–A personable, middle-aged, traveling salesman, he is married to the boss's invalid, spoiled daughter. His life and marriage are at a dead end when he unexpectedly meets Irene Kent.

Clinton Maxwell–An artistic young man back home from Denver, Clinton struggles with the confining small town atmosphere of Merritsville. He focuses his designer talents on Irene, and turns her into a stunningly modern woman.

Ellen Kent–Irene's daughter watches her mother's struggle, and observes and evaluates the culture and lives of her family and fellow townspeople. She grows into young womanhood critically examining time-honored beliefs versus her deep desire to forge a different life for herself as a woman.

Simone Hamilton–She moves to Merritsville with her strange family. Simone both fascinates and repels Ellen. A completely uninhibited and daring Simone draws Ellen into new and frightening experiences.

Addie Kent–Mother-in-law to Irene and grandmother to Ellen, she is a wise, kind, and strong widow, a woman of faith and endurance. Addie is the center of all her families' lives.

Doris Kent Walker–Aunt Dosey is a typical Mormon woman whose entire focus is her large family and the many positions she holds in church. She and her husband struggle to cope with the loss of their business and livelihood. Kind, cheerful, and generous, she provides encouragement to Irene, her sister-in-law, as long as she can.

Everett Gordon–Son of a prominent family, his unfulfilled great music and literary talent drive him to despair and drink. The close mentoring relationship he had with Ellen's talented father Laurence transfers to Ellen as he sees these talents within her.

Ferrin Hallsworth–The physically handicapped son of a rough, wealthy rancher, Ferrin is handsome, intelligent, and kind. Ferrin falls in love with Ellen and hungers for the rich family life she takes for granted.

PART ONE

CB

December of 1930 was very cold and bleak in Merritsville, Utah. The snow had not been deep but the spell of freezing weather had lasted for more than a month. It had been hard for Irene Kent whose husband Laurence was herding sheep on the far western hills. Alone with her daughter Ellen, she was able to keep a fire only in the kitchen of the small frame house several blocks off main street.

This evening, two weeks before Christmas, Irene was in the rocking chair close to the stove crocheting edges for pillow cases. In her early thirties, with a handsome figure and beautiful face, she wore her chestnut brown hair in a glossy coronet of braids. Deep blue-grey eyes were fringed with dark lashes that cast shadows on her fair skin. Her fine hands, those of a pianist, worked the lace design gracefully.

Ellen sat at the kitchen table cutting out decorations for Christmas. She did not look like her mother. At nine-going-on-ten, she was small, slightly plump with a round face and a pert nose on which there was a sprinkling of freckles. Her mouth had a certain determined set indicating a strong will. Straight light brown hair with a reddish tinge was cut in bangs across her forehead. Light lashes and brows framed greenish-grey eyes; people said she favored her grandmother Addie.

"Mama, can I read to you now?" Ellen asked. She liked to read her school books to Irene who was not always interested in the childish stories, but liked to hear Ellen read aloud.

She nodded. "Come over here where it's warmer and I can hear better," indicating the little chair beside her.

Ellen settled herself happily. Already in fourth grade, she was reading sixth and seventh grade books, when she could get them from the library. She read in a clear, precise voice.

Irene was not much of a reader herself. "She gets it from her father," she explained to people who praised Ellen, not understanding how anyone could find so much pleasure in the printed page. She herself read the church publications and other church literature as well as women's magazines like *The Woman's Home Companion* chiefly for dress patterns, recipes, and decorating hints. Women were discouraged from reading fiction–novels and frivolous love stories. Their hands were always supposed to be busy with useful work.

Her favorite magazine was *Finer Homes* of which she saved a stack on top of the Hoover cabinet. When she was "blue" about Laurence being away from home so much at the sheep herd, she poured over magazines of beautiful homes, dreaming of the fine house they were going to build if the sheep business prospered.

Although more than a year had passed since the big Stock Market crash, threatening a wide depression, the full impact of it had not reached Merritsville. Irene knew things were not going as well as they had hoped, but Laurence never talked about business to her. Tonight, although a little downhearted, she was still sure things were going to be all right. The fire snapped and sighed; the kettle rocked on the warped stove lid, and she and Ellen were still comfortable and safe.

At nine o'clock, she folded her crocheting neatly and Ellen put away her book. Irene checked the stove, put out kindling for the morning fire, then filled a hot water bottle from the kettle. Hurrying into the bedroom, she tucked it into the bottom of the icy bed. While the bed was warming, they got into long flannel night gowns, then rushed into bed, cuddling together like "spoons" under heavy covers until the heat of their bodies created a cavern of warmth.

Ellen slept in her mother's arms or curled at her back. Long after, she would remember this time as one of happiness that belonged to another world, a world in which everything was right. She would recall the fragrance and silkiness of her mother's hair, the softness of her arms, the tenderness of her embrace.

This was before the beginning of the Great Depression had deepened into stark tragedy for them and many others.

Blue winter light awakened them; the walls glistened with frost and their breath made clouds of "smoke." Irene got the fire going while Ellen wrapped her arms about herself and kept warm until

Irene came shivering back to bed. When the fire had time to warm the kitchen, they ventured out. Irene started the oatmeal mush simmering on the stove and then they faced the really big problem of the morning–the race to the outdoor toilet where they brushed snow off the seat. Poising themselves cautiously above the sharp coating of ice crystals, they got the chore over as quickly as possible. Teeth chattering, but laughing, they raced each other to the house.

Irene longed and planned for the day when they would have an indoor bathroom. She had been used to one at Aunt Delia's and this was a real hardship to her fastidious nature, but marrying as young as she and Laurence had, they were not able to afford a house with indoor plumbing. Few houses in Merritsville had it, but against the day when they could build their dream house, she collected pink towels and washcloths and crocheted lace edges on them. Ellen thought the nearest they could come to the Celestial Kingdom–a Mormon's highest goal for heaven–was an indoor bathroom.

Although the day seemed frozen into one solid, cold chunk, time moved across the big Washburn calendar that hung on the kitchen wall. Every day when Ellen came home from school, she marked off another day, depositing a new Christmasy item on the table–cutouts of bells, stars, trees, sleighs, and Santa Claus. Irene hung them on the walls and cupboard doors and the room began to take on a bright holiday atmosphere.

Irene had moved her sewing machine into the kitchen and was busy all day on gifts that she carefully hid before Ellen came home. But as the days grew closer to Christmas, she became more nervous; sometimes she was even impatient with Ellen. Every night she would look longingly toward the western hills as she moved the red and pink geraniums in camouflaged coffee cans and pulled down the blinds. In the morning when she raised them, she would peer through the dazzling frost pictures as though she might penetrate the cold distance between her and her husband. But she said very little to Ellen; she was never very good at talking about her feelings.

One night as they were finishing the dishes, Ellen, who could feel her mother's mood, asked, "Will Daddy come home for Christmas?"

Irene burst into tears. Ellen put her arms around her and they held each other, crying together. Finally Irene dried their tears, "It's no use to cry, Honey. It's the way Daddy makes our living and we have to put up with it, that's all."

"But couldn't the sheep stay alone for just a little while, just for Christmas?" Ellen pursued.

"No, the old things can't stay alone a minute. They wander off and coyotes get them."

"Then, maybe we could go to the sheep camp and have Christmas with him."

Irene smiled. "I guess that would be a fine Christmas," she said as she put the dishes in the cupboard. "Maybe Uncle Aaron will take a turn and let him come home. He's been out longer this time."

The idea cheered them. Irene got out her crocheting and Ellen her book and they settled down for the long winter evening.

☙

"Mama, what is a depression?" asked Ellen Kent. She had just come home from school and taken off her galoshes on the back porch, standing them neatly together as her mother had taught her. Putting her books on the wash stand, she removed her brown coat, trying to untangle the string that ran through her sleeves to keep her mittens together.

Irene Kent, poking at the coals in the kitchen stove, looked at her daughter with surprise and faint annoyance. Lately Ellen was in the habit of troubling her with questions she couldn't answer and didn't want to think about.

"Why... what makes you ask that? Did you have a good day at school?" She shook some coal from the scuttle into the fire box. "My goodness that's nearly the last of the coal. I'll have to see Aaron tomorrow about some more. Here, don't pull so hard on that string, you'll break it." She helped Ellen the rest of the way out of her winter things and hung the coat on a peg behind the door.

"Hal says we're gonna have a big depression and we're all gonna starve to death. He says...."

"Oh, that Hal," Irene burst out impatiently, "He's always trying to stir up trouble. I don't know what Dosey's going to do with him."

There was such a worried, earnest look on Ellen's small, round face that Irene forced a smile and patted her cheek reassuringly.

"I don't think Hal knows much about it," she soothed.

"But Miss Hunter says there are lots of people out of work in the East and starving and it's coming here."

"I don't know anything about that," Irene evaded. She didn't read any newspaper but the Merritsville *Guardian*; she hastened to do the thing that seemed most natural to her in a disturbing situation–feed someone or clean something. "Do you want a piece of bread and jam?" She was already slicing a fragrant loaf of newly baked bread, spreading it with butter and apricot jam. "Grandma brought this jam over today. Maybe Daddy can tell you about it when he gets home," she added thoughtfully. Laurence could always explain things like that.

Ellen sat down resignedly at the table by the west window. Something was happening between her and her mother; every time she wanted to talk about grown-up things, Irene got nervous and changed the subject.

Her mother brought the "piece" over to the table on a little dish to keep the crumbs from messing up the table. With a troubled, almost angry look on her face, she began to poke about the geranium plants in the window sill above the table.

Years after, Ellen would think of her mother in this time of her life like the rustic flowers. They had a certain fragility combined with hardiness–lacy, pink and red blossoms on thick stalks, with scalloped leaves that tasted like lemon when she bit them secretly. They provided a romantic grace to humble homes.

Irene touched the blossoms lovingly, broke off a few dead leaves and shifted the pots. They seemed to restore her spirits, to remove her from the immediate moment. This irritated Ellen who, with a willful perverseness, continued to prod her mother.

"Did you ask Uncle Aaron today if Daddy is coming home for Christmas?"

The frown deepened on Irene's brow. "I don't know, Aaron wouldn't say." She moved one of the geranium cans a little and gazed out toward the western hills where the red winter sun hung sulkily in a dirty cloud. It looked like a storm might be coming; out there somewhere her husband was alone on the frozen winter range with a herd of dull, gray sheep. How she wished he were home; life and Ellen were becoming more than she could cope with alone.

"I wish Daddy didn't have to be away so much," Ellen spoke with the faintest, unconscious malice what she surmised was her mother's thoughts as she gazed so achingly into the murky evening. Tears started to Irene's eyes and she turned away from the window, moving toward the stove to hide them from Ellen. It had been a long, dreary day; ordinarily she was an even tempered woman who kept her spirits up by thinking of other things: the happy past, the bright future they had been promised these recent years. But today had been longer than usual and she had given in to the "blues," noticing the ache for Laurence in her body and spirit more intensely. And now Ellen was on one of her "streaks." It seemed at times that she just wanted to torment. Irene wished sometimes that she wouldn't go around to the Walkers after school even though they were family and so close. Lately Hal was always tormenting the girls and upsetting them with some wild story. Ellen took things much too seriously, like this depression thing....

The truth of the matter was that Irene had begun to feel a strange anxiety. Never one to concern herself with affairs of men, politics, business, still she had been hearing rumors about the crash. She had heard about the stock market last year but had only the foggiest notion of what it meant. "Stock" had always meant animals to her, "livestock," like the ones from which they made their living. She had had a funny vision of cows, sheep, pigs crashing through an old pole fence but she didn't dare mention it to anyone. She was used to leaving things to Laurence and the authorities of the church. Recently there had been mention of the depression in the Fast and Testimony meetings. The old men who were always talking about gloomy prophesies said it was the Lord's anger with our wicked ways. She tried not to listen to them too much since they could always find something to be depressing about; she knew they would run things to suit themselves. The Lord would take care of them.

Yet there were troubling things. Although nothing had changed noticeably in Merritsville in the year since there had been a fuss about the stock market crash, there were small signs that disturbed her world. Laurence and Aaron had to let Parley Mack, their hired herder, go; that was why they had to take longer turns at the herd, why this winter had been harder for her. With Parley to spell them, it had been possible for Laurence to spend more time at home, and he had often talked about how they would be able to expand the business and hire even more herders. Then they would be able to run the business pretty much from town like the other big Sheep Men. He hadn't mentioned that lately, had never said in so many words why they had let Parley go, just something about "expenses," but she guessed all was not going well.

Irene wiped her tears away; she knew she had to keep hold of herself. Ellen had just touched a raw nerve with her obstinacy that she couldn't really understand.

Ellen finished her snack and carried the dish to the kitchen cupboard. She knew that she had finally got at her mother and she felt uneasy and guilty in spite of her success. She didn't know what to do; it was too late and cold to go out to Grandma's as she usually did when things didn't go right at home. The other rooms were chilly and dark, so she got her school books out and hunched up on a kitchen chair with her foot hooked around a rung. She held the book close to her face so that she had to keep sweeping her brown bangs out of her eyes to see. Something was happening to her eyes so that she could only see close-up, but she was afraid to tell anybody.

Irene busied herself about the kitchen looking at Ellen huddled there with a feeling of love and irritation. The child read too much; it was ruining her eyes–if she had to wear glasses it would spoil her looks. Her mind was growing faster than her body and that was frightening in a girl. She might never be able to find a man to take care of her. Irene had wanted a boy first but Laurence was happy with a girl. They had planned to have more children–it was a man and woman's glory in the next world, especially a woman's. She had had several miscarriages but they were still hopeful. After they got the new house, there would be room.

The new house–that was the worst of her fears–the depression or whatever it was that was happening might ruin the dream. It wasn't that she wanted a mansion like those of the Washburns and Cottingtons on the other side of town; just a nice modern brick bungalow with a pink bathroom. Ellen's questions had made her unformed fears seem much more real, much closer.

When Irene was upset she had two main comforts: she could play her piano or clean and straighten. Since the piano was in the cold front room, and she couldn't afford to build a fire in there until Sunday, she had to find something to do. She went over to the Hoover cupboard that stood on the wall opposite the window, a marvelously contrived object with a place for everything she needed. Her cooking utensils were in the bottom cupboard, her embroidered dishtowels in a drawer beneath the kitchen knives and forks and above the bread can. The basic supplies were in the lower part of the upper half and there was a sizable flour bin with a built-in sifter, a special detail that Laurence had insisted upon even though it cost more. Her everyday dishes were in the upper half of the cabinet and the doors had little racks for spices. There was an enamel-coated shelf that pulled out to make a generous work table where she mixed her bread and rolled her excellent pie crust. She liked the cabinet so much that she wasn't sure she could part with it when they got those fancy built-in cupboards in the new house. Working about it now to prepare their simple supper made her feel better and she began to hum, "When there's love at home...." Ellen looked up relieved from her book and smiled.

"I don't think there will be much of a depression," Irene said as she set out the supper plates. "We will always have each other and the family. Grandma Addie has the farm and your daddy can always do something ... if we just live the gospel and trust in the Lord."

"I wonder what other people will do, if it's like Miss Hunter says?" Ellen was eager to reopen the subject seeing that her mother had been thinking about it.

"Oh, for goodness sake," Irene broke off abruptly, "I don't know. Your dad will tell you all about it when he gets here. Stop worrying and come eat. Think about something happy. It's your turn to say the blessing."

Ellen pulled up her chair and, bending over her plate, she squeezed her eyes shut, rattling off the familiar blessing on the food. Hesitating before the "amen" she hastily added, "Please, Father in Heaven, don't let there be a depression, and let Daddy come home for Christmas."

Just before they went to bed, Irene made some cocoa. Ellen watched her mother's hands, stirring the cocoa and pouring it into the steaming cups. The gold band on her left hand glimmered in the pale light. It gave her a warm feeling. It meant that her father and mother had been married in the Temple for all eternity and they would be a family forever: Grandma, dead Grandpa, Aunt Dosey, Uncle Aaron, the Walker cousins, even the Salt Lake cousins. Even though her father was so far away that she could not even imagine the distance, a hundred miles or more, she felt close to him.

"Maybe Daddy's having cocoa in the sheep camp tonight," she ventured. It was a custom when he was home. Irene nodded and patted her cheek lovingly. Whatever the depression was, it seemed a long way away.

CB

About a week before Christmas Uncle Aaron Walker came to the house with a small load of coal, a sack of flour and some other groceries. He brought the flour and groceries into the house and sat down beside the stove where he could spit his chewing tobacco into the coal bucket, much to Irene's distress.

He was a fat man with a handsome ruddy face and a head of black wavy hair. His stomach hung over his faded Levis and strained the buttons on his dingy flannel shirt. He was neither a jolly nor loud man as his appearance might suggest, but there was on his face an expression of imperturbable good nature. It was as though a thick layer of fat had insulated him against the minor irritations of life. He was an incurable optimist, a perpetual "figgerer" as his mother-in-law, Addie Kent, had labeled him. He was always "figgerin'" that tomorrow would correct the mistakes of today. The repeated failure of his incessant figuring to produce the results he most desired–to get rich quick–seemed not to bother him greatly. He was always ready and willing to set out on some new venture that would prove more successful and lucrative than the last, and, like so many in this year, he did not believe in the depression. It was only a temporary slump. The fact that in the previous fall the sheep business in which he and his brother-in-law, Laurence Kent, had invested all their money and eight years of hard, lonely work, had all but failed seemed not to have dawned on him.

He chewed his tobacco, spat into the coal bucket, wiped his mouth on a blue bandanna and cleared his throat.

"Me'n Dosey talked it over last night," he said calmly, rubbing his dry, calloused hands together. "We decided I better let Laurence in for Christmas. I was in last year and I figgered you was gettin' a little lonesome maybe...." He grinned and his gold front tooth shone. Irene, who was standing in front of the stove toying with the lid lifter, looked up in glad surprise; then her face crumpled like wadded tissue paper. Ellen leaped off her high stool and threw her arms about Aaron, kissing him on his unshaven cheek.

"I'd be so glad, Aaron," Irene said in a low strained voice, "I've had the blues so long this cold winter, I...."

"Well, I figger I could go out and stay 'til New Years, then he could take it a bit longer in February. I can't get out much before Christmas, though, might even be Christmas Eve."

"Oh, that would be all right, anything, just so...." Irene clasped her hands together almost like a child; her face glowing. Ellen was so happy she hopped around the table, singing "Jingle Bells" at the top of her voice.

Aaron rose, slightly embarrassed, "Well, I'll be gittin' along. I b'lieve there's enough coal out there to last you through Christmas. You c'n look for 'im most anytime after Thursday."

After the truck had pulled away, Irene burst into tears, covering her face with her hands. Ellen put her arms around her mother's waist and tried to comfort her.

"What's the matter, Mama, aren't you happy Daddy's coming home?" she asked, almost afraid. Suddenly, Irene put her arms around her and hugged her violently, "You just don't know ... you just don't know how happy," she cried.

Irene plunged into her Christmas preparations with feverish energy. She and Addie baked fruit cakes all one day and made dozens of cookies and pans of fudge and divinity. The kitchen table was piled with tissue paper, ribbon and boxes so that they had to pull out the kitchen cabinet leaf to eat on. The roll of music that she had ordered for Laurence came in the mail and she wrapped it in a larger box of an odd shape so that he could never guess what was in it.

All that Ellen wanted for Christmas this year was a lady doll– one with a waist–for which she could make pretty, grown-up clothes like those on the models in Washburn's store or in the catalogues. There was one in the window of the big store on main street, graceful as a fairy, with a beautiful, dreamy face and long blond hair. Ellen dreamed of her day and night–of the scenes from books which they would play out together, of the fine clothes she would make from her mother's and grandmother's scrap bags. She would call her Lady Lillian, and the doll would be like she would be someday when she grew up.

She had pointed the doll out to Irene and her grandmother and talked about it constantly, drawing designs for clothes on brown wrapping paper or the backs of envelopes. When the doll disappeared from the window of Washburn's, she was quite sure that Mama had put her away for Christmas, and she went busily and contentedly about her own Christmas preparations, making gifts for her cousins, mother, father and grandmother.

In all her spare moments Ellen labored on a book of poems and drawings for her father. On the first page, elaborately bordered by crayoned holly, bows, bells and Christmas ornaments was inscribed:

Daddy Dear, it is true
That we love you
When you are away,
We miss you every day.
We hope you will soon
Come home to stay.
Your Loving Daughter, Ellen

When she read it over, as she did several times a day, she had chills of pride and anticipation. How wonderful Christmas time was. How wonderful life was when you were nine years old and your mother was happy and your father was coming home for Christmas.

Two days before Christmas the mercury dropped even lower than before. Ellen and her mother had put all the extra covers on the bed they could find and filled the bottom of the bed with hot bricks, along with the water bottle, but somehow during the night Ellen had got her arm out of the covers. She awoke the morning of Christmas Eve with a numb, burning sensation. The room was filled with blazing white light, and frost glittered like splintered glass on the wallpaper. She looked at her hand and tried to move it; the fingers were white and transparent looking like the light in the room, and she had the strange sensation that she had dissolved into it. Perhaps she had died; she moaned a little and woke her mother. When Irene saw her arm, she cried out with fright and sat up, rubbing it frantically.

"Elly, oh Elly, how did you do it?" she wailed. "It's probably frostbitten, oh Lordy, keep shaking it while I get a fire going. Oh, what'll we do?"

It seemed a very long time before her mother returned. Ellen rubbed and shook her harm in the blistering cold. At last her mother came back, her teeth chattering, and supported her into the kitchen. She ran outdoors in her long flannel gown and brought in a pan of snow with which she rubbed the hand and arm vigorously, and, as soon as the water had warmed a little in the kettle, she dipped Ellen's hand in the warm water. All the while she was shivering and crying. Ellen, half dazed, wondered if her arm would fall off. In the excitement they failed to hear the truck drive into the yard.

Laurence Kent, with a fragrant desert juniper tree on his shoulder, banged at the kitchen door and called loudly, "Anybody up in there?" They both rushed wildly to the door and suddenly it was CHRISTMAS.

Laurence Kent was not a big man and the fact that he was small boned and fine featured made him seem even less suited to the rugged life he led. He had light brown hair parted on one side and combed back into a slight wave. His eyes were blue-gray with sunburned lashes and brows and his skin, which would have been fair under other circumstances, was brick red from the hot suns and harsh winds in which he spent most of his time. But there was an air of strength and confidence about him. His most attractive feature was a well shaped, generous mouth that was set with a certain pride and air of defiance. This contradicted a kind of melancholy shadow that had crept imperceptibly into his eyes this past year. Neither Ellen nor Irene had noticed it yet and he was determined to conceal the worries and pain that he had been trying to face these last, hard months.

Forgetting her aching arm, Ellen flew to him. He had dropped the tree and was already kissing Irene, who laughing and crying, was trying to protect herself from his stiff beard. "Didn't want to take time to shave," he murmured, "Had to get home to you two." He extended one of his arms to take in Ellen who buried her face in his rough coat that smelled of sagebrush and sheep camp.

It was a while before they could settle down for breakfast. Laurence had to hear as much about what had been going on and what they had been doing and thinking as they could tell him in their excitement. Ellen's arm had begun to feel all right, but he examined it lovingly and shook his head with distress.

"We won't have anymore of that; we'll get a stove for that bedroom, you bet." He stroked her hair with tenderness and Ellen thought she would simply burst with love and joy. She loved her mother, but how much more it expanded when her father was there. How right the world was when they were all three together.

The stove was glowing now and the kettle bubbling. Laurence put his coffee pot on, and the room had that very special smell that she associated with him, a sort of outdoorsy, rough smell, that added completeness to the house. Pretty soon it seemed that the kitchen was just too small to contain their joy, so Laurence threw open the front room door and built a fire in the round stove with its shining curved-out skirts in which Ellen laughed at her face stretched out wide and comical. While the room was warming, he made a stand for the juniper tree, and Irene got out the trimming box. They all three trimmed the tree, singing, kissing, hugging and stumbling over each other in a frenzy of happiness.

By afternoon they were all tired out, but Ellen was far too excited to rest, so she ran to Grandma's to tell her that Daddy had got home. Laurence and Irene lay in each other's arms, murmuring words of deep, almost anguished joy.

Grandma came for supper, as happy as anyone that her only son was home where he belonged, and they all four went over to the Ward Christmas Eve program. First there was the sacred pageant in which angels in white nightgowns and tinsel crowns and Wise Men in long bathrobes and colored towels wrapped around their heads hovered about a crude stable above which a big tinfoil star hung on the blue gauze sky. A local Madonna looked tenderly on a well-swaddled doll, and this year there were two real sheep on the stage, courtesy of Aaron Walker. Ellen's cousin Hal, a chubby shepherd in his mother's old blue robe, hung on to their collars nervously. Back stage the choir sang all the old Christmas songs and Bishop Comber read the Christmas story in a solemn voice. Ellen seated between her Grandmother and Father had little prickles of happiness all over as though she were wrapped in tinsel.

After the pageant sleigh bells rang somewhere outside the hall. A delighted shriek arose from the front benches where most of the children were crowded together, and Santa Clause came loping in –ho-ho-hoing and jingling loudly. Ellen knew by now that he was just Brother Bennett dressed up, but she was still as excited as anyone. She marched up happily along with the rest of the children and got her red string bag full of nuts, candy and orange.

Laurence had to shake hands all around among his friends and exchange talk about the state of the sheep business. Ellen was growing very sleepy before they started home. The snow squeaked and crunched as they walked on it and was covered with what looked like a million broken stars, but there were plenty more in the dark blue sky. They all walked close together, each feeling in a deep and wordless way what a magnificent place the world was. They walked Grandma to her gate and then quickly home.

The house was still warm since Laurence had banked the front room fire. The red glow around the isinglass door of the stove reflected in the tinsel and balls on the bushy little tree. The room was full of a strong deserty smell from the juniper tree and Ellen had to draw a deep breath and put her arms tightly about herself to keep from bursting wide open.

Laurence yawned and stretched his arms, "Well, to bed, young lady, or Santa Clause won't come," he threatened.

"Laurence," said Irene quietly as though she had been thinking about it for sometime, "I wish you would play something for us on the violin, a Christmas song. I've missed hearing you so much."

"Please, Daddy," Ellen joined in, glad to postpone bed.

"All right, just one piece. It's been a long day since four o'clock this morning." He went to where his things were still piled in the corner of the kitchen and took the old violin lovingly out of its blue plush-lined case and red flannel sack.

Seated beside the Christmas tree, where the firelight reflected on the smooth, satiny curves of the instrument, he made it sing out "Silent Night, Holy Night." The notes of the music broke over Ellen like a shower of stars; she trembled with pleasure so sharp that it hovered precariously close to sorrow. Afterwards, though she remembered many things about her father, the image that remained closest to her heart was this one of him bending over his violin in the dim Christmas firelight.

☙

The Kent family always got together for Christmas dinner. Even Bertha and her husband and two daughters came down from Salt Lake City on the Interurban. This year the feast was at Dosey's. In the early afternoon Irene, Laurence and Ellen bundled up and walked through the snowy streets to the big house just across the railroad tracks north of the business district of Merritsville.

The morning had been full of delights. In the wintery dawn Lady Lillian was sitting serenely under the juniper tree as though that was exactly where she belonged. She was even lovelier than Ellen had dreamed, slender and gently shaped, she had small perfectly formed hands and dainty feet in little white kid slippers. Her blue glass eyes were lashed with long, thick gold lashes, and her blond hair was real! She was wearing a blue taffeta party dress with a very full skirt; there was a small gold locket around her neck. She was, Ellen thought on that Christmas morning, the most beautiful thing she had ever seen. There were other packages too–two new dresses that Irene had made, books, paper and pencils and watercolors from Grandma and surprise presents from all her cousins.

Laurence and Irene were pleased with their gifts, too. Laurence had fastened a string of pearls around Irene's throat and, kissing her, told her that they were real pearls, not imitation. He was happy with the roll of music that she had so cleverly wrapped. He went to the piano at once and played all the pieces through. Then Irene sat down and tried them. She played the piano and organ, not as well as Laurence, but well enough to accompany him and to be the substitute organist at church. Then he got out his violin and played some more; the house was full of music.

Ellen danced around with Lady Lillian for a while then put on her coat, wrapped up the doll and ran about to her friends' houses, comparing presents and exclaiming over theirs. Everybody had had a good Christmas; there was still credit at the stores and plenty of homemade gifts to which everyone had been accustomed anyway. Irene explained that she had charged the doll at Washburn's and, although it cost more than she ought to have paid, it was all that Ellen had wanted. Laurence kissed her again, assuring her that she had done just right. Things were going to be all right if they could hold on for a year or two. He didn't tell her how deeply he feared that they might not be able to, nor how his mandolin was in a Salt Lake City pawn shop where it had been left in exchange for the pearls she wore around her lovely throat. How right they looked there, he thought as he gazed at her with despairing love. She deserved good things; by God, he would get them for her someday, somehow.

When Irene, Laurence and Ellen arrived at the Walker's, festivities were in full swing. Addie had been there since early morning helping with the puddings and settling the squabbles of the young Walkers. Bertha and Albert had arrived and the two city cousins, Eileen and Darlene, were flaunting their city manners and fashionable clothes in the midst of the happy riot. Ellen, who always felt self-conscious with these cousins, who, it seemed to her, belonged to a strange and superior world, was immediately conscious of the difference between her brown velvet dress cut down from one of her mother's and trimmed with hand-crocheted lace and the crisp, maroon, store-bought taffeta in which Eileen twirled and swirled to show off the flare skirt.

She stood awkwardly holding the doll which she had brought wrapped in an old doll blanket to protect her. The smaller Walkers were crowding around her to see it, and she uncovered Lady Lillian's face carefully. Darlene, who was only a year younger than Ellen, dressed in a red wool suit with pleated skirt and white pique collar that made her, with her blond curls, look much like a doll herself, peeped at the doll disdainfully.

"We decided I was too old for a doll this year," she said primly.

Ellen was suddenly overcome with humiliation and wished she hadn't brought Lady Lillian. She wanted to explain that she only wanted a doll to make grown-up clothes for it and to take part in grown-up dreams, but she could not find the words that she thought Darlene would understand. Her cousin Lorraine, Dosey's oldest girl, came to her rescue.

"I don't think you're too old for dolls if you like 'em," she said. "I know this woman who has millions in a cupboard."

"Oh, well, that's different," insisted Darlene with an air of boredom, smoothing the pleats in her dress.

At that moment Hal Walker, the only big boy in the crowd, came bounding through the room, brandishing a gleaming new gun.

Bang, Bang! Bang! He shot them all with deliberate and cold delight, then coming over to Ellen, he jabbed the gun fiercely in her side.

"C'mon, I'm takin' you in and don't try anythin'."

"I don't want to," Ellen shrugged him away irritably. Ordinarily she loved to play with Hal. She and Hal and Lorraine had been inseparable since they were babies. Dosey and Irene were close friends, even as sisters-in-law, and they had raised these children practically together. At the moment, though, standing there with his round, red, freckled face and unruly, black, curly hair, his lip turned back in an ugly outlaw grimace, he was a fearful stranger to her. She was confused and had not made up her mind what to do about the doll and the city cousins, so she gave Hal a violent push. His face flushed with real anger, and he grabbed the doll from her arms, racing down the hall into one of the back bedrooms.

Ellen, very close to tears, leaped after him, knocking down one of the twins. Hal jumped around the bed, holding the doll above his head so that the exasperated Ellen could not reach it. He laughed with huge delight, now, when she had caught him, switching the doll behind his back. They fell onto the bed rolling and tussling. Ellen lunged and almost succeeded in reaching Lady

Lillian, but Hal threw her backward, cracking her pretty face against the iron bedstead. Ellen screamed in fury, and Irene, Addie, Dosey and Bertha appeared in the doorway all at once.

Hal was standing by the bed with the broken doll in his hand. His round face, a miniature of Aaron's, had settled into a stubborn and guilty look. Ellen was screaming and stomping her feet. Dosey leaped for Hal and began to thump him furiously, while Irene put her arms around Ellen, her face distorted with pity. Addie finally succeed in pulling the unfortunate Hal away from his irate mother and disengaging Ellen from Irene. She pushed the mothers out the door and drew the miserable children together, sitting down on the bed with one of each side of her.

"Now what was this all about?" she demanded sternly.

"He ran away with my doll and smashed her," wailed Ellen.

"She pushed me," Hal muttered.

"Why did you take the doll, Hal?" Grandma asked, wiping Ellen's tears on her apron hem. She put her arm around Hal to draw him closer, but he held himself stiffly, his chubby face averted.

"Dunno, I was just playin', I didn't mean nothin'" he muttered.

"Well, you better say you're sorry to Ellen," Grandma admonished, " Of course I don't want you to think that mends the doll, Hal Walker. Didn't either of you remember that this is the Lord's birthday? This is a fine way to celebrate it, quarreling."

"I ain't sorry." Hall jerked himself away. "I ain't sorry and I hate girls and dolls!" He tore out of the room.

Ellen picked up the doll with the cracked face and looked at her through tears that sparkled and stung. She looked so different. It wasn't only the jagged crack running through the cheek and forehead so that the eye was caved back into the socket; it was something about what the doll had meant, something about the whole day and time that has changed in this last half hour. Perhaps even if Lady Lillian hadn't been broken, she wouldn't have looked quite the same after Darlene had said Ellen was too old for dolls.

"Never mind," said Grandma soothingly, "I think I can fix her almost as good as new."

"But she won't ever be the same again," Ellen said thickly,

and the thought struck her oddly as though she had discovered something new about life.

"No, she won't, but maybe you'll love her better because she ain't just perfect," Grandma said patting the mutilated plaster face. "That's when we need to be loved the most, when we have been cracked and hurt."

But the doll isn't hurt, it's me, thought Ellen clearly and coldly. She knew she would never love this doll, no matter how well she was fixed. She could not love anything which had been broken and proved to be different than she had imagined or hoped it would be. The image of love was locked tight and pure, deep within her, and all the cruel accidents of life would only thicken the walls.

But this storm passed, and presently Laurence had them all gathered around the piano singling Christmas songs and laughing, while dinner was being placed on the table.

They gathered hungrily and happily around the big oak table, stretched the full length of the dining room and loaded with a variety of good home-produced food. Uncle Albert solemnly blessed the food, the family, the church authorities and sundry other items much to the distress of the children. Then the bowls of potatoes, sweet potatoes, parsnips, turkey and dressing, cranberry and stuffed celery, pickles, hot rolls, all the wondrous holiday foods, began going round and round. When everyone was about to burst, Ellen helped her grandmother serve the English rag pudding with thick caramel sauce. This was her special job that none of the other cousins were allowed to do, and it made up a little for the earlier bruised day.

The day ended at last with everyone in an advanced state of satiety and weariness yet glowing with the warmth of human companionship and love. Uncle Albert and Aunt Bertha and the two city cousins were hustled off to the last Interurban, the signal that Christmas was almost over.

At dusk when the bluish shadows lay thick on the white snow, and lights in the houses had begun to glow like squares of melting butterscotch, Laurence, Irene and Ellen walked home. Ellen was carrying the broken doll wrapped in the blanket, her injuries forgotten for the moment in the pleasure of being a family together at Christmas.

CB

The week between Christmas and New Years was perpetual holiday in the little frame house. Fires roared so that even the bedrooms were warm; the piano or the violin or both together sang for hours. There was a great deal of talk, friends dropping in and Irene, Laurence and Ellen talking together about the future, remembering funny things that had happened in the past, making big plans.

Irene was wondrously happy, but she had a strange feeling there was something a little feverish about Laurence, about the way he plunged into every sensation and activity as though the long months alone on the winter range had starved him to the bone for companionship, warmth, love, more than they usually did. But she was not a woman who could look too deeply into things or understand what she occasionally glimpsed beneath the surface of human life.

She and Laurence talked a lot about the dream house, and she got out some of the magazines in which she had marked rooms, plans, color schemes. But when she suggested that perhaps they could start next year, Laurence was evasive and joking. He had inherited the old nineteenth century idea that money problems and business belonged to a man's world, that women were meant to be protected, provided for, sheltered from cruder things. He had seen his own mother work so hard in the fields and house and barn, growing old and worn that he determined never to let a wife of his endure these humiliating hardships. When Irene needed things she asked him or charged them at Washburn's. She had never written a check in her life, or had more money in her possession than a ten dollar bill. This late in the twentieth century, Laurence clung to the notion that woman belonged on a pedestal in the midst of man's dream of a better life. To keep her on that exalted prominence, Laurence had gone into the sheep business with his father and Aaron, instead of continuing with the study of music, the education that he wanted. It seemed to him that if he could get a good solid investment in something, he could go on with his plans later. The sheep business had been, in the previous decade, the most promising of ventures. It was sheep money that had built most of the fine, big homes and comfortable fortunes for a few families in Merritsville. Everybody thought that the prosperity of the Twenties was the natural fulfillment of the American Dream, the blessing of the Lord on his Chosen People.

There was plenty of rich grazing land in the Wasatch mountains just for homesteading. Laurence's father, J.L., and Aaron had enough capital to provide the stock and Laurence came in with his right to provide land and labor. For a while it looked as though Aaron's "figgering" was going to make them neighbors of the Washburns, Cottingtons, Haleys, all big sheep men. Laurence had intended to stay in active partnership just long enough to get something solid under him for Irene and his children. Ah yes–his children–now he was glad there was only one, for the sheep business, far from providing the education, security and elaborate new home that had grown steadily in Irene's dreams, was not even going to keep this thin roof over their heads. If what Aaron had said was true–and they had sat a long time talking and figgering the night Aaron had come to relieve him for Christmas–six more months would finish them. Except for a miracle, the bank would take over everything from the big camp horses down to the granite washbasin in the camp. Their only hope was that they might hire on as herders or foremen on slim wages with the Deseret Livestock Company.

Driving home over the lonely rough frozen roads that December night, Laurence had fought off the bleak despair as best he could. He wondered if he should prepare Irene, but by the time he reached home, he had resolved that they should have one more untroubled Christmas. The rest of the winter was going to be long and lonely enough without leaving her with that. Part of the reason that he could not tell her was his own unwillingness to believe what had never at any time in the past five years seemed possible, did not seem possible now. He made his own brave, defiant gestures in the face of the nightmare.

"Tell you what," he said one morning after breakfast, "We're going into Salt Lake and get a stove for that bedroom; we don't want no more frozen arms around here, so get into your warm duds, both of you." Ellen hopped up in delight. How she loved to go to Salt Lake City–the sounds, sights, even the smells of the big city were intoxicating to her. Long after, when she had lived in the city for many years, she was to remember the metallic grinding sound of the electric street cars as a strange and wonderful music that opened the stage on a different world, an unreal, enchanted, movie-place world. From the beginning she loved the city as only a country girl can.

Laurence went to the bank, deliberately drew out almost all of the money in a small personal account which he had maintained separate from the business and they set off joyously, the three of them, in the cab of Aaron's big truck.

It was a wonderful day. Ellen was never to forget it: it was the last day in her life for more than fifteen years that there was abundance and untrammeled reveling in the good things that money could buy. She could not know how desperately the pleasures of the day were grasped by her father nor how precariously purchased. He seemed in the highest of spirits. They wandered gaily from store to store. Ellen had never imagined there were so many different kinds because in Merritsville you bought almost everything in two stores–Washburn's and J.C. Penney's.

They lingered in several music stores where Laurence jokingly imagined them taking home a huge piano that he called a "baby grand." Ellen like the big department stores best where there were stairways and elevators and such a variety of things that it seemed like Christmas stored up forever.

Laurence bought almost every trifle that Irene indicated she might want and insisted on her having two new dresses. Ellen noticed how his face lighted up when Irene came out of the dressing rooms and nervously surveyed herself in the long, gleaming three-way mirrors. Ellen was intrigued by these mirrors in which she was multiplied so many times and wondered what it would be like if there were so many of herself. Her father teased her when he caught her pressing her face into the mirror as though she could push through the bright surface to the magic world beyond. He said he would buy her a book about a little girl who had gone through a looking glass. He did buy her some new patent leather shoes and gave her a whole dollar to spend; she clutched it anxiously, not wanting to part with it all at once. She didn't believe that a whole bunch of dimes, nickels or quarters could really be the same thing, but he persuaded her to exchange it for a fine scrapbook with a leather-like cover in which she could keep her poems. He had praised the one she wrote him for Christmas so much.

Hungry but glowing with joy, they had lunch in a fine restaurant which was dark and greenish inside with deep, high booths like caves. Ellen drank in the wonders of thick carpeting, polite waiters, padded white table cloths and a long string of gleaming silverware by her place that confused her. How could anyone need so many things to eat with? Daddy amused them by making designs with the little round oyster crackers that filled a cut-glass bowl on the table. She thought there had never been such a wonderful world and such happy people.

Later in the afternoon they found and bought a small bedroom stove. In the same big furniture store there were some radios, those magical boxes that were just beginning to make their way into the lives of most Americans. It was there in the corner that Laurence found *the radio*. He spent the rest of the afternoon fascinated with it, turning the dials, listening to it turned up loud and turned down low, looking inside, stroking its satiny walnut finish. Irene said that it cost too much and they didn't need it. Laurence's eyes grew even brighter, more determined. He dickered some more with the weary salesman, and at last succeeded in getting what he considered a bargain price. The radio went home to Merritsville in the back of the sheep truck alongside the stove.

He talked about it all the way home, how it would keep Irene and Ellen company all the time while he was gone, and how they could keep up with what was going on in the world a lot better, especially how they could hear good music programs. A symphony orchestra, the latest dance bands, comedy shows like "Amos 'n Andy;" they could have the whole world right there in their front room in Merritsville, Utah. He made it sound as though the radio would cure all the aches, pains and loneliness in the world. Ellen was inflamed by her father's glowing enthusiasm.

"It would be all right if you could have one in the sheep camp, too," Irene said. She was snuggled up with Ellen in an old quilt to keep warm since there was no heater in the truck.

"Someday we'll have that, too." Laurence patted her fondly, "You just wait, this is a great time, marvelous things happening, when you think you can just turn little knobs and get peoples' voices and sounds from all the way across the continent. Maybe I'll study electricity and get out of this sheep business."

Laurence uncrated the radio in the front room with great care. It consisted of two pieces, a rectangular box that looked like a small coffin with a narrow window in front and a table of the same shape with a round cloth-covered hole. On a metal plaque on the front of the upper box it said "RCA SUPERHETERO-DYNE." Ellen, who loved long, strange words, was as fascinated with the word as with the instrument itself. When Laurence had attached the cord of the radio to an extension cord that ran from a double socket in the center light fixture and down the wall, he opened the lid of the box and let Ellen look at the glowing, humming tube, the fans of metal that meshed in and out when one of the dials on the front was turned.

"Now you're looking at one of God's great miracles," he said and there was great reverence in his voice. He tried to explain the principle of the radio to her but Ellen could not understand. She preferred to think of it as magic and, when she listened to it afterward, for many years she pictured miniature creatures inside performing on a small stage like the one in the church recreation hall. Voices belonged to bodies, not to wires, tubes, and metal plates.

Of course friends and relatives had to come and see the new radio. It was one of the biggest and finest in town, eleven tubes; few people had any kind of radios and none which could pull stations in from so far. For several nights the house was full of people; Ellen was proud and felt that they were very important people.

Several evenings before Laurence had to go back to the herd, they had planned one more small farewell party. He had prepared a list of programs in a fine, old-fashioned script listing the times they could be heard by turning one of the knobs until a number was opposite the small pointers. The guests were to have their choice. The Christmas tree was still up, and Irene had shined the small room. She was dressed in a dark silk skirt and loose pink crepe blouse with silver trimming. The pearls were around her throat and the dark rich braids of her hair wound in a coronet around her head glistened. Laurence, dressed in his Sunday white shirt and tie that contrasted with his sunburned face, making him look a little uncomfortable, was crouched in front of the radio, turning the dials and listening, like a doctor to a heart patient. Someone had told him he could get Los Angeles at night.

"Listen! listen!" He held up a finger in agitation as Irene approached him.

"Oh, listen yourself," Irene said playfully as she put her arms around his neck from behind. "I'd rather listen to you while you're here. You'll soon be gone again, and I can listen to that thing all the time."

The look of agitation passed quickly from Laurence's eyes, he stood up pulling her to him.

"By gad, woman, you look gorgeous; you get more beautiful every year. I don't think it's safe to leave you here alone." He put his wind-roughened lips on hers, and they kissed for a long time; then he pulled her gently down beside him on the couch. At that moment Ellen, who had been reading in the corner between the Christmas tree and stove, looked up; a shock of surprise went through her at the sight of the couple locked in each other's arms. They were like strangers who had completely forgotten her presence. Suddenly she dropped her book. Irene looked up embarrassed, her cheeks glowing and her eyes strangely bright.

She got up quickly, smoothing her skirt and hair nervously.

"Oh, ...Ellen ... I didn't know you were there ... listen, why don't you run down to Grandma's and see if she can bring some extra cups–three or four, maybe, old ones, just in case we don't have enough ...You can stay and walk back with her when she's ready to come."

Ellen could tell the errand was made up on the spur of the moment, and she got up resentfully, almost on the verge of angry tears. It was the first time that she realized there was something in the life of her father and mother from which she was excluded.

"I don't want to," she said sullenly.

"Go on, be a good girl," her father coaxed, and there was something pleading in his voice that made her obey. She put on her coat and boots and went out, but she lingered on the porch for a moment where she could see through the lace curtains on the door. Laurence Kent had taken his wife in his arms again and was kissing her hair, her neck, her ears. Ellen was deeply disturbed by the look on her mother's face of being completely absorbed by something so powerful that it obliterated the ordinary world. It was a sight no one else can endure but the person who has inspired it–the face of a woman deeply in love, in love without pain or shadows. Ellen never forgot the look, she never saw it again on her mother's face.

She plodded on in the crisp winter night to get the cups which were not needed, flushed with resentment and anger. She wished she could tell Grandma Addie about her feelings. Oddly enough her distress settled on her mother, who with her beauty and superior position, seemed to have some kind of power which Ellen imagined denied to her forever. Her father seemed to be a victim of something which she could not name, but it was dark and evil. His face had not been glowing and triumphant like Irene's when he asked her to go away so they could be in secret together, but as though he had been stricken with a sudden pain which he could barely endure. She clenched her hands inside her thick mittens in fury and almost wished she could stay at her grandma's away from those two who didn't want her around.

By the time she reached Grandma's house, most of her irritation had dissolved. She explained her errand cheerfully.

When they arrived an hour later with the cups and some cakes Addie had baked just in case there wasn't enough, everything seemed normal again. Irene was bustling about in the kitchen, counting sandwiches, but her cheeks were still suspiciously flushed. Laurence was absorbed in some sputtering and crackling on the radio that he thought might be Los Angeles. Ellen went timidly and stood by him; he drew her down beside him, hugging her warmly. Her uneasiness evaporated; she sighed with relief–home was all right again. But deep truths, once seen, have a way of alerting the inner eye to be on the look out for them constantly.

As Ellen remembered it, there was only one other dark note in the week. It was the day before Laurence was to go back to the herd. They were sitting at the breakfast table–there had been hot biscuits and strawberry jam and all the good special things that Mama fixed when Daddy was home.

Laurence sat fiddling with his knife and fork, drawing designs on the table cloth and tapping out rhythms on the glasses. At last he said without looking at Irene, "I guess I ought to go see Everett, if he's home."

There was a curious silence and Ellen noticed the shadow that came over her mother's features. She knew that Everett Gordon was that drunk man who lived in the big, spooky house on the other side of town, and that he had played some mysterious part in her parents' life. She knew that her grandmother sometimes took bread and jam and things to him, that kids were afraid to pass his place because he talked crazy to an old donkey that he kept. Hal and some of the other boys sometimes tormented the donkey or played tricks on Old Ev.

Her father pushed himself away from the table and got up. He looked almost angry. "I owe him that much," he said as though Irene had objected, although she had not said a word. She began to stack the dishes together.

"Let me go with you," Ellen suddenly cried, jumping up from the table. Laurence looked at her oddly as though he had forgotten she was there.

"No," he said shortly.

"Oh, let her go, at least as far as your mother's," Irene said unexpectedly, averting her eyes. "She needs some fresh air."

Again Ellen had that left-out feeling as though her parents had a secret world from which she was excluded.

Laurence was hunching into his old sheep-skin coat. He looked at Irene with a beseeching, puzzled expression.

"Oh, all right, get your things on," he said to Ellen, who hustled her coat and mittens and tried to smooth the lumps that her long legged underwear made in her tan-ribbed stockings. They set out, crunching along the snowy paths. Ellen clung to her father's hand, but he seemed almost unaware of her. Whether he forgot to take the lower street that went by her grandmother's house or had decided to take Ellen to Everett's, she couldn't tell, but they arrived at the old Gordon mansion shortly.

Stopping at the entrance to the grounds where all the heavy foliage covered in snow half concealed the massive, dark house, he looked at Ellen hesitantly.

"Maybe you could run on back to Grandma's. Oh well, come on, he may be all right. Remember, Ellen, he might be sick." He gave her mitten an anxious squeeze. Ellen was puzzled but half-suspected it was about Everett's drinking; that was probably what upset her mother. She thought best not to ask.

The snow on the driveway was perfectly smooth. No tracks of any kind going in or out. "Maybe they've taken him away again," murmured Laurence, but he plunged ahead, Ellen stepping in his tracks as best she could. As they drew near the house, Laurence stopped and looked around. It was very big and quiet. The snow and icicles came down over the dark windows and there was no sign of life in the front of the house, but after a few moments, they could see a thin wisp of smoke coming from somewhere in the back. It was only a faint movement of gray in the wintery sky.

"Must be somebody there," Laurence said pushing ahead. The drifts of snow came up to Ellen's knees, but she didn't complain. There was something fascinating about the big, dead, dark house. It was as though she and her father had entered a new world. The snow-covered bushes and trees looked like strange creatures enchanted in a silent white forest, the house brooding and sinister as in fairy tales. It didn't even seem to belong in Merritsville.

As they came around the house, they saw a shaggy misshapen beast tied to an old hitching rail under the big trees of the back yard. He had trodden out a hard circle stained with brown and yellow clumps and there was a pile of hay at one side into which he had nibbled judiciously. He lifted his grotesque head with its long flapping hears and gave a ludicrous bray as he saw the two figures.

Leaving Ellen standing in his track in the snow, Laurence made a great leap toward the animal. "Brahms, old boy," he cried. "How are you?' He patted the shaggy head and the donkey snorted happily.

There was a high rickety wooden stairs leading up to a screened porch on this side of the house. Although it, too, was covered with snow, there was a narrow groove made by a single set of footprints down one edge of it. Someone pushed open the sagging screen door of the porch. Ellen had seen Everett Gordon from time to time at a distance, but she didn't remember the sad figure that stood on the steps, clinging to the rail and swaying slightly. It was the figure of a thin, aging man with disheveled gray hair and a mottled, reddish face, a fine face, but she couldn't see that at the moment. He was dressed in a very shabby red velvet bathrobe with loose carpet slippers on bare feet. Around his neck was a dirty white rag, creased and sagging as though it had been there for days. In one hand was a pipe from which thin blue smoke coiled upward.

"What the ...?" he cried blinking into the light, which was strong even though the sun had not come out from behind thick, gray winter clouds.

Laurence turned and seeing him, bounded up the stairs. "Everett," he cried, almost knocking the older man off the stairs with his embrace.

"Laurence, Laurie–my God–" Everett rasped. "When–where–how'd you come?"

Ellen was still standing knee deep in the snow. She began to shove toward the stairs and her father turned toward her.

"My girl Ellen," he said reaching down to help her up, "Everett Gordon, Mr. Gordon, Ellen, you remember?"

Everett stooped and took her mittened hand gently and, fixing his cloudy eyes on her said, "How do you do, my dear. I hope you will excuse me, I've not been very well, I wasn't expecting company, Laurence, you know. I hadn't heard from you in so long." He held the screen door open for them and they passed through the cluttered porch.

"I'm not company, you know." Laurence tried to ease things as they entered the small, warm, incredibly crowded and dirty room where Everett lived most of the time.

Ellen was unaccountably taken by this mysterious man who wasn't like any of the other men about town. He fussed about almost like a woman, finding a place for them to sit by removing piles of papers, books, junk and bottles from two old brocade chairs. And he talked so politely. Not anybody else she knew would have said "How do you do, my dear?"to her. The words echoed in her mind with a peculiar rhythm. All other grownups would have said, almost as though she weren't present, "My she's a nice little girl." or "She looks like her father, doesn't she?" or if they acknowledged her, something like "What grade are you in now?"

She sat uncomfortably on the chair, however, looking about at the clutter and filth in the narrow room which had apparently served once as a sort of pantry or second kitchen to the house.

Shelves lined one wall from ceiling to floor and were full of a fantastic collection of items; prominent among them, Ellen noticed, yellowed rolls of music and a violin. She did remember that Everett had helped her father with his music, that sometime in the distant past her mother had played with them at their house or on some public occasion. She wondered what had happened that Irene was so upset when Daddy mentioned Everett. She knew her mother would have been driven into hysterics by the disorder in this room. It would be best not to tell her about it.

The table in one corner was almost half full of empty bottles and there was a pile of dirty dishes so deep that Ellen could not imagine where space could be found to eat. Everett was hovering nervously over a very black, old-fashioned kitchen stove.

"You will have a cup of coffee with me, Laurie?" he urged. "How on earth have you been? My God, it has been a long time. You're looking damnably good, old man." He rambled on poking up the fire. Ellen saw that he was not such a really old man as she had imagined, maybe not so very much older than her father though she couldn't tell for sure. But his hands shook so bad that when he lifted the stove lid, it clattered fearfully before he could get it back in place. She glanced at her father who had a peculiar look in his face as though he were about to cry. In fact he took out his handkerchief and wiped his eyes.

"Had a touch of the flu," Everett explained. "Must've caught it in the city. Sisters insisted on dragging me up there for Christmas. Been a bit better the last few days. Guess I'm going to live though I can't think what for." He gave a harsh laugh that ended in a fit of coughing.

In a while, with considerable poking and fussing, he managed to get the crusted coffee pot to boil and then, after rummaging around in the shelves, shuffled out of the room muttering something to himself. Presently he came back with several beautiful tea cups, dusting them with the corner of an old curtain. All the while he kept up a stream of incoherent questions, answers, ejaculations, comments which Laurence tried diligently to order into something like conversation.

Taking an armload of bottles and cans to the back porch, Everett dumped them down with a crash and made room on the table for three cups.

"Will the young lady have coffee?" he smiled at Ellen and she was charmed. She felt inexpressibly important and grownup, even womanly when he spoke to her.

"No," put in Laurence hastily, "perhaps she better not." Everett looked distressed. "Maybe just a little *café au lait*, if I put in a lot of milk?"

Laurence nodded, smiling a bit uncertainly and Everett drew a can of milk out of the untidy shelves. Punching holes in it, he filled the beautiful cup, whose iridescent colors had already mesmerized Ellen, half full of thick condensed milk and added the steaming hot coffee.

"These are pretty cups," she said timidly.

Everett's face lighted. "You like them? Ah, Laurence, she has an eye for beauty. You must cultivate it. Yes, these are from my mother's set of Sevres. I would give her one you know," he turned seriously to Laurence, "except that my sisters still inventory me from time to time."

Laurence shook his head. "It would be wrong to break up the set. She'll have pretty things of her own one day."

A long time after Ellen remembered the strange sweetness of that warm, pungent, but slightly bitter drink in the steamy, filthy, cramped room. The wintery light from a long, thin, dingy, uncurtained window falling on the faces of the two men showed a panorama of emotions, most of which Ellen did not understand, but which burned into her memory so that these two faces became the permanent masks of her view of the masculine world. The familiar, good, young face of her father and the unfamiliar, entrancing, rather disturbing face of Everett Gordon. Both faces, though they lit up from time to time with the joy of shared memories, were stained with deep sadness.

They talked mostly about music at first then, when it seemed the subject was no longer of interest, Laurence began to talk about the hard times and the sheep business. "I was always sorry that you went that way, Laurie, when you had so much talent." Everett said.

"Well, it looked like a good way to make a lot of money fast and then I always planned...." Laurence was looking at the table and picking at the oilcloth. "but the best laid plans of mice and men...." He grinned ruefully.

Ellen had found a book among the piles on the window sill and moved close to the light to read, but she heard snatches of the conversation from time to time.

"Well," sighed Everett, "Spilt milk...as my mother used to say. We have all chosen the wrong path from time to time. Who am I to have regrets over wasted talent? Do you really think this depression is going to last?"

There was that word again. Ellen pricked up her ears.

"Don't know, Ev. It sure don't look good for the sheep business. I doubt we can last much beyond this winter. Aaron figures we might get out with our homes if the bank don't get too hard."

Ellen dropped her book and stood up. She had grown restless and alarmed at this conversation. This startled Laurence who, slapping his knees briskly, rose and made motions to leave. It seemed a long time, however, before Everett Gordon would take his trembling hand off Laurence's sleeve and cease his entreaties for him to come again soon. Turning at last to Ellen, he picked up her hand and squeezed it, urging her to come see him when she could. Ellen, though she was already aware that it was not likely she would, promised mildly. They left Everett standing at the top of the snow-covered stair, waving to them.

The sun had come out; the glare from the snow hurt Ellen's eyes so that she couldn't see her father's face clearly, but she had the impression that there was still a gray wintery shadow over it. He walked along, without even holding her hand, in deep silence. Ellen dared not ask many questions, but she ventured.

"Daddy, why does Mr. Gordon keep that funny old donkey?"

Laurence looked at her quizzically for a moment before he answered.

"Because he's lonely, I guess, and can't talk to people around here much. Always had an odd sense of humor."

"What was that funny name you called him?"

"The donkey, oh yes, Brahms. That's the name of a famous musician that Everett likes. Sometime you must hear him play from Brahms' violin concerto."

Ellen was intrigued. What curious words and names she had heard this morning. Was there a world outside of Merritsville that she had never even dreamed about that was even bigger and different from Salt Lake City? In her grandmother's back room was a set of small grayish-covered books that she had got in pay-ment for helping to clean the school house. On their backs was the gold lettering, *Carpenter's Geographies*. Grandma said they were all about the world. She must look at them soon.

CB

On a slushy day in late January Ellen stopped off at the Walker's on her way home from school. Her cousins Lorraine, Louise and Hal had always been her closest friends. Grandma Addie was there minding the little ones and mending for Aunt Dosey who had to go to a meeting about the ward bazaar. She got up from the big, round oak table heaped high with clothing much the worse for long, rough wearing and greeted the girls. Ellen gave her a hug and kiss; she loved her grandmother dearly. Sometimes the other grandchildren suspected she was a bit the favorite.

Putting her small gold spectacles and thimble in a safe place, Addie bustled into the kitchen to oversee the after-school snack-ing; whole loaves of bread and jars of jam disappeared at this time of day. The twins came racing out of a back bedroom where they had been at play and Joey, the baby, awakened, trudged crossly into the kitchen, his sodden diaper down around his knees.

"Now you mind the baby," Grandma directed Lorraine and Ellen, "while I spread the pieces." Ellen hesitated. She liked Joey but not when he was all wet and smelly. Lorraine, since she was the oldest girl, picked him up matter-of-factly and stripped off the dirty diaper, throwing it into a pan by the stove. She put him on the corner of the kitchen table and fastened on clean britches, tickling and cooing at him until he regained his happy good na-ture. Sometimes Ellen envied Lorraine; she seemed more grown-up although they were the same age. Ellen took Joey from her. She liked to feel his little fat hands patting her face and even endured the slobbery kisses he planted affectionately on her cheek.

Hal, the oldest Walker child, slammed through the back door; throwing his books on the table, he slumped into a chair. Two years older than Lorraine and Ellen, he had assumed the airs of the masculine leader of the bunch. They had played happily to-gether from the time they were very small, but now Hal was getting to be bossy and smart-alec. There were times when Ellen disliked him like now when Grandma tousled his hair as she passed by and he pushed her rudely away.

"You ought to wipe your feet better, Hal," she scolded mildly, "Look how you've tracked up your ma's clean floor." She handed him a large slice of bread and jam and he grinned, knowing that he was not really going to be punished. Grandma never got mad at him; only his pa but not about tracking up floors. However, he did turn his shoe sideways to make sure it was his muddy track on the worn linoleum and flicked an additional cake of mud under the table. "Ain't there no more milk?" he asked his mouth full of bread and jam. Grandma filled him a glass from a pitcher and brought it to the table.

"Why don't you get your own milk?" Lorraine sputtered at him; she was getting sick and tired of the way everybody waited on Hal.

"Yah, yah," Hal mocked back with a malicious grimace, "Pickle-face, you're just jealous."

"Now, children, let's not fight," Grandma soothed, but Lorraine was cross about something Hal had done that morning. He had extracted a quarter from his mother that morning when she had asked for some money.

"I'm just tired of the way everybody waits on him and lets him have his way all the time. He just thinks he's so big and smart. He gets everything like this morning when I wanted some money for an autograph book."

"Sure, sure." Hal looked very satisfied and superior. Even Ellen wanted to break his smug expression. "Boys are supposed to be the boss and get money first. Girls ain't nothin' much," he sneered.

"Now you hush up, both of you," Grandma admonished more sternly. "Brothers and sisters ought not to quarrel and fight like you two have got to doing. You ought to love each other and take care of each other like the Lord tells us. Here, Hal, you go out and get a bucket of coal. If boys are big bosses they have to do the big work, too."

Hal grunted and stomped out with the coal bucket. Lorraine smiled triumphantly at Ellen.

Louise appeared in the doorway of the dining room. She was in her worn flannel nightgown and had a thick, grayish rag around her throat. She had been home from school with a bad cold and her face was swollen and red. She rubbed her eyes and sniffed.

Grandma drew her over to the table, "Now there, Honey, you sit right up here and Grandma will get you a piece of bread and jam. Are you feelin' better? Oh, my goodness, you ought to have something on your feet. Lorraine, get some of them socks off the table and put on Louise. She might take more cold and get pneumonia."

Louise was not quite two years younger than Ellen and Lorraine, a pale, smallish girl, quiet and submissive who followed them around worshipfully, trying to do everything to please everybody. She was easily upset when there was any friction or unhappiness. Ellen always felt sad about Louise and wanted to protect her from the rest of the wild Walkers. She just didn't seem to belong to that robust bunch gathered around the table devouring their snacks greedily. The twins, Beth and Bobby, were fighting although they usually got along very well, sticking together against the others. Beth had spilled her milk on Bobby and he had hit her. She was crying loudly. Grandma was trying to wipe her nose. Joey was splashing in the milk and chuckling, and Lorraine was trying to find a rag to mop it up.

Families were awfully messy; Ellen thought it was a good thing her mother didn't have to put up with all this confusion and litter. But some days Ellen liked to be here in the midst of it all. It seemed more like life should be than the quiet, almost dull order in which she and Irene spent their time. She went over to help Louise put on the stockings that Lorraine had found. Louise's thin feet were blue and pitiful; there was a hole in the stocking and one of her toes stuck through it. They both laughed and Ellen gave her frail cousin a hug, longing to make her warm and well.

Aunt Dosey came through the front door and into the kitchen. Joey held out his arms and began to whimper. The twins rushed to her, clutching the skirt of her long, shabby coat. She gave them a squeeze. "Oh, laws, Ma, I'm sorry I couldn't get back sooner. Maddie Peterson wanted me to help her with the program after the meetin', and we don't have all the sacks made up for the fish pond ... now Bobby, look you got Mama all sticky. Here sweetums...." She picked up the baby. "What's this? Oh, Lorraine, couldn't you find another diaper? This is that piece of old bedspread. Lordy, I hope you ain't had too bad a time, Ma."

Aunt Dosey was awfully thin, Ellen thought, and not as pretty as her mother. Her hair was coming loose from its pins, and she didn't have her lipstick on straight. Her shoes were run over and some thing on her dress was, as usual, held together by a safety pin. She was always hurrying, doing this and that and coming and going to all the church meetings. But she made you feel good, like now, giving each one a hug and kiss and saying something that let you know you were special. She gave Ellen an extra pat, "That talk you gave in Primary sure was good, Ellen," she said.

Hal, who had lugged the coal bucket in, dodged her arm when she tried to catch him, but Ellen could tell he wasn't unhappy when she caught him and planted a big kiss on his forehead. He became sullen again when she reminded him that he had some chores to do for his dad before it got dark.

"Don't forget you was supposed go over and take care of Brother Smith's goat, like you promised," she called after him as he went thumping through the living room. The front door slammed and Dosey sighed. He was becoming a handful.

Addie had fixed Dosey a cup of Postum which she drank sitting at the table with Joey on her lap. "I guess Aaron ain't been home yet?"

Grandma shook her head.

"He had to see about some supplies. I guess he's goin' to have to go out to the herd. He thinks Laurence might need some relief."

At the sound of her father's name, Ellen pricked up her ears.

"Has he heard anything from the bank yet?" Grandma asked.

"Not yet." Dosey put Joey on the floor and stirred her Postum. "Bobby, don't crumbled the bread up like that, Honey. Eat it now like a good boy. We can't waste food. Laurence didn't say when he left what he wanted to do about his share. Aaron can't find out what is goin' on. He heard last week that the Clark Brothers were goin' under."

"Oh dear," Grandma sounded worried. "What will they do with all them mouths to feed?"

"What will *we* do with all these mouths to feed?" Dosey spoke almost in a whisper.

Grandma got up and began to clear the table. Ellen helped her, sweeping up the mud that Hal had tracked in. Finally Grandma turned back to where Dosey was still puddling in her drink.

"I guess we'll have to trust in the Lord like we've always done. We've always had trials and tribulations long as I can remember. I never expected no different."

"Oh, Ma," Dosey remonstrated. "Sometimes I wonder if the Lord pays much attention to what's goin' on with us poor folks. Irene said the other day that she was almost out of coal, and they told her at Washburn's that she couldn't tick no more until the bill was paid. Aaron said he would try to get some wood chopped for her. We ain't got the Christmas bills paid up yet, either. I don't know how we're goin' to. We won't have anything comin' in until the wool gets sold. Aaron says he can't sell anything until the bank makes up its mind whether to foreclose or not."

Aunt Dosey sounded so discouraged, not like herself at all, that Ellen felt a shadow of fear cross her heart. All during the month since her father had gone away, there had been intimations that something was wrong. Suddenly she felt that she must go home to see if Irene and their cozy life was still there. "I guess I'll go home now," she said. "Thanks for the piece, Aunt Dosey and Grandma."

"You're always welcome, Honey. "Aunt Dosey gave her a pat. "Oh, would you take that magazine on the piano home to your ma? I hope it ain't ripped up too much by them kids. It's the one with the bathroom picture in that she wanted to save."

"I think I better be goin', too, stir up the fire before it gets too dark and cold. Wait a minute, Ellen, and I'll walk with you. Why don't you get my hat and coat while I gather up my other things?' Grandma said. "I'll take some of this mendin' home with me, Doris, and bring it back on Tuesday. Can you send Hal down on Friday to help me with the chickens? Now, Louise, dear, you go back to bed or that cold might get worse. Doris, don't you think she ought to have a mustard plaster?" Louise had begun to cough deep, phlegmy, jarring coughs.

"I'll put some of that mustard ointment on her that I got from the Raleigh man last week," Dosey promised. "Thanks for everything, Ma. Don't know what I'd do without you."

Adeline Kent, a woman in her early fifties who had been widowed for more than ten years, was still a vigorous woman, short and stocky like her Scottish ancestors. She had thick, graying hair that showed glints of the original reddish-brown, and she wore it in a plain coil on the back of her head as she had always done. Her face, that had never known any kind of make-up, was a ruddy color from so much outdoor work; its distinguishing feature was bright, bluish-green eyes that looked on life with a generous willingness to accept and care.

She pulled on her neatly mended gloves and wriggled into the sensible galoshes. All bundled up in her old winter tweed coat with the shabby hat she always wore, she was a bit of a comical figure, but Addie had no self-consciousness about her appearance. Like most other women of her age and circumstance, she had relinquished vanity. Ellen never compared her grandmother to anyone else; to her she had a special kind of identity that didn't include young or old, beautiful or otherwise.

The two of them set off down the wintery street toward home going east on the main street past Penney's, the drugstore, the shoemaker's shop and Washburn's. Addie had to stop several times to speak to people she knew; sometimes Ellen got impatient. Grandma knew everybody and their families from way back and cared about them all. But finally they reached Ellen's house. The kitchen light was on, and they could see the shadow of Irene moving about.

"Guess I better stop a minute," Grandma said as they stamped their feet on the doorstep, "see if your ma needs anything."

"My goodness," said Irene as she saw them, "I thought you were never coming home, Ellen. Hello, Ma. Here, Ellen, come over here and take your galoshes off on this paper, I just finished mopping this afternoon."

"Just give me a piece to stand on, Irene," Addie asked, "I can't stay but a minute. Just wanted to see if you was all right."

"Oh, come on in, Ma, and have a bite with us. I've been kinda blue this afternoon."

Irene, who had no mother of her own, had always loved Addie, partly because of Laurence, partly because of the older woman's unfailing kindness. She had never been an interfering mother-in-law.

"Well, it's gettin' a bit late, and I hate to walk on these icy streets when it gets dark, but it is good to have somebody to eat with." She was already unwinding her scarf.

Addie sat in the rocking chair by the stove and talked about Dosey, the kids, the townspeople while Irene set the table. There was a delicious smell in the kitchen.

"Hmm, smells like you made one of them good stews of yours." Grandma sniffed in anticipation.

"Yes, I got a good soup bone at Washburn's today real cheap. Did you know they laid off some of the clerks down there, said business is falling off?"

Grandma clucked in dismay and shook her head. "Seems like it's gettin' worse and President Hoover says prosperity is just around the corner. Wonder which corner?"

Irene laughed. It was hard to believe there was anything wrong with the world, except that her father was not home, Ellen thought as they pulled their chairs up to the little table laid so attractively. Irene even put her embroidered napkins out, the ones she usually saved for company.

Addie bowed her head and said the blessing. Ellen tucked her hands between her knees and bowed her head; catching fragments of the familiar prayer, she felt a joyous warmth pour over her. "Heavenly Father, we are grateful for the food of which we are about to partake. May it nourish our bodies and give us the strength we need. We are grateful for thy blessings on this family, for the chance we have of gathering together in love and harmony. Bless those who are not with us this hour and watch over them...." Grandma always prayed a long solemn, prayer but tonight Ellen didn't mind. She did feel all the words of the prayer and, in spite of the clouds gathering in their life, she could see a long vista of happiness stretching all the way out over the hills to take in her father and the world.

╣

On the thirtieth of December Laurence had packed his clothes that Irene had washed and mended, his violin and a few supplies and started back to the herd. It was only fair to let Aaron join the New Year's day dinner; New Year's eve was seldom an occasion for parties in Merritsville. Most Mormon families didn't drink liquor and besides Prohibition made it risky to obtain enough spirits to celebrate. On the chilly porch Irene and Ellen clung to him. He forced himself to be bluff and hearty, making jokes to reassure them, but the prospect of the cold, weary months ahead were extremely disheartening.

"I'll be back before you know it," he kept telling them. "Middle of February Aaron's going to take over–time will go like Billy Mac's old mule."

Ellen laughed through her tears. Irene let him go reluctantly. "I know, Honey, I don't know why this winter's seemed longer and worse than the others but we'll be counting the days."

"Look," Laurence said firmly, "I'm going to take the music Mama gave me and the book you made with me, Ellen, and I'm leaving the radio with you to keep you company until I get back. We'll think of each other every day, all day. I'm gonna read that little poem you wrote me over and over. You keep writing them for me." He kissed her and got into the truck.

Irene stood at the south window for a long time after the truck had gone out of sight, picking dead leaves off the geraniums and shifting the cans so that some of the flowers would get more sunlight. Ellen wandered around the house which seemed suddenly, cold and empty.

The hills of western Utah are long rolling swells–yellowish-green in the summer time and yellowish-gray in the winter. In the evening they turn mauve and blue and finally black like great, lazy waves on an ancient ocean swelling toward the horizon. Ragged patches of shadow mark the numerous gullies and ravines. They are a perfect allegory of monotony for, unlike the sands of the desert in southern Utah, they do not drift and form weirdly poetic shapes. There are few trees except scattered scrub juniper and cedar squatting close to the dry hungry earth.

Coarse, tough vegetation– dull greens, yellows and browns– blends the scenery together. Year after year there is no apparent change. Some man-made trails, which could hardly be called roads, wind around among them: some fences have been strung and the lean shadows of telephone poles shift across the rough earth. But the vast expanses are contemptuous of these small human marks. Given a year or two they would be rotted and covered and the desert would never acknowledge their passing.

The first week that Laurence was back on the winter range after his brief, bright respite were difficult. He was often bored and depressed as he rode around the dormant hills, and his feeling of futility seemed to be expanded by their aimless repetition of the same dull theme. No matter how many miles he rode, there were so many more of the same kind of miles to ride. Sometime, however, his unquenchable sense of beauty welled up from the hidden springs of his being, and he found comfort in the subtle changing colors, the flowing patterns of the hills. He took sustenance from the great calm indifference with which the desert tolerated him. He thought once that these hills must look like the face of God; God would have to have this same vast imperturbability to endure the world as it was.

But thinking about God always brought him to the thorny problem of religion which he generally tried to avoid. This was not easy. He had been raised in an atmosphere saturated with it and, though he could put it out of his mind for long periods of time, it would spring up in unlikely places to disturb him. He realized that the vision of God which he had come upon in the desert was very unlike the one of the God who ran the church. That one was a congenial but indefatigable bookkeeper with such an immense and complicated filing system that it staggered the imagination. All the souls living and dead that inhabited the earth were slowly but surely being filed away in their proper and carefully labeled niches. He didn't like the idea of his soul being flattened up and stored away with all the proper entries, and he could not accept a personal God as erratic as the power which ruled the earth he knew–the one which allowed huge fortunes to be made and hoarded away by a few men who could wipe out the lives and dreams of millions of other men in a mystery called a depression. He guessed he had come to that state that Everett called "agnosticism," a kind of bleak place like these endless hills. Laurence had read a little philosophy and some literature but not enough to help him to know that many men in many times had come to the same state of mind by many different routes. He and Everett had talked about it a lot in earlier years; Ev had influenced him more than he dared admit, especially to Irene. It was not a systematic, reasoned position, more just a feeling. He couldn't really say that he didn't believe in the church anymore, although he had come to question so many things, but he had never even considered severing ties with the church which bound him so strongly to his family and his whole life. He had married Irene in the Temple and she and Ellen were his for eternity; whatever that was it gave him a lot of comfort out here.

His for eternity–the thought gave him a feeling tinged with a sickening fear; what if he couldn't even keep her in this world? It wasn't likely that they would starve. There would be some way of eking out an existence, but existence was a pretty grim prospect after what they had dreamed of through the Twenties. Laurence rode his wintry hills like a man in the grip of a heavy nightmare.

One late January afternoon almost a month later, he noticed that some ewes had strayed and he set out to find them. As his horse sidled down a ravine where sheep often became lost, he noticed the bones of a bleaching skeleton. The ribs of the animal, apparently a sheep, still attached to the ingenious links of the backbone, curved up in rigid, macabre memory of their former role, that of containing living viscera and supporting warm furred hide. Laurence had seen hundreds of such skeletons, some smaller, some larger, strewn about these hills in the years he had spent on them, but this one struck him as being curiously poignant. Among people death was attended by such a lot of false pageantry and self-deception. Here it was taken care of swiftly and cleanly. In another year there would be hardly a trace of this creature. The shadscale would be a little more profuse perhaps and cacti would fatten; it seemed altogether right in a way. The desert would dispose of a man fallen here in much the same efficient and impersonal way. For himself he wouldn't mind so much; the thought of a coffin and vault sealing him away from the earth gave him a nauseous sense of claustrophobia. It would be better to be released here in the open, completely wild and free.

Then he caught himself up and grimaced at such morbid thoughts. Not sighting any sheep in the gully, he spurred his horse out to the flat land and galloped toward camp. On the way he located the delinquent ewes and got them back to the bedding ground. The light was falling fast and it was growing colder. He was anxious to get in and start supper. The plaintive bleating of the sheep in varied tones and tempos filled the evening as they gradually subsided onto the cold ground for a night's rest. Their gray backs looked like a creek full of smooth rocks.

Such dumb creatures to have staked one's whole life on, Laurence thought. The shepherd and sheep have ever been the symbol of the humblest man—"The meek shall inherit the earth"—perhaps the last man on earth would be a stupid shepherd herding his stupid animals on a cold hill far far away from anything and anybody. He would probably be the last to hear that the world had ended and the last to care.

A sheep camp makes a cozy home. In the thirties it was still built on a wagon bed which was always painted green. The canvas top was stretched over high curved ribs. Inside at the back was a high double bed with storage space underneath, which could only be reached from outside. Storage bins, the tops of which covered with linoleum made a seat, ran around the sides. Near the door was a small iron cook stove and above the stove were high, open shelves filled with dishes, pans and almost always, the sour dough jar. A small table which, in case of company could hold three enamel plates and cups, let down from the opposite wall.

Sheep camps had a particular smell which varied from camp to camp but was basically the smell of cooked or cooking mutton and cold mutton grease. In the background was the odor of unwashed bedding and clothes. Greek sheep camps smelled of garlic; some herders smoked and theirs reeked of tobacco. Laurence's camp smelled strongly of black pepper, which he used profusely on the mutton, and sometimes of raisins, of which he was inordinately fond.

Tonight he built up the fire as usual before tending to the horses so that it would be warm and cozy when he settled in. He fed the dog, old Gyp, who whined and crawled under the wagon contentedly. Then he climbed into the camp, fastened the two parts of the door between him and the cold night and set about preparing his simple sheepherder's meal.

He put the coffee on. Coffee was a bad habit that he had acquired from his rough life, contrary to his early teachings. It distressed Irene and his mother, but he couldn't quite face life in the sheep camp without it now. He rolled out sour dough biscuits and opened a can of tomatoes. Mutton chops were sizzling away in the pan and every so often he would douse them with more pepper. The small canvas room was full of good warm smells.

Laurence ate his supper wishing his wife and daughter were sharing it with him. He had never grown used to the pervading loneliness; he was a man poorly fitted to this kind of life, a man who thought and felt too intensely. The solitude, while sometimes good for his spirit after the stimulation of people and cities, was bad for his active and inquiring mind. The past weeks since his trip home at Christmas had been one of tumult and torture, but it seemed to him tonight that, although he had not reached any decision about the future, he had calmed some of the fear and bitterness that had churned about in his mind night and day. He wondered if he should have prepared Irene a little more for what might happen.

In his dismal mood he thought it might help him to work on his music tonight, take his mind off his troubles. That was one of the things with which he had to come to terms; the dreams of continued study he had so foolishly nursed had been wiped out in the past few months. He saw now that even if he had money, he had let the time in which a man could lay the groundwork of his talent go by. Could he hope to go on dallying with his gift or must he courageously renounce it? He had meant to ask Everett's advice when he visited him, but couldn't bring himself to approach the subject.

After he cleared the dishes away, he got out his violin and a large portfolio of yellowing papers. He spread the curled papers out on the camp table and adjusted the kerosene lamp. How pitiful they looked. What in God's name had ever made him think that he might write music or play it the way he had learned and sensed it could be played? Everett Gordon, of course. Looking back sharply and clearly he could see that he had been the agent of another man's dream.

Laurence, in his long association with the older musician, had never understood the tragedy of his life. Everett Gordon was the only son of what had once been the wealthiest and proudest family in Merritsville. He had been educated in the best eastern schools, had traveled all over Europe, and had had every opportunity to develop a splendid musical talent. But before he was thirty he was a ruined man who had come back to live like a shadow in the decaying mansion on the west side of town. Once in a while he could be persuaded to come out and perform musical chores in the community, and on one of these rare occasions, he had met young Laurence Kent who had been taking music lessons from the German shoemaker on main street. There had been something in the young man's playing and in his face that aroused his interest and a fragment of his lost dreams. Laurence responded to his gestures of friendship and was shown into a world of books, art, music, ideas that he scarcely dreamed existed.

Now Everett's handsome, drink-ravaged face stood out in Laurence's troubled mind as he had seen it on that last wintry day, and he thought that there was an aura of darkness about it. Gordon had shown him a world which made him forever restless and unhappy in the narrow one into which he had been born, and from which there had never been, in spite of all his fancies, the slightest chance of escape. Laurence had been born into a time and place that denied the validity of true artistic experience. Of course musical performance of hymns and popular sentimental music was greatly encouraged, reading of sentimental, religious verse was widely practiced and church works, informational documents, light fiction were read, but the real experience of "art" belonged to the wicked world which the Saints and pilgrims before them had renounced. Besides such interests were considered effeminate and impractical, contributing nothing to the consummate goal of getting rich and remaining faithful to the church. Laurence, who did not have the fiery impetus of genius and was not at home in the broad reaches of thought and idea, did not fully understand what had thwarted Everett and now himself. He only felt a dull, deep sense of futility.

Sometimes Laurence, who had been so rigidly trained against the evils of alcohol, became disgusted with Gordon and resolved to stay away from him. Not that he was ever tempted or that Everett had tried to corrupt him; on the contrary, he spoke sadly and ashamedly of his affliction. But Laurence puzzled, how could a man who had what Gordon had had in life waste it? And yet he exerted a powerful fascination for Laurence and drew out of him a bitter kind of love which was second only in strength to his love for Irene. Only his mother defended his friendship with this sad man–his sometimes exasperating, but brave and wonderful mother whose moral behavior was impeccable. Only she could make room in her world for Everett as she made room for all the tragic and errant people that others coldly excluded. Of course, at one time she had worked for the Gordon family, even helped raise Everett. He smiled to think of her, odd obtuse, but completely right way of meeting life and handling all comers. Surely he could not fail her courage. Together they had often talked about Everett and pondered the mystery of his debasement that neither of them could understand. Now suddenly a veil had been lifted, no, torn aside and he knew.

At some time in Everett's life the world in which he had believed had collapsed, and he was simply incapable of living in the one in which he found himself. Perhaps he found his talent did not measure up in the larger world; he had hinted as much at one time. Perhaps it was the marriage that failed. Drink provided the most convenient adaptation to a situation for which he had been totally unprepared. Laurence found himself now in just such a place, a shadowy limbo, a place more barren than these cold, windswept hills with no landmarks. A world in which he had placed all his hopes and faith was on the verge of collapse. Irene and Ellen, his mother, his family, all seemed to belong to a world much farther away than a couple of hundred rough desert miles. Only Everett had been here before him and he had found a desperate way out. But that was not a way that Laurence could take; from several youthful drinking sprees, he knew he could not get drunk enough to forget his troubles. Alcohol separated his mind and will, but his relentless mind never lost its power to ridicule and condemn. He could not shame his family that way. But what to do?

After the sheep business was gone, he would have to rebuild his life from what was left, but this cold night he could not see how that would be possible.

The devil that haunts the night winds of despair whispered a seductive thought to him–there is a way out. But his strong young mind and body recoiled. Not that, Dear God, only cowards take their own lives, and his church firmly taught that he who took his own life could never regain it. There could be no resurrection, no eternity, no wife, child, no nothing. There it was, the thing troubling him more than the mere fact of adjusting to the hardship of making a living. Nothing. His faith had failed him utterly in the hour of his greatest need.

He looked at his music again. There in a system of notations, most of which he had learned from Everett and part of which he had devised, was the sound of the pines in summer in the high Wasatch mountains, the crystal clarity of the air, the gleam of the white Mountain Columbine spilling down the slope back of their cabin where he and Irene had spent summers homesteading. He played the music sketchily on his violin, and his mind filled it out into the wondrous orchestration of love and hope they had once shared. He had lived and felt these things so deeply that he wanted to preserve them, pass them on. Was this not more real than the despair he was feeling tonight?

Of course there were other passages in the music to balance the optimism and joy for he knew life had a harsh, often terrifying side. He had marked down sudden wild thunder storms, the murderous flashes of lightning that split giant pines in two. He had noted the cold, shrieking winds and oppressive melancholy of the desert. He had heard these contrasts in the music of the great masters that Everett had played for him on his phonograph; knew that he had caught this in his own composition. He wasn't afraid of the struggle, the conflict; it was the meaningless of it all that shook him, the grotesque fact that thousands of men like himself and Aaron could be deceived to build on something so precarious, promises that a great, abundant nation held out to every young man and woman but could never be fulfilled. And yet the country was still what it had always been, full of everything man needed or could want. There was an abundance of forests, of land, water, plants, animals and strength in mens' arms and backs, and abundance that staggered the imagination and yet a man could build no security on it? People were homeless, unemployed, bewildered and eventually they would be hungry in the richest land in the world. Something that in Laurence's mind was sheer fantasy, "the economic system" that existed only in the minds of certain high-placed men, was more real and powerful than all that God had provided. Neither by experience, training or temperament was he able to understand it. It is likely that no one really was.

As Laurence played tentatively through his music, it became more and more apparent to him that he had taken a wrong turn somewhere. He could barely see, shining through the mist and fog on a distant hill far across a thorn-filled ravine, a home for the spirit of man. He would never reach it this time, but he had seen it at least. Could he be grateful for that and go on? He laid the violin, wrapped in its red sack, back in the scarred case and folded up the music with a long sigh.

As he prepared for bed, he became aware of the howling of coyotes in the distance, a familiar, dark thread in the tapestry of desert sounds. It sawed across his already exacerbated nerves.

For all his years in the desert he had never ceased hating the nasty whine-shriek-bark of the coyote on a winter night. He reached for his 30-30 which stood by the stove and checked it. It was loaded and he might need it. He decided not to remove his clothes, for if the wailing came closer, he might have to ride around the sheep. Putting one more stick on the fire, he lay down drowsily on the bed; he must have fallen asleep for suddenly he started up. Gyp was barking wildly; the horses were thrashing around and the shrill noise of the coyotes sounded as though they were just outside the camp. He leaped to his feet, shrugged into his sheep skin coat and angrily reached for the gun.

Aaron made a trip to the herd every two or three weeks with fresh supplies. He thought there was something strange about the camp that morning when he bounced the truck to a stop near it. The camp horses were stamping restlessly and the saddle horse was wandering about dragging its bridle. Gyp crawled out from under the camp whimpering and beating his tail on the ground. There was no smoke coming out of the stove pipe; Laurence must be sick or something this late in the morning when usually he would have been out riding around the range.

Aaron yanked open the upper half of the door and yelled, "Hey there, anybody home?"

There was no answer, so he reached inside and unfastened

the rest of the door, poking his head into the gloom. In the cold yellowish light seeping through the canvas he saw a dreadful sight. Laurence, still wearing his sheep skin coat and boots now covered with dried blood, was crumpled down between the stove and projecting bunk, the whole side of his head blown away. The gun lay across his legs. Gobbets of blood, flesh and hair spattered all over the camp, had frozen on the linoleum, the cold stove, canvas and quilts.

Aaron backed off the wagon tongue, swearing in horror. Shouting long strings of incoherent oaths and half sobbing, he staggered back to the truck. Leaping in he roared away to get help; he could never enter that camp alone. Out on the desert the sheep that had scattered aimlessly for the past three days, nibbled at the sparse grasses and bleated forlornly at the cold gray February sky.

CB

Under a February sky filled with heavy gray clouds like bales of dirty wool, Laurence Kent was lowered into a muddy hole on cemetery hill overlooking the broad valley. His grave made the fourth mound in the family lot.

A sizable crowd milled about; among them on the fringe, and quite apart, was a rather slightly built middle-aged man in an expensive but old-fashioned overcoat. His Mephistophelian face was averted from the scene, and the wan light shown on his dark curling hair which was streaked with gray. He held his black hat to his chest in a finely gloved hand and supported himself on a gold-headed mahogany cane. He was so drunk that he could hardly keep himself erect even with its help. He had debated a long time about coming to see the last thing he had genuinely loved obliterated by earth and time; it had taken several stiff drinks in fact; now he knew that the gesture was quite futile and a trifle melodramatic. But he had been prone all his life to futile and empty gestures. Cursing silently to himself, Everett Gordon turned and cautiously made his way down the slippery muddy road before the graveside rituals were finished.

Ellen looked up and noticed the dark, retreating figure that, even from the back and staggering a little, showed a distinction which did not belong to anybody else in Merritsville. She whispered to her grandmother to whose hand she was clinging tightly, "There goes Mr. Gordon."

Addie looked up in surprise; "I'm glad he came," she said fervently.

Dosey and Bertha were supporting Irene, whose tear-swollen face was buried from the sight of the tan casket slowly descending into the earth in the big fur collar of her best black coat. Before the first shovel full of earth was tossed into the hole, they had gently guided her to the waiting car and driven away. But Addie stood firmly, holding Ellen by the hand. She intended to stay to see that the flowers were placed right and all was in good order. This was the last thing she could do for her last son.

Ellen looked on with wide bewildered eyes, trying to understand. They said that box contained her father, but she had not seen him. Her mind, heart, body, everything rejected this strange day. The long funeral with interminable speeches sounding like church, the sad music, smell of carnations, had nothing to do with her father as she remembered him. For the rest of her life Ellen would hate the smell of carnations. The sound of sobbing, sniffling, people, talking in unnatural voices and her mother looking terribly ill–all of it was strange, frightening, but she could not connect it with her father. He was still out there somewhere on the hills; he would be home, as he had always come home after long absences.

She had cried when they told her, from fright and because Irene was crying, and she was terrified when she heard the words, "accidental gunshot wound." Hal had told her in his crude offhand way that the reason she couldn't see her father was that his whole head was blown off. She had screamed at him but she knew it must be true. When other people had died, you could go look at them in their coffins. They looked like they were sleeping, but all Ellen could see was the big tan box, covered with flowers that they all said contained her father.

Her love stood between her and this awful fact to protect her from a blow which would be devastating if accepted all at once. The truth would make itself known over a long, long time in small, unexpected ways when the heart had time to gather strength.

The clouds grew heavier and it began to snow big, wet flakes. Addie and Ellen went home to Grandma's house with bouquets of funeral flowers. A lot of people were there eating and talking, saying things that they had said a hundred times on occasions like this–he's with his father now preparing a home for his family... he led a good life and will get his reward in heaven... the Lord will bless you in your hour of need. Ellen was too confused to understand and wished she could run away home and hide in her bedroom, get away from the teary hugs everybody was giving her and think about her father alone.

Presently, by dark, they were all gone, even the cousins who had acted like it was some sort of picnic, Hal stuffing himself, Lorraine trying to tend the baby while Aunt Dosey was busy with the food. Only Louise stayed close to Ellen seeming to share her feelings.

At last Irene, Ellen and Addie were alone. Irene sat in the padded rocker by the kitchen stove, her eyes closed and her face white and waxy. The harsh light from a bare globe which hung by a cord from the ceiling cast hard black shadows on her exhausted features. From time to time tears would slide from under her thick lashes spilling down her cheeks onto her new black dress. She seemed not to notice and sometimes gave a queer, harsh sobbing noise as though she were choking. Ellen went over and touched her hand; it was cold and she moved it feebly with a tremendous effort as though trying to reach out to her daughter.

Ever since they had heard about Laurence, Irene seemed oblivious to anyone else, as though she were in some kind of trance. Addie and Dosey had had to take over all the arrangements.

Grandma made some hot tea and urged her to drink it, but she shook her head weakly.

"Poor, poor thing, she's worn right out." Grandma stroked her hair and tucked some of the stray strands back in the braids. "We must leave her be awhile," she said and turned out the light which seemed unusually cruel in its exposure of her sorrow. Addie lit one of the kerosene lamps which she still kept in spite of the fact that she had put electricity in the house; its mellow shadows were kinder to Irene who had gone halfway into the darkness with her husband. Addie had been there before her, several times. Not as deeply, she knew, as this woman, for although she had loved strongly, she had never been as dependent on another person or as vulnerable. There had always been too many other claims that life made on her.

She had feared for Laurence and Irene when she had seen long ago how, at the first, from their high school days, they had made a complete world for each other–how for Irene especially everything outside her love for Laurence was unimportant, even unreal with the possible exception of Ellen who was, of course, part of their love. Yet Addie knew secretly that if Irene had to choose between her husband and child, she would have chosen her husband. She could not by nature have done otherwise; some women are like that. Their love, which is their being, is like a vine which has to wrap itself around something firmer in order to live at all. But it has a formidable strength and vitality which remolds the object upon which it is fastened and becomes an inextricable part of it. If one is removed the other withers or, at least, suffers the change deeply.

Poor things, they had both been so innocent. Knowing their love sanctified by the church and approved by the community, they thought they were right in letting it fill their lives to the exclusion of all else. What a crime they had committed against each other. Laurence, if he had been left, for all that he was a man and supposedly stronger, might have been as stricken as the pale woman he loved, who sat where he had sat so many times in his mother's warm kitchen.

But life must go on. If God had permitted this terrible thing to happen, Addie was sure that He had made some provisions for the consequences. She had learned that the most saving thing besides prayer was the ordinary ritual of life–eating, sleeping, mending, washing, cleaning, visiting, church going, attending to whatever had to be done at the moment. Although there was a lot of other food left, she set out bread and milk bowls in the lamp light and she and Ellen had their favorite bedtime snack. She locked the doors, banked the fire and helped Irene to bed, tucking her in as tenderly as she did Ellen. As she kissed Ellen good night, Ellen put her arms around her grandmother's neck and held on tightly.

"Grandma, where's Daddy tonight?" she whispered.

"In heaven, I s'pect," said Grandma, gently disengaging Ellen's arms.

"Already?"

"It isn't far for good people to go." Addie patted her cheek. "Now you say your prayers and go to sleep. That's what he'd like you to do." She tried not to let Ellen feel her cheeks were wet with the tears she had held back all day. She would cry a little alone and carry on with the extra burden that the Lord had put on her this day–the care of Irene and Ellen.

Ellen mumbled off the little prayer she had learned ending with "and please take care of Daddy wherever he is." When Grandma had left the room, she pulled the covers over her head to close the darkness down to a size she could stand.

I said that same prayer the very night he was dead, she thought with a chill, I said "please take care of Daddy." What if I didn't say it soon enough? Maybe God was taking care of him now like they said in the funeral; if heaven were such a wonderful place, then surely everybody ought to be glad to go there and to have people they loved go there. But why did it seem so awful and ugly to get there? The words "accidental gun-shot wound" and what Hal had said, "head blown off" called up tormented pictures that raced through her mind. She felt very cold and curled herself into a tight ball, wishing she could creep out of bed into the one with her mother. They could cuddle up like spoons they way they did and talk about when Daddy would be home. It seemed like such a long time ago that everything was all right though it had only been a week since Uncle Aaron had brought the terrible news.

℃ℑ

February slipped into a nasty March and March oozed into a cold rainy-snowy April. Time moved as cumbrously as an old wagon on a muddy road. Ellen went on to school, shutting, as best she could, the awful week out of her life. Irene sat about the house in her bathrobe most of the day, her face dull and white as plaster. Her hands, which before had always been busy with embroidery, tatting, crocheting or sewing, lay quiet and cold in her lap, and her hair–the hair that had been Laurence's pride–hung down her back in a heavy braid. She had lost weight and looked as gaunt as a fence post; Irene was a woman in whom ten or fifteen pounds made a great deal of difference. Her well-formed large bones made her a handsome woman when they were padded with flesh; when they were not, she looked emaciated. From force of long habit she managed to take care of the essential household chores and prepare food for Ellen of which she ate very little and frequently threw up if she did. Everyone was concerned about her, most particularly Addie and Dosey. One of them made a point of dropping in every day or so. One spring day Dosey made her way through the puddled streets with a special pudding that she knew Irene liked.

Doris, Laurence's older sister with whom he had been very close, had nevertheless been an affectionate exasperation to him. It was Laurence's belief, perhaps because of his unusual artistic sensibilities, that all women ought to be beautiful, or at least attractively groomed. Dosey, as he had nicknamed her very early when she cared for him as a child, had been a pretty girl with fine dark eyes, an abundance of rich brown hair and a good figure when she married Aaron Walker. At no time had she every cared a great deal about her appearance, fancying herself quite homely, and the demands of marriage to a poor man who kept children coming every two years or so had destroyed most of the womanly vanity that she had.

Today she was wearing a shabby brown coat, probably one of Bertha's or Irene's cast-offs because it stretched too tightly across her unsupported breasts. The hem of a plain house dress showed unevenly below the coat, and her hair, which had begun to show gray streaks, was bound up loosely with no attempt at style, into a messy bun. Carrying a chubby over-bundled baby in one arm and a covered dish in the other, she walked briskly in run-over black Oxfords, crooning pleasantly to the baby and bouncing him much to his delight, as though everything in her world was all right.

She pushed open the door of Irene's house and called cheerfully, "Anybody home?"

Irene, startled, answered from the rocking chair in a voice that sounded as though she might have been asleep. "Oh, come on in, that you, Dosey?"

Dosey plumped the baby down on the braided rag rug in front

of the stove and put the dish on the cupboard.

"I want you to eat some of this, right now," she ordered and went to the cupboard. Spooning some of the pudding into a dish, she thrust it at Irene. "Lands, girl, you look like sin on Monday. Now I don't mean to be hard on you, but you know how bad Laurence would feel to see you like this. Come on, I fixed it special for you, and I want to see you eat some before I go. I got a meetin' of the Primary teachers in half and hour." She put the spoon in Irene's hand who waved it away in distress.

"Not now, Dosey." Tears of weakness flooded her eyes. "I tried to eat just a little while ago and it all came back up. Dosey, I'm scared. I've missed two periods now."

Dosey set the dish and spoon down in surprise.

"You don't mean it?" she gasped. "Oh well, I've heard these bad upsets sometimes cause you to miss and go all wrong. You don't look like you got enough blood to make a good period."

Irene smiled weakly at her blunt sister-in-law and shook her head. "No, I think it's for sure, Dosey. I know the feeling. You know I've been pregnant before, and it's not like anything else."

Dosey nodded in agreement, momentarily stricken speechless, but she quickly recovered. "Oh my good land a goshin!" she exclaimed looking sympathetically at Irene.

"Dosey, what am I going to do?" Irene wailed.

Dosey pursed her lips and shrugged her shoulders. "Do? I guess you're gonna do what every other woman does when she's pregnant–you're gonna have a baby. Oh you poor sweet kid." She put her arms around Irene and held her tight against her full bosom. Then she sat back with a falsely bright face. "Maybe it'll be a boy and look like Laurence. You know how he wanted a boy. No matter how hard it comes a child is always a blessin' from the Lord."

"But how will I take care of it?" Irene pursued with trembling lips; it seemed more real and frightening now that she had actually said it to someone. " I haven't got money for doctor bills and there's not even going to be anything to feed it." She knew by now that she was practically a penniless widow.

Dosey, too, knew what desperate straits they were all in. After the funeral Aaron had told her that everything was gone, except the sagging old house they lived in, but that was mortgaged and might still be lost. They were going to have to start all over again with six children and Irene and Ellen to take care of as well. But even in the years of apparent prosperity Dosey had never become accustomed to plenty. Most of their resources had gone into the business; she had always had to make do on less than she needed. As in most of the families in the mountain and desert communities the only thing they had ever had in abundance was hard work and optimism. In the Mormon communities this was reinforced by faith that the Lord would provide. The thought of another mouth to feed did not frighten Dosey all that much. Babies had always been welcome.

Little Joey Walker, who had been forgotten for the startling news, had crawled under the table and pulled the table cloth off. A vase of artificial flowers came crashing down.

"Oh, Lardy." Dosey leaped up. "Joey, come out from there, naughty boy. If you don't want the baby, you can give it to me. I haven't got enough," she said wryly. Irene had to laugh, cheered in spite of herself.

Irene was grateful for her indomitable sister-in-law, had many times wished she were more like her. Hardly anything seemed to upset her for very long. The more she took on her shoulders the easier she seemed to carry it. Dosey was one of those people who can never do anything unless they are doing a dozen things at once. She held responsible and demanding positions in all of the church organizations, and was always in the process of preparing a program or a "lesson." Her sewing machine was always piled high with mending, her ironing board with ironing and her laundry basket with laundry to do. She house-cleaned perpetually, but no more than one room of the large old house was ever straight at one time. She embroidered, tatted, crocheted, made quilts, doorstops out of cans filled with sand and dressed like dolls, flowers out of crepe paper dipped in wax, fancy pot-holders and aprons out of scraps, dolls out of men's socks and painted designs on scarves with metallic beads to name a few of her projects and hobbies. She was never too busy to start a new project. The only way she kept her sanity was to call on Addie frequently for help.

Irene's house and life, by contrast, had to be in nearly perfect order for her to endure the world at all. She attacked and completed each task meticulously. If things got out of hand or beyond her, as now, she succumbed to depression or illness.

Dosey replaced the table cloth and vase and retrieved the mischievous baby. Jogging him on her hip, she turned seriously to Irene. "Well, now, you've got to snap out of it and start taking care of yourself. There'll be a way to take care of this baby. We'll all help, you know that. I got some of Joey's clothes left over. Remember you got something else to live and be glad for now. That's the way Laurence would've wanted it, wouldn't he?"

Irene nodded with a wan smile with just a trace of disbelief in it.

Dosey patted her affectionately. "Now you try to eat some of that pudding soon's you can. I've got to go now. I'm already late for the meetin', but I'll look in later or again tomorrow."

Irene saw her to the door and watched her striding down the street. Tears began to stream down Irene's face; how good Dosey and all her family, Laurence's family were. She must try hard to welcome this poor baby.

CB

There was not much to be done in preparation for the child of Laurence Kent. A small insurance policy had paid for his burial, with only a little left over. Irene, who had never understood the economic arrangements of life, leaned heavily on her mother-in-law and Aaron for help. Between them they arranged for a small widow's pension from the county; the church pledged help and friends and neighbors brought in bits of produce–a sack of potatoes, a piece of meat. It was the way they had always done things in Mormon towns. A few years of relative prosperity had not disturbed old habits or the Protestant cast of mind that had seen them through almost a hundred years in the mountain-desert land where life at best was a struggle. It was better so, many of the church leaders preached. The forces of evil triumphed where minds and hands were idle. A depression was not really a new experience to these descendants of the Pioneers.

Addie planted her vegetable garden, for which she had long been famous, and there were plenty of fresh vegetables all summer, which she never tired of urging on Irene for the "sake of the baby," and she shared eggs and milk with her and Ellen. Out of her egg money she bought some batiste and flannel and set Irene to work on small clothes.

After the fourth month Irene began to feel better, to eat and regain some of her color, but she did not pick up all of the vitality she had lost. Through the summer she remained pale and tired, moving as though in a soft haze. She sat in the rocking chair working on the little garments with her fine pale hands in which the blue veins stood out. There was some peace in handling the soft fabric and taking fine even stitches. She had always liked to sew, but she could not think of the clothes in connection with a baby. She hardly thought of the baby at all and looked at herself occasionally with distaste and disbelief as her stomach began to swell. In fact she did not dare think about anything much, backward or forward, but let her mind rest in a quiet, featureless twilight zone. Whenever she tried to understand what had happened to her, that Laurence was gone, a severe panic gripped her. The future seemed so empty in spite of what Dosey and Addie kept telling her about "eternal marriage" and the Celestial kingdom. But there was Ellen... she knew she had to go on for her sake.

One day she noticed the house magazines and plans. She took them out and quietly burned them one by one in the kitchen stove to heat the kettle.

The spring, which had been long, rainy and cold, suddenly in May burst into radiant bloom. The old apple tree by the privy was loaded with fragrant white blossoms around which bees wove a golden net of sound. For years Ellen thought that bees blossomed out of the trees and were the sound trees made in their happiness with spring. The lawn was a tufted quilt of yellow dandelions, and lilacs by the gate feathered into a lacy lavender-blue haze. Irene put off telling Ellen about the baby. Things like that, confidences about the mysterious process of life, had always been difficult for her. She could never talk about her periods like Dosey and some other women; her sex life had always been a deeply personal secret. She knew she must explain to her daughter somehow about having a baby after its father had died; she simply didn't know how. But Ellen already knew.

Hal and Lorraine had taken care of that one afternoon when she was at the Walker's. She was playing "boo" with baby Joey, whom they were tending while Aunt Dosey was away at one of her hundred meetings. Joey was a delightful baby, fat, round healthy and very good natured. He puffed himself and wriggled and gurgled with joy as Ellen put her hands over her face and then suddenly removing them, cried "boo"! When she held them over her eyes a little longer than usual, he patted her cheek and tried to pull them away. Ellen had a sudden pang of love and hugged him fiercely.

"I wish I had a baby brother," she said impulsively.

Hal and Lorraine, to whom baby brothers or sisters were no longer a delight or novelty, looked at each other. They had overheard their mother and grandmother talking about Irene.

"You're gonna get one pretty soon," Hal said without taking his eyes off the flipper he was fixing.

Ellen looked up in surprise. "Whata you mean?'

"Your ma's gonna have a baby," said Lorraine.

"I don't believe you," Ellen cried irritably. Her cousins were always tormenting her with things they knew that she didn't. Louise was listening, her big eyes wide.

"But you have to have a Mama and a Papa to get a baby, don't you?" she put in.

"Oh, he made it b'fore he got his head blowed off," Hal replied, calmly aiming his flipper at a robin in the apple tree.

Ellen leaped up and began to beat on Hal with both fists. He put up one arm to defend himself, grinning maliciously.

"He didn't, he didn't!" she screamed, infuriated and frightened anew by the terrible words that Hal had discovered upset her.

The baby began to cry and Lorraine pulled Ellen away from Hal.

"I hate you, I hate you, you're all mean liars." she sobbed.

Lorraine put her arms around her, "Don't cry," she soothed. "It's all right. Babies are made a long, long time before they're born–years and years up in heaven. They can get born after the daddy dies. Sister Stockton's did, remember?"

Ellen looked interested. "They can, how?"

Lorraine was suddenly filled with confusion. "Well, I don't know 'zactly, but they just can."

"Mothers have 'em in their bellies," Hall supplied the information with an air of superior knowledge.

"In a nest, like birds, Mama told me," Louise added anxiously, trying to soften the shock and keep peace as she always did.

Ellen, stunned, looked from one to the other of her wise cousins. "But why didn't Mama tell me?"

"I don't know," Lorraine said nervously. "Maybe you better not tell her we told you; she might be mad. Older people don't like to have kids know things like that, I guess." Then more urgently, "Don't tell her we told you, cross your heart."

Ellen slowly, incredulously, crossed her heart, and when she looked at baby Joey again, trying to coax her back into the happy game, it was as though there were something strange and sinister about him.

"Guess I'll go home," she said, gathering up her sweater and books.

For several days Ellen looked at her mother suspiciously. Irene hadn't looked like her usual self for a long while; the loose clothes she wore concealed the swelling of her figure so that Ellen couldn't tell the difference. Her mother hadn't dressed up pretty like she used to ever since her father had died. Several times she tried to open her mouth to ask the tormenting question, but finally realized that a barrier like a the thick plate glass windows in Washburn's store had arisen between her and her mother through which she could see her plainly but never touch her. But the secret, of which she was still uncertain, fearing the Walker cousins were making fun of her, troubled her constantly. She became restless and uneasy around Irene.

One bright Saturday morning Ellen arose before her mother, fixed something to eat and wandered around the house wondering what to do. She went into the front room and her eye fell on the radio. It was seldom turned on; Irene seemed to have an aversion to it; she imagined it consumed a great deal of power. Sometimes Ellen turned it on very low and sat with her ear close to the speaker listening to the voices and music. A cheerful breakfast show was on and Ellen was entranced by the jocularity and music so foreign to Merritsville.

When Irene arose, irritable and depressed, with traces of nausea as well, she glanced into Ellen's room which was more than usually cluttered. This, added to her misery, was enough to spoil the sunny day already. When she spotted Ellen snuggled happily by the radio, which was a particularly vivid reminder of her dreadful loss, she lost her temper.

"Ellen, I want you to pick up that room like I told you to last night, right this minute," she said sharply.

Ellen didn't answer at once.

"Ellen!" repeated Irene, setting her teeth. By this time the harsh tone of her mother's voice aroused a flush of antagonism in her. She didn't want to see the face that went with it, so she stubbornly kept her ear to the speaker.

"Ellen, do you hear me?" she all but screamed.

Ellen turned a face to her filled with hatred and contempt which shocked Irene to tears. She sat down by the table, tears streaming down her face. She had begun to notice the estrangement between her daughter and herself; just lately there had been such a change in Ellen that she hardly recognized her as her own child. She was either feverishly engaged in some project like making scrapbooks, littering the house with clippings and all sorts of mess or curled up with a book oblivious to everything around her. It was as though they lived in two different worlds. Her round freckled face with its snubbed nose and straight brown hair cut in Dutch bangs looked secretive and defiant to Irene, who was disturbed to find that she thought her own child distressingly plain and at this moment didn't like her at all. Worst of all, for the first time she felt like slapping her.

Irene was one of those women whose love for her children, for the whole world in fact, flows through the man she loves. Her capacity for love had come from Laurence who had given her that sense of herself and her worth as a woman which she had needed to unlock the resources of her soul. With him gone, the circuit closed– her affections were dammed; her normal channel of expression clogged and she had not had time to find a new one.

She was frozen in horror at the hatred she saw in Ellen's face, not realizing that it was a reflection of her own. One of the sacred myths of Motherhood was shattered in one unexpected moment. She was wholly a product of the nineteenth century which had insisted that ALL mothers love their children ALL of the time, and ALL children love their mothers ALL of the time.

This had been firmly and dramatically taught her by the maiden aunt who had raised her from the death of her own parents at the age of six. Aunt Delia, a successful teacher of music who never presented herself as a substitute for Irene's own mother, had built an immaculate shrine for her sister, Irene's dead mother. She constantly retouched the picture of ideal Womanhood (Victorian pose) which had as its prime end Chaste Motherhood. Nowhere in it had been the slightest suggestion that a good and virtuous (now bereaved) mother could provoke disobedience and open dislike. Irene was shattered.

Ellen was stricken for a moment and wanted to go put her arms about her mother, but the resentment she had nursed in her confusion and humiliation about the secret welled up inside her and she could not. After all, her mother had shut her out first and, even though she knew she was terribly sad about her father, Ellen felt that she too deserved to be pitied. Both of them were tangled in the meshes of their love and ignorance, so close that neither could see that her own overwhelming need was the need of the other.

Ellen turned the radio off in exasperation. "Oh, all right," she said petulantly and went into her room.

Irene continued to sit in the chair, feeling infinitely sorry for herself–horribly alone in a world that continued to crumble at every touch. Now the ties between herself and her child were breaking. Indignant at the loss of her stature as a mother, she was even more frightened by the change in her own feelings. She wondered if she could ever love the child she was carrying. She had not felt much life and the first stirring of the poor little creature had given her no pleasure or sense of anticipation. It had been, if anything, a more discouraging confirmation of what she had kept hoping was not true. The only emotion she felt with any strength at all was the desire "to get it over with." She wondered if perhaps she ought not to tell Ellen. Maybe the idea of a baby would make her happy, but before Irene could summon the courage, Ellen had stalked out of the room with her straw hat.

"All right–I picked up my room," she said belligerently. "Can I go to Grandma's now? I promised I'd help her clean the chicken coop today."

"Yes, go ahead," said Irene. "Bring home some milk when you come, if Grandma has any left over."

Once out of the gate in the strong May sunshine Ellen had a lift of spirits and a sense of freedom. She resolved as she hopped and skipped along the weedy sidewalk that she would ask her grandma about the baby. Grandma would tell her the truth.

Addie was already down in the coop when Ellen arrived at the small farm on the lower edge of Merritsville. She was in her old blue coverall dress and heavy man's shoes, her hair covered by a shapeless man's hat drawn down the full length of its crown. She was scraping away at the rough cement floor of the coop. Ellen got a shovel and began to help her. She worked happily although she disliked the musty, feathery smell of the coop. She was big enough now to push the small wheel barrow full of manure down to the pile back of the barn and bring back a load of fresh straw. It gleamed in the sunshine and reminded her of the story about the princess who had learned to spin gold out of straw. Grandma and she spread the floor of the coop with clean straw and let the chortling hens back in from the run. They tiptoed around inspecting their new carpet like Relief Society ladies.

It was time for lunch. After Addie had removed her rough clothes, washed and put on a clean apron, she set out the simple lunch.

Ellen had taken several bites of the good home-made bread and jam before she ventured, "D'you know what Hal and Lorraine said the other day?"

"No, what?" Grandma said suspiciously.

"They said that Mama is going to have a baby." she blurted.

Addie didn't answer immediately, but finally she said, "Well, she is."

Ellen had a thrill of gladness which was soon displaced by the memory of the troubling problems that Hal and Lorraine had brought up.

"But don't babies have to have fathers?"

"Your father is the baby's father."

"But he's dead."

"Yes, but he's still a father." Grandma seemed in no mood to pursue the subject, but even though Ellen hesitated before she let loose the real problem that troubled her; she was determined to find out as much as she could. "Hal said that mothers have babies in their bellies."

Addie was seldom annoyed, but now she got up from the table and Ellen could see that she was agitated. She rattled the stove lids and poked chips on the little fire to heat her tea water.

"Oh, that Hal," she muttered. "I don't know what Dosey's gonna do with that child. He's too smart for his britches."

It was true then. Ellen turned the startling truth over in her mind before she asked a very risky question.

"How do they get there?"

Addie pursed her lips and looked steadily at her tea cup.

"The Lord puts 'em there with the help of the father. There's some things that good little boys and girls don't need to talk about. There will be a time to learn about all that."

Ellen knew she was squelched, but she was far from satisfied. "Mama's awful cross anymore. Does having babies make mothers like that? I don't think she loves me much anymore. Maybe she's just going to love the baby?"

"Now, Ellen." Grandma set her tea-cup down and fastened her gold-spectacled gaze firmly on her. "You mustn't say or think things like that. Of course your mother loves you just like she always did. It's somethin' of a trial havin' a baby and it's a double trial to your mother, her bein' left alone at a time like this. I know you ain't quite old enough to understand a lot of things, but you must be good to her. Your mama's not a strong woman, never has been. I don't mean she's sickly or anythin' like that; it's just that she needs somebody strong to lean on and, with your daddy gone, all she has is you and me. We must help her a lot these next months."

Grandma's careful and serious words had a curious effect on Ellen, something like the magic in Alice in Wonderland, that caused her to feel grown suddenly very large and disproportionate in her world. After lunch she went out and sat in her favorite place in the crab apple tree, thinking about the whole strange thing. She had to take care of her mother! It was funny. She thought grownups took care of children, but somehow, very obliquely, she could see what Grandma meant. Her mother did seem sad and lost as though she needed someone to take care of her, not all strong and reliable the way she had been before her father died.

Ellen felt a calm superior strength in herself; she resolved, crossing her heart secretly, that she would be good to Irene and help her with the baby.

The baby! What wonderful fun they would have taking care of him. It would be a boy. She picked a large leaf off the tree and formed it into a cradle with a small apple bud in it, rocking it gently as she imagined she would. But eventually the thought of the baby and its mysterious location in her mother cast a shadow from which she could not fully escape. Ellen had stumbled upon a world behind the world–a place which even her good honest Grandma couldn't talk about. It was a world full of things which you couldn't see until you bumped into them and got hurt and dreadfully shamed like the time she had accidentally opened the door of Grandma's privy and seen Uncle Aaron with his pants down. But after a while she grew tired of puzzling over it so she went back to pleasanter dreams of the baby. How she would love it and take care of it; it wouldn't grow up to be like Hal and the other rough boys she knew. Mama could never stand a boy like that. Presently she jumped out of the tree and went into the house.

"Grandma, can I make something for the baby?" she asked.

"Why, I think that would be fine," Addie agreed. She was mending socks for the Walker family, but she laid them aside, found some white flannel, her sharp scissors that nobody else ever dared touch, and cut out a little white petticoat hardly bigger than for a doll. Then she got out a curious box which fascinated Ellen. It was full of designs stamped on paper with small holes. Selecting a border of flowers and dots, she placed the pattern on the cloth and rubbed it with a felt pad dipped in blue powder. A fine blue tracing of the flowers came off on the cloth.

"But if it's a boy maybe he won't like flowers and fancy things, will he?" Ellen, watching closely, suggested.

"All babies like anything. They're all little and sweet," Grandma assured her. "Now you do this nice."

Ellen disliked embroidery work; she had had something else, she didn't know quite what–in mind, but she sat down obediently and began to untangle the snarls of thread in the sewing box that Grandma kept for her. Sitting on the cushion in the deep window sill that was her private corner, she worked virtuously the rest of the afternoon, producing on the small garment, which Grandma had quickly stitched together, an uneven row of multi-colored daisies. She thought it boring to do them all in one color as Grandma had suggested.

Addie, glancing from time to time at Ellen's intense face, the short, brown hair falling forward on her cheeks and her tongue caught between her lips as she struggled over the embroidery frame making crooked flower petals and frayed French knots, had a sharp pain in her chest that almost brought tears. She, too, was worried about the little broken family to which the new child was coming.

Late in the afternoon Addie filled a lard bucket with milk she got from her steady old cow, wrapped up the petticoat and walked home with Ellen. When they came into the house, Irene was sitting at the kitchen table looking calmer. She had done her hair up and put on a pink house dress that gave her pale cheeks a touch of color.

Addie sat down, unrolled the parcel and laid the little garment on the table between them.

"Ellen made this for the baby," she said simply. "I told her about it. I told her about it this afternoon."

Irene looked relieved, almost happy, from one to the other and then smiling, she held out her arm to Ellen who went into its curve awkwardly.

"My, it's nice." Irene ran her trembling fingers over the childish embroidery as though to make sure it was real. "Maybe we can put some lace on the bottom."

Ellen had a warm feeling as though something of the former love and serenity were restored to the house, but the relationship between her and her mother had changed. In some ways it was better; she grew to understand, without knowing why, that not all women can carry the heavy burdens of love.

ᗢ

June and July passed. The heat was hard on Irene; many days she lay in the cooler bedroom with the blinds drawn. Ellen moved quietly about the house doing what tasks she could or spent time at Grandma's. The summer holidays came and went without the usual high excitement. She did not go to the Walker's as much as she had been accustomed to.

Irene had explained that the baby would come sometime in September but one hot, sticky night in August Ellen heard her mother cry out. She leaped out of bed and ran to the door of the bedroom. Her mother was moaning and tossing on the bed. "Go get Aunt Dosey, quick!" she gasped. "Tell her to get the doctor, I think the baby's coming."

Ellen put on her dress and shoes and ran, stumbling and praying, the seven blocks through the sleeping town—past all the clawing shadows with huge echoing footsteps following her all the way. She pounded frantically on the Walker's front door.

When Dosey answered it, clutching her nightgown around her nervously, Ellen stammered, "Come quick, Mama's going to have the baby, I think. She's awful sick."

Dosey shook Aaron, got him yawning and grunting to his feet and dispatched him for Doctor Wardle. She and Ellen trotted swiftly back to the house where they found Irene crying hysterically. Dosey made up a fire, got out dishpans and filled them with water, found the clean old sheets which had been torn into squares, and told Ellen to get newspapers off the back porch. Scared and anxious to help her mother in some way, Ellen followed Dosey into the bedroom, but Aunt Dosey pushed her out firmly. "Now you just go back to bed and be a good girl; everythin' will be all right."

Ellen didn't go back to bed. She went out and huddled in the corner of the couch, her thin nightgown pulled around her feet, shivering in spite of the warm night as she listened and tried to understand what was going on. In the turmoil she was forgotten. She sat with her head pensively resting on her knees wondering why, at the last minute, she was excluded from this most important event, why getting born was so terrifying. She cringed every time she heard the sounds from the bedroom and began to cry softly.

Uncle Aaron and the doctor arrived. Aunt Dosey kept rushing back and forth between the bedroom and kitchen with pans, and Uncle Aaron had his instructions to keep the fire going. Irene screamed wildly once or twice and then Ellen heard her sobbing; once the doctor swore. There was a strong thick smell of chloroform which made Ellen feel sick. A little breeze stirred the lace curtains on the windows and touched Ellen's cheek; she looked up and saw a star fall across the deep black sky.

Before the dawn of another hot August day Irene had given birth to a stillborn baby boy. Aunt Dosey came out of the bedroom with a little blanket bundle, tears streaming down her face. Ellen leaped off the couch and rushed to her. "Is that my baby brother?" She reached out to touch it. Dosey drew back with alarm.

"No, no. You can't see him yet. Ellen, go to bed now. You'll catch cold out here."

Ellen crept, frightened and lonely, into her bed. It was quiet in her mother's room. The doctor was still there, and the smell of chloroform mingling with the rising heat was dreadfully oppressive. Ellen felt herself pushed down into a deep troubled sleep.

She saw her brother the next day lying on a pillow in the living room where all the blinds had been pulled down and the warm light was greenish like underwater. He was dressed in one of the soft white dresses on which her mother had tatted a deep lace hem. It was far too big for him and she thought that the little wizened face and tiny claw-like hands looked like a bird she had once seen before it got its feathers. The only real thing about him was a curl of dark moist hair that showed from under a yellowing tatted bonnet on either side of which fresh rosettes of blue ribbon stuck out oddly, making the face appear even smaller.

Aunt Dosey was with her; she rearranged one of the bows tenderly. "This was your daddy's bonnet when he was a baby; you wore it, too," she said gently. "Here, look, Ellen, he's wearing the petticoat you made for him." She lifted the dress and Ellen could see the daisies over which she had labored. She caught a glimpse of thin blue legs in white crocheted booties that were much too large. She could only stare, her throat drawn so tight that she could not speak.

Ellen wanted to touch him, but she couldn't. She knew the tiny dark claw of a hand would not feel at all like the fat warm one of Joey's that she had visioned in all her dreams of the baby. Aunt Dosey drew her gently away, and they went into the kitchen where Grandma was busy fixing some food and tidying up.

"Poor little thing," said Aunt Dosey, "Maybe it's a blessing after all. He would have had a hard time in this world startin' out so poorly and all."

Grandma nodded and patted Ellen. "Yes, he's with his daddy now in heaven. You better come and eat something, Sweetheart, It will be all right in a while."

They told her that her mother was very tired and must not be disturbed but once in the late afternoon when Aunt Dosey had gone home and Grandma was resting, Ellen tiptoed to the bedroom door which was slightly ajar. In the dim light she could see Irene's pale exhausted face turned sideways into the pillow. She looked like she would never wake up either. It scared Ellen but she did not dare ask Grandma if her mother might die, too, so she went out and sat in the swing in the apple tree. It seemed that the world had rudely changed again. What you thought was there was not at all. She tried to think of her father and the baby in heaven where things might be counted on to be always what you thought they should be. But it was very hard.

The next morning Uncle Aaron came with the small pine box he had built and which Grandma had lined with cotton batting and white satin. The baby was placed beside the grave of Laurence Kent and again Ellen climbed with her grandmother up the cemetery hill for graveside services. The sun beat down on the thick yellow clay as mercilessly as the snow and rain had fallen the last time they were here. Grandma held her black umbrella over them, tears running from under her glasses and down her cheeks. Ellen, whose stomach felt as though it were too full of hard, green apples and whose face was burning from the heat, wondered why the passage to heaven had to be so hard and dreary.

Almost a month later Irene still lay in the big brass bed with its smooth white cover, her face in its frame of dark hair only a deeper shade of white on the pillow. She had only glanced at the dead baby when Dosey had brought him to her all dressed for burial; touching him lightly, she murmured, "Poor little thing" and turned her face away. She had never spoken of it since; in fact it seemed a tremendous effort for her to speak at all. The doctor didn't know what to do for her though he looked in every day or so. Her long, thin hand with its wedding band reflecting the little light that seeped through the drawn blinds, lay motionless for hours outside the cover. He would pick it up and listen for her pulse, shake his head, "Just too much shock for her system, deep depression... nature will have to take its course." He advised Dosey and Addie to keep trying to get her to eat and take an interest in things.

Ellen would bring things to show her and read to her; once in a while Irene would smile weakly and try to respond, but then close her eyes and drift away. Dosey, Addie and some of the neighbor women took turns caring for her, carrying trays of food which they tried to tempt her to eat into the bedside and carried them out with only a few bites eaten. Addie and Dosey grew worried. Had death camped at this house? They were sitting listlessly at the kitchen table one hot morning.

"I'm afraid for her," Addie said shaking her head. She had just tried to coax Irene to eat some custard. She had looked at her mother-in-law as though she were a stranger, setting her bluish lips against it.

"I know, I hate to say it, but I think she wants to die," Dosey sighed. "I don't believe she has any desire to live at all."

"She can't give up and leave Ellen alone." Ellen heard her grandmother say as she came in from the back porch. She stopped, her heart beating rapidly, and pressed herself against the door jamb. Not her mother now, no, Heavenly Father. She listened breathlessly to hear what Addie and Dosey were saying.

"Well, I think it wouldn't hurt to call a prayer meetin' of the sisters." Dosey said.

"The elders have been in twice now and they said a prayer for her in church last Sunday," Addie said.

"I know, but I don't think it would hurt to call on the Lord a little more to strengthen her... I b'lieve Sister Bates and Knowles'll come."

"Yes," Addie agreed. "I don't think it would hurt a bit."

Ellen had come into the room and she turned to her and said, "Get your hat, Ellen, and come for a walk with me. We'll go see who we can round up, Dosey, and you keep tryin' to get some of that broth down her. She looks like she ain't got a bit of blood."

That evening three of the town's women came to the little house–Sister Bates, a heavy, untidy woman with kind gray eyes and straggling gray hair; Aurelia Knowles, president of the Relief Society, tall, handsome, forceful and neatly dressed who lent a solid air of authority wherever she was, and Maddie Thurman, a little snag of a woman whose long life of hardship and trouble reflected in her child-like, plain face. Together with Addie and Dosey they knelt down around the bed on which Irene lay apathetically staring at the ceiling. Addie had leaned over and told her that they had come to pray for her to get well and she must help them. She had only nodded feebly, making neither protest nor acquiescence.

Aurelia Knowles began to pray in a low firm voice that, if it were the will of the Lord, the life of this woman be spared, that her strength and health be restored to her for the sake of her child and her suffering family. It was a no-nonsense, straight-forward petition to God. Tears ran down all the homely weather-beaten faces of the women as the losses and suffering of their own lives, the mystery of life and death that hovered in this room was borne down upon them. The genuine tenderness and concern which they felt at that moment for the tired, beautiful woman on the bed caused their hearts to melt together in a miracle of sympathy that carried them all out serenely on the great ocean of human misery. Each woman lent a little of the strength of her heart and soul to lift Irene's out of the valley of shadows. There was a deep stillness in the room when Aurelia finished. Their soft "amens" went around the bed like a gentle breeze. They remained kneeling for a few minutes. Sister Thurman sniffled and, having forgotten a handkerchief, was obliged to wipe her eyes and blow her nose on her dingy petticoat. Sister Bates had to press down hard on the side of the bed to raise herself and the springs creaked loudly. Irene opened her eyes and looked about as though she had only awakened from a very deep sleep and was not quite sure where she was. Then she smiled as though she were greatly rested.

Ellen was surprised and delighted when she came home from Aunt Dosey's where she had been sent to help Lorraine with the kids, to find Irene sitting up in bed in a peach-colored satin bed jacket drinking a cup of milk-tea. She held out her hand and Ellen went and sat on the bed and laid her freckled rosy cheek against her mother's thin white one.

"Oh, you are going to get better," she whispered, "aren't you?"

"Yes," said Irene, "yes, I think I am going to get better." From that hour she slowly, but steadily regained her health.

CB

It was 1932; the great depression was in its third year. Everybody talked about it—women over their quilting frames and at their gatherings, men in restless knots on the street corners of Merritsville, voices on the radio to which Irene and Ellen listened more frequently now, teachers on the schools, even children—without any of them knowing quite what it was or what had caused it. They sang "Happy Days are Here Again," and repeated that "prosperity was just around the corner" as though it were only playing hide and seek with them.

One stormy February afternoon Hal, Lorraine, Louise and Ellen were seated at the big oak table in the Walker's cluttered dining room making valentines. The girls were carefully cutting out hearts and flowers and neatly fitting them together in bright little tokens of affection. Hal smeared the home-made flour paste lavishly on red construction paper and pounded hearts and other decoration in place with his fat fists. He made valentines like he would make berry crates in the summer.

"Hal, don't paste the hearts so crooked," Lorraine said in despair as she held up one of his messy products. "Look what a mess you've made and we don't have much paper left. Mama says we have to make all our valentines this year because of the depression."

Hal's face flushed with that stubborn, hateful look which he got whenever he was crossed or scolded. "Ah, I don' wanna make valentines anyway." He pushed the paste away and tipped back in his chair the way he had seen Aaron do.

"What's the 'depression' anyway?" Louise asked thoughtfully, holding up for inspection a double heart on which she had been tracing a lacy design.

"It's when people are out of a job and starving to death and there's no money or nothin'," Lorraine explained calmly.

"Are we gonna starve?" Louise's eyes widened with fright.

"We might," said Hal ominously without the slightest idea of what it meant to starve, as his plump cheeks evidenced.

"Oh, we won't either," Lorraine said irritably. "The church'll take care of its people. I heard the Bishop say it last week and, besides, we can grow food right here on the lot and the farm like always."

"But what caused it?" Ellen put in a troubled word as she finished a pretty valentine.

"It's the Republicans' fault," Hal pronounced loftily. He had been tagging Aaron around and listening to the talk of the men. "A million vet'rans are gonna git together and go up to Washington and if ol' President Hoover don't give 'em their bonus, they're gonna shoot 'im. Dad's gonna go with 'em."

Aaron Walker had served in the First World War though he never went overseas; his small veterans pension was all that he had to count on in the way of solid cash this stringent year.

"Oh, he is not and you don't know what you're talkin' about, Hal Walker," Lorraine protested.

"I do too," Hal pounded on the table and made the girls stop their work to look at him in disgust.

"Anyway, we're gonna vote 'em out this year, we're gonna get ol' Hoover voted out this year sure as shootin'. I heard Dad and Seth Peck talkin' about it the other day." He puffed out his chest and stuck his feet up on the table in the manner of Sheriff Peck. There were holes in the bottom of both shoes.

"Get your feet down, you'll ruin everything," Lorraine scolded. "And look at your shoes again. Ma'll scream when she sees them holes, old boy. It ain't your turn to have new shoes either," she added resentfully.

"Ah, shut up," Hal said scornfully and, tipping his chair down with a thump, he left the room thoroughly disgusted with girls. He didn't know why he bothered to go around them anyway.

If the depression was symbolized by anything in the Walker household, it was the constant and persistent shortage of shoes. First one and then the other was discovered to be "out on the ground." Shoes were one of the few items which could not be produced by ingenuity and effort at home. They cost money at the store, there was very little of that in the Walker home. Aaron could put new soles on them if the tops were not too worn and some material could be found, but it was a recurring nightmare for Dosey and the girls. It was so hard to go out in shoes that were shabby, run-over and filled with cardboard to mend the holes.

After the loss of the sheep, Aaron had cast about for some

kind of job, but he was approaching forty and this, added to the fact that there were no jobs anyway, was against him. But he had two assets–a capacity and willingness for hard work and a half-ton Dodge truck paid for which the bank had not confiscated.

He also had a piece of bench land on which, like other farmers, he planted fruit trees and berry patches. Later Lorraine, Louise, Ellen and others of the young girls and women of Merritsville spent much of their summers in these patches and orchards. Aaron picked up odd jobs of hauling with the truck for which he usually received produce, odd pieces of furniture, even clothes, instead of money. Many others subsisted in the same way, but with Dosey's managing and scraping the Walker family kept well within the margins of hunger. Hal did not lose any weight. In fact no one in Merritsville went hungry or suffered severe physical deprivation. It was more the loss of the American dream of getting ahead which had driven them all at top speeds for the past few years that caused deep humiliation and frustration, especially for the men who lacked meaningful and challenging employment.

The women, who, with the exception of a very few, had never changed their way of life, went on practicing the old thrifty habits which where a part of their upbringing and religion. They pieced and patched and turned and handed down and passed around clothing, bottled and preserved and dried fruit. They scrimped and shared and buoyed each other up with new patterns for quilt blocks, crocheting and embroidery and found ways of using everything several times from cans and bottles to old Christmas cards. The optimism of their pioneer mothers prevailed; most of them had always been poor with little money to spend. The depression was only a deepening and reinforcing of a way of life from which, of course, they hoped and prayed to be delivered. But they went on practicing, more or less cheerfully, the habits by which they had survived, even flourished in these desert-mountain valleys.

Dosey, Addie and Irene were no exceptions. Irene's small widow's pension was stretched out with the contributions of neighbors who were always dropping in with a piece of meat when they killed a mutton or pig, a basket of fruit, a bunch of vegetables. Addie cut off one of her milk and egg customers to share with Irene and Ellen and Aaron brought a load of stove wood when he chopped for his own family. Irene had always had a flair for clothes: she missed the charge account at Washburns' where she had been accustomed to shop freely before Laurence's death. She discovered, however, that she had a supply of clothes quite beyond her needs so she used many of them to make over for Ellen. Her talents as a seamstress made Ellen often better dressed than her classmates and she always had *two* pair of good shoes much to the envy of her cousins, Lorraine and Louise, who frequently had only one pair of Sunday shoes between them. Since their feet were near the same size, Dosey bought a size into which Lorraine could squeeze and Louise could manage with thicker socks. They took turns wearing them to Sunday school. Their main point of friction was which one had put the most wear or scratches on the precious shoes.

But neither the Walker children nor Ellen were more unhappy nor less because of the depression. Like all children, they lived in their dreams and they were surrounded by adults who cared and loved them. The violent squalls which come quickly and pass quickly are part of childhood in any time and place; children are a long time becoming aware of the perils of the larger world when the smaller one of the family holds steady as it did in most cases in Merritsville and especially with the Walkers and Kents.

In spite of the sad events that had fallen to her and her mother in the past two years, Ellen did not think of herself as unhappy. Having a vivid imagination, she sometimes frightened herself with visions and memories as now, this February evening she went home clutching her coat about her, trying to imagine how it might be to starve, to be homeless, cold and unloved, to be part of the depression that was going on in the world, but she found it very difficult. She stopped off at the store to look at the "boughten" valentines. Irene had given her a whole quarter to buy some. She felt guilty now that she had learned that the Walkers could not buy valentines. Perhaps a lot of other kids couldn't either; she would be acting "stuck-up" to send out boughten ones. So she selected three nickel ones all lacy and crowded with cupids, hearts and lace, one for Addie, one for Irene and one for her teacher. She spent the rest of the money on red and white paper and went home to make her own valentines.

While all over the United States that gloomy February evening thousands of people were wandering hungry and cold in the streets of big cities, thousands of men were contemplating suicide as a way out, thousands of other men and women were puzzling over the disastrous phenomenon, trying to figure a way to survive, Ellen sat at the kitchen table under blooming geraniums and cut out paper hearts. Irene crocheted in the rocker nearby and they listened to music on the radio which she had moved into the kitchen since they could only afford to heat one room most of the time.

Irene had come slowly to enjoy the radio, although she felt embarrassed at owning such a big and expensive set when she had become an object of charity. She wondered at times if she should sell it, but it was the last thing Laurence had bought. He had been so happy that day–that week, Thank God. She was occupied, amused and frequently cheered by the shows and music, but that spring of 1932 she, along with the rest of the country, was saddened by the story of another woman who had lost her son. Day after day she turned on the news hoping to hear the Lindbergh baby had been found, but finally with the rest of the shocked country, gave up hope and mourned with the bereaved family.

Sometimes Aaron and Dosey dropped in to listen to political speeches and campaign news that crucial election year. The Walkers had a radio but the reception on it was not as clear as Irene's. The radio was becoming a strong binding force in American life, both reassuring and alarming, but giving people the sense of being together in their struggle, their hopes and fears.

Americans have always been a mobile people. It was settled by the horde who felt there was always something better somewhere else, not the least of these the Mormon pioneers. Having arrived at "Zion," however, few of them wanted to leave. The rest of the country was in motion like an ant-hill which Hal might have stirred up, as he frequently did, with a stick, laughing in glee to see the disturbed creatures scurry about in the chaos. Was there some mischievous demon sitting above the world holding the stick with which he had toppled the carefully contrived ant-hill of American and world economy, immensely enjoying the sight of thousands of people hustling and bustling across the continent in rattling Ford automobiles, or bumming hazardous rides on the great railroad systems? This part of the story has been well and vividly told. There were others who stayed at home and toughed it out.

Few people left Merritsville and there was a good reason for this. Many of them had homes there and all had relatives and friends. Most of the homes were poor, but without mortgages, due to the fact that some, not all, had heeded the often repeated advice of the church to avoid indebtedness. With these homes—poorly built, without plumbing, meagerly furnished and having as their only "modern" feature bare electric light bulbs hanging from fly-blown cords in the center of each room and an ugly black meter box in one corner—was usually a half acre of ground or more on which one could raise a garden, keep a chicken coop, a pig and a cow. The cow could be fed by grazing her up and down the weedy ditch banks or driving her to the outlying pastures in the summer. Getting her through the winter was a tougher problem, but most managed.

Some of the fine new solid brick bungalows which had been built in the 20's on the promise of the livestock business had changed hands and some of their occupants went elsewhere in humiliation or of necessity. For the most part they were able to make other arrangements such as renting half of an older home or moving in with parents. Quite a few young couples set up housekeeping this way. Many people picked up a few dollars by installing a cook stove in their back bedrooms and renting the rooms. Later on newlyweds were able to dig basement or foundation homes, which roofed over with tar paper, waited sometimes ten or fifteen years for the house to be added. All in all among the Mormons strong interlaced family and religious ties operated in a way, not easy to trace out, by which most "managed to get by."

More people came to Merritsville than left—impoverished relatives generally, hoping to ride out the storm by camping in grandpa's back room or converted outbuilding. Some few adventurous or desperate city dwellers imagined they could survive if they had a little ground to raise something on so they rented or leased unused property. They generally found themselves unsuited to farm life and, being "outsiders" who did not understand the complex system by which "Mormons" existed, moved on in hostility so there were always a few vacant houses and dormant farms. One of these stood on the lower fringe of Merritsville, southeast and about a quarter of a mile from Addie Kent's house where small farms of twenty, thirty, seldom more than forty acres stretch down to the swamps that bordered Utah Lake. The farm houses were scattered out with long spaces between, connected by rutted roads that were bordered and criss-crossed with the ubiquitous irrigation ditches, slouching rusted fences and dotted with clumps of wild roses, hawthorn and squaw bushes. Here and there huge, ragged cottonwood trees dropped tassels and cotton in late spring and big leathery yellow leaves in autumn.

The Anderson place it was called although the last Anderson, a son who had little inclination for farming, had moved away late in the twenties. Part of the land and water rights had been sold and only a few acres and the house remained. Vacant, sad, it had almost become the haunted house of Merritsville. It had started out to be a fine big Victorian house with bowed front window, white pillared porch and a fashionable cupola, but ended up with a frame lean-to at the back. It was falling into neglect and decay. Late in the spring of 1932 a strange family, driving a dilapidated car with a Kentucky license plate, moved into the house. Apparently because they had so few possessions, they occupied only the lean-to at the back and one of the other rooms for sleeping.

There were two tall, gaunt men with grim dark faces, brothers obviously, who looked so much alike that they might have been twins except that one, who called himself Frank and seemed slightly younger, had a long scar running down the side of his face that gleamed white and eery through his black whiskers. The other one, Arthur, apparently had a wife and children, a tall, thin scared looking woman who looked older than he, and a girl and boy about the same age as Ellen.

The girl's name was Simone, which she pronounced through her teeth when she and Ellen met, as "Seemoan." It was a long time before Ellen found out how to spell it. It was an odd name, one that nobody in Merritsville had, but it fitted her wild gypsy-like appearance. She had thick, dark naturally curly hair like her father and his glittering, oily black eyes. Her skin was a rich brown, but there were deceitful black freckles under it sprinkled along the bridge of her nose. She was extremely nervous and bit the nails of her brown, often dirty hands, to the quick except when she was close to someone; then she kept running her hands all over them, feeling their clothes, their skin, even their hair in the oddest most intense way.

Robert Lee, as they called him, was such a contrast to Simone that it was hard to believe them brother and sister as they stoutly claimed. He was tall for his age, extremely thin, but pale and quiet. His face had the frightened shadow of his mother over it; his thin, long, brownish hair fell in his eyes so that he was always jerking his neck like a horse in fly time to throw it back. He had pale gray eyes fringed with dark girlish lashes and a long crooked nose. Ellen thought he had the saddest face she had ever seen, but when he smiled, in spite of blackened decaying teeth, a strange sweetness lit up his face.

Ellen wondered if these people were some of the gypsies who came through Merritsville from time to time begging and stealing and scared all the children into minding their mothers, but Simone said they were from the South, from "Kaintuckee."

The family had the elegant last name of Hamilton, and they excited, as strangers do, the suspicious imagination of the townspeople. Their secretive, unfriendly attitude gave rise to all sorts of wild stories, among which was the speculation that they were fugitives from the law, maybe like the Barker gang. But their manner was so menacing that not even Sheriff Pack dared to inquire outrightly as to their origins and intentions.

Word got around that they were distant cousins of the Andersons who had been given permission to live on the place. It was recalled by some of the older folks that the old Mrs. Anderson had been from somewhere in the South: "Old Peter Anderson brought 'er back from his mission somewhere around '87." It did appear that they had come to "prospect." Brigham Young had once said that the mountains around Merritsville were filled with enough gold to pave the streets of Salt Lake City, when, of course, it had been much smaller. None of the gold had ever been found but silver, lead, and zinc had turned up and there were hopeful holes all about the hills. Two or three times a week the Hamilton men did get in their ramshackle auto with picks and shovels and their big red chow dog and headed for the hills. Nobody was sufficiently brave or interested enough to follow them or inquire how their prospecting was coming. "Long's they mind their business and don't do no harm, guess it ain't none of ourn to interfere," Seth Peck said. "Ain't heard from Bud Anderson what he intended to do with the old place anyhow; guess if he cares a hoot, he'll come find out what's goin' on down there."

The church did, however, dispatch a couple of Elders to find out if the Hamiltons were, by any chance, Mormon converts or interested in becoming members. They were definitely put-off by the snarling dog and the hostile manners of the two Hamilton men, as well as the long black rifle standing conspicuously in the corner of the kitchen. Though it was hard, the residents of Merritsville left the Hamiltons pretty much alone. When the Federal Relief rolls were finally established and beans, canned goods, potatoes and other "surplus" commodities were handed out of city hall every other Thursday morning, Mrs. Hamilton, Robert Lee and Simone were seen there regularly. Mrs. Hamilton scratched about in a pitiful vegetable garden which she tried to grow in the back of the Anderson place, but its cultivation was too hard for her. She got little help and encouragement from the two lanky men who, when they were not away in the hills, lounged about under the wild, old fruit trees in the weedy yard, smoking their pipes in silence. Occasionally they made some cryptic remark to each other that sent them into spasms of ribald laughter.

It was hard to see how the family subsisted, but since they didn't mix and didn't seem to want to, nobody offered them any help. Sinister stories kept circulating, as they will, as long as people's curiosity is thwarted by secretiveness or reserve. Some said that Frank must be some kind of an outlaw because of the scar. Some said the woman lived with both brothers and was married to neither, when in truth she seemed estranged from both. Some said, and this was the most plausible, that they were bootleggers, but no effort was made to find their still and none was ever found. They did get liquor from somewhere, which wasn't hard to do even in Merritsville during Prohibition, and went on long, wicked drinking bouts during which they sometimes abused and beat the woman and boy—but Art Hamilton would never permit anyone to touch or discipline Simone.

On summer nights across the fields Addie could hear them

cursing and laughing, sometimes singing–Frank played an ancient guitar. Her soul was chilled with pity for the woman and children for she abhorred drunkenness with true Mormon, nineteenth century zeal. One night at dusk of a long summer Saturday, having finished her Saturday cleaning and had her Saturday bath in the tin tub by the stove and changed her clothes from the "garments" outward, as she was about to sit out on her porch full of the peace of a virtuous life to watch the stars, she looked up to see a figure stumbling across the fields.

All afternoon she had heard loud shouts and curses interspersed with sounds of the guitar; she knew the Hamiltons were at it again, so she guessed, before she could see, that it might be Mrs. Hamilton. She would stop and look around, wringing her hands in her apron, then run on. When she reached the outer fence of Addie's stack yard, she hesitated but finally crawled under the wire and came timidly up to the back porch. Addie could make out that the woman's face was full of despair and she had been crying. Her hair was straggling down her shoulders and she kept rubbing her bony hands together in agitation.

"What's the trouble, Mrs. Hamilton?" inquired Addie, awkwardly, for she had guessed what the trouble was although this was the first call that her neighbor had made.

Mrs. Hamilton stuttered, choked and turned as though to go.

"Well, wont you come in a spell?" Addie held the screen door open. "I'm here all alone this evenin'; wouldn't mind a bit of company."

The woman came warily into the house, trembling, and sat down gingerly on a chair by the door.

"Ahm ashamed, oh ahm ashamed, Miz Kent to be a troublin' yew," she stammered, trying to smooth her hair into place. There was a big red welt across her cheek. "Mah man, mah man, he's on one again and that Frank, oh, Miz Kent, he's a bad one, that one, and when he gits Arthur like this, you cain't do nothin' with either uv 'em. He started after me with the butcher knife this time." She sobbed great gulping sobs.

"Now, now there, you try to calm yourself and I'll make you a nice hot cup of tea." Addie began to pile some chips into the stove. "Where're your kids? Ain't you afraid to leave 'em over there when your menfolks are like that?"

Mrs. Hamilton had got hold of herself, wiped her face on her ragged apron and tried to hold her head up with some pride. "Oh, Robert Lee, he lit out arly for the crick like he allus does when his pa starts likkerin' and he won't come back till he knows it's good and safe."

"He stays in the creek all night alone?" Addie clucked her dismay.

"Oh, I reckon he's a lot safer thar than with his pa like this; he's a smart boy, that Robert Lee." There was weak pride and affection in her flat voice. "An' Arthur won't never harm Simone. He won't never do nothin' to her even when he's drunk." Her voice trailed off and she shook her head in despair. "He wouldn't let me brang her away anyway... Oh ahm ashamed to put my troubles on yew, Miz Kent."

"Now that's all right, never you mind." Addie poked the blaze under the kettle and got out the tea cups. "Now you just calm yourself and then we'll walk over and talk to the Sheriff about this."

The woman started up in obvious alarm, "Oh, no, no... Ah couldn't do thaat."

Addie looked at her quizzically, discovering that her terror was real.

"He'd kill me fer sure," she went on. "He's got that mean a temper. If I ever set the law on him, oh my goodness!"

"Well, well, all right, just you set right down there and rest a bit. You can stay all night if you're afraid to go home," Addie assured her, cutting some slices of bread with which she served raspberry preserves she had made that morning.

"Oh, they'll quiet down in a bit." Mrs. Hamilton picked nervously at the bread and jam; it was apparent that she was hungry. She drank the tea with little choking noises and her eyes wandered admiringly around the kitchen. "You shore have a nice little place here, Miz Kent. I wish I could get a place fixed up nice for a while, but we all move around so much."

"Yes, it's pretty comfortable. The Anderson place used to be right nice; maybe when times get better...." They had both become easier with each other and exchanged some of the small confidences that women do, but Mrs. Hamilton kept looking out the door and fidgeting. Addie wondered if by chance the drunken men might follow the woman. Then what would she do? But she dismissed the thought and was glad to see Mrs. Hamilton relaxing.

Crickets were chirping loudly in the summer night, there was the faint fragrance of new mown hay. Presently the woman stirred and sighed. "Ah want to tell yew how much ah 'preciate this, Miz Kent. Ah hope yew wont think too bad uv us. Mah man ain't really bad, ah want yew to know; it's jest likker...."

"I know, it's a terrible curse." Addie nodded in fervent agreement. "I'm glad you dropped by; I'm lonesome in the evenings. You come anytime you can. Now don't you go if you're afraid...."

Addie walked to the fence with her; there was a deep silence in the direction of the Anderson house. Mrs. Hamilton stooped to get through the wires. "Oh, they's most likely drunk stiff by now and sleepin' it off. It'll be right peaceful for a day or two now," she sighed. "Ah sure do 'preciate your kindness, Miz Kent." With that she went off across the dark fragrant fields to the thicker darkness among the trees where the decaying house brooded.

Addie stood in the warm darkness watching her figure as it melted into the night, wondering how a woman managed to live with such brutality and evil. Her good heart swelled with pity. She must try to lighten the burden her sister had to carry.

Ↄ

Irene's life settled gradually into a familiar routine, a round of household tasks and church activities. She yielded passively and gratefully to Dosey on one side and Addie on the other as they persisted in their efforts to keep her "getting out and not giving up." She went to Relief Society and made rounds of her neighbors as a "visiting teacher;" she went to quilting bees and showers for brides and babies, to Daughters of the Utah Pioneer meetings; to Sunday School and Sacrament meeting, Fast and Testimony meetings and conference and ward socials, all with the quiet manner of an invalid who had only partly returned to the land of the living. From substitute organist of the Sunday School she had succeeded to full time when Sister Taylor resigned to have another baby. This was the only thing that she did with animation.

Ellen always felt a thrill of happiness when she heard Irene practicing or playing at home; it was the only time the house came close to the life they had once known.

Although she remained a little too thin, Irene had regained much of her beauty; in fact the aura of sadness that surrounded her added a touch of romance which did not go entirely unnoticed by the males of the congregation who watched her at the organ on a Sunday morning. But she gave no sign of being aware of any of them, the eligible suitors of which there were few, or the ineligible ones who could only offer her silent tenderness or an occasional sack of spuds.

Although on the surface her wounds seemed to be healing, she lived with a sense of emptiness, her days precariously shored up by her family. From the wreckage of her emotional life, she had salvaged only two intense feelings. One was a need for absolute order in the small house. Only when everything was in its place, dusted, scrubbed, polished, could she endure the world. Little by little Ellen moved her "projects," playthings and books to Grandma's house where she could make a mess without causing her mother the nervous distress that often ended in sick headaches.

The other emotion which Irene actively displayed was a curious kind of fear about Ellen, a fear that she expressed vaguely as "getting into trouble" which Ellen began to sense was more than skinning her knees or breaking her bones. Only seldom and generally after long sessions of pleading or assurances, usually from Aunt Dosey or Lorraine, could Irene be persuaded to let Ellen take part in long hikes, weeny roasts, slumber parties or house parties where there were *boys!* On those rare occasions when she did get permission to go to such affairs, her mother saw her off with such an anxious look on her face and such painful admonitions as "Don't you let those rough boys take advantage of you," or "Be careful of those nasty boys," that the party was already spoiled. Ellen was constantly apprehensive of something dreadful and sinister for which she must be alert, although she had little idea of what it was. She was usually the only girl besides Marissa Clements who didn't have a "beau." Even though the kids didn't date, parties eventually ended up in pairs or involved kissing games, another thing against which Irene had warned her.

Half the time Ellen knew the kids didn't invite her to their parties, and the rest of the time she didn't want to go anyway.

When she talked about it to her grandmother, Addie had tried to explain that it was because she was all her mother had left and that she was afraid to lose her. "You must be good to your mother, you might not always have her," Grandma said many times and that only made Ellen feel worse.

There was something darker in Irene's fear of boys, and Ellen was becoming aware of the fact that there was a difference in the worlds that were marked off by accident of sex. She had seen the difference between boys and girls in helping to change the diapers of the little Walkers, but had not made connections between the physical facts and the behavior of adults. The only male in her personal life, Hal, had changed a lot in the past two years. Time had been when he had played happily with her and Lorraine and Louise, sometimes more boisterously than they liked, but all the same congenially. Hal had always seemed to like her and take her part if there was a quarrel. She had forgotten the broken doll. Lately he had become insulting and rough, and never wanted to be around the girls. He said dirty words and swore when he thought grown-ups weren't listening; he never came into Irene's house anymore.

It all had something to do, Ellen was sure, with the disturbing secret of which she had become aware in the feelings of her parents and the dead baby. What she couldn't know was that Irene did have a deep dislike and fear of the opposite sex properly instilled in her by Aunt Delia. Laurence had been the only male with whom she had had any relationship that could be called sexual. The fact that he had been different, gentler, musical had broken through the diffidence with which in the best nineteenth tradition, her maidenly virtues were safely and securely bound. Aunt Delia had approved of him and the idealism and tenderness in which he held Irene led her to give her blessing to the marriage even though her niece was very young.

Both women believed in the sanctity and safety of Temple marriage where innocence and chastity were protected from the coarseness of the ordinary world. Laurence had been like the Prince Charming who had cut through the thorns of inhibition, and Irene had awakened to him, responding with modest passion until that very last week when they had been together. Then they had experienced more intense physical desire for each other than any time of their marriage, loving each other so passionately, almost with a forbidden lust, that they were left feeling some guilt but even more hunger. It was the more tragic and bewildering that he had left her so suddenly alone. Sometimes she wondered if they had sinned and she was being punished. The thorns had grown back thicker than ever and she, having been fully awakened to sexual love, was even more aware of their cruel confinement.

Now that Ellen was approaching womanhood, Irene feared for her daughter in a world where men, as she had been warned by Aunt Delia, were wicked monsters out to destroy a woman's virtue then cover her with shame and ridicule. The picture of the poor outcast girl with an illegitimate child facing the storm, forlorn, disgraced beyond redemption haunted her. Now a widow, a woman without resources or strength, how could she provide for a daughter who fell into "a fate worse than death." But Irene didn't know how to talk to Ellen who seemed to be growing away from her; she could only make oblique reference and point out sad examples of "fallen women," exercising such control as she had.

Ellen had already read some stories on this theme in the cheap paper-back novels and the *True Confession* magazines that some of the girls traded around furtively. They had a place near one of the irrigation culverts where they stashed the forbidden literature and read and giggled over the lurid tales. Ellen never knew where they came from, but she was as curious as the rest. She didn't dare take them home, but could read them at Grandma's who never seemed to worry about what she was doing. The girls talked about Hazel Dykes in veiled language that she didn't really understand, like they said she was a "whore." Hazel lived down by the Turkey Plant with her kids of whom it was said that each had a different father, and she didn't know which was which. Ellen knew better than to ask Irene about any of this; it would only upset her, but she guessed that her mother's fears had something to do with that dirty word, "sex."

Although Ellen's welfare, her material needs and her uncertain future, were constantly in Irene's thoughts, she was not always happy when Ellen was around. In fact much of the time she was wearied by the energetic, restless, imaginative child. The only other place which she considered that Ellen was completely safe from harm and evil was at Addie's, so Ellen was often to be found there. Summer days when Irene had to spend all afternoon in the darkened bedroom with a sick headache or that vague feeling of malaise which often overtook her, Ellen spent reading in the apple tree at Grandma's, drawing, writing or working on one of the many scrapbooks she kept. These were happy and contented hours for both of them, but what Irene could not know was that she could never keep her safe from the evils Irene dreaded.

It was inevitable that she should get to know the Hamilton children since they were the only ones near her age on the several farms adjoining Addie's. She was aware of them because they had been seen about town. She had heard stories about them, but it was not until a warm day in early summer that Simone and Robert Lee thrust themselves into her life.

She was meandering along the hot, dusty road to Grandma's, a bit bored and lonely, when she noticed footsteps behind her. Turning she saw two odd figures who had, it seemed, appeared from nowhere. They were grinning curiously and, taking positions one on either side of her as though they had planned it all, fell into step without saying anything. Ellen was extremely uncomfortable and increased her pace, holding her chin up nervously. Suddenly the girl grabbed her sleeve and jerked her to a stop.

"That's a purty dress you're wearin'," she said, fingering the dress greedily. Ellen could not tell whether she was sincere or making fun of her. It was a pink flowered rayon that Irene had cut down from one of hers and had a ruffle on the bottom. It was not especially suitable to Ellen who did not look good in ruffles or bows, but contrasted with the shapeless, gray washed-out cotton with a dirty ragged once-white collar which the other girl was wearing, Ellen decided it must look pretty to her. The dark girl continued to examine the dress in detail, running her hands sinuously over Ellen's shoulders and even down her chest.

Ellen noted that the girl was wearing run-over boy's shoes with no stockings and that her feet and legs were dirty. There were black callouses on her heels that looked like cakes of mud, but her black hair lay in "naturally curly" waves and hung in ringlets down her back. On the subject of curly hair, Ellen was extremely sensitive. Hers was stubbornly straight and resisted all Irene's efforts to put it into curls or waves. They had given up on the Saturday night rag-curler ritual.

The boy, who stood on one side with his hands behind his back, obviously admiring the dress, too, was wearing a pair of faded bib overalls hanging precariously on the protruding blades of his bare brown shoulders. He had no shoes at all and his long bumpy feet were caked with mud. Ellen began to flush with embarrassment and tried to shrug away from the hands that were crawling over her like some nasty insect.

"My name's Seemoan," said the girl fingering one of the buttons on the back of Ellen's dress. "What's yourn?"

"Ellen, Ellen Kent." Ellen brushed the hand away irritably, but Simone grabbed the ruffle of the dress and jerked it up maliciously. Ellen tried to push it back down and backed away quickly. The ruffle tore away from the dress with a dismal ripping sound.

"Mine's Robert Lee," said the boy eagerly stepping forward as though he had been awaiting this moment to introduce himself. Ellen, very close to tears, looked at him in bewilderment and then at Simone who had at last retreated and was regarding the ripped dress with something like surprise mixed with satisfaction. She seemed to have no remorse.

"Now just look what you've done!"

"I didn't mean to," Simone said defiantly.

"No, she din't mean to," Robert Lee advanced anxiously "Will yer ma be real mad?"

"Oh Grandma'll sew it up, I guess," Ellen said sulkily and began to walk rapidly down the path. Simone and Robert Lee trotted a few steps behind.

"If you come to our house, we'll get Ma to sew it up for ya," Simone offered. They had reached the lane which turned off to the Hamilton's. She grabbed Ellen by the arm.

"Yeah, come on," coaxed Robert Lee who had taken hold of the other arm. "Come on down and see our playhouse; we got sumpin' you ain't never seen, I bet."

Ellen felt herself being pulled down the lane, half afraid, half angry and yet somehow curiously excited, between the two dirty children.

As they opened the rotting gate, a rusty-colored chow dog leaped up and sniffled at Ellen warily. Robert Lee patted his head. "She's all right; she's our friend now, Red, so you be nice to her," he said proudly. Ellen patted the dog's stubbly head timidly, and he accepted her calmly but without affectionate display.

The front of the old Anderson house containing eight or nine rooms in its two stories was boarded up. The Hamiltons occupied only the small frame addition at the back which made a cramped, kitchen-living room and the whole family slept in one large bare room of the main house. Robert Lee and Simone guided Ellen around to the back and pushed her through a rusted, sagging screen door. There was a strong, thick smell of frying grease and coffee. Two dark complexioned men with ragged beards were slouched at an oilcloth covered table, and Mrs. Hamilton was standing at the old stove which was red-hot and enveloped in clouds of bluish smoke. The perspiration dripped off the tip of her nose.

Ellen was all but overcome in the sweltering heat, feeling that she had blundered into a strange, unfriendly place. Simone pulled her by her sleeve over to the table. "This here's Ellen Kent, her granma lives over yonder," she said perfunctorily to everybody. "She tore her dress so I said she could come down here and ma'd fix it. See?" She jerked Ellen's dress up. The two men looked at her and grinned.

"Howdy," they said in what sounded like a mocking tone to Ellen.

Mrs. Hamilton turned from the stove, wiping her face on her apron. "Well, howdy, Ellen," she said. "Your granma's a right fine lady. Glad to have ye call, set up an' have a bite with us, now make a place for her, Robert Lee. I'll see what I can do 'bout fixin' that tear right after we eat."

Robert Lee had already slid to the far end of a long bench that ran along one side of the table under the windows. Simone nudged her onto the bench and, very ill at ease, she slid alongside him. Simone followed. Ellen felt the perspiration running down her neck and tried to avoid the glittering eyes of the men which she could feel on her face like hot lights.

"Wal, so ye got a friend naow," said Frank leering at Simone. "A leetle Mormon friend, no doubt. You a Mormon, eh?"

He directed the question at Ellen with a sarcastic drawl.

"Yes," said Ellen, shivering. She had been raised on the gruesome tales of the persecution of the Mormons, especially by the Missourians and she wondered if the Hamiltons were some of these.

"She's my friend, my very best friend," Simone flared back at Frank. "You jest leave 'er alone."

"Better not go makin' friends with them Mormons," drawled her father, a wicked gleam in his eye, "They'll lock you up in that big gray temple up thar in Sal' Lake and marry you up with some ol' bishop with farty wives."

Ellen was paralyzed with fear and embarrassment. She looked about frantically trying to discover a way to get away from this awful place, but she was hemmed in on either side. She felt as though she were going to burst into tears, but she knew she must not let them see that they had got her goat.

"That isn't true," she choked out. "We don't have polygamy anymore and we don't lock people up in the Temple."

"Oh, it ain't true," Art Hamilton mocked. "They don't have poleegamy anymore, she says." He poked Frank and they both broke into loud, crude laughter, rocking back in their chairs so they almost upset the table.

Simone leaped up and flew at her father. She began to beat on him with her little brown fists. "You stop that, she's my friend; you leave her alone. If you scare her away, I'll hate you," she screamed, her face flushed with fury and her black ringlets dancing up and down.

Ellen was even more frightened. It was all she could do to keep the tears back. She looked at Robert Lee who had shrunk miserably into his corner of the bench and was watching her furtively. She could tell that he was scared of his father.

Arthur Hamilton settled his chair and looked at Simone with amusement as though she were no more than a fly that had been bothering him; then he swept her into his long arm and began tickling her. She wiggled and screamed with laughter. When she was almost breathless, he set her up and began stroking her hair.

"That's awright, Chickadee, if you wan' a little Mormon friend, you kin have one." Simone nestled against his chest and began running her fingers along his cheek. Then she reached up and kissed him directly on the mouth and resumed her seat with a sly, satisfied smile.

Ellen was astounded. She had never seen anything like it; she felt like some ragged toy that had been awarded to Simone though she had never even said she wanted to be their friend. However, she sensed it was better not to dispute it at the moment. She just had to sit quiet and watch her chance to get away.

Mrs. Hamilton, who seemed to have ignored the whole thing, brought a pan of smoking curly brown things to the table and a big blue enamel pot of coffee which she began pouring into the cracked mugs at each plate. Ellen looked dismayed.

"I don't drink coffee," she ventured timidly.

"You all gonna drink it today, little Mormon girl," Frank said pinning her with his fierce ugly gaze, the scar on his cheek gleaming, his knife and fork poised menacingly. "It ain't nice manners to turn down what folks offer you, now is it?"

"Shut up and leave 'er alone," growled Arthur and Frank subsided.

Mrs. Hamilton poured the coffee back in the pot and filled Ellen's cup with tepid water from a grimy water bucket. Ellen nibbled at the strange brown stuff which Simone had heaped on her plate. It was cracklins or chittlins, pork fat fried to a crisp, she learned later; but she had never seen it before and the greasy taste nauseated her. She stuffed it down with some sour gray biscuits and jam, wondering if she would survive this curious meal in the broiling hot, poverty-stricken room. Surely Hell could not be more miserable, and the devil must resemble Frank Hamilton who, like Arthur, ate with loud, uncouth noises and watched her with an inquisitive sneer.

At last Simone finished and, abruptly clutching her by the arm, dragged her off the bench. "C'mon, let's go play outside," she said. Ellen stammered her thanks for the meal and followed Simone with relief. Robert Lee tagged after them.

Simone guided Ellen to an old shed in the weedy back yard.

"This is our playhouse," Robert Lee said, pushing open the door of what had been a place for storing coal. It still had the acrid odor of carbon. Long slits of light gleamed in the darkness where the boards had shrunk apart. In the gloom Ellen could see some boxes and pieces of broken furniture. Robert Lee pushed one toward her. "Set down," he said shyly.

Simone was dressing herself in some old curtains and rags in the corner. Presently she turned around with a flourish.

"I'm the queen," she announced imperiously, "and you have to do what I say. I can tell fortunes, too."

"You can?" Ellen asked with interest, forgetting her misgivings for the moment, "Show me how."

Simone came nearer and crouched over her, grabbing her hand and Robert Lee crept up to watch.

"You're not gonna live very long." Simone shook her head sadly as squinted seriously at Ellen's sweating palm. "Your lifeline's not very long, see." She traced a line on Ellen's hand with her dirty fingernail. Ellen jerked her hand away in annoyance. "I don't believe you," she stuttered.

"Don't pay no 'tention to her," Robert Lee said in alarm. "She allas tells lies."

"I don't, I don't," Simone shrieked and slapped him so hard that he fell over backwards. She grabbed Ellen's hand fiercely again.

"Maybe I made a mistake," she soothed. "I could probably change your fortune to something real good for some money, maybe even a penny?"

"I haven't got any money," Ellen said and drew her hand away firmly hiding it behind her back. "Besides I don't believe you can really tell fortunes. Anyway it's wicked."

"Well, I can tell 'em lots better with cards," Simone said sulkily, moving away and rearranging her musty draperies. In the semidarkness her glittering eyes and wild hair and the oddly grown-up pose which she had assumed made her look like the pictures of gypsy fortune tellers that Ellen had seen. There was something both fascinating and frightening about her. At that moment Ellen half-way believed that she might be able to tell fortunes; Simone seemed to have a kind of power that Ellen had not encountered before.

Simone had begun to rummage around in an old chest. "Dammit, where're the cards?" she demanded.

"Frank took 'em," Robert Lee offered.

"Well, go get 'em." Simone stamped her foot and Robert Lee leaped out of the shed, coming back quickly with a greasy pack of cards. Simone spread them out on the floor and they knelt around them. Simone flipped them over and back with her nervous thin hands, chattering rapidly about kings, queens, aces, spades, diamonds in a weird jargon that impressed Ellen in spite of her uneasiness. She had seen cards, of course, had played Old Maid and other childish games with the Walkers, but these were different cards almost alive with evil portents. As Simone puzzled over them expertly or flipped them angrily, muttering dire prophecies, they were like a mysterious book in which all the secrets of life were concealed.

"You're goin' on a long trip and meet a tall, dark handsome man, soon," she said solemnly.

"Oh, you tell that to everbody," ventured Robert Lee.

"You just shut up," she turned on him furiously, then back to Ellen triumphantly. "And he's gonna strangle you." She ground out the words between her teeth; her face was such a mask of hatred that Ellen almost fell over. She jumped up and backed toward the door.

"I gotta go," she said weakly.

Simone scattered the cards with a wild whoop and fell back on the floor screaming with laughter.

"Why'd ya do that?," Robert Lee said with genuine distress. "She's our friend, remember? And then to Ellen, "Please don't go; she jist likes to tease, she does that all the time. It don't mean nothin'"

Simone stopped laughing, shrugged and then leaped to her feet. She threw her arms around Ellen and hugged her tight. "Don't be mad, I'se only teasin' like Robert Lee says. Please be our really friend, 'sides you ain't got your dress fixed yet."

Ellen extricated herself as soon as she could, confused by the extremes of Simone's moods, but for all that, fascinated.

"I really got to go," she said, "but I'll be your really friend. Just give me that safety pin you got there and I'll pin it up. Grandma'll fix it for me."

They walked to the gate with her, hanging on to her arms.

"You'll come back tomorrow, maybe?" Robert Lee begged wistfully. "You're the only friend we got here. I got somethin' I wanta show you down the crick sometime, maybe tomorrow."

Ellen shook loose of their arms and began to run across the

field calling back in answer to their repeated invitations that she would come back maybe even tomorrow. In spite of the queer mixed-up feeling of fear, irritation, even revulsion, she knew that she would come back.

❧

Ellen began to see a great deal of Simone and Robert Lee Hamilton. They were almost always waiting somewhere along the ditch banks as she came to her Grandmother's, or she went, uneasily edging around the suspicious chow dog, to their place. They proved to be exciting and adventurous playmates, willing to do anything that Ellen could think up. They were full of strange bits of knowledge about places and things which sounded tantalizingly romantic to Ellen. When they talked about "back thar in Kaintuck or daown in Noo Orleans, the tobacco and cotton fields, the niggers," she envied them experiences that seemed to make them much older and wiser than she. But she was better than they at inventing games and writing stories and plays for them to act in. Simone especially liked to act in the plays if she had the part of a queen or beautiful fairy. She loved to dress up in a bridal gown fashioned out of some old clothes Grandma had given them to play with and get married, although she would never let Robert Lee play the bridegroom. She said he was too ugly, besides you couldn't marry your brother, so Ellen drew a face on a shovel and tied a bow on it. Simone was married a dozen times to it with a different movie star name every time.

Although Simone was often capricious, even vicious, as she had been on that first day, Ellen, like Robert Lee, learned to ignore her mercurial tantrums and as soon as they were over, they all went back to whatever they were doing with feverish zest. At the same time she enjoyed being with them, Ellen was aware that there was something not quite acceptable about the Hamiltons, that she ought not to be associating with them. She hardly ever mentioned them to her mother. Grandma seemed not to mind them, handing out bread and jam to all three of them when they were playing there. All the same, Ellen did not invite them to join her when she went to the Walker's or played with some of the other girls.

Sometimes they played at the Hamiltons in the old coal shed which Ellen helped arrange into a fine playhouse; sometimes they spent the afternoon in Grandma's stackyard playing hide and seek, follow the leader or using the hay rack and sheep loading chute as a stage. Sometimes they played in Stone Creek.

Stone Creek was one of the small streams that wandered out of the mountains to the east of Merritsville and fed the criss-crossing network of irrigation ditches with melting snows from sharp granite peaks. Although full to the brim in April and May with foaming, swirling muddy water, by June it was wet only occasionally by a little surplus of the precious irrigation water which was the life-blood of the valley or a flash flood. It was bordered by tall, frowzy mountain ash and cottonwood trees and thick clumps of wild rose. Dry and quiet most of the summer, the clean grayish white stones glowed in the soft light filtered through the trees. Now and then the stillness was broken by the sudden rush of wings or a dislodged stone: the sound wandered up and down the twisted dim corridor like a shattered ghost.

It was a wonderful place to spend summer afternoons. There were long satin-smooth patches of the finest sand along the edges, rocks of all shapes and sizes which formed patterns for jumping or tagging, all sorts of treasures that the water had gathered up, carried a ways then dropped in unlikely places, big smooth logs to ride or carve on and, above all, a cool, mystical, secluded atmosphere from which adults were excluded. At one time or another all the kids of Merritsville played or wandered there.

Stone Creek curled around the lower edge of Grandma's farm, passing within several hundred yards of the Anderson place. Robert Lee had discovered it soon after his arrival and spent most of his time there, partly because he loved it, partly to avoid his father who was easily infuriated by the quiet awkward boy. He had found a place on a smooth sand bank protected by bushes and logs where he often spent summer nights, especially if Art and Frank were drinking.

One hot, muggy afternoon Ellen met Robert Lee as she was on her way from Grandma's. It was unusual to find him alone. He was shuffling along watching his bare feet when he raised his eyes and saw her. He stopped squarely in front of her on the path and spread his arms out teasingly, touching the big cottonwood tree at the corner of the lane so that she could not get around him on the narrow path unless she jumped the ditch which was full of water. The only other way was to squeeze under his arm by the rough tree.

Ellen was out of sorts and bored. The heat made her feel itchy and cross. Grandma had not been home and the door was locked; her mother was in bed with a sick headache. She had been picking berries in the morning with the Walkers but didn't want to spend anymore time with them. Lorraine was getting so silly about boys and Hal had been rude and unbearable.

"Get out of my way," she said to Robert Lee irritably, giving him a little push but he only grinned and began to dance back and forth across the path in front of her.

"I got somethin' I want to show you down the crick," he coaxed.

"I don't want to see it." Ellen tried to dodge under his arm and he caught her and held her. She struggled away and pushed him so hard that he fell back in the path. Still grinning amiably, he continued to coax from a squatting position.

"Ah, com'on, it's something' like you ain't never seen before, I bet." There was something so pitiful and honest in his sad face that Ellen felt sorry for him.

"Oh, I bet I have, I been down to the creek lots more than you have," she retorted.

"Betcha ain't never seen this."

"What is it?"

"You have t'come see it, I can't tell ya." Robert Lee was pleading earnestly.

"Is it bad like a snake or a bug or something?" Ellen searched his face for a trace of the maliciousness which she knew in Simone, but there was none.

"No, it ain't, it's purty, real purty and I made it mostly for you," he added shyly scratching in the dirt around his toes.

This last bit of information aroused Ellen's interest.

"If it's bad, I'll never speak to you again," she warned as Robert Lee leaped happily to his feet, grabbed her hand and set off for the creek across the fields.

The bank of the wide bend that went just below the Hamilton's was steep and weedy and the two of them had to slide and stumble through the scratchy burdocks, stickweed and wild briar. The creek bed at this point was narrow and secluded because of the sharp bends, but at the side where the water had been slowed and forced to drop some of its silt and debris was a wide expanse of white sand. This small, perfect beach was sheltered on one side by a thick clump of wild roses; along the other was a huge fallen log stripped of its bark, smooth and gray.

Robert Lee led Ellen across the stones and stopped proudly in front of what, when her eyes became accustomed to the gloom, was the most fantastic thing she had ever seen.

"What is it?" she asked in bewilderment. Then as she squatted pointing with a stick, she could see that it looked like a miniature city. The streets had been marked out with a sharp stick on the smooth sand and using the polished white and gray rocks of all shapes and sizes, Robert Lee had made buildings of every shape and description, some long flat open plans of houses, some piled up like two or three story buildings. Some were even furnished like real houses. Among them were wilting branches for trees and he had made a garden of chips and broken bits of colored glass. On one side, quite out of proportion but ingenious, was a car with a small brown twig for a steering wheel. It must have taken hours and hours to find the right stones and fit them all together so carefully.

"This hyere is like the cou't house at Lexin'ton and this hyere is the jail house like where uncle Frank wuz in." Robert Lee was excitedly conducting her around the little city.

"Why was your uncle Frank in jail?" Ellen asked.

"Oh, he all the time gettin' in fights and trouble. Hyere's where the Colonel live. He a fine genleman." Robert was crawling around fussing with the trees and shrubs. Ellen knelt down in the sand to help him.

"Did you make this all by yourself?" she asked incredulous.

He nodded with self-conscious pleasure. "Yeah," he admitted, "I tol' you it was purty, din't I?"

"I like it." She was intrigued and wondered why she had never thought to do something so delightful and clever. "Let's make some more buildings over here. You can show me how."

Robert Lee agreed, quivering with happiness, and began to gather rocks from the creek bottom. "You have to git these flat kind mostly," he said showing her a piece of slate," and these long thin pieces."

"I know, instead of a city, let's make one big house with all the furniture and stuff in it," suggested Ellen, her eyes glittering with pleasure.

"Yeah, that's real good and we an make believe we live in it, eh?" Robert Lee danced about. Carried away with creative energy, they gathered cans, bottles, sticks and wire and pressed them into objects resembling furniture. Ellen made a lamp with a real shade of leaves, a table cover and a decoration for the table of the red berries from the rose bushes.

Robert Lee's excitement mounted and he pranced about the house with the glee of a ragged elf.

"You sure are smart, Ellen. You sure are the smartest girl I ever seen," he cried as she finished the lamp and stood it in the living room area. "I never would a thought uv that." Ellen was enjoying his admiration immensely.

The house completed, the two of them sat down to survey their creation. Ellen had a deep sense of elation as though she had discovered a secret all by herself. She scarcely thought of Robert Lee as part of it, forgetting that it was he who had provided the inspiration for her creativity. He was kneeling in his ragged overalls patting the sand with pride around the walls of the house. His lank blond hair fell into his eyes and he was chewing his tongue in the corner of his mouth. He looked comical to Ellen. At last he sat back and glanced up shyly.

"I sure would like you to be my woman someday," he stammered.

Ellen was jarred out of her sublime mood. "You what?"

"I'd like you to be my woman someday." Robert Lee brushed his hair back and grinned. "I sure do think you're smart and purty too. It'd be a long while, but I'm gonna learn about buildin' things and I kin draw purty good, too. I'm gonna git a good job and then...."

Ellen stared at him, feeling herself flushed with embarrassment at his pitiful, pale gray, red-rimmed eyes, his thin hunched shoulders and bare cracked toes. When she realized what he meant, the feeling of revulsion for him that swept over her prevented her from repulsing him directly. The vision of poor Mrs. Hamilton loomed darkly in her mind.

"Well, I'm not going to be anybody's woman," she said haughtily, tossing her head. "I'm going to grow up and write books and make lots of money by myself. I'm not ever going to get married."

"Not ever?" Robert Lee asked sadly.

"Not ever!" She got up crossly; he had spoiled the whole afternoon that had been such fun. She began to run across the creek but slipped on the uneven rocks and twisted her ankle under her. The moment that Robert Lee had leaped to help her, they heard the sound of crashing rocks and laughter echoing down the creek. Three boys appeared around the curve. Hal Walker was one of them, his fat face shining red under his thick thatch of curly dark hair. He shouted with malicious glee when he saw Ellen and Robert Lee kneeling in the rocks.

"Hey, watcha doin' down here with old Robert Lee, Elly," he prodded one of his companions who giggled knowingly. "Betcha they been havin' a little fun, betcha."

"You shut up, Hal Walker," Ellen said, furious now with shame and anger for she half guessed what they thought. "We just been building things."

"Buildin' things, what things?" Hall grinned wickedly.

Ellen pointed to the house and Robert Lee's city.

"Hah, look, Jack!" Hal went over to the sand bank. "Lookee at this. You been buildin' this baby stuff, Ellen?"

"Robert Lee might," said Jack Benton, " 'cause he ain't got all his marbles anyhow." The three boys crouched around the rock designs laughing and saying crude things. "Hey, Robert Lee, this here house, it got a bathroom in it?" Where's the toilet?" Jack proceeded to pee on the creation.

Ellen's face felt like flame; she turned away but could not move. She could not look at Robert Lee who still squatted beside her.

Hal kicked at the playhouse; then he scrubbed the whole thing to chaos with a sneer on this face.

"You mean thing, you mean old thing, you wait 'til I tell Grandma on you," Ellen cried.

Hal turned and gave her an ugly look. "You wait 'til I tell Ma on you. She'll tell Aunt Irene," he drawled triumphantly. Suddenly something like a blinding flash of light filled her with an awful sense of despair. She got up and started to hobble out of the creek and when Robert Lee moved to help her, she turned on him furiously, "It's all your dumb fault," she hissed. "I wish I had never seen you. Leave me alone."

Robert Lee's face crumpled and he turned and lunged at Hal; the two of them went down in the rocks. With savage cries the other two pounced on top of them. Ellen ran as fast as she could, dragging herself up the bank, getting her clothes full of burrs and stickers and scratching her arms and legs. She made her way across the field to Grandma's, seething with hatred for the whole world, especially the world of boys which she now perceived was, as her mother hinted, a dark and evil place.

But the blurred vision of Robert Lee bending over his childish dream city, the tender look on his face when he looked at her, did not quite fit. It bothered her a little, but then after all, Robert Lee didn't count in the real world. He didn't belong to her life or the life of Merritsville. Yet she shivered a little as she thought of the pathetic look on his face as he leaped like a cornered animal on the cruel boys; he would be beaten to a pulp in the creek bottom. She couldn't help him; what was worse she didn't even want to. The incredible idea of being his "woman," sharing the dreary strange life that the Hamilton's lived, made her shrink with disgust.

Grandma had not returned home, so Ellen rinsed off her arm and soaked her ankle in the tub by the hydrant in the back yard; then she crept into the seat under the arbor to pick the burrs and weeds out of her clothes. She thought about the queerness of this afternoon. The more she thought about it the more helpless and furious she felt. What if her mother found out, what could she say to convince her that she and Robert Lee had been down in the creek just playing baby games, building things like in a sandpile? There it was, that awful secret about what went on between boys and girls for which there was no name; a secret that you knew and yet didn't know, one that was all around you and yet you couldn't get hold of it. It was always popping up to spoil your world. She writhed with shame. Maybe Robert Lee was planning to make her do something awful that he knew about all the time. How she hated him.

By the time Addie came home from her Relief Society rounds, Ellen was weeping with chagrin and pain. Her ankle had begun to swell and hurt and, although she had never told her grandmother a lie before, she could not bring herself to tell her where she had been and what had happened. She said that she had tried to jump a ditch and had fallen in.

"Where on earth was that?" Grandma demanded, binding up the ankle and examining the scratches on her legs and arms. "It looks like you been playin' with wildcats."

"Oh, over by the Anderson's lane. Robert Lee wouldn't let me go by so I...." she trailed off, feeling even more miserable and guilty that she had mentioned him.

"Well," said Grandma, "Accidents will happen. Now let's stir up a pitcher of lemonade. It's been a scorcher today. I think I'll stir an egg and some cream of tartar in, I'm about done in."

Slowly, but surely, the world began to come right in Grandma's cool kitchen

The next few days Ellen retreated to her books as was her habit when things became too confusing. She went to the library, traded in one arm load and brought home another. She took a salt shaker and sat in the White Transparent apple tree, her book propped among the thick green leaves, eating tart, salted green apples, as she immersed herself in the safer world of fiction.

Absorbed and content, she was still aware of an ominous silence filled with echoing versions of the story that she was sure Hal would tell about her and Robert Lee. It was like waiting for a crime to be discovered, hoping that Hal and the other boys would never tell. She heard nothing but didn't go over to the Walker's or back to Grandma's for the rest of the week. Sunday, five days later, when some of the memories of that unhappy afternoon had become blurred, normal events sifting over it like dust, Ellen saw her cousin Hal in Sunday School. She tried to avoid him but he managed to get a seat behind her in the class where he kept slyly poking her and making suggestive noises.

Ellen felt her stomach knotting and face burning. She could not concentrate on the lesson which was something about the innocent boy Joseph Smith and his visit to the forest where he saw the angel who told him where the golden plates were. Ellen's disturbed imagination kept seeing him in the creek looking like Robert Lee kneeling among his rocks with the light filtering through the trees on his poor head. About the time that Sister Beckett, who had kept sending nervous glances in their direction, reached the dramatic point of Joseph's vision, Hal leaned forward and whispered hoarsely so that Ellen was sure everybody around heard, "Boy, we sure did beat up your boyfriend, Robert Lee. You oughta see him."

Ellen could endure it no longer. She turned around and slapped Hal resoundingly on the face. He reared backward, tipping over his chair, and Ellen jumped up and ran out of the classroom. The class exploded. Ellen could hear the laughter following her as she ran down the hall. She tore out of the church and ran all the way home in the bright sunshine, holding the hot, dry sobs in her chest.

When Irene came home an hour later, she found her sullen, red-eyed daughter crouched in front of the radio. The music issuing forth from the round, cloth-covered hole from hundreds of miles away was soothing to Ellen. Of course Sister Beckett had reported her disgraceful and unladylike behavior to Irene who was understandably upset. The two looked at each other with anguish and embarrassment, not knowing where or how to begin.

"We weren't doing anything," Ellen said at last, her lips quivering.

Irene was confused. "But Sister Beckett said you hit Hal right in Sunday School and knocked him off his seat."

"I did, but he's a fibber and a meany–Robert Lee's not my boyfriend."

"Who? What's this all about?" Irene looked more distressed than ever.

"I was going to tell you." Ellen's throat was constricted; she could scarcely talk and when she began, it came out so wrong that she felt more guilty and ashamed than ever.

"The other day I went down to the creek with Robert Lee Hamilton, you know the boy that lives down by Grandma's, and we made a house in the sand–that's all we did." She described the city in detail, hoping to persuade Irene of its reality which she herself had begun to doubt. "We weren't doing anything wrong at all and along came Hal and Jack Benton and Bill Burton. They said a lot of nasty things and messed everything up. I didn't stay to see what happened to Robert Lee, but Hal said they beat him up something awful. I ran over to Grandma's; that's the day I hurt my ankle."

"But why did you hit Hal in Sunday School today?" Irene asked. She had not been able to understand the story which Ellen poured out breathlessly.

"Because he said Robert Lee is my boyfriend; he said, 'We sure beat up your boyfriend.' He isn't my boyfriend and I never want to see him again and I hate Hal, I hate boys." Ellen finished, clenching her fists and pounding her knees.

Irene sat quietly for a moment, twisting the gold ring on her finger. "But why did you go down in the creek with him if you hate boys?"

"I was going to Grandma's and she wasn't home, that was the day you had the bad headache. Robert Lee was there by the lane and he said he had something to show me real special–this little city he made–he had all these little rocks fixed around real cute. Hal and Jack messed it all up." She was about to tell about Jack's peeing but thought that would upset her mother more. "He just kicked it all to pieces and the house we made too. It wasn't wrong, was it?"

"I guess you're a little too old to be making playhouses in the sand," Irene looked at her piteously.

"It wasn't like playhouses," Ellen pleaded. "It was, it was like art work, you know, like making designs or something."

"Yes," Irene said distractedly, "but you ought not to go off with a boy alone in places like that... it looks bad."

"But we weren't doing anything bad, just building in the sand, Mama. Don't you believe me?" Ellen's eyes filled with tears.

"Yes, oh, yes, I believe you." Irene passed her hand over her eyes. "It's just what other people think, it's just the way it looks."

"But why does it look bad when you don't do things bad?" Ellen persisted. Irene sighed deeply; she had such an agonized look on her face that she knew she would get no answer.

"You're getting to be a young lady now, Ellen, and you just can't go off and play with boys anymore. You must learn to behave like a lady." As Irene said this the cold, prim words in Aunt Delia's precise voice echoed in her mind and she felt their hollow inadequacy. But she knew nothing else to say to her distressed child in whom she could see the budding woman surrounded by all the fearful shadows of shame. She wanted to reach out to her and hold her back in the safer world of childhood, but her arms were paralyzed by her own revulsion to the dark and secretive curse of womanhood. With Laurence's death she had been thrust across the chasm on the further side of her own innocence. Now that Ellen was finding her way blindly but inevitably into this tumultuous realm, she felt the gap widening between them. She arose wearily. It was very hot and her Sunday girdle and dress were sticky; she moved into the bedroom, calling back to Ellen.

"Well, you better go tell Sister Beckett that you're sorry. I don't want you to play with that Robert Lee or whatever his name is anymore."

But Ellen was not sorry she had hit Hal; it had given her a wonderful sense of release. She would have done it again and twice as hard if she had the chance. Whenever she thought of Hal, she was filled with such fury that she clenched her fists and teeth and imagined all sorts of horrible ways to get revenge on him. All her imaginings ended in a helpless frustration, a desolate feeling of being defeated, surrounded by impregnable forces against which she had no defense. She had no witnesses other than Robert Lee whom she genuinely despised for his weakness, for his allowing Hal, Jack and Bill to beat him up. She already sensed the weight of the word of a person like Hal. Hal was a "real boy." She'd heard Uncle Aaron brag about him, and Aunt Dosey said he was a "Holy terror"–this was a kind of special distinction. Furthermore, he was "one of them;" Robert Lee was an outsider, a "furriner," with his disreputable family against him. When most of the elders in the town heard of the beating which the boys had given Robert Lee and the occasion for it, they smirked with satisfaction that "them damn trash had been put in their place." The boys had been defending one of their own girls who had been lured down there in the creek with evil intentions. Ellen gained nothing from the righteous indignation that cloaked the instinct of violence in all humans, even the "saints."

This warm spoiled Sunday Ellen pressed her ear to the radio speaker where sounds of a great orchestra spoke to her of a larger, more magnificent world where the human spirit could find meaning, dignity and self-realization. It was a place from which both

Hal and Robert Lee could be excluded.

♃

It was a hot July morning. The mountains sparkled in clear intense light and the sky was a bluish-white as though the heat had drawn out its vitality and wadded it up in white cotton balls of clouds wandering listlessly around the horizon. The cheat grass on the low hills was dry and yellow; even the green of the valley was beginning to get that faint tinge of ocher that announced the ripening of summer and the advance of fall.

There was a great deal of bottling, preserving, drying, pickling and other sorts of food preservation going on. A housewife's virtue and prestige hinged on how many bottles of fruit she had on her pantry shelves and how many bushel of peaches she could bottle in a day. Although normal activity for rural areas in Utah, this year it was even more necessary. In spite of the hope that a new administration would change things, the coming winter was likely to be another hungry one for the whole country.

Addie and Dosey were making raspberry jam. In spite of the heat Dosey's stove was roaring hot; she stood over it stirring the rich, ruby-colored liquid in an enamel pan. Addie was washing more bright berries at the kitchen sink. One row of jars with paraffin seals gleamed dark red on the kitchen table. Along with the jam-making Addie and Dosey were talking over the news and family problems. Ellen was just now the topic of conversation.

"... and Ida Beckett said that Ellen just hauled off right in Sunday School and hit Hal in the face, knocked him right off his chair, for no reason at all," Dosey said setting her mouth in firm disapproval, "tore Hal's best shirt on the corner of the bench; then she just got up and ran right out of Sunday School. It's a disgrace for Irene to let her act that way."

Addie ducked her head to hide the smile that threatened to turn up the corners of her mouth. "I don't suppose it's Irene's fault. Ellen's pretty much a mind of her own. But what was Hal up to?" She tossing a handful of berries into the colander.

"Well, he says he wasn't doin' nothin' but puttin' his feet on the back of her chair," Dosey said.

"Now, Doris, you know Hal better'n that."

The screen door slammed and Lorraine came in carrying Joey.

"I thought I told you to stay outside," her mother said crossly, "and keep him out of the way."

"Well, his face needs wipin'; he eats dirt all the time," Lorraine replied defensively.

"Lorraine," said Addie carefully, "why did Ellen hit Hal in Sunday School?"

Lorraine hesitated. "I don't really know, but I think it was becuz he was teasin' her about Robert Lee Hamilton."

"Robert Lee Hamilton?" Dosey looked puzzled.

"Yeah, that boy that lives down by Grandma's, you know, them funny people that moved there last spring."

Dosey set the jam off the stove and looked at Lorraine intently. "Yes, and what about him?"

"Well," Lorraine stumbled, "nothin' except last week Hal and Bill and Jack found Ellen and Robert Lee alone down in the creek, and–well–they beat Robert Lee up somethin' awful, they said. I think that's what she's mad about."

"Well, I never! What on earth business did they have down in the creek–the two of 'em–alone," said Dosey, very much agitated. She began to plop the hot jam into jars, splashing some of it on her hands and arms. "Goodness, Irene should watch that girl better, I declare. Here, Lorraine, wipe up that baby and go on out. Yes, you can have some bread with jam skimmin's."

Addie sat silent, thinking about the bruised ankle, the scratches and the lie that Ellen had told her about falling in the ditch. She was both hurt and frightened. Why had the child had to lie to her? Dark suspicions crossed her mind, but she put them aside resolutely. It was Hal who annoyed her most. Of all her grandchildren she had the hardest time feeling affection for him lately. Was Ellen now in his camp? There was something here she dare not look at in the light of her own emotional leanings.

When Lorraine had gone out again, Dosey said with an ominous note in her voice, "That's a fine thing, Ellen gettin' mixed up with that bunch of trash, criminals most likely, Aaron says."

"Now, now, Doris," Addie remonstrated with her daughter. "You know Aaron picks up a lot of nonsense from that bunch he hangs around with down on the bank corner. For all I can tell, they're poor people like the rest of us. Them men ain't up to much, I admit, but that poor little woman sure does have a hard row to hoe and them kids don't seem no better, no worse than most. I let 'em play around with Ellen in the orchard, and the little boy seemed real nice and polite, kinda bashful.

"All the same, they don't seem like decent people, not the kind for Ellen to take up with." Dosey was vigorously scraping the last of the jam into a jar.

Addie had no answer for this. By all standards that she knew, they did seem like dangerous and disreputable people but her heart was as stubborn as her mind. Why should children be condemned for their parents' shortcomings? She recalled the pitiful look of gratitude, the shy one-sided smile that Robert Lee had given her with his "Thank you, ma'am," for the bread and jam and how he had sat on the steps, eating it as carefully as though every bite were gold. The little girl, who was a bit cheeky, aroused her dislike ever so faintly, but they and Ellen seemed to have a fine time playing together. Still and all, Ellen was *hers* and if she were to be harmed by this, they must be separated.

It was difficult to imagine what two children of different sexes almost past their childhood would be doing that was innocent in that secluded, dimly lit place. She could not bear to think of Ellen doing bad things. What a sad and frightening moment to see the child you love pass out of innocence; innocence was so perilously close to ignorance and ignorance to evil. She sighed deeply.

"Well, it's a sad thing, I guess, yet we mustn't be hasty. You know, Doris, all that looks bad, ain't always so and all that looks good, ain't good, either. We all tend to see what we want to, don't we?"

"Yes, and that's the worst of it, Ma. You got to live with what it is people see. It ain't the way things are, it's the way they look that makes the difference in this world and it looks bad no matter how you put it for a growin' girl to be goin' off alone and playin' with a strange boy."

"That's so," agreed Addie, "and I'll talk to Irene and Ellen about it. I know she didn't think about it bein' wrong and I know she didn't do anythin' wrong."

"Oh, Ma, you always stick up for Ellen; she don't do nothin' wrong in your eyes. It's because she's like Laurence, I guess."

Addie took this thrust calmly. She knew that in spite of her efforts to be impartial, her daughters had always felt that she favored Laurence. Perhaps it was so; some parents and children have more natural sympathy for each other, although she would have sworn stoutly, and truly, that she loved them all equally.

"I guess," she said thoughtfully, busying herself to clean up the kitchen, "but I take any of my grandchildren's part if I think they're right and I don't defend 'em if I think they're wrong. And I think Hal was wrong to help two other boys beat up one poor skinny boy who han't no friends to help him. No matter what Ellen and that boy was doin' it was a mean and ugly act." She looked Dosey straight in the eye and Dosey lowered hers, picking at the corner of a dishtowel.

"Oh, kids!" she finally exploded, "Lordy, what a trial, if I ever get 'em raised in these times...."

"Yes, we need to pray for constant guidance, It ain't an easy world." She took off her apron and folded it into her bag.
Still bothered by the lie Ellen had told her, she stopped on her way home and talked to Irene and Ellen. Ellen tearfully told her grandmother the whole story. Addie knew she was telling the truth. From watching Ellen many hours at work and play and knowing how uneven the pattern of growth is in any child or grownup, she could see how easily Ellen could have fallen in with the curious game that did seem a bit childish. Ellen seemed different than other children her age, more inward-looking and with a curiosity about things that maybe she shouldn't have.

Irene listened more intently than she had the first time and was moved to say, "What a funny little boy he must be. Don't he have any boy friends at all?"

Ellen hadn't thought about it before but now she realized that he didn't. They didn't. She was the only friend that Simone and Robert Lee had but the thought did not make her happy. In fact, she could see it now as something humiliating. How had she been taken in by these ignorant, poor outsiders? She prickled with shame.

Addie, watching Ellen's mobile, freckled face filled with the stress of conflicting emotions, glimpsed the perils of childhood. Although her heart ached for the poor boy, and she was loath to thrust him out without a hearing, still and all the strong pattern of social custom, the uses and abuses of the past by which everyone in the community is ultimately judged, prevailed. Ellen was her own; she belonged here and must be protected against any outside influence that came uninvited and unwanted, threatening her. She thought it best that Ellen stopped playing with the Hamiltons. Ellen agreed fervently and hugged her grandmother, vowing she hated Simone and Robert Lee.

"Now, now," Grandma soothed, "we mustn't hate. The Lord tells us to love our enemies and forgive them. But it's best to stay away from temptations. Those folks don't seem to be our kind."

Safe in her grandmother's love and approval once again, the burden of falsehood lifted, Ellen was greatly relieved and mentally composed a sharp speech that she would deliver if either of the Hamiltons pestered her.

For a few days Ellen felt free and light hearted. She picked up her old acquaintances among the girls and spent more time at the Walkers. She found a new way to go to Grandma's that went past the Gordon house where she sometimes caught glimpses of Everett Gordon but thought little about him, only vaguely remembering the visit she and her father had made. But the Hamiltons pervaded her consciousness. She found that her older friends were less imaginative and pliable than Simone and Robert Lee. They had never heard of wonderful places that Ellen had read about that the Hamiltons had actually lived in or been to. They didn't like to play "make-believe" games anymore or act out plays. The Merritsville kids were caught up in their own Mormon dominated world; the girls paired off into "best friends." Instead of a gaggle of small chattering girls with front teeth missing who changed pals indiscriminately two or three times a week or played happily in clumps of three or fives, they were now seen slumping around in pairs, their arms locked about each other and their heads bent close together in whispered confidences. They were almost wholly occupied in writing notes about their boyfriends which they posted in secret mailboxes, changing their hairstyles to look like some movie star, or appraising each other's clothes. They giggled furtively about naughty things they discovered in true confession magazines, older sister's diaries and anonymous sources. A lot of the information had to do with "coming sick" (menstruation was a word not current in their vocabulary) and getting babies.

Ellen had been closest to her cousin Lorraine, but she now discovered that Lorraine and Helen Bates had become "thick as thieves." When Ellen was around the two of them, they acted as though they didn't want her. They made silly remarks to each other that Ellen couldn't understand and then laughed hilariously at her looks of dismay. If she happened on them unexpectedly, they stopped talking and hinted that they knew all sorts of fascinating secrets. They had a secret mailbox that Ellen could not discover and both of them had a boyfriend. Lorraine was stuck on Jack Benton though he acted like he didn't know her sometimes, and Helen had a case on Ray Whitney who was stuck on her.

To make it all the more poignant, Ellen had found *Anne of Green Gables* that summer and succumbed to its lavender spell. She imagined herself to be Anne Shirley, and wished she had a Diana but, as she began to hunt for one among the dozen or so girls her age, she found that Marissa Clements, a thin sickly girl who had had polio and was small for her age as well as crippled, was the only one not paired off. Marissa was too frail and slow to keep up with anyone and far too dull, Ellen discovered, to comprehend the romance of "make-believe." Gradually the thought of Simone crept back into her consciousness; there was something seductive about the Hamilton's and Simone had dark hair like Diana Barry.

The boys had grown tired in a short time of tormenting Ellen about Robert Lee, making a pantomime of avoiding her blows when they taunted with such nonsense, "When you and Robert Lee gonna get married?" knowing that such teasing would prod her into a rage. Irene had told her just to ignore them and keep a straight face as if she didn't hear. It had worked. The fad passed: the memory became less painful every day.

One day she decided to take the old road back to Grandma's, not admitting to herself that she really hoped to meet up with Simone. She didn't want to encounter Robert Lee, afraid of what she might see, even though it had been several weeks since the incident. She had had awful visions of what he looked like after Hal and the boys had beaten him up, and she was ashamed of many things for which she could find no reason. Yet she was curious. She was not disappointed for she had hardly reached the old cottonwood where they had first met when she saw the two of them dawdling in the lane. She almost turned and ran the other way, but Simone had already sighted her before she could put the impulse into action. She came racing up to the tree, Robert Lee hung back a little plowing his toes through the deep dust.

"Whaer you been so long?" she demanded grabbing Ellen fiercely, her eyes dancing with pleasure.

Ellen tried to pull away but Simone held fast. "We been lookin' for you ever day, we even went over to your granma's and she said you wasn't supposed to play with us anymore."

"No, I mean, yes."

"Why," Simone asked, a menacing curl to her lip, "ain't we good enough fer ya?"

"It's about that day Robert Lee got beat up." Ellen, embarrassed, wriggled out of her grasp. "My cousin Hal told everybody and they think that me'n Robert Lee...."

Robert Lee had come up to the tree now and stood fiddling with an old pocket knife. His face was bleaker than ever and there was a red scar across his cheek under his faintly bluish eye.

"Yeah," said Simone, "them boys is gonna git it someday. Robert Lee he gotta knife and he gonna drive it right in 'em if he catch 'em 'round here." She made a descriptive gesture and Robert Lee lifted his head with a jerk that sent his hair flying back. He drove the blade of the knife deep into the tree. Ellen jumped back. There was a look on his face which she had never seen before–one of such painful hurt and helpless hatred that it frightened her. It was the look of the weak and gentle who cannot fight back. But she knew Simone could have driven the knife into flesh with steely joy. Ellen felt the old thrill of fear that she had known on first meeting them; she turned to run away.

"I gotta go," she said, but Simone jumped in front of her and Robert Lee made a move as though to block her from the back, although when she turned to look at him, he gave her a sad, appealing glance and dropped his eyes.

"Come on down and play with us," wheedled Simone. "We got new things in the playhouse you ain't never seen. Ma makin' cawn pone t'day, too."

Ellen looked from one to the other almost in tears, "No, I can't; Mama says I can't play with boys anymore," she burst out, pronouncing "boys" with such intensity that Robert Lee fell back, stumbling over the root of the tree. "They're too rough," she added on seeing his distress.

"Well, I'm not a boy, you can still play with me," Simone persisted. "Robert Lee can go on down by the creek."

"But I can't come to your house anyway," Ellen stammered.

"I'll come over to your grandma's house." Simone was not to be put off.

Ellen hesitated, flushed with fear and desire. She wanted to play with Simone, too. She had worked out a play based on *Anne of Green Gables*, and she needed someone to help her. Playing with Simone suddenly became very urgent.

"Well, I'll tell you, I'll ask Grandma if I can play with you if Robert Lee don't come. I'll meet you down by the bottom of the orchard after lunch time if she will let me."

"Don't ask her," Simone said cagily, "just come by yourself."

Ellen didn't answer this, for she knew she could not risk being out of her grandmother's grace again. She thought she knew a way of getting around her any way. She began running down the path, Simone calling after her, "I'll be in the orchard anyway."

Addie was busier than usual; she was the chairman in charge of the stand that was to be set up back of the church as part of the celebration of the Twenty-Fourth of July, which, in Merritsville, as all over the state of Utah, was the big day of the summer. When Ellen arrived she was set to crimping red, white and blue crepe paper in which the stand was to be trimmed. Ellen sat fluting the paper with her stained thumb and finger wondering how to approach the subject of Simone. Finally, there seeming no way to edge into the subject carefully, she said abruptly, "Simone Hamilton might come over here today."

Addie, whose mind was occupied figuring out who should help freeze the big freezers of home-made ice cream and who should tend the pop tubs, just murmured, "uumh." Ellen could not tell whether it was a sound of approval or not and, knowing her grandmother, she thought she ought to make sure.

"Can I play with her if she comes?" she asked warily.

Addie laid her pencil down and looked at Ellen, "Now what was it you wanted?"

Ellen kept her head bent over the crepe paper and twisted the edges extra carefully, but she said distinctly, "If Simone Hamilton comes over here, can I play with her?"

Addie looked troubled for a minute, "Well, I suppose it wouldn't do no harm if you stayed around here. Is the boy comin' over, too?"

"No, I don't think so," Ellen answered, trying to conceal her excitement.

"Well, it seems all right for little girls to play together. I don't know that I trust that girl too much, she seems kinda sneaky. We got a lot of work to do today. Maybe she could come some other day?" Ellen's heart sank but she didn't dare go any further. She would just have to hope things would turn out.

Addie did not have the morbid dislike of boys that Irene harbored nor the clear-cut sense of who was and who was not decent that Dosey had. She still had the vague notion that little girls were made of "sugar and spice and everything," and that something in their makeup was inherently more innocent and virtuous than boys. She had never known any "Wicked Women," outside the stories in the Bible and other rumors. She certainly was not aware that some little girls are born with the primitive wisdom and temper of witches. Age had mellowed or obliterated many of her fears about sexual differences. In the back of her mind there lingered a sense of pity for the Hamilton children. They were, after all, only children and all precious in the sight of the Lord.

As soon as her grandmother had given approval, Ellen began to wish fervently for Simone's arrival. She finished the crepe paper job rapidly and began to gather up some old clothes and props. As soon as she had eaten her lunch, she was down by the orchard fence, looking anxiously across the fields. At last Simone appeared, dark hair glistening in the sunshine, face glowing with pleasure. She threw her arms around Ellen and they danced around gleefully. It began to seem to Ellen that Simone just might be her "Best Friend," her Diana with black hair like in the book. How Ellen wished that hers were bright red like Anne Shirley's.

Ellen had been planning to ask Simone if she would swear to be best friends but an odd premonition prevented her from asking it at once. She was not sure that Simone would understand *Anne of Green Gables*. Books were one thing for which Simone had little interest. She liked to have Ellen tell her stories particularly about beautiful girls who got lots of jewels and presents and married the prince. Simone always made up stories about stabbings, shootings, beatings, all sorts of gory things. She would never play at dying gently, as Ellen sometimes did, imagining herself pale and frail with long hair spread dramatically on the pillow; if die she must it was dramatically with awful ear-splitting shrieks or moans.

Ellen decided to postpone asking Simone to be best friends until she was sure of her mood. She hoped to put her in a good temper by producing an old lipstick that Irene had given her. Simone had a mania for lipsticks.

"Well, what'll we do?" Simone had sprawled in the orchard grass.

"I made up this show about these two girls, Anne Shirley, that's me and Diana Barry, that's you. They're in this book and they're bosom friends."

"They're what?" Simone sat up with interest. "Do they have boyfriends and get married?"

"No, not right at first, they have all these adventures. They're not old enough...."

"What do they do? Are they rich?"

"Well, no, Anne's an orphan and she comes to live with this old couple, Matthew and Marilla. They don't want her at first because she isn't a boy, but after a while they like her. She makes friends with this other girl, Diana and they pledge to be bosom friends and to love each other until they die. Then they do all these things like Anne gives Diana this raspberry stuff and it makes her drunk and she dyes her hair green and then she gets on this raft and floats down a stream...."

Ellen stopped for Simone was looking at her disgustedly. "That sounds crazy, that's not nothin' fun to do. How you gonna do that thing like dye your hair?"

"You just imagine that you do, you...." It began to dawn on Ellen that never in a million years could she explain the magic of the book to Simone who was not, in spite of her dark curly hair, a Diana Barry. She could see that the dramas and dialogues she had thought up in bed at night and under the apple tree belonged to a world into which Simone could never be brought. Somewhat deflated Ellen said, " I got some lipstick."

Simone sat up with interest, "Where? Let's put some on."

"There isn't much left, so don't smear it all over," Ellen said irritated now that her dream bubble had been pricked and her prize forced out of her prematurely. Reluctantly she went over to the box of things she had brought down to the orchard to play with and dug out an old purse, from which she fished out the stub of a lipstick. Simone seized it and the purse on the flap of which was stuck a cracked mirror and began to paint her mouth.

"Hey, let's play dance today. Let's play like we go to this dance and we meet this big handsome rich man and we both like him and he takes us for a ride in his big swell car. We can go in the old buggy, c'mon." Simone was already pawing through the dress-up clothing, selecting the fanciest pieces for herself. Ellen was put out but Simone's feverish animation soon overcame her resistance. She began to fill out the rambling plot.

"We can pretend that he loves one of us more'n the other and we have to decide which one."

"Yeah, we can have a fight to see who gets him," Simone grinned maliciously.

Soon the two of them arrayed like caricatures of the '20's moved the scene of their fancies to the stack yard where the haystack provided shade and they were closer to the buggy that served as carriage, bus, car, train even airplane when they dared travel by this new dangerous means.

After the dance and the car ride and an episode in which they quarreled over the favors of their imaginary escort and Simone ended up shooting him, they decided to be "best friends" after all. In the middle of the afternoon Grandma came down to see how they were getting along, bringing some cookies and lemonade. They were driving the buggy at full speed, giggling hilariously. Addie was glad to see Ellen enjoying herself so much with innocent play, comical as the two looked. After all the young didn't have a long time to play; she recalled how she had had to go out to work when she was their age, had never had much of a youth at all.

"I have to take these things over to Sister Clark's, Ellen. I'll be back soon. Can you two ladies stop your trip now to have some refreshments?"

Munching the cookies and drinking grandma's lemonade

in the shade of the straw stack, Ellen and Simone were filled with the happiness of childhood freedom, but all afternoon both Simone and Ellen had prodded each other to new flights of imagination and so stimulated each other's nerves that they were hot and exhausted. Simone threw herself down on the straw slide at the base of the stack where the shade was deepest. She was wearing an old red crepe dress of Aunt Dosey's from the flapper era with ragged fringe and broken beads. Her dark curls protruded from under a black satin cloche, and she had a smear of lipstick on her mouth like a wound. With her legs spread out and her feet in run-over high heels turned inward, she looked like a beautiful but dilapidated doll. Sweating and feeling slightly irritable, Ellen plopped down beside her in a flowered chiffon that had once been her mother's and threw off the droopy hat with its faded roses. It was oppressively hot; some dark clouds had begun to gather over the east mountains. The musty smell of the barn yard seemed to have grown thicker and Ellen felt as though she could hardly breath. All at once Simone began tearing off her clothes. She threw off the hat, kicked the shoes high in the hay and peeled off the dress, her own flimsy cotton one at the same time and stood panting in a pair of dingy rayon panties that barely clung to her hips.

Ellen was spellbound. In the greenish light caused by thick clouds rolling toward the mountain Simone looked like a queer little elf who had appeared in answer to a careless and weird wish. Laughing excitedly she lunged at Ellen and began pulling her clothes off too. She ripped the chiffon right down the front and scooped Ellen's dress up over her head. Ellen jumped up, hugging herself in dismay, then suddenly she caught the wild spirit of the game, tossed her muslin petticoat over her head and faced Simone in home-made bloomers across the back of which could be faintly seen the brand of a local flour mill. She could feel a fierce and furtive excitement boiling up in her. Secluded in the warm, clean space between the back of the shed and the haystack, they were screened on one side by an old sheep loading chute, its warm gray boards reflecting the sunlight, and on the other by the end of the chicken coop. Acutely aware of themselves and their privacy, they looked at each other intently. The contours of their small bodies were only here and there swelling into womanliness; across the chest were slight bubbles of flesh tipped with little pink, wizened buds of nipples. Ellen was very white with firm round legs and arms but Simone was a warm brown and her ribs and shoulder bones showed sharply through the flesh. She wriggled and her panties fell off her skimpy hips. She looked like a starved bird or some queer, brown wood creature; she kept her glittering eyes fastened on Ellen who giggled nervously, as she stepped out of the panties and flung them aside with her toe.

"Take yours off, too," Simone urged. Slowly, as though hypnotized, Ellen pushed the firm elastic down over her round white buttocks. With a little gurgling laugh Simone leaped forward and pushed her down in the hay, dragging the bloomers off the rest of the way. The heat flooded over Ellen's body making her painfully, but at the same time almost deliciously, aware of her nakedness. Simone flung herself upon Ellen who recoiled at the shock of feeling the warm flesh. Almost suffocated she managed to thrust Simone off and sat up, chills running down her spine and making her jaw tight.

"What you tryna do?" she asked nervously.

Simone stared at her, narrowing her eyes and brushing dark curls off her shining face. "Ain't you never fucked before?"

Ellen shook her head stiffly.

Simone put her head back and laughed; then she looked around furtively. Ellen had drawn the old dress half over her naked body, feeling both hot and cold.

"Oh, everbody does that when they're just babies. You mean you ain't fucked with nobody, your cousins nor nobody?"

Ellen had heard the word and knew that it meant something awful; she continued to shake her head miserably, quivering with anxiety which, in spite of the fact that she knew she ought to get up, put on her clothes and get away from here, kept her paralyzed on the spot. Overwhelming desire and curiosity had consumed her so that she was a flame of agony.

"How, how do you do it?" she murmured.

Simone moved over close to her and thrusting her hand between Ellen's legs began manipulating the little fat folds of her genitals. "There's lots of ways. Pas and Mas get on each other like this." She threw herself on top of Ellen and began wriggling like a fish.

Ellen pushed her off in irritation. "That's no fun." She struggled to get up.

"Yeah, I know better ways," Simone breathed. She had picked up a weed with a long feathery frond and, pushing Ellen back down, began tickling her. The pleasant tingling sensation spread all over Ellen and allayed the apprehension she felt. Simone watched her intently, her face catlike in its concentration.

"It's fun, ain't it?" Ellen, swallowing the lump of fear in her throat, nodded. She had never felt a more gripping sensation. Every nerve in her body was quivering with unbearable excitement when Simone bent down quickly and began to run her tongue deep in the fold. A suffusion of shock sent Ellen weak all over, and she moaned and squirmed with pleasure. Simone raised her head and grinned.

"You like that, huh?" she asked but Ellen could not speak. She felt like crying or screaming and an intense wave of fear flooded over her. She began to wiggle away but Simone clutched her, digging her fingers deep into her flesh.

"Now you gotta do it to me," she hissed and threw herself backward beside Ellen spreading her legs. Their warm bodies touched again and Ellen jerked away. She sat up and looked at the thin brown body. Simone's legs and feet were very dirty but on the rest of her body a fuzz like peach down glowed in the slanting cloud light. There was a sour smell of urine about her. Ellen was overcome with a feeling of aversion and nausea so powerful she thought she was going to throw up. She clutched her stomach and bent over.

"I won't, I can't," she cried, "I don't want to, you're dirty, Simone Hamilton." She leaped up and began gathering up her clothes in panic.

Simone's face blackened with fury and she sprang up at Ellen. "You got to, you cheater," her dirty fingernails dug deep into Ellen's arm. "I did it to you, you're a stinkin' cheater.

Ellen had burst into tears and pulled herself away. "I can't, I'm afraid, besides it's nasty," she whimpered and began getting into her bloomers which she put on backward.

A clap of thunder rolled against the mountain and even Simone looked frightened. Ellen began to sob. She had heard wicked people got struck by lightning and she knew for sure now that she was wicked. She felt wicked because she liked what Simone had done to her, and she felt mean and guilty because she could like it and not do it back to Simone. Things were all so mixed up inside her.

"I hate you," she burst out at Simone, tears streaming down her face. "I don't ever want to play with you again."

Simone, who had put on her meager clothing, turned around and darted her tongue out like a snake. "I hate you, too, you're just a dumb, Mormon baby cheater," she said venomously and ran out of the yard. Ellen, numb and miserable, watched as she ran jerkily through the fields, her black hair bouncing crazily.

Listlessly Ellen began to gather up the discarded costumes and props. She found the half-melted lipstick among the straw and threw it as hard as she could in the direction in which Simone had disappeared. But after she had put everything into the box, she couldn't think what to do with herself. She was afraid to go up to the house for fear Grandma had come back and would see that there was something the matter. There was no way that she could tell her the truth this time. She dried her eyes and sat down again in the straw, examining the red welts that Simone had left on her arm. When she thought of Simone, the trail of associations led back to that stupendous event. Curiously Ellen put her hands between her legs where she had always been thoroughly taught not to put them, at first touching herself through the cloth, then hesitantly stretching the leg of her bloomer. Something like the previous shock went through her and she withdrew her hand guiltily, but she could not rid herself of the stupefying memory.

As she sat there in the dark, pre-storm heat, it came to her that she had been led at last into the presence of that dreadful secret, strangely enough, by a girl, not a boy as her mother feared. She was deeply confused and ashamed. What was it that happened between boys and girls that was so much worse than this? Of course, it must be worse the way everybody fussed about it. Then the horrifying thought came to her: What if Robert Lee had been going to do something terrible like that to her. She shuddered and was flooded with a new sensation of shame—everybody must think that he did anyway. Ellen was never to know that she had awakened in Robert Lee the most tender, ideal emotion he was ever to know, the idealism of a young boy, so much more fragile than that of a girl. At that time of his bleak life, she was never in his thoughts connected with what he knew as a common woodshed experience. Alone in his misty creek haven he had dreamed of her as his star that would lift him out of the pain and ugliness of his life. Like a star, the ideal is often most clearly apparent in darkness and even after the beating, the meaning of which Robert Lee clearly understood, he clung to his image of her. Long accustomed to deprivation, abuse and unkindness, he had spent that same afternoon in the shadows building another house of stones and sticks, saddened but not daunted by the news that she could not play with him anymore.

Ellen, brooding alone in the straw stack as the summer storm gathered, hated them both, hated all the Hamiltons and wished that they had never come to Merritsville. She had begun to agree with Hal who had said that some of the men said they ought to be chased out of town. Surely they were *worse* than other people; she imagined all sorts of dark things about them, and they had dragged her into their evil world.

She felt like she could never face anyone again. Guilt would be written all over her. What Ellen, sheltered as she had been and isolated from most ordinary experiences, did not know was that most of the kids her age in Merritsville had made the same discoveries long before. They had eagerly explored the forest at the edge of which she had just arrived and having less imagination, less sensitivity and less tense adult vigilance, had assimilated it casually. It had been a joke among the girls for sometime that Ellen was "real dumb" about some things even if she was so smart in school.

What Ellen had only dimly perceived from the time of her father's death and the baby, was that there were two worlds–the world of grown-ups and of children. There was an unbridgeable gap between them. Children learned that it was necessary to conceal such knowledge and activities from grown-ups who had forgotten that the exploration of their own and each other's bodies and feelings was an urgent and natural part of the child's world. When adults had crossed the chasm, they looked with horror on their own lost innocence and feared the time it would happen to their offspring.

Ellen sat disconsolately, her dress pulled tightly down around her knees, trying to decide how she was going to face the grown-ups in her life now that she knew what they knew only did not know what to call it. Above all she must not let her mother know what had happened to her. It was a secret she must bear herself; this was the first burden of maturity. She was now precipitately in the lost world between worlds, adolescence, where one cannot turn back to innocence nor go forward with certainty to knowledge. From morning to afternoon her whole perspective had changed.

Forked tongues of lightning flickered across the sky and deep claps of thunder rumbled ominously. Ellen remembered sadly how Grandma used to tell her that it was the Devil's wagon going across a bridge, and how she really believed it, picturing his terrible black face with peaked red ears and a tail with a burning fork on the end of it. Now she imagined he might be grinning at her, having got one more soul on the way to Hell.

She moved her things under the shed and listened to the great drops of rain as they hit the tin roof. In the dim shadows she began to recompose her new self with the knowledge that the bad and the good resided together in her, and she would have to watch out for those people and things that would so easily lead her astray. For sure she was going to avoid Simone.

 C3

The Twenty-Fourth of July dawned hot and bright saluted by twelve blasts of dynamite to simulate festive cannons announcing a day of celebration in Merritsville. Old Jake Healy was down by the creek setting off the explosions with immense pride at fifteen minute intervals. It was eighty-five years since the pioneers had come into the Salt Lake Valley. Later on there would be a parade; girls dressed in long, plain gingham dresses and old-fashioned sun bonnets and boys in overalls, big hats and false whiskers would pull coaster wagons on which white sheets had been draped to make covered wagons. There would be a few kids on crepe paper decorated bicycles. Ellen had refused to dress up this year like an "old pioneer" although Aunt Dosey had wanted her to help pull the Primary float. Most of the young people were tired of the "old pioneers" and liked the prettier, more up-to-date floats like the one draped with white satin and sparkling stars on which Helen Bates, "Miss Merritsville," rode. Ellen didn't really want to be in it at all this year, but she would go to the festivities and try to remember the pioneers who seemed so remote.

After the parade there would be a program in the park with hymn singing and speeches about them and their great hardships and "our wonderful heritage," which bored most of the audience, especially the younger ones who were anxious to get back to their firecrackers, popsicles and hot dogs. Once the pioneers had their due, the Twenty-Fourth became a riotous, typical country festival with plenty of furtive drinking, even in this abstemious community, noise, dirt, surreptitious love-making, quarreling and finally the satiation and fatigue which made it a relief, if not a pleasure, to go back to the ordinary routine of life.

Ellen woke irritably on the second of the blasts and lay listening to the dull echoing against the mountainside. Other years she had awakened to the prospects of the Twenty-Fourth with an unbearable feeling of excitement and happiness, but this morning she felt more like crying. For one thing her head ached from sleeping all night on tin curlers she had persuaded Irene to buy in a renewed effort to train her stubborn, thick brown hair into curl "like the other girls." She sat up and began to feel the sore spaces on her scalp and unwind the curlers. On the fifth "boom" she climbed out of bed and went to the dresser where she finished extricating the punishing instruments of beauty and dumped them in a heap. The result was far from satisfying. Some of the hair had become loosened in the night and was as straight as ever; other curls were odd shaped sausages sticking out at various, unbecoming angles.

Leaning on her elbows, chin in hand, she studied her image disconsolately. How ugly she was she thought, rubbing the freckles across her nose as though she could erase them. Tears began to fill her eyes. It was going to be a terrible day! She was going to look stupid and there was nobody for her to go around with anyway. All the other girls had had slumber parties last night; their plans were all made. Aunt Dosey had made Lorraine ask Ellen to join hers and Helen's, but Ellen had said no; Ellen didn't want that kind of invitation. She grabbed the comb and raked angrily through her hair; the curls separated and stood up in a spray of fuzz that looked even worse. In despair she threw herself back on the bed. Maybe she could just stay home and read and pretend she was sick, succumbing to her misery.

An hour later when the last salute from Stone Creek had resounded against the mountains, Irene came to the door of the bedroom holding up the flowered dimity dress which she had made for Ellen; it had a flare skirt and broad yellow sash. She had been worried about Ellen who had moped around all week and hoped the dress would make her feel better. She had a lot of faith in the power of pretty clothes to affect a girl's mood. The day brightened as Irene brushed and tucked at the stubborn curls and tied them with a yellow ribbon to match the sash. By parade time Ellen was almost pleased with the reflection which smiled warily at her from the mirror. Irene looked fresh and lovely and as the two of them walked hand in hand up the street, Ellen felt some of the old happiness flooding over her. In the bright, sparkling light of summer filling the valley it might have been that the ugly events of the past two years had not really happened. She told herself that she was far happier walking with her mother than with those silly girls.

After the parade Irene had to work in the stand with Grandma, and Ellen found herself alone once more, wandering about in the noisy crowd of harassed grown-ups and greedy, demanding children taking advantage of their parents' holiday mood and public good nature. She dodged malicious boys whose wicked firecrackers filled the air with ear-splitting explosions and sickly odor of burned powder. She tripped over the feet of the old folks smiling tepidly on the benches that had been placed under the scattered trees back of the church. Some of the girls passed and said "Hello" with superior smirks. For a while she helped Louise look after Joey and the twins, but that became tiresome and she decided to spend some of the quarter she had tied up in her salt-sack handkerchief with the crocheted edging that Grandma had made her.

The park to the south of the church was dotted with stands draped in red-white-and-blue bunting set up and attended by the various church organizations to raise funds for their treasury. Ellen felt obliged to patronize the one in which her mother and Grandma were dispensing pop, ice cream, candy bars and gum, so she wedged up to the pine board counter and tried to catch Irene's eye. Irene was dashing about the enclosure busily. Ellen noted with surprise how happy and pretty she looked. She was wearing a soft blue dress with a full skirt and a wide flowing cape collar; the pearls Laurence had given her were gleaming on her fine, white throat. Her cheeks were flushed a delicate pink and her dark hair glistened in the light that slanted through the trees. Ellen had grown used to her mother moving or sitting in quiet tired sadness these past years, and this sudden, bright animation made her seem almost strange. For a moment she felt bewildered, forgot what it was she intended to buy. Her mother finally noticed her and came over, leaning over the counter affectionately to straighten her hair bow.

"Are you having a good time?" she asked. Her voice had the hint of laughter and excitement in it.

Ellen nodded absently and asked for a popsicle, still staring at the vision of her transformed mother that she faintly resented. Irene brought her the popsicle and said, "When you get tired go over to Aunt Dosey's. We're all going to have dinner over there. Here—here's the rest of your money, now tie it up and don't lose it."

As Ellen pushed away, licking the orange popsicle, she heard a man who was lounging against the tree, the corner of which supported one side of the stand, say, "Boy, she's some looker, that Irene Kent. Wonder why somebody ain't took up where old Laurence Kent left off?"

"Hear she don't give nobody an openin' at all," said his companion who was supporting the other side of the tree.

"Can't be shot for tryin'," said the first, grinning lasciviously in the direction of the stand. "Think I'll give it a try later on...."

Ellen stared angrily at the two men, one of whom she recognized as Dub Peck, the Sheriff's son; the other looked ugly and strange, probably somebody from out of town. A chill of apprehension went down her spine, followed by a flush of hatred at the idea of him even thinking of her mother, but she had no more time to think about it for she felt a hot, sticky hand clutch her shoulder. She knew before she turned that it was Simone Hamilton.

She had not seen her since that awful afternoon; the memory of it still made her burn with shame, and she had resolved firmly not to have anything more to do with Simone or the Hamiltons.

But Simone, her face sparkling with glee, acted as though nothing at all had happened and they were still good friends.

"H'lo, whaer you all been, I been lookin' all over for ya," she beamed. She had on a cheap, new red taffeta dress which was too old for her and too big, but the color heightened the rich darkness of her skin and hair; she was fairly dancing with excitement.

"Oh, I want one of them, gimme a bite." She grabbed Ellen's popsicle and bit a large chunk out of it. "Let's go git me one an' I'll pay you back a bite," she said handing it back. Ellen felt like throwing it away, but she was being dragged toward the stand, once more caught up in the violent whirlwind of Simone. There was a larger crowd around the stand now, but Simone managed to wriggle and push a place for them. Old Sister Bates came to wait on them.

"I wanan orange popsicle," Simone ordered, holding out a nickel. When the old lady brought the popsicle, Simone took it and held out the other hand impatiently. Sister Bates peered at it quizzically through her bifocals.

"I want my change, I gave you a dime," Simone said firmly.

"Did you?" stammered Sister Bates in confusion and waddled back to the change box bringing Simone a nickel. Ellen opened her mouth to say something then closed it as Simone gave her a rude push toward the fringe of the crowd.

"That was only a nickel you gave her," Ellen said in wonderment when they had found a bench and sat down. Simone, licking her popsicle greedily, gave her a sly sideways look, then shrugged her shoulders.

"So, I got the popsicle and I got the nickel," she replied archly.

"But that's cheating, it, it's stealing." Ellen began to edge away from Simone nervously.

"It's short-changin'," Simone said coolly. "Here, you wanta bite a my popsicle?" Ellen shook her head feeling suddenly very hot and scared, but she didn't know where to go or what to do. The noisy crowd milling around all seemed like hostile, stupid strangers. Only Simone seemed real and alive, the very spirit and heart of excitement. In spite of her fear and dislike, Ellen felt a certain admiration for her.

Simone finished the popsicle, examined the stick to see if it said "free" which would entitle her to another one and when it didn't, flung it away. "I'm thirsty," she announced. "You got any more money?"

Ellen was about to say "no," but somehow found it impossible to lie to Simone. She nodded unhappily.

"Listen," said Simone, "give me a nickel and I'll go get a pop and a nickel change like I just did and then we can both have a pop and you can have your nickel back."

Mesmerized, Ellen untied her handkerchief and mutely handed Simone the coin, but she remained seated on the bench, her hands and neck sticky with perspiration as Simone wriggled her way up to the stand again.

This time one of the men, Brother Egdel, who had been pressed into service, waited on her and caught her trick, so Simone came back with the pop but without the nickel, an ugly defiant look on her face. She turned and stuck her tongue out toward the stand. "Old smarty," she hissed and took a long gulp of pop.

"But it's mine," said Ellen, holding out her hand though she hadn't wanted the pop just then. Simone guzzled a third of the bottle before handing it nonchalantly to Ellen.

In the stand Martin Egdel said to the women, shaking his head, "Better watch that little dark haired snot over there. She tried to short change me just now–would you believe it, a kid that little?"

Ellen looked at the pop with distaste and thrust it back at Simone. "Here, I don't want it," she said jumping up and starting off alone. Something warned her that she had better get away from Simone before she was dragged into another frightening and humiliating experience. Simone followed her and grabbed her arm. Ellen jerked away. "I gotta go home," she said fiercely on the verge of tears.

"All right. You ain't mad again? You sure ain't no fun anymore." Simone finished the pop, tossed down the bottle and walked away. Ellen turned, not sure which way to go, and saw that Simone was running toward her father and Frank who were standing alone by the fence. They were grinning drunkenly. As Simone came up to her father, he put his arm around her and patted her hair, then leaned down and whispered something in her ear that made her laugh. She whispered something back and he reached into his pocket and brought out a coin. Ellen couldn't see what it was, but she was filled with boiling rage and envy as she squeezed the fifteen cents wadded up in the damp hanky; Irene had told her that was all she could afford to let her spend that day. To think that Simone had calmly tricked her out of a nickel then walked over and got money out of her father as easily as that made her furious. For a hot, excruciating moment she thought of running at Simone and pulling out that gleaming black, naturally curly hair that bounced down her back as she loped toward the hot-dog stand. But, as usual, she was paralyzed by some strange force that seemed operative only in the presence of Simone Hamilton. It was as though she always wanted to do two things exactly opposite; the two desires pulling so strongly against each other made any motion impossible.

At last, however, she started off in the direction of Aunt Dosey's feeling very dejected, hot and soiled.

Even during the depression, holidays were the occasion for big delicious meals; in spite of the heat and the other things she had had to do that morning, Dosey spread her dining room table with an abundance of good things to eat much of which had been raised in their own garden. There were little new potatoes and peas with a sprig of mint, small sweet carrots, radishes, new let-tuce surrounding the roast of beef which Aaron had produced somehow, plump hot rolls with Addie's butter and for dessert, a huge bowl of gleaming red raspberries and one of Irene's famous cakes. The meal was noisy but happy, Ellen forgot the irritations of the morning, surrounded by a large and affectionate family. She sat between Addie and Irene and ate so much that, like ev-erybody else, she became drowsy after the meal.

When the children were shooed out of the kitchen, she and Lorraine wandered out and curled up on the old broken-down sofa occupying one corner of the porch. Hal, who had been fairly civil to her that day, followed them but sprawled in the cooler grass under the apple tree amusing himself with a solitary game of mumble peg. The rest of the children strewed themselves lazily about the yard, steeped in the euphoric atmosphere of a holiday when everybody, including the grownups were good natured. For a while there was a lull in the overcharged tension of the Twenty-Fourth, but the energies of children recover rapidly and suddenly overcome by boredom, Hal leaped up shouting, "Hide and Seek!"

The twins were ready and Louise and Betty, a friend of Louise's who had joined them, sat up with interest but Lorraine sniffed scornfully at the childish game. Ellen was not really anxious to join, but Louise and Betty tugged her off the sofa. Shortly she was running wildly through the yard hunting a place to hide from the wily Hal.

At the back of the Walker's large untidy yard was a row of old sheds built of adobe. They were low, dark and cool and full of odds and ends of tools, wood, old furniture; they had been wonderful to play in other years. Feeling the sun beat down on her head and arms, Ellen ducked quickly through the furthest of the splintery doors and flattened herself against the wall back of the door. A sticky cobweb fell across her face; she tried to brush it away, listening nervously for footsteps, peering into the darkness which was crossed by a single bar of hot yellowish light from the crack in the door.

She could hear the excited shouts of the other children as Hal discovered them and raced back to the apple tree counting them out, "One-two-three–for Louise." She held herself very still, smiling secretly until she heard the stumbling against the raised door sill and loud breathing. Her heart began to beat very fast at the thought of Hal finding her; she suddenly realized she had forgotten to find a way out so she could get back to the goal first. She tried to hold her breath as Hal fumbled along the wall, unable to see in the gloom. When he touched Ellen, she gasped with a frightened chill. He gave a low gleeful laugh and instead of running to the door to beat her back to the goal, he pressed her further into the corner and kicked the door shut with his foot. She opened her mouth to yell, but he whispered "Ssssh" so loudly that she was confused and only tried to struggle against him. But still holding her firmly, he breathed his hot breath into her face and whispered, "When you gonna fuck with me?"

That word again! Ellen, suffocating with shock and hatred, tried to beat him with her fists, but Hal, a older and considerably stronger, had the advantage. Her struggling seemed to excite him more. Grasping one of her hands firmly, he thrust it into the unbuttoned fly of his overalls where it touched his naked penis. Again, as with Simone, she felt that violent shock of discovery that swooped over h vhole body and left her trembling, full of scorching unbearable emotions. She renewed her struggle with Hal, choking out, "I hate you, I hate you, Hal Walker, you let me go." Abruptly he let go but pushed her brutally against the wall where she struck her head on something sharp and was all but stunned.

"Yah, you'd do it with that old trashy Robert Lee Hamilton. I don't see why ya won't fuck with me, yer own cousin," he whispered petulantly, buttoning the fly of his overalls. He jerked open the door and leaped out into the sunshine, leaving Ellen still pressed against the rough, cool wall where she stood motionless for what seemed a long time, waiting, absurdly to hear him shout, "One-two-three for Ellen." When she failed to hear the strident triumph, she stumbled out of the shed, feeling as though she were a different person and no one would recognize her. Her mind had not fully admitted the stupendous accusation that Hal has made, the very thing that she had been dreading, she knew now, the very thing that everyone had thought about her and Robert Lee. She was so crushed with the utter futility of ever making the truth known that she could not even face her little cousins who, of course, could not know or understand. She walked slowly, painfully aware of herself to the hydrant and leaned over to get a drink from under the faucet. She held her mouth against the cooling stream a long time, avoiding the gaze of the children who sat about under the apple tree bewildered that Hal, who was swinging aimlessly from a low limb did not count her out. Finally one of the twins jumped up and patted the tree goal, "One-two-three–Ellen's it!" he yelled.

"I'm not gonna play anymore," she said sullenly over her shoulder as she started toward the house. "It's a baby game."

Disappointed, all the little Walkers looked from her to Hal, sensing that something was wrong between them. Hal swung himself up into the tree. "Yah," he mumbled, "it's a baby game; you go on play it by yourselves." But nobody wants to play baby games, especially babies, so they all subsided into the grass to await the next inspiration. The front gate slammed on its hinges as Ellen made her way rapidly down the hot street toward her own house.

After the seven long blocks in the blazing sun, the house was a cool, quiet haven from the burning confusion of the day. Ellen went to her neat room where the green blinds had been pulled and through fine cracks and small holes the light shone like a map of stars. She took off her dress; there was a brown smudge on it where Hal had pushed her against the wall and she brushed at it irritably. But as soon as she had hung it on a hanger, turned back the bedspread as Irene had taught her and picked up the library book she was reading, she had thrust Hal and Simone out of her life.

In the world of books she was comfortable, safe, at the same time that she was free to experience all sorts of adventures and emotions. In the world of books you could find out what was happening. There were surprises, of course, but you were always somehow prepared for them, and then you could look back and see how things fitted so neatly together. In life you could never tell how anything was going to end; you could not tell who was good and who was bad. You were always stumbling over something that you hadn't known was there, like Hal and what he had said today. Yet when you looked at it, you realized it had always been there waiting to trip you.

How strange it was that one minute you felt safe and happy as though everything was all right and the next moment everything was all wrong. It was like the clouds that gathered and shifted some days so that one minute everything looked so radiant and beautiful–leaves sparkled on the trees, mountains were iridescent blues, greens and purples, the flowers had such sweet faces and then the cloud passed over the sun and everything faded into dull, depressing gray. It was the shifting of the light she could never endure; her nerves were too responsive to light and color and grayness dragged away all memories of beauty even though it lasted for only a moment. Although there was this same pattern in books, you could move hurriedly on to the good parts. So Ellen lay and read in the dim light, straining her eyes until they grew tired and she fell asleep.

The oppressive heat grew heavier as the afternoon went on, inducing a nightmare which Ellen had had before and would have again. It seemed that the house was enclosed by a screened porch extending all the way around it. She found herself on the porch listening to ominous scratching on the screen and knew that she would soon see the cause of that ticklish noise–a tall red figure looking like the picture of the Devil on the cement sacks in Uncle Aaron's shed. He grinned at her and she ran around the other side of the house, but he appeared as quickly there, leering at her with his fanged mouth. He glowed all over like a red-hot stove. Ellen could feel the heat enveloping her body. All that stood between them was the thin screen wire and, though she ran frantically from one side of the house to the other, her companion moved as easily and agilely as she, switching his tail with glowing forks on the end of it. His eyes were like bright, hard, green marbles and they stood out of his head under sharp horns. The oddest thing of all was that over each horn was a little gold halo just like the one painted over the infant Christ in the pictures in church. These little rings of light were suspended in the air and moved always in a position to be slipped down easily over the horns. Ellen became so fascinated with these little twin halos that she stopped running and stood staring intently, his hot breath searing her face. Finally she pointed to the halos and asked what they were; the Devil gave a weird chuckle and scratched the screen with his long pointed nail, cutting it through with a burst of smoke. At this moment Ellen woke up thrashing and crying strangled cries. She sat up on the bed, damp with perspiration, horribly depressed. Gradually the dream faded and the quiet of the room, darker now, settled peacefully about her. She rubbed her face, which felt as it had when the cobweb had stuck to it in the shed, and slid off the bed. She could hear the sound of water being splashed in the basin in the kitchen and knew that Irene must have come home.

Her mother, also weary with the heat, had taken off her dress and was combing her long hair with cool water. It hung below her waist in thick brown waves and, as she bent to comb it, sprayed out catching the light with extravagant beauty. Ellen stood watching her mother from the doorway; in the gold evening light, it was as though she were looking at a stranger. She was as pretty as the pictures in catalogues and magazines with her full smooth bust and hips, her long well-shaped legs and slender arms. Ellen touched her own body wonderingly. Would she ever be so pretty? She could feel the beauty of her mother entering her own limbs, swelling, filling, changing them from the horrid pudginess into something lovely. The physical identification permeating her in this transfixed moment also opened her heart to the deep, turgid emotions of womanhood.

How lonely her mother must be, she thought, remembering

what that awful Dub Peck had said that morning. She chilled both with anger and excitement. What if her mother should marry again? It had been a long time now since Ellen had thought about her mother and father together, thought about him as real and alive. Yes, he was there forever in her memory, a shining beloved, almost sainted figure now but with only one dimension like the beautiful picture of him that stood on the piano. At this moment she realized they had made a life without him, and it struck her as cruel, unfair, but still and all, her mother was real, alive and beautiful.

Irene caught sight of Ellen in the dim mirror and smiled, "Been asleep, Honey?" she asked unnecessarily for she had come home earlier, puzzled when the other kids said Ellen had gone home and found her sleeping. She ran her hands through her long hair and brushed it back from her temples, lifting it up off her shoulders and neck. "Oh this hair, it's so hot and heavy I can hardly stand it this kind of weather. I think I'll have it cut."

Ellen gasped, "Oh, don't do that, I couldn't stand it," she said vehemently, unable to picture her mother without the thick braids that she wore like a crown but more deeply afraid of any change in the tranquil life that had become too vividly desirable this day.

Irene looked at Ellen in surprise. Her face puffy with sleep and her hair tangled in the limpness of uncurling, she looked very childish and sad. Startled by the strong outburst of emotion, Irene had a painful surge of affection for her odd little daughter. Dropping her hair, she went to her, putting her arms about her.

The silken hair fell about Ellen's face and bare shoulders and she could smell the slight odor of perspiration and dust that it had picked up during the hot day mingled with the sweet warmth of her mother's flesh. She could not understand the curious emotion that filled her. It was as though she had never before realized that her mother was a living separate person. The shock of intimacy of her flesh, so warm and pulsing soft and having about it the faintest odor of unpleasantness, sweat and soil, mingled with the fragrance of talcum powder, made Ellen tremble so that she hugged her almost hysterically about the hips.

"Why did you come home alone today? Don't you feel good?" Irene asked, tenderly stroking the disarrayed curls. Ellen leaned gratefully against her mother's body, wanting to confide in her the encounter with Simone and the tormenting reason why she had left the Walkers. But she could find no words; anyway it seemed like a long time ago since it happened. It was as though she and Irene had moved into a different world, a quiet, neat world in which there were no men or boys or other disturbing persons. The two of them could live together and be happy forever. She rubbed her cheek against the satiny material of Irene's slip and for the first time in a long time, perhaps since before the death of her father, found comfort in that tender, generous body.

∞

As the summer of 1932 drew to a close a feverish excitement penetrated even the small communities of Utah. The depression had spread and crept deeper into the lives of everyone; the conviction grew that it had all been the fault of the "gover'ment." The gover'ment was Republican and the arch Republican was the mild Herbert Hoover whose conservative attitudes reflected the basic Mormon philosophy of a tenacious optimism, "All is Well." If one ignored bad things and maintained a belief in "good old ways," all would come right again. It was a matter of faith and patience, but belief in the good old ways was slowly but surely eroding.

The Mormons had always been actively concerned in government since church and state often overlapped in Utah. Merritsville, like many other Utah towns, had been predominantly Republican for many years although the church had tried to maintain a decent opposition for political reasons. There were a few maverick Democrats, but it amounted to heresy almost for a sheep or stock man not to vote Republican. However, the edgy sense of deepening disaster that every man carried in his stomach urged the old belief that change was always bound to be good when things got this bad, even a change of name or popular image. The stagnation and bewilderment in Washington led many of the party faithful to defect, and the men gathered in small groups on the street corners of Merritsville began to predict that the Democrats would win the fall election.

Aaron Walker was one of the most vociferous of these although he had decided not to join the bonus march on Washington because he had planted a new raspberry patch that summer and had to stay home to see that it was watered. Hal was not to be depended on and he was surrounded by women all looking to him for support. At times he felt overburdened and discouraged but Roosevelt gave him hope. He was sure that the man with the broad cheerful smile and rich voice conducting his political campaign from an invisible wheelchair was to be the savior of the country.

In that year of worsening depression the mountains still took on misty blue-green tones in early September preceding the extravagant burst of yellow-oranges and reds. Autumn in Merritsville was as exuberant as it had always been. In the orchards apples, pears, peaches, plums hung abundantly among curling yellow leaves and the silos droned all afternoon in the thin blue air. School had opened and summer-satiated children slouched in their desks, shuffling their feet in irritation at the confinement. The oily-chalky smell presaged a long winter ahead.

Although children heard about the coming elections, listening to heated arguments they heard at home which they scarcely understood, there were far more important things in their lives that fall. In the sixth-grade room where Ellen, feeling dull and sleepy, leaned on her elbows and stared at the geography book in front of her without seeing the words at all, it was the annual Weenie Roast. Everybody was supposed to have a date for this last outdoor event marking the end of summer which took place the second week-end after school began. Notes about who was dating whom passed furtively up and down and under and around the desks and were only occasionally intercepted by Miss Frandsen who was trying to interest her thirty students in the rivers of China. None of the notes were for or concerned Ellen who did not have a date, was not likely to get one and pretended not to care.

Ellen had always liked school. Learning was not only exciting to her, it was essential; she felt happiest where there were plenty of books. Always prepared and expressing the kind of pleasure in learning that delights teachers, she was generally a "teacher's pet," but this year had started out badly. Some of the bitter residue of the summer lingered, especially when Robert Lee and Simone appeared in school. They had been brought in by the authorities and, although it was not certain which grades they had completed in their moving about, it had been decided that Simone should be in the fifth and Robert Lee in the sixth grade. Robert Lee could read and write along with the lower portion of the class, but he had a great deal of trouble with arithmetic, so Ellen, who always finished her problems early, had been delegated to sit in his seat with him and help him. Miss Frandsen, a little nervous woman with frizzy blond hair, ignored or did not understand the imploring, reluctant look that Ellen gave her as she hesitated about moving into the seat with the shabby, poorly washed boy.

Robert Lee gave her that shy, sad little smile that she had first seen on his face early that spring and moved over eagerly but Ellen returned it with a stare of cold hatred and tried not to look at him as she sat down as far from him as she could manage. He was a trial to help. Sometimes he picked his nose and rubbed it on his shirt sleeve, and he squirmed around nervously. Instead of looking at the paper where she was working out the problems, he watched her face with intense admiration. She almost felt sick at the smell of stale tobacco and grease that clung to him and took elaborate pains not to touch him at all. She wished she could slap him hard. When she finished the problems, he took the paper and carefully folded it into a very small square, tucked it in the bib pocket of his overalls.

This had happened at the beginning of the week and Ellen had had to do it several more times before she learned to dawdle along with her own work so that she could avoid the enforced tutoring session. She often felt Robert Lee's eyes on her; he sat one seat back on the next row; once she turned and gave him an ugly look.

Once a week Miss Frandsen "rewarded" her student with an art period usually on Fridays. The sixth grade was old enough to use water colors and they were permitted to splash around happily painting things like a bouquet of autumn leaves on the teacher's desk or when they finished that, they could do something else of their own choice. On these occasions Robert Lee had produced some astonishing drawings, full of delicate but hectic lines which gave Ellen a queer feeling when she looked at them but surprised her into the admiration she had felt for his creek architecture. Miss Frandsen praised his drawings and hung them with the best on the board. At recess he stood staring at the tacked-up pictures with a sublime expression as though he could hardly believe his good fortune.

Since this was Friday and it had been a trying week, Ellen was glad when the bell rang for recess. She tucked the geography book and the rivers of China in her desk, but she was slow getting out to the playground, partly because she didn't want to join the other girls who were all talking and whispering about the weenie roast tomorrow. She hesitated on the lower step of the school porch, trying to decide whether to swing or just sit in the sunshine. Joe Hammond and Bart Van Kamp came out and stopped on the step above her. Joe Hammond was the spoiled, dark-eyed son of a widow with a mean glint in his eye; he was followed around by Bart Van Kamp, his cousin, a shy, awkward boy with curling blond hair who took orders from Joe and tried unsuccessfully to imitate him. Joe was going steady with Leila Beckstead, one of the most popular girls in school even though she was skinny and had buck teeth.

Joe gave Bart a push and he bumped rudely into Ellen.

"Gwan," Joe whispered loud enough for Ellen to hear, "Gwan, ask her, she ain't got a date, I bet, there's only Marissa Clements and her left."

"Aw, I don wanta ask her, she's too ugly," said Bart, "besides she's old Robert Lee Hamilton's girl."

When Ellen realized that they were talking about her, something inside her contracted with such a painful shock that she had to lean against the rough stone wall. Tears filled and burned her eyes, running down her cheeks; it was as though someone had hit her hard in the chest. She turned her head and dug her chin into her shoulder so that no one could see the tears, but Joe and Bart were already at the other end of the school-yard, Ellen forgotten, unconcerned that they had been cruel. Ellen had grown far too sensitive to the power of words, half-child, half-adult that she was, she took far too seriously the callous brutality of the young. Most of the other girls would have run screaming and calling names after the boys or shrugged it off with an insult of equal harshness. As Irene's daughter she had learned a certain reticence, but the chance words of Bart and Joe had confirmed for Ellen what she had long suspected that she was hopelessly unattractive and that there was something wrong with her because she wasn't popular and didn't have a date. This was made worse by the association with the despised Robert Lee. Bursting with misery, Ellen ran into the school building and locked herself in one of the lavatory cubicles where she stood sobbing even after the bell rang.

When Miss Frandsen missed her, she sent one of the girls to look for her. Peggy McDaniel found her, but Ellen would not come out nor answer Peggy's question as to what was wrong so Miss Frandsen came herself and coaxed her out. Reluctantly Ellen opened the door, her face swollen and red.

"What's the matter," asked Miss Frandsen gently. Ellen burst into tears again.

"I, I don't feel good," she stammered.

Miss Frandsen wiped her eyes with her own handkerchief and led her out of the lavatory.

"Well, come lie down in the office and I'll have somebody take you home, Ellen," she soothed and led her into the small principal's office. She put her on the leather couch and patted her forehead. "You don't seem to have a fever. Now you lie still and rest and maybe you'll feel better in a minute. I'll come back as soon as I can."

It seemed a long time to Ellen that she lay staring at the ceiling, feeling as though she could not ever face anyone again, but after a while her eyes wandered to the high deep window where there was a plant she had never noticed before. It had lovely pinkish blossoms that looked like little dancers with turned up skirts over full pantalets. She began to imagine that they were taking part in a fairy ball. She pictured herself as one of them and presently drifted off into an ethereal world where she had been transformed into a glorious beauty. She was swathed in soft, filmy pink material that floated out behind as she walked; on her feet were dainty white slippers. All the kids of Merritsville were in rags, dirty and hungry, and Joe Hammond and Bart Van Kamp were the dirtiest and hungriest. She had come to bring them all presents, but she would make Joe and Bart wait the longest, maybe not give them any at all. It was a soothing vision and she began to feel better. She got up and knelt on the sofa, examining the blossoms of the fuchsia plant. They were just like little dancers! Delighted, she wanted to write a poem about them. She looked around to find something to write on and with. A pencil lay on the desk and there was some waste paper in the basket which she smoothed out and wrote:

On the plant
Are little dancing ladies
with pink bloomers
and turned up skirts
and tiny shoes
that hang loose
so their toes
never touch anything but air.
I wonder if they are happy there.

It was not exactly right, but it had helped to catch and keep a little of the beauty of the fragile pink blossoms miraculously hanging there in that dingy office to heal the wound to her pride.

She was reading it over when Miss Frandsen came back and showed it to her shyly. "My, that's nice," Miss Frandsen assured her, not really thinking about it for her mind was busy with a dozen other problems including the puzzle of Ellen's behavior. She knew very well that Ellen was not sick, had only been badly upset about something, which now, as was usual with the young, seemed to be all over.

"Maybe you could use a nicer word here than 'bloomers,'" she suggested, not unkindly. "Do you feel like coming back to class? Maybe you could copy your poem nicely instead of painting since the time is almost over."

Ellen went back into the room, not looking at anyone and bent over her desk laboriously recopying the poem.

"Time to put the paints away," announced Miss Frandsen, going up and down the rows, praising the efforts of the young artists as best she could. When she came to Robert Lee's desk, she held up his picture and praised it in front of the whole class. "Now look how pretty Robert Lee has painted the autumn leaves. They look real, don't they?" Robert Lee squirmed with self-conscious joy. Ellen ducked her head and hated him even more.

When the bell rang, everyone scrambled out of the room, but she remained, diligently rounding out her letters and making curlicues on them as though she had no other concern in the world. When she thought she could quite safely leave without meeting any of the sixth grade on the way home, she got up, put a copy of the poem on Miss Frandsen's desk and went slowly down the stairs.

As she came out of the heavy battered doors, the late afternoon sun blinded her still tear-swollen eyes and for a moment she did not see the figure pressed into the shadows of the porch against the dark red brick, so it was not until she was almost opposite the park that she realized Robert Lee Hamilton was following her. She walked more swiftly, a solid knot of anger in her throat, but before she could turn the corner, he had caught up with her.

"Ellen," he wheezed, out of breath, "I want to tell ya, I want to–I got somethin' fer ya." He thrust a folded sheet of paper into her hand. It was the picture he had worked on all during the art period, the one the teacher had praised, making it even more special.

Ellen stopped on the path, her face distorted with wrath. Without even looking at the painting, she ripped it into small pieces before his eyes. "I hate you!" she hissed, "and I don't even want you to come near me again." Her own eyes were so full of tears of humiliation and rage she could not see the stricken look on Robert Lee's face as she flung the pieces of his picture into the muddy water of the irrigation ditch. Stamping her foot, she cried, "You and your sister stay away from me, do you hear?" Before he could answer or move, she turned and ran wildly down the street.

Robert Lee thrust his hands into his pockets and blinked in bewilderment as he watched the little pieces of his painting whirl around and glide away on the dark ripples of the shallow water. He could never understand what it was that he did to Ellen; he never meant any harm at all. Today when he sensed she had had some trouble, he was anxious to sooth her. The only way he knew was to do the picture for her. He had thought it was one of his best even before the teacher said so.

He shuffled on down the path, overtaking some of the scraps of paper but felt no particular emotion about them. They were something that no longer existed so he had to let them go. He guessed that Ellen just didn't like him and that was that. His life had been mostly like that anyway, torn up, scattered, nothing, ever lasted very long. He hadn't been able to make many friends since they moved around so much; nobody seemed to like him very much except his mother, so he had learned to live by himself. He guessed he would go down by the creek and swing on the rope he had strung up between the yellow cottonwood trees. It gave him a wonderful, free, flying feeling; he didn't have to think about anything at all.

C8

The Saturday morning of the weeny roast dawned cold and gray; Ellen felt almost happy. It looked as though it might rain on that hateful affair which had caused her so much distress but she resolved not to think about it. She planned to spend most of the day helping her grandmother who was in the process of fall house cleaning. This meant transferring all the rug rags, quilt blocks, doilies and hoops, boxes of thread and yarns into other rooms temporarily, attacking the room furiously with broom, scrubbing brush, dust cloths and polish then hauling all the clutter back so that in the end the room looked about the same. But Addie *knew* it was *clean* and this, like church going, was one of the solid pillars of her philosophy.

Ellen got a lot of satisfaction out of sorting through all the wondrous things her grandmother collected. They were working in the back bedroom today, and Ellen came across the big collection of scrapbooks and clippings that Addie kept for her genealogy work. There were fascinating pictures of all sorts of family including herself, her father and mother. The odds and ends of souvenirs like the program of a musical event her father and mother had given with the accompaniment of Everett Gordon gave her a curiously poignant feeling. She had not looked at the these scrapbooks very much during the past two years.

Her grandmother was busy elsewhere at the moment. One of the nice things about working with her, she didn't stand by you and keep telling you how to do the job like Irene did, and she never seemed to have to get things done in such a hurry. So Ellen, who was supposed to be sorting and stacking the bulky books, sat down and opened one. The yellow paper crackled and a dusty smell arose from the pages; there were the serene and smiling faces of young people who had grown old, old people who had died, babies with no resemblance to the ungainly children they had become. Ellen found herself numerous times and smiled with indulgence. As she turned over a page toward the end of the book, a yellowing newspaper clipping fell out. She picked it up. The name at the head of it in dark type caught her eye and she read:

LAURENCE JOHN KENT

Laurence John Kent was born February 9, 1899, at Merritsville, Utah. He died of a gunshot wound on or about January 28th near Emmett. He was the son of Adelaide Winward and John Laurence Kent. He was a member of the L.D.S church, holding the rank of Elder in the First Ward of Merritsville. He was active in musical circles both in and out of the church. He served in the United States Army from Sept. 1917 to Jan. of 1919 stationed at Camp Hood in Oregon. On November 15, 1919, he married Irene Ferris in the Salt Lake City Temple.

He is survived by his wife and one daughter, Ellen, his mother and two sisters, Mrs. Albert (Bertha) Monson of Salt Lake City and Mrs. Aaron (Doris) Walker of Merritsville.

Services will be held Feb. 3 at the Merritsville L.D.S. First Ward, Bishop Charles Comber officiating. There will be no viewing of the body. Friends may call at the Frandsen Mortuary until the time of the service.

Pinned to this was another small clipping with a cryptic caption:

SHEEPHERDER FOUND DEAD NEAR EMMETT

Laurence Kent was found dead of a rifle wound in his sheep camp January 30th by his brother-in-law, Aaron Walker. It is believe that he had been dead several days of what appears to have been an accidental discharge of a 30-30 rifle.

Ellen read the fine black words on the dingy paper with goose bumps breaking out all over her; it was chilly in the room but this was a different kind of cold. How funny, she thought, this is my father's whole life here on this tiny piece of paper. When a person dies, this is all that you can tell about him in the newspaper. It wouldn't have been very much longer if he had lived to be an old man. She realized with a clenching of her stomach that she had never really known her father. Now that she was beginning to grow up and find out how confusing life was, she understood, although vaguely, that the memories she kept of her father were part of herself, part of her childish self. She would never really know him and, had he lived, both of them would be different at this hour.

The grayness of the day, the chill of the cluttered room, the immense sadness of it bore down on her until she thought she must be crushed. How cruel life seemed compressed, disfigured, almost obliterated on a thin piece of poor paper that would soon crumble to dust. She wondered if she might do something about it someday, if she could write something that would make him seem warm and alive again, but she was overcome by an awful sense of futility. For a terrifying moment she could not even remember how his face looked or his voice sounded. That was the worst loss. Pictures could help her remember his appearance but not his voice. What she remembered most was a feeling of enveloping warmth, of safety and rightness of the world when he was around. He was associated with the sound of music, the sound of his violin. Perhaps that would never die. Carefully she put the clipping deep in the crease of the pages and laid the book back in the drawer as Addie called from the kitchen for her to come get a bite to eat since it was past lunch time.

They were sitting at the kitchen table finishing their lunch of bread and butter and jam and milk tea when they heard a rush of footsteps on the back porch. Without even knocking Simone Hamilton burst into the room, her face wild and flushed.

"Miz Kent, Ma says would you please come quick?" she gasped.

Addie jumped up, "What's the matter, child?"

"It's Robert Lee...he fell out'n the tree in the creek. I think he's daid, come quick," Simone panted twisting her hands in her skirt. She did not look at Ellen but kept her eyes fastened imploringly on Addie who was already putting on her rubbers. "You best get your coat on, Ellen, and come along, maybe you can run for help," Addie said and then turning to Simone, "Ain't somebody sent for the doctor?"

Simone shook her head, "No'm, we don't know no doctor."

"What on earth did he do?" queried Addie in agitation as they set out rapidly across the damp fields, Ellen trailing a little behind, not wishing to get too close to Simone.

"He's been swingin' on this old rope all the time way up high in them trees," Simone stammered. "This time it busted and looks like he's done for."

I wonder if she's going to cry, Ellen thought, feeling the tight constriction in her throat as she remembered Robert Lee standing by the ditch yesterday while his torn-up painting floated away; she could feel no remorse, only the cold fright of disaster and death. But Simone did not cry then or after.

Mrs. Hamilton met them at the gate, wringing her hands in her soiled apron, her face crumpled and horrid with terror. They went into the kitchen where Robert Lee lay straight out on the smelly, ragged cot in the kitchen, his head turned slightly to one side, his face the color of lard. There was a smudge of bluish-brown on his temple running into the stringy hair and a small trickle of blood ran out of each nostril. There was no sign of motion; one dirty brown hand hung limply over the edge of the cot. Ellen could not bear to look at him.

Art Hamilton was standing at the head of the cot, his dark face drawn into a scowl which might have been sorrow, anger or bewilderment or all three; Frank sat in the corner, his long hands hanging between his knees.

Addie went resolutely to the bed and picked up the hand. It was warm and she could feel a faint pulse. As she leaned over the boy, she saw the slightest tremor of the blue lips.

"You sent for the doctor yet?" she asked brusquely, looking up at Art Hamilton who only moved slightly and grunted. It was Mrs. Hamilton who whined, "We don't know no doctor and we cain't afford one, Miz Kent."

"That's no matter, it can be straightened out later; you go for Dr. Carlton," she commanded.

"Don't know where he live," grumbled Art. "We ain't got no money fer doctors."

"Never mind that, Ellen'll show you where he lives. This boy's hurt bad and you better get the doctor here quick!" There was something in Addie's manner that moved the man. Ellen felt herself get weak at the thought of riding into town with these awful men. Simone jumped up and came along and she was almost grateful for her. They bounced into town in the old car and brought back the doctor who examined Robert Lee carefully and shook his head. All he could tell was that the boy had had a severe injury to his head, probably had broken his back or neck and would most likely never regain consciousness. There was no use trying to get him to a hospital twenty miles away, but he sat down patiently to watch as the small, sad measure of life seeped slowly from the thin frame. Robert Lee died shortly after sundown.

Addie Kent stayed a little while longer with Mrs. Hamilton who sobbed the same deep, gulping sobs as she had done on the first night she had come terrified across the fields. She could not seem to stop shaking. After the doctor gave her some pills and told her to go to bed, he left, saying he would send the undertaker down right away. Art stoked up the fire and made some coffee while they waited in thick silence.

Ellen and Simone had gone out into the yard long before. They sat silently side by side on the rough gray bench under a poplar tree, the leaves of which rustled crisply in the cool evening breeze. Ellen was cold and miserable but she didn't want to go back into the kitchen, and she didn't want to sit close to Simone, who hunched up on the end of the bench, made no sound.

At last she ventured, "When did you find him?"

"This mornin', he hadn't come in last night but that was no different. He stayed down the creek lotsa times by hisself. When he didn't come for breakfast, Ma sent me down... he was there by that big tree." She was biting her nails fiercely.

There was nothing more to say. They sat in silence until Frank came out, told them that Robert Lee was dead and lit his pipe. Simone got up and walked over to where he stood smoking. He laid his hand on her shoulder. The old chow dog barked sharply, and the smoke from the chimney curled up into the gray sky that was fast growing black. Across the fields Ellen could see the bonfire that was being lighted for the sixth grade weeny roast.

The death of Robert Lee created a special problem. In Merritsville death, like life, was a church affair and the Hamiltons had tenaciously resisted any connection with the Mormon Church. There were no other denominations represented there. The

Hamiltons were without friends, relatives or funds. When Dr. Carlton summoned the undertaker Clyde Barton, there was some confusion. It was not that Clyde was a difficult or heartless man, but he couldn't quite see himself shouldering the whole burden of disposing of this seventy-odd pounds of alien human flesh in a professional manner. Dr. Carlton rubbed his big stomach reflectively, then reached for the phone and called Bishop Ed Washburn of the Second Ward, who was also manager-owner of Washburn's Department Store. The Bishop in turn summoned his counselors, Jacob West and Andrew Cardon, and with several other prominent members of the ward, they held a meeting. It was decided that the counselors would call on the Hamiltons immediately though the hour was late and find out what could be done.

The two men went warily up to the darkened house at the back of which was a faint glow from the kitchen window. Old Rusty leaped out from behind the lilac bush as they pushed open the gate, growling viciously. Brother West hesitated then spoke gruffly to the dog about the same time that a tall figure came around the house.

"Lay down thar, Rusty," said Frank, "lay down. Now what you all want?" He advanced toward the men who held our their right hands. Frank shook hands with them gravely. "We just heard about your trouble, Brother Hamilton," said Andrew quietly. " We come to see if we could be of any help."

"Why, that's right decent of you," Frank said. "Come on right this way."

It was hard to see in the small kitchen lighted only by a kerosene lamp, the wick of which was turned down very low, and the air was full of tobacco smoke. Simone and her mother were huddled against the kitchen table. Arthur rose stiffly from his chair by the stove, shaking hands morosely with the two men. The little body on the cot had been covered by a dingy piece of muslin. Frank found chairs for the two men and Jacob cleared his throat.

With a great deal of hemming and hawing on the part of the elders and gruff monosyllables and grunts from Arthur and Frank it was discovered that the Hamiltons were completely at a loss. They had no means whatever to bury the child. They had relatives in the South as poor as themselves and burial lots in some obscure southern town but no way of getting the child back there. From time to time Mrs. Hamilton, who said little, made a strange noise like a hiccup and Simone clung to her.

"Well," said Andrew at last, sighing and rubbing his hands together, "we'll do all we can to help you folks." He rose to go, then hesitated. "It's the custom in families hereabout to pray together in times of trouble," he said, "and if you are willing, we'll kneel with you and ask the Lord to comfort you at this time."

Before the men could agree or object, Mrs. Hamilton jumped up from the table and ran to him. "Oh, we'd be much obliged, oh, I'd be so glad," she cried clasping her hands together fervently. With an acquiescing grunt Arthur and Frank bent their long legs beside their chairs and the two elders knelt down on the hard, dirty floor. Jacob West offered a short solemn prayer for the newly departed soul of Robert Lee and his bewildered family. For a moment the room seemed a little warmer and brighter; the hearts of the believer and unbeliever, the native and foreigner were blended in their common humanity, the enveloping humility that attends the presence of death, especially that of a child.

The town of Merritsville pitched in and helped bury Robert Lee on a cool bright day the last of September in a plain box paid for by donations and church funds, dressed in neat white clothes which the Relief Society had gathered under Addie's supervision. There were a few late flowers gathered largely from gardens and even one hot-house spray of red carnations bought with the nickels and dimes of the sixth grade. The Bishop, who had ascertained that the family had had some connection with the Southern Baptist Church, conducted a short, simple grave side service from the Bible with only muted references to Mormonism.

Only a few of the townspeople turned out for the service, but the whole sixth grade had been allowed to come and lay the carnation spray on the casket. Addie stood close by Mrs. Hamilton for whom she had provided a neat black dress and hat and the two men with dark, ill-fitting suit coats over trousers that did not match stood awkwardly behind her. Simone in her red taffeta summer dress made a strange splash of color as she squirmed nervously at her father's side; her eyes were bright with excitement at her family being the focus of attention.

Some of the Relief Society women sang a sweet sad song and

there was a short prayer; then Addie began to urge Mrs. Hamilton away from the open grave. She had begun to sob again, that tearless dry sob, but managed to say, clinging weakly to Addie's arm, "I want to thank you folks, Miz Kent, I want to say you folks're right Christian people...."

Addie patted her and guided her soothingly through the weeds and among the humps of earth, trying to get her far enough away that she need not hear the first shovels full of earth that thudded on the coffin.

Simone stayed with her father and Frank while they conferred about a simple marker giving the dates of Robert Lee's birth and death. It could only be a card in a small metal holder reading Robert Lee Hamilton, b. June 14, 1919, d. September 27, 1932. It would soon disappear among the weeds.

Ellen waited until Addie had parted from the Hamiltons and then they walked home together. It was one of those radiant Autumn days in the mountains when the sky is so blue that it hurts the eyes, and the yellow leaves of elms, sycamores and birches along the streets catch the slanting rays of sun in such a way that they look like huge bouquets of concentrated light–magnificent lamps lighted from within rather than without. Great heaps of leaves had already fallen. Ellen shuffled through them loving the sharp prickling against her legs and the dry crackling sound.

Like most of the people who live in the desert-mountain country, Ellen loved the autumn best of all. After the hot, enervating summer, the fall comes as a true rebirth. The crisp sparkling air not only restores the zest for living but fans it into greater intensity than does the milder atmosphere of spring. Today the exhilarating beauty of the year was heightened by the recent somber presence of death. Ellen could not feel grief for Robert Lee, but she could feel the sharp sadness of not being alive.

She struggled in her mind with the strangeness of his having been alive so short a time ago. The vision of him standing on the path helpless as she tore up his paper hovered on the edge of her conscience where it threatened to exact some pity from her, but she could not remember him very clearly. She could not remember how his face had looked that day, so blinded had she been by her own anger. The thing she recalled most vividly was that the toe of his shoe was broken and she could see his bare, dirty toe.

She didn't want to admit that last bitter cruelty to Robert Lee.

She turned her mind back to the perplexing problem of being and not being–herself here, alive, healthy, kicking the leaves and breathing deeply of the air slightly tainted with the smoke of bonfires and Robert Lee there in a box in a narrow hole in the dirt. For this she pitied him immensely at the same time that she was afraid for herself. Could she, too, in a few days, weeks, not be here but there? No, it could not be. She could not die.

"I wonder why people have to die," she said addressing the question as much to the universe as to her grandmother.

"Well, we each have our work to do and when it's done we must go to the other side," Addie explained. "We don't really die; someday we will all be resurrected perfect and the earth will receive its paradisical glory. That is if we all live right and obey the Lord."

"What's para-dis-ical glory?" asked Ellen, liking the elegant sound of the phrase.

"Why it's when everything will be perfect and our bodies will be restored to us perfect and we'll all live together in peace and love."

"But how will our bodies be perfect," Ellen persisted, "if we're old or crippled or little like the baby. Will Daddy have his head all fixed perfect where it was shot?"

Addie frowned at her sharply. "Of course, the Lord will take care of all those things; they're not for us to worry about. Sometimes you do ask too many questions, Ellen."

Ellen knew when her elders had closed the conversation so she was silent all the rest of the way. Perhaps Robert Lee would wake up perfect and be a great artist in that far, glorious time.

CB

Saturday, March 4th, 1933, Ellen's twelfth birthday, Franklin Delano Roosevelt was inaugurated President of the United States. Irene, Ellen, Addie, Dosey and Aaron Walker were gathered in front of the RCA Superheterodyne radio in Irene's cozy kitchen. Along with a birthday cake she had baked some cinnamon rolls. Their fragrance added to a sense of well-being as a splendid reassuring voice emanated from the round cloth-covered speaker:

President Hoover, Mr. Chief Justice, my friends. This is a day of consecration, and I am certain that my fellow Americans expect that on my induction into the Presidency I will address them with a candor and decision which the present situation of the nation impels. This is preeminently the time to speak the truth, frankly and boldly. Nor need we shrink from honestly facing conditions in our country today. This great nation will endure as it has endured and will revive and prosper. So, first of all, let me assert my firm belief that the only thing we have to fear is fear itself–nameless, unreasoning, unjustified terror which paralyzes needed effort to convert retreat into advance ...

Aaron, bursting with emotion, kept smacking his lips and wiping his eyes on his blue handkerchief as he listened to the solemn crackling of the air waves bringing this heartening message from clear across the country! He took the triumph of the Democrats personally. He had joined the party defiantly and worked and talked for them all summer, sure like many others that he had exercised his rights as a free citizen. He figgered that if a man fulfilled his political responsibilities conscientiously things were sure to be put straight.

The women in the room, listening without quite the same conviction, were none the less cheered by the rich, warm, encouraging voice. Addie and Dosey were mending some stockings, Irene was crocheting; even though things were taking a turn for the better, it was best not to waste time.

Ellen, who was expecting a quiz on the election in school next week, was kneeling in front of the radio, scribbling on her notebook and munching on one of the cinnamon rolls. While the words were filtering loosely into her mind, she was thinking of the birthday party that she was to have later in the day. She, too, was deeply moved by that voice sounding as though the new President really did care about each one of them personally. In years after she was always to thrill to the memory of the sound of that voice materializing like a shaft of sunlight in the heavy gloom that had settled over their lives the past few years.

When the ceremony had finished and the impressive sounds died away, the little company dispersed and, in spite of the soggy, uncertain spring weather, went about the tasks of the day with renewed hope. Ellen felt important that her birthday had fallen on such a day, and the little party that Irene gave for some of her girl friends came off without a mishap even though some of the girls were disappointed that boys hadn't been invited.

As the spring wore into summer, Aaron was more heartened than ever along with the rest of the country, as the new President and the 73rd congress set into motion a series of actions to counteract the heavy despair that had settled over the nation. In Utah the banks had been closed on the day before the inauguration and continued closed for the next week. President Ballard of the Merritsville bank, a tall, handsome man with a shock of white, waving hair who Ellen thought looked like the angel Moroni, kept assuring everyone that the Bank of Merritsville would reopen and no one would suffer. Since he was also the Stake President this was comforting; there is no more formidable figure in the Mormon society than a religiously prominent man who is also a successful business man. The bank did reopen; Brigham Ballard was also a compassionate, honest man and cared about the community, but there was little he could do in the long run to offset the enormous losses of the past years.

Aaron opened his paper hopefully each evening for the first hundred days of the new administration, listened to the fireside chats and exchanged optimistic predictions with the men on the corner. The confident headlines, the genial, reassuring voice sounding far and wide in the land; the outpouring of vigorous and positive legislation; the scourge of the "money-lenders" under that guy with the funny name, "Picolo" or something–all combined to make the summer of 1933 one of renewed energy and hope.

Aaron figgered that in another year or two they would be back on top; he wasn't sure just what he would or could do. He didn't expect to go back into the sheep business. He knew now that the land had been disastrously over-grazed; the livestock business had expanded far beyond the capacity of the western mountains and deserts to sustain. At first he had thought that he might get a job with the Deseret Livestock which was still in business; he had been a foreman there before he and Laurence had struck out on their own. But he was past forty; they would want younger men now. He would have to depend on the small amount of land that he owned on the outskirts of the city and the home and lot. He feared the loss of even that; there was still a residual mortgage on his property for the sheep losses. Laurence was lucky to be out of it.

He had gone ahead and planted berries and fruit trees on the land, hoping that he could make a go of it. Secretly he had always wanted to work on the railroad, and there was a new act in congress to help railroads but that was a remote possibility. His age was against him. Meanwhile he had seven hungry mouths to feed and Ellen, Irene and Addie to look out for.

By early fall Aaron had to admit that not much of all that exciting recovery was filtering into Merritsville. The papers reported that the highest number of people in the history of the country—nearly eight million—were receiving emergency relief under the FERA.

The thought of having to take outright charity, to stand in long ragged lines like those in pictures which appeared more frequently in the *Deseret News*, made his stomach gnaw with fear. Public charity had always been looked upon in Utah as a disgrace; it reduced a man to nothing in his own and others' estimation. Where there was little land to scratch on and a place to keep a few animals a man like Aaron was going to try to hang on to his self-respect. But you couldn't watch your wife and kids starve, could you? By late fall Aaron had to admit that, in spite of all the exciting legislation, all the soothing reassurances, not very much was different than it had been the past three years. Thank God he had a few spuds in the cellar, a healthy milk cow and his old Dodge half-ton truck. He picked up a few odd jobs hauling things and had a lucky break of landing the job of shoveling sixty tons of coal from the railroad cars in Lehi and distributing it to the school buildings. The $75.00 he got was a bonanza that helped them through the winter.

Irene listened to the radio more and more, not only because she felt vaguely that she ought to try to understand more things for herself now that she didn't have Laurence to explain them to her, but because she had come to rely on it for the presence of a male voice in her house. She did miss that—the quality of a man's voice, deep, firm, was comforting in some inexplicable way. She spent so much time in women's gathering where the high pitched chatter and nervous giggling of women often made her feel depressed.

It was almost impossible to make any sense of the fury of activity going on in Washington. There was veritable explosion of programs with long, complicated names reduced to initials so that it seemed a giant pot of alphabet soup had been poured over the land–NRA, PWA, AAA, FERA, HOLC, NIRA, FIDIC, CWA. The welter of new names–Johnson, Tugwell, Perkins, Ickes, Morganthaw, Wallace, Berle, so many that it made Irene's head ache to try to think of them all. Ellen had to memorize them for school; she seemed to grasp things so quickly, Irene came to depend on her for help.

There was a great deal of fussing about the NRA. A comical man named Hugh Johnson was whipping up a great storm with posters, signs, stickers, parades, songs, slogans–all appealing to the women who were the shoppers to never buy anything from a store that didn't display the "Blue Eagle."

"When every American housewife understands that the Blue Eagle on everything that comes into her home is a symbol of its restoration to security, may God have mercy on the man or group who attempt to trifle with this bird," Johnson boomed passionately over the radio.

Irene thought it sounded very fine and made her feel important as the controller of the purse but, in her case, it made little difference. She didn't have much money to spend. The few stores in which she did spend her meager widow's pension had all signed up by late summer, conspicuously displaying their big Blue Eagles. She just had to remember that they closed earlier and were closed on Wednesday and Saturday afternoons.

She couldn't afford to take the Salt Lake papers and with no man to talk to except Aaron who wasn't used to sharing important information with women anyway, Irene didn't hear too much of what was going on in the spheres of male activity. So it wasn't until he came to tell her about it that she realized a government relief agency had come to Merritsville. It had been set up discreetly in a back room of the City Hall next to the fire station.

The Mormons had always been staunchly against federal and state relief, feeling there was a stigma to accepting hand-outs without doing honest work or at least some work. Hadn't Brigham Young kept a pile of boulders in the tithing office yard which he would have a welfare applicant move to the other side just to make him feel he was earning his bread? The next one would move them back again. It was the principle of the thing: every good Mormon knew that welfare soon led to interference by the government, loss of freedom, especially religious, and self-respect, eventually the collapse of the whole moral structure. Mormons were used to helping each other and the Church tried to provide, but the problem had become overwhelming. The people of Merritsville were slow to apply for the government relief, but there were many who were getting hungrier and more discouraged each day.

Aaron had vowed that he never would. By sharing what they could raise on his land and Addie's place with persisting hard work, they had been able to scrape by. It looked like they might manage but gradually even Aaron had to admit that the slump could be harder to pull out of than expected. He had never considered Irene and Ellen a burden, but he had an uneasy feeling about being responsible for so many now. He thought he had better try to put Irene on to anything that she could get just in case.

One evening Aaron stopped by to see if she needed anything. He sat in his usual chair by the stove and cleared his throat. He had given up smoking and chewing as a small sacrifice to the hard times, for which everyone was grateful, and chewed a straw or toothpick instead. After shifting it a bit and stumbling for words, he advised her that, as a widow, she was certainly entitled to some of that government surplus they were giving away. It was not that he thought they weren't going to make it, but there was no sense in not getting what was coming to you. Every little bit would help out until things got back to normal. He was thinking that the small check she got every month was more than he could count on coming in regularly and, although he didn't begrudge it, he figgered she might as well do a little to take the pressure off.

The idea shocked Irene. She had caught a glimpse of the relief line once or twice recently when she was going down town and had felt scared. She couldn't think of herself as reduced to that;

she was making her pittance stretch, even paying some tithing out of it, but she caught the note of worry under Aaron's casual, forced cheerfulness.

"Now you go on down there, Irene, on Tuesday next and sign up. It ain't all that much but it might help tide you over the winter if things get tighter. You won't have no trouble qualifyin' because widows and old folks is automatically entitled," he admonished as he got up to go.

Irene hung her head, picking nervously at the collar of her dress. She didn't reply immediately.

"Now, you will, won't you?" He patted her shoulder anxiously.

"I thought I'd never come to that," she said in a choking voice. "I thought things were going to get better after...."

Aaron was sorry he had brought it up and he was nervous that she was going to cry. Crying women upset him no end but you had to stand firm with them. His voice was a little rougher than usual.

"Well, it's got pretty bad for all of us. It might take a little longer than we figgered to pull the country outa this. A lot's gone wrong; this is a big country so we got to be a bit patient. The President and Congress is workin' as hard as they can, but we gotta do what we can to get by. It ain't no shame, Irene, to take things that is goin' to waste. These things is surplus, *surplus*." He repeated the word as though having trouble convincing himself. "I heard that farmers in other parts of the country're throwin' food away, dumpin' milk in the gutters, throwin' oranges in the ocean out there in Californy. Just the other day I heard they was goin' to burn piles of wheat in the Midwest 'cause there ain't no market. It seems a damn shame to let people go hungry when there's so much in this land." He had worked himself up to such a pitch that he had to extract his blue bandanna and wipe his eyes.

Irene was convinced and agreed that she would go over to the city hall and sign up for the program next Tuesday. As she watched him go down the walk, looking old and tired though he was still a youngish man, her heart squeezed with pity. Laurence might look like that if he had still been here. Some tears started to her eyes but she forced them back. She had to learn to be strong, depend on herself; Aaron couldn't bear the burden of her forever.

Men were not as strong as she had once thought.

The following week Irene prepared for her ordeal. There had been a late October rain, and it was chilly so she got out her old brown, second best coat that, though bought in 1928, still looked good on her trim figure. She was glad there was an excuse to wear her galoshes over her every day shoes that were getting shabby. With her heart thumping uncomfortably against her chest, she trudged down the street toward City Hall feeling finally, hopelessly and even resentfully, a widow.

Ten or twelve people had assembled and were shivering in the bleak yard behind the building where rain puddles were glimmering in the cold light of morning seeping through wet trees. Irene knew most of them, and they greeted her as she took her place. Some of them were exchanging good natured complaints about the weather or the news; a few were making feeble jokes about the depression but most of them stood, like Irene, miserable and angry, hoping to get it over with. She could only smile wanly and answer in strangled monosyllables when some friendly greetings were addressed to her. Always a proud, shy woman she could not identify herself with humanity at large. At last they left her alone. Somehow she had expected to be able to slide into the office without being recognized, pick up her allotment and speed home. She had deliberately come late, but they were slow opening up so she stood hands in pockets, her face burning with shame, staring at the ground.

Presently she was aware that quite a few others had come straggling into the yard, among them that Hamilton woman. The poor woman's coat was actually ragged, its fur collar worn down to the greasy pelt. There was a hole in the old black man's hat she had pulled down over her straggling hair and she was wearing a man's shoes. She took her place apologetically in line. A few of the regulars acknowledged her but, like Irene, she tried to make herself invisible, staring at the gravel. Irene's spirits plunged even lower. Was it possible that she, too, could sink so low in poverty and despair?

It seemed an eternity before the door was opened. They all filed silently into the big, gloomy store room to fill out the forms and receive bags of beans, rice, and other odds and ends of surplus commodities. There was a large poster on the wall of the dank, grayish room describing who was eligible. Irene could hardly read it, her eyes were so blurry. she was hoping that something would say she didn't qualify, and she could turn and flee. People behind the tables handing out the sacks were people she had known all her life, people with whom she had grown up and whose opinions made her world.

Although Irene was not vain, she had always had a comfortable sense of her family's status. Her parents had both died young, but they came of a good early Mormon line and had left enough money for her to be raised comfortably by her Aunt Delia, a highly respected music-school teacher in the community. The Kent family into which she had married was one of the "old families" in Merritsville and, though she and Laurence had had to struggle along in their early years, they had never felt really poor and humiliated like this. This morning the final shred of his promised protection had been ripped away. She turned to leave, but an old friend, Bert Robinson who was helping hand out the commodities, grasped her hand.

"Hello there, Irene. How're you doin' these days?" He acted like they were meeting at church or somewhere. "Don't get to see you much anymore since we moved into the other ward. Sure do miss your music." His affability shocked her out of herself. She had known that the Robinsons, who had been in the sheep business too, were in bad straits. They had had to move in with Elva's folks, and she had heard that she wasn't too well after the last baby.

"Tough times for all of us," he said sympathetically as he thrust some of the brown paper sacks marked in ugly black letters into her arms. As their eyes met, she knew that he understood her distress.

"Say 'Hello' to Elva." She managed a stiff smile. "I'll try to get over to see her sometime soon."

"She'd like that, Irene." Bert pressed her hand. She moved on abruptly, afraid she would cry, and hastened out.

"Cheer up," he called after her, "The gover'ment's goin' to look after us all now." He handed several sacks of commodities to Mrs. Hamilton without any comment, and she moved out after Irene. Head bowed, she crossed quickly to the opposite side of the street and trotted briskly away. Irene stared for a few minutes after the retreating scarecrow figure with a strange feeling of guilt. She might have said something friendly to her at least. They were all in the same fix.

As she made her way home on the wet sidewalks–some paved with treacherously cracked and buckled cement, some just dirt paths full of puddles reflecting the gray sky, she was more acutely aware than she had been of the shabbiness of the town. Many of the houses were in need of repair; some were boarded up; yards were neglected and fences sagging. No new houses had been built in the town for a long time except here and there some desperate young families had dug basements which projected a foot or so above ground. Roofing them over with tar paper, they made a home, hoping that sometime they could build the rest of the house.

Irene had always liked this place where her life had begun and would end, she had thought, in the peace and security of a loving family and friends. Now she felt alien as though she had come to a strange, unfriendly land. How long those three blocks form City Hall to her gate! She imagined everyone along the way peering at her from their windows, noting her humiliation. She had to jerk hard on the gate to open it because of a broken, rusting hinge that she could not fix; she hated to put more on Aaron. Going into the back porch, she dumped the hateful sacks on a bench. The kitchen was cold. Without removing her coat, she slumped down at the table. She was hungry and exhausted but too drained to stir up the fire. It had only been an hour and a half since she had left by that relentless old alarm clock that ticked away as though nothing had changed since she and Laurence bought it so long ago, but she had gone through another time zone, it seemed, into another frightening dimension.

PART TWO

Cℬ

On Tuesday mornings Irene awoke with a hard knot in her stomach; she continued to go for her commodities, but it never got easier. Each week she came home depressed, stacked the brown sacks on the porch and often cried. She used very little of the stuff, giving most of it to Addie and Dosey, but she felt that Aaron would be mad at her if she didn't go. Irene had always bowed to masculine authority. As winter came on, Irene caught the flu and was very sick in bed so Bert Robinson arranged for Ellen to pick up their allotment after school.

Irene was able to get out of bed a little before Christmas, but she was weak and depressed. Not since the death of the baby could Ellen remember her mother not getting dressed all day, just sitting in the rocking chair, staring at nothing. Neither Addie nor Dosey could interest her in preparing for Christmas and it came and went without her even going to Christmas dinner. Ellen thought it was the most dismal Christmas they had ever had.

As winter wore on, it became apparent that there was something very wrong. Irene wouldn't sew or crochet; she wouldn't play the piano at home or in church; she didn't want to go anywhere or do anything. What was worse, she began to neglect herself and her house. This really worried Addie and Dosey who tried to lecture her, telling her she must snap out of if for Ellen's sake. They reminded her of all her blessings, of her duties and tried to cheer her up in every way they could. She would usually just cry. The Elders administered to her; the Relief Society teachers called regularly, bringing food and little gifts. Aaron and Dosey even took her on a shopping trip to Salt Lake and tried to get her to buy some new clothes. All to no avail.

Finally Dosey made her go see Dr. Wardle who examined her completely and could find nothing wrong. "Seems like she's just gone into depression," he explained to Dosey while Irene was getting dressed. "Sometimes these sicknesses bring it on; we don't know why and there's not too much we know what to do for it;

no medicine that I know of. Mostly it's mental, but I don't think we ought to send her over to the State hospital yet...." Dosey shuddered at the thought of Irene or anyone she knew in the State Mental hospital. He scratched his chin reflectively with his pen. "Just have to keep a close watch on her. They have these psychiatrist doctors in some of the bigger places. Might be some in Salt Lake soon, but they cost a lot of money."

As he helped Irene on with her coat, he felt a wave of sadness he didn't often permit himself. She was such a beautiful woman in spite of looking so washed out and helpless. Added to all the shocks she had had in the past few years the flu had drained her strength away. He had not seen too much of deep medical depression in his rural practice, mostly happened to women in menopause and Irene was nowhere near that. She was young and in good physical condition; just have to hope that nature would take over and she would pull through. He patted her shoulder. "Now you come see me anytime you feel you can't handle things, Irene." She nodded, her eyes full of tears.

As they were leaving, Dr. Wardle pulled Dosey back into the office. "I don't want to upset you, Doris," he said in a low, confidential tone, "but try not to leave her too much alone. Cases like this sometimes get suicidal."

Dosey *was* upset. They couldn't be with her every minute of the day; she wouldn't come stay with either her or Addie and Ellen had to go to school. Still they would try to manage. One of them could go over every day or so.

On February third, Irene remembered that it was the anniversary of Laurence's burial. It was the same kind of day as that one; nasty as only February can be. She had risen and made the fire for Ellen to get off to school and then gone back to bed. Ellen called good-by from the door, pausing to look at her anxiously.

"Is there anything I can get you, Mama?" she asked. Irene shook her head. "I'll come home at noon if you want me to."

"No, don't bother," Irene raised her head painfully, "I might be asleep. I didn't sleep very well last night. I'll be all right."

Later in the morning she arose; the fire had gone out and she was hungry but without appetite. She got out the butcher knife to slice some bread. It was an old knife worn thin and concave but very sharp. She stood looking at it as though mesmerized. Slowly she raised it to her throat and pressed the cold blade against her skin. She had a curious, excited feeling, more emotion than she had felt for many months. It was exhilarating to think of escaping from this dreadful, dark existence. She could be safe with Laurence if.... Irene was not aware how long she had been standing by the cabinet with the knife in her cold hand when there was a loud knocking on the door.

Startled, she dropped the knife; when the knocking resumed, she pulled her old robe about her and went to the front door.

Addie and Dosey were used to coming right in. Who could it be on this miserable morning? It was the Raleigh Man, Brother Schmidt, who greeted her cheerfully in his thick German accent.

"O, I am sorry I bother you, Sister Kent. I chust vondered if you needed anyting dis mont'? I got a special on d'vanilla vot you like most. I like to come in and show you." He had his old brown corduroy cap in hand and he peered at her anxiously from his thick glasses.

Irene opened the door wider; for a long time she had had a curious feeling that there was a thick pane of glass between her and the rest of the world. Kind Brother Schmidt was on the other side of it, strange, unreal. Vanilla? What did she want with vanilla?

"Vell, I see you don't feel so good, I call nex' mont'." He had started down the path with his wire basket of products.

Irene panicked; she thought of the knife and suddenly didn't want to be alone anymore. "Oh, no, come in, do come in. I think I need some vanilla."

Brother Schmidt tried not to notice that there was something wrong in the cold kitchen as he took out his spices and medications and explained their virtues to her. She examined each one quizzically and deliberately, hoping to prolong his visit. Brother Schmidt usually dispensed a little news along with his selling, and he managed to spin out his call to almost an hour, working in a little sympathy and philosophy. He had heard that Irene was in a bad way and felt for her. A lot of the folks he visited on his route were having troubles but few had given up to despair. At last Irene decided to take a bottle of vanilla and some mentholated ointment. When he left, the terrible spell had been broken.

She cut a slice of bread and put the knife way in the back of the drawer. After a meager lunch, she went back to bed and sobbed until she fell asleep.

When Ellen came home from school, she was struck more forcibly than usual with the cold, untidy house. It was so unlike what their home had always been. She noticed that several geraniums had died and stood brown and snarled in their rusting cans. She could not hold back the tears and sat disconsolately at the table wondering what to do. Her first instinct was to go to Grandma's, but something told her that she must grow up now and try to do things on her own. As Grandma had said long ago, Irene was not strong, that they would have to take care of her.

Resolutely, Ellen got up, stirred up the fire and heated the kettle to wash the dirty dishes. She straightened the kitchen as near to the way her mother would have done as she could and then found some canned soup to heat for dinner. It made her feel very good and important and, when Irene appeared in the doorway disheveled and dazed, the table was set neatly with a cloth and nice dishes. Ellen had thrown out the dead geraniums and watered the others, setting one that was blooming on the table. There was some apple sauce cake that Grandma had brought, and she opened a bottle of fruit.

A warm light penetrated Irene's deep lethargy.

"My, but I've been lazy today," she apologized weakly, attempting to fasten up her hair that was dull and matted. It hurt Ellen to look at her but she knew she had to be calm.

"Come on and eat supper, Mama. I fixed us some chicken soup and things."

Irene sat down and tried to eat the soup but her hands trembled and the tears started down her cheeks.

"You're such a good girl, Ellen," she sobbed, "I wish I knew what to do...."

"Never mind, Mama," Ellen begged, feeling tears in her own eyes, "Just try to eat so you'll get strong again. Things'll be all right again. You'll get better."

Irene made a great effort and presently finished most of her meal. After dinner when Ellen had cleaned up the kitchen again, she dragged in the galvanized tub in which they bathed by the fire and, filling it with hot water from the stove reservoir, made

Irene a bath. Just like a grown-up she hunted up clean garments and a nightdress. When Irene had bathed, Ellen brought out the ivory hair brush that Laurence had given her mother on their first anniversary and brushed and brushed her long hair until some of its sheen was restored.

As she brushed, she said fervently to herself, "Dear, Lord, make her better, please. She must get better."

By the time the spring had begun to break tentatively over the valley in April, Irene began to recover. The "bathroom" might have had something to do with it.

Among the many urgent plans for putting people back to work, especially able bodied men, was the Public Works Administration. Under the cautious direction of a man with a name that sounded to Ellen like a hiccup–Ickes–this project was for upgrading American cities and towns by putting money into building and much needed improvements like sanitation. In hopes of getting some of these funds, the city fathers of Merritsville decided to enact zoning laws that required the removal of all outdoor privies, barns, coops and animals for six or eight blocks in either direction of main street. This area took in both the Walker and Irene's home. At first Aaron was dumfounded. He had not foreseen this interference with his living arrangements. In addition to having to move all his livestock out to the farm on the edge of town, he was going to be obliged to install two bathrooms, one for his family and one for Irene. He feared this government might be going too far.

He grumbled with the other men on the bank corner for a week or two then hitched up his overall straps and went to work figgering how to accomplish the task. Sewers would make a big improvement in the town and provide some employment. Irene, who was just beginning to regain her hold on life, was both worried and delighted at the prospect of getting a bathroom, finally, something she had dreamed of ever since she had left Aunt Delia's. But where on earth would she get the money? The government was going to provide funds for labor and larger materials but each householder had to furnish the fixtures and remodel the space. Aaron went with her to the bank where Brother Ballard treated her kindly and arranged a small loan to suit her circumstances.

She was dreadfully afraid of going in debt but there was no alternative.

It took several months for Aaron and some of the other elders putting what time they could spare into partitioning off the back porch which was the only space she had. Aaron gathered up some second-hand fixtures–a big, narrow tub on claw feet, a toilet that had to be flushed in a special way or it would flood over and a basin that was rather elegant in spite of a chip in it. Together he, Irene and Dosey covered the walls half-way up with oil cloth that had a rose design in it. Irene painted the rest of the walls and ceiling a pale pink, feeling pleasure in her new strength. On the day that Aaron inspected the pipes, tightening them a little more and tinkering with the toilet, then standing back fairly pleased with himself, Irene felt a real surge of pleasure in her home again. She surprised herself and embarrassed Aaron by giving him a hug and kiss on his rough cheek.

The room was not like the one she had once dreamed of with pink and white tiles in the picture she had burned after Laurence's death, but it was a genuine advance. She, Aaron and Dosey congratulated each other for almost half an hour before Aaron gathered up his tools and promised to come back and haul the old outhouse away next week.

Irene and Ellen put out the pink towels with crocheted edges, the pretty washcloths and scented soap and reveled in their first baths in their very own first bathroom.

The next week as Irene watched Aaron pull out of the yard with the old back house on his truck, she felt that a new day had indeed dawned for them.

As her strength and interest in life returned, Irene's main diversion from a monotonous round of house and church work was the daily walk she took uptown in the afternoons when the weather was good. She dressed herself carefully, almost ritualistically, for these strolls and, with her fine figure and fragile beauty, she aroused warm comments from the gangs of men who were put to work under the WPA and other make work schemes of the New Deal. Some of them were chopping down the rows of dying Lombardy poplar trees long a feature of Utah towns; cleaning weedy ditches and streets or building culverts, bridges and other improvements. A few of them still preferred to loaf about the streets, hoping for other less humiliating work.

It was impossible in so small a town that she would not be noticed and speculated about by both men and women; the comment was varied. Some still pitied her for what they imagined or knew to be a lonely, empty life; others of the women envied her for having the time to "parade around the streets looking like Lady Astorbilt." Many of the men had other thoughts and wished they were able to offer her some male consolation. The widower Frank Farely with five children and an impoverished farm had indeed made her a tentative offer and was so coldly rebuffed that his reports discouraged others who might have been interested in filling the heart and life of Irene Kent.

Irene had learned to live with her loneliness in the way that one learns to live with the loss of an arm or leg or an eye–no matter how well she seemed to be getting along there was always a dull, aching sense of something missing. It was worst at nights when she frequently awoke with a feeling of acute despair and fear. She could scarcely remember having been a whole woman; her memories of Laurence had begun to fade like an old photograph. Although she remembered how he looked, she had difficulty recalling how his voice sounded, how he had felt in her arms or smelled. Her former life seemed like an old movie she had seen long ago and of which she recalled only vivid jerky snatches. But she had never thought of remarriage or a man in that sense at all. She moved like a dreamer through timeless time, ignoring the attentions of Merritsville men with cool indifference.

One of the men who noticed Irene with a deep and unusual interest as she made her rounds through the stores and down the main street was Clinton Maxwell, manager and buyer of Washburn's Ladies-Ready-To-Wear and Drygoods Department. Part of it was boredom, part loneliness and part the peculiar creativeness of a man like Clinton who was badly out of place in this earthy, small Mormon town. It was an accident of the depression that had brought him here, the fact that his wife was Helen Washburn. When he had lost his own exclusive Lady's Shoppe in Denver, he had been forced to take this as the only possible way of supporting her and their daughter.

There were days when ordering for the dowdy matrons and frowzy housewives nearly drove him to drink or worse–pouring over catalogues to find a line of dresses that would cover up the longish sleeves and high necklines of the garments, yet would keep the females of Merritsville from looking like the last plague of a Puritan God. There had to be style and beauty in the world for it to be endurable to Clinton, especially in the female. Clinton was an artist with some leanings that he had learned to repress to survive in a world where his gifts were redundant if not scorned.

It was as though a shaft of redemptive light had struck through the gloom of the dark oak paneling of Washburn's Ready-To-Wear department when he became aware of Irene Kent intently ruffling through the dress racks. Practically no one in Merritsville, least of all the stalwart farmers or ranchers in whom aesthetic appreciation of beauty had atrophied, could have understood Clinton's feeling for Irene. He was not and never would be in love with her or would want her in the ordinary ways of sexual or practical male-female relationship. He felt like a sculptor looking at a splendid new piece of marble ready for his hand to form into a work of art. She would fulfill his thwarted ideal of beauty.

Gradually as he began to look forward to her almost daily visits, he became consumed with the dream of her potentials as a fashionable, physically beautiful woman. Emaciated from her recent illness, she had the exotic look of fashion models. To amuse himself in long dreary days, he began to imagine how he would fit certain dresses and fabrics to her gently sloping hips and thighs; from the fashion magazines, he chose necklines to display her fine throat and arms and studied the colors he thought might flatter her coloring. He could see that she had a sense of clothes from the ones she wore though they were out of style and a bit shabby.

Although Irene had always enjoyed clothes and had had some good ones a few years ago, she was aware that they were growing outmoded as she rummaged thoughtfully through the dresses in the stores. Presently she became aware of Clinton's special warm interest in her, sensed the eagerness with which he awaited her visits and shyly confided in him that she was saving up for a new dress. Assuring her that there was nothing on the racks to suit her at the moment, Clinton discussed the whims of fashion with her and showed her his catalogues and magazines. It became something of a game for her to drop in and look over the sales books. He asked her opinions and found that she did have a good eye for line and detail.

Due to the depression, Clinton's staff in the women's department consisted of only one other full-time saleslady, Bertha Washburn–maiden aunt of the present owners–so heavy and crippled and racked with arthritis that she could hardly get around. But she was possessed of the qualifications of a good saleswoman, infinite good nature and a knowledge of the special needs and desires of her various customers. During the busy seasons there was a part time sales lady who came in Friday afternoons and Saturday. One day when Arlene Simpson could not come as she had promised, it struck Clinton that he might work Irene into her place.

His imagination dared to go even further; perhaps she could be worked into a full time position since surely Bertha could not hold out very much longer. From that moment he began to trip more lightly around the dingy glass cases and among the depressing dress racks, humming snatches of popular songs under his breath. He vowed to start sympathizing Bertha right out of the place by reminding her at every turn how hard it must be for her to stand on her feet the way she did and how she must sit down as often as possible and not go downstairs to the stock room. In a few weeks he had Spencer Washburn's permission to bring Irene into the store on a part-time basis.

Irene could not believe her good fortune. She had often thought, with crushing discouragement, of trying to find a job; but totally unfitted and untrained to do anything else but domestic chores, she had not known where to start looking. She did not feel able to go out to do housework as a stronger, less fastidious woman might. She thought of sewing for people but few could afford to pay her; besides most women sewed for their families as a matter of course. When Clinton asked her if she would like a part-time job one day in late spring, she was so elated that she rushed home, played the piano and sang all the rest of the afternoon. When Ellen came home from school, she was astonished to hear her mother sounding so happy. When Irene told her the news, they hugged each other ecstatically. Clinton had said that she would have a discount to buy hers and Ellen's clothes and groceries, too. It was as though the clouds had lifted and a strong ray of sunshine warmed the small house that had long had a chill upon it. Although Clinton had warned Irene that she would not make more than fifteen or twenty dollars a month for a while, he had hinted at better things. Then there was a certain amount of importance and glamor in working at the biggest department store between Provo and Salt Lake City.

Many people were happy to see Irene in the store, a little uncertain and awkward at first, but gradually, under Clinton's warm and patient tutelage, to blossom like a carefully cultivated rose. She was surely a fresh and pleasant addition to the gloomy old store which had not been redecorated since the early 1900's. Her instinct for order and cleanliness began to be apparent in the careless shabbiness that had long marked the atmosphere. Eventually Clinton found more and more excuse to bring her into the store for a few hours in the afternoon while the desultory Bertha perched on her old brown stool at the lingerie counter where she helped some of the older women with their purchases of L.D.S. garments because they had been accustomed to buying them from her for so many years that it seemed indecent to confide one's size to anyone else. Bertha was relieved to have someone younger and sprightlier to attend to the merchandise.

Before the year was out Clinton's dream had materialized. Irene was the full time sales lady and Bertha, whose arthritis had progressed until she could scarcely move about, came in only occasionally, wheezing and groaning with pain if she had to get down into the cases or reach the higher shelves.

The change in Irene came about so imperceptibly that few realized how cleverly Clinton was remaking the simple country beauty into a svelte woman of fashion. With his instinctive good taste, he knew how to dress her so that she would not be obviously overdressed for Merritsville, yet point up her best features.

He maneuvered so that even Irene was only barely aware of what he was about as he picked out a piece of jewelry from the case for her to wear during store hours or purchased a dress especially for her but hung it towards the back of the rack until he could conscientiously take a markdown on it and casually suggest that she slip it on. As his slender hands smoothed, tucked and fitted, she was never aware of the slightest impropriety. There was little sexuality in their relationship. To Clinton she was a piece of artwork upon which he was constantly working for the sheer pleasure of working at that which he loved, his salvation in the sea of dreariness that surrounded him both at work and home.

The only thing that distressed Clinton about Irene was her hair. Magnificent as it was, its length and abundance made it extremely difficult to shape into a stylish coiffure. Those "Swedish milk-maid braids" will have to go, he thought to himself but when he suggested that she cut it, she looked so unhappy. Laurence had always loved her hair, and she was still half afraid of the elders in the church. Scarcely a Fast and Testimony meeting passed without some querulous old man arising and admonishing, with threads of agitated spittle on his indignant lips, the women of Zion to keep their crowns of glory as the Lord had intended. Makeup and short hair were still incipient signs of depravity in little towns like Merritsville. She finally agreed to wear it in a softly waved frame about her face with a smooth chignon at the nape of her neck. This gave her an exotic look that disturbed her somewhat; on Sundays she put back the coronet of thick braids that she had worn since she was a girl.

The only thing that distressed Irene about Clinton's pervasive interest in her appearance was his insistence that she wear higher heels most of the time. He had a horror of so lovely a leg terminating in heavy-heeled oxfords, but he saw, by way of compensation, that she was permitted to sit down as much as possible.

She came to regard him as a fine and warm friend and to depend on him for many things. She liked the work better all the time; besides the welcome addition to her income, it restored her zest in life. She shared Clinton's interest in fine fabrics, beautiful clothes, handsome jewelry; as she gained confidence, she became a tactful and proficient sales person, learning which customers needed a little more persuasion, which to leave alone until they had decided.

Although she was slightly aware that Clinton was not like most men of her acquaintance, she did not feel antagonized by his effeminate manners and was, for the most part, unaware of the snide remarks and shady rumors that inevitably made the rounds of the street corners and work gangs.

She was more content than she had been since Laurence's death; yet there were still times at night when she felt a deep sense of deprivation that she knew neither Clinton nor her work could fill. The woman whom Clinton had succeeded in partially reawakening to life was, in a deep part of her, agonizingly hungry for the love she had once known. It was this elemental need that gave her beauty a kind of patina, a glow that kept it from hardening into the slick fashion-magazine gloss of a sophisticated mannequin. Even Clinton noticed and approved, knowing that he could never compensate: it was like an unexpected quality in the medium which rendered the gifts of the artist even more effective.

૪

When Ed Barker first saw Irene almost a year after she had become a saleslady at Washburn's, it was the fine sheen of sadness underlying her beauty which, without his knowing it, attracted him. He saw good looking women frequently but none who looked as though they needed loving so much. It is easy enough to resist the appeal of physical beauty though one takes pleasure in it, but to deny the appeal one human being makes to another's capacity and necessity for love takes a strong or heartless person. Ed Barker was neither and he was as vulnerable at that hour as Irene. Traveling representative of the largest wholesale hardware company in the state, Fancher and Sons Wholesale Hardware and Farm Machinery Company of Salt Lake City, he was a country boy who had made good in the city by diligence of hard work, congenial personality and marriage to the daughter of the original owner of the company.

He had come up to the city from a farm-ranch in western Utah, a clean-cut, ambitious and personable young man, one of the many who had to leave rural areas in the first half of the century because there was really no room for them and exciting things were happening in America. He had found a job almost at once with the Fancher company and gained the favorable attention of his father-in-law-to-be because he possessed those solid, western virtues that old Fancher had unwittingly bred out of his sons by affluence and an eastern education. Contrary to what many afterward thought, Ed had made his way by grueling hard work, strict honesty even when it meant opposing the boss on occasion and a kind of old-time romanticism about individual enterprise and initiative.

When he married Emily Fancher with the approval of her father, if not that of her brothers, he had married for what he sincerely considered love. Bill Fancher had a heavy emotional investment in his daughter, for, although beautiful in a quiet way and intelligent, she was crippled. One hip protruded awkwardly and when she walked, dragged her left leg conspicuously. She had been that way since birth when her mother had died leaving her to fill the abyss in her father's life as best she could. All the medical help he could find had failed to correct Emily's deformity, but she had overcome some of her handicap and blossomed into an agreeable and accomplished young woman. She played the piano and sang, did fine needlework and had learned how to run the household and manage her father and brothers skillfully.

Bill Fancher would never have consented to anyone marrying her who did not have something of the same reverence and awe of womanhood along with the tender, protective idealism toward Emily that he did. He was not wrong in discerning these qualities in Ed whose mother had been a semi-invalid and had instilled in him those gentle emotions.

Emily and Ed were married in 1916 and the union seemed to him about what it should be in light of his limited experience and observation. Having few amorous experiences beyond mild flirtations since he had been brought up with the strict ideals of his mother in the church, he was not sure for a very long time what it was that troubled him about his marriage. He felt vaguely that it would have been better if they hadn't continued to live with her father in the big old house on Oak Avenue, but it was Emily's firm wish. Besides there was no way Ed could have provided her with a similar home on his salary.

He had always regretted not enlisting in the services as war engaged the country, but Bill Fancher, at Emily's insistence, had maneuvered to keep him at home. Emily was pregnant and ailing so he had stayed to help on the home front while her brothers went off to glory. One of them came home with a wound and medal that galled Ed.

Emily relied heavily on the affection and attention that Ed gave her, but she was shy and cold in bed. He had thought it right that a virtuous woman would find some of the realities of sex difficult, but he was disappointed that, as time went on, she was not able to overcome a fear and distaste of the physical relationship. Edward Junior was born early in 1918 and after the birth of Clifford in 1920, the doctor advised him that more children would jeopardize her life. As her health gradually declined, Ed resigned himself to the situation as best he could.

Emily, who had dominated her father and brothers most of her life on the strength of her affliction, developed the despotic temperament of the invalid. She had to have complete control of time, place, and the people who formed her small, pale world. Ed soon learned that opposition was not only repugnant to her, it was incomprehensible. She took over their lives from her bed or chair, directing the raising of the children through their nurses and seldom allowing Ed much say. Although he had permission to take them to the ranch and introduce them to the things that red-blooded western boys did–hunting, fishing, riding, he soon learned that they were city kids, Emily's boys. When she insisted on sending them away to school, the estrangement was completed.

In the wild, inflated years of the twenties, Ed, like so many other men, was occupied with the booming, expanding business world. Although there was some friction between Ed and the brothers who had taken over the business on the death of Bill in 1927, things worked out well on the whole because Ed was especially adapted to handling the outlying territories. Neither of the brothers liked that part of it. Ed traveled the length and breadth of the state and into neighboring ones, Idaho, Arizona, Nevada, contacting small businesses, farmers and ranchers. He was a successful and resourceful salesman and, in spite of the fact that he knew Emily's brothers would be just as glad to have him out of it, he felt that he had a real stake in the business. He knew Emily would never permit them to release him.

One of the advantages of his work was that he was away from the big, gloomy ostentatious house a great deal. Emily's health became steadily more precarious, so Ed had moved into a bedroom-study where he spent most of the restless hours when he was in town. That the intimate side of his and Emily's relationship had all but ceased appeared inevitable to him. Although he felt a nagging sense of loss and unfulfillment, it never occurred to him to him that there was much he could do about it. His view of things included, even in the chaos of the depression, a deep sense of honor toward contracts, business and otherwise. Having married her for better or worse, he avoided those temptations that might have caused him to forget his vows.

Then came the great crash. Although life in the Oak Avenue house was scarcely disturbed on the surface, the perspective of it was. Ed, who had always felt that there were many possibilities in life and a man was free to choose liberally among them, came to see that he was trapped. He never permitted the awareness to come to the surface of his mind, but the changed circumstances of the country showed him that many things he had held to be absolute and permanent were fragile and false.

Fanchers felt the depression keenly enough, but the business had been solidly based and carefully managed so that, though there was a tightening of belts all around, some layoffs and temporary readjustments, there was little danger of it foundering. Ed knew his position was reasonably secure but, as he traveled among the familiar towns and stores, some of which had to cut their orders drastically, others had simply had to close their doors owing Fanchers and many other wholesalers substantial sums of money and others who apologetically showed him merchandise which had not moved since he had been around the previous time, he became increasingly worried. It was wooden comfort to him to know that even in a time of serious widespread unemployment, he couldn't get fired because he worked for his wife's brothers. He felt guilty and depressed, never more so than when he went back to the shabby opulence of Oak Avenue. Emily refused to believe in the depression cloistered as she was with her money safely invested, but she did agree to take the boys out of their expensive private schools. Edward Jr. began work in the company; Clifford went to a local high school. They were strangers to Ed and, always ill at ease and nervous at home, he felt a sense of release that was as close to happiness as he could remember when he packed his cases, crawled into his Buick and hit the road. In the crumby little hotels and boarding houses where he had long been accustomed to staying without enthusiasm, he began to find a new man, a man he scarcely understood.

In 1934 he was thirty-nine, better looking in his genial, solid way that he had been when he was younger. He was still well-liked wherever he went; this perhaps accounted for his unspectacular but enduring success with the store-keepers and merchants of the small towns who were still suspicious of a "city slicker." Now he listened with a sympathetic ear and genuine concern to long tales of financial woe all the way from Arizona to Idaho and back again.

He began to feel more at home in the seedy lobbies of the make-shift hostelries and run-down front rooms than in the over-furnished parlors on Oak Avenue. Irrationally they reminded him of the front-room at home on the ranch with its shabby, ungraceful mail-order furniture, doilies and ubiquitous pots of molting ferns. He could relax in his shirt sleeves and socks without feeling guilty. But most of all he enjoyed breezing along the highways or bumping along rutted country roads, letting his thoughts ride easily along crazy fence lines or picking out familiar landmarks like friendly old faces–lunch stands, odd old houses, curious formation in the landscape, old gnarled trees–all of which had become a part of him. Still and all he felt that most of his life was over, that he was drifting with the ghosts of past hopes and dreams.

Even though he wasn't fond of being at home in Salt Lake, he found the week-ends when he had to stay in one of the small towns irksome. The long dead hours from Saturday afternoon, when the stores closed, to Monday morning when he could pick up his orders and hit the highway again were tedious. Saturday nights he would roam around the meager streets as late as he could, frequenting whatever places of amusement or businesses that remained open after dark. Most small western towns "rolled up the sidewalks" at nine or ten. On the week-ends the only places open in Utah were the grubby beer and pool-halls reopened since prohibition had been repealed, those dens of iniquity which haunted the dreams of wives and mothers, and some movie houses and dance halls.

Almost every town the size of Merritsville had a public dance hall, a big barny structure with a fanciful name like the Apollo or The Coconut Grove, its crudeness relieve by amazing arrangements of crepe paper. Crepe paper–that cheap, immensely versatile material was a symbol of those shabby years. Used profusely to recreate vanished dreams, it softened reality and created cherished illusions of South Sea Islands, sentimental Victorian gardens, exotic moonscapes where to the poignant wail of a saxophone, the tinny thud of a piano from which the front panel had been removed and the rattle of drums, despair and loneliness could be forgotten for a few hours. The Mormons encouraged dancing. These dance halls, except for a few rowdies who brought their bottles and drank in their darkened cars and occasionally stirred up a fist fight, were respectable enough places for lonely people to go in search of company.

Ed, who had liked to dance when he was younger but had given it up, of course, when he married, discovered that he could pass Saturday nights pleasantly dancing with the local girls, flirting mildly with them for an evening then dropping them from his life and memory. Once in a while he took one of them out for a drink or sandwich and drove them home after the dance. There had been a few disturbing incidents with the more attractive and aggressive ones that troubled him for a while, but not one of them aroused the feelings which, in truth, he considered to have passed out of his life. If anyone had asked him or if he had asked himself, he would have declared that he never expected to fall in love again having made a bearable adjustment to the conditions of his existence. And he had always been wary of casual sex. The dancing tired him sufficiently so that he could sleep late on Sunday, and the week-end was reduced to a drowsy Sunday afternoon during which he read, did his accounts and passed the weary time.

The summer of 1934 had been hot, dry and unusually discouraging. Business in general had tapered off after the first hopeful surge of the New Deal. The month of August had always been a slow time for Fanchers since the farm work was finishing up and the hardware departments no longer needed a heavy stock. The heat lasted into the first week in September and Ed, just finishing a particularly grueling week in southern Utah, arrived in Merritsville late on Saturday Afternoon, tired, sweaty and depressed. For once the cool high-ceilinged bedroom in Salt Lake seemed desirable. But he had to stop at Washburns, one of his best customers, to check on a small order which George Hansen had all but promised him earlier in the week.

George, the hardware manager, was out of the office when Ed arrived and, as he sat down in one of the misshapen old leather chairs, his eye fell on the large calendar above it. Sunday was Em's birthday he remembered with a start of guilt! By the time he got to Salt Lake now the stores would be closed. He couldn't be caught empty-handed. Em, though she wouldn't have said so, was sentimental about birthdays and anniversaries. Ed had learned to be most punctilious in his observances of them to avoid the silent recriminations and little digs that he would have to endure as a result of his neglect. Since George was not in the office, Ed thought he might as well go across to the main store and see if he could find anything in the lady's department that would do in a pinch–a nightgown, bottle of perfume.

After the blinding light of the street, Ed could hardly see in the greenish darkness of the Ready-To-Wear section. The air was very thick and warm in spite of the whirring of two large fan blades above the center aisle and he stood mopping the perspiration from his forehead and neck uncertain just where to start looking. The low, rich feminine voice startled him. "Can I help you with something?"

He turned nervously and looked into the most beautiful and disturbing face he had seen since Emily Fancher had walked into her father's office so many rusted years before. In the greenish, watery shadows there was something of the same haunting quality in this face as in that other–a look of suffering so long endured that it had produced a magnetic essence although Irene was smiling brightly. She was wearing a pink and blue-flowered voile dress with a low neckline and a string of pearls that had the same soft glow as her skin, almost seemed to be made of the same vibrant substance. A shaft of light which forced its way through a chink in the high green blinds touched quivering glints of bronze in her thick brown hair. Ed felt slightly dizzy as though he were floating in a strange warm lake of green water; he was afraid to move for fear his legs would melt out from under him. He stammered an answer to her question, "Yes, yes, I guess–that is I was looking for a birthday present for a woman," he added not knowing why he was reluctant to say, "for my wife."

"Well, fine," said Irene, beaming as Clinton had taught her and gently leading the customer's attention to the merchandise.

"We just got some lovely fall things in, some jewelry maybe?" Ed shook his head, having slightly recovered his equilibrium, "She doesn't use much jewelry, she don't go out much."

"Well then, some pretty lingerie?" Irene was proud that she could pronounce it the French way, but she could see its effect was lost on the customer who seemed extremely ill at ease for a nicely dressed man obviously from the city. Never mind, most men were uncomfortable in the women's part of the store; she was used to smoothing over their anxiety. She spread some boxes of peachy colored satin slips on the counter and held them up delicately so that their relation to the feminine figure was not too obvious.

"This one has the new adjustable straps." she leaned over the counter to show him the little gadget that slipped up and down the ribbon, and Ed breathed the warm, womanly fragrance of her hair. It flooded him with a sensation he had not had for years, a longing so acute that for a moment he thought he might faint.

"Awful warm," he murmured and mopped at his neck again. "No, no I don't think so, she, uh she's something of an invalid, not, not very well most of the time." He had a sudden impulse to turn and run, but Irene was looking at him with a curious half-amused, half-sympathetic expression which he felt penetrated the inmost secrets of his soul, secrets that he had so long ago stored up and forgotten that he couldn't even remember what they were. Oddy, he felt as though he was being unfaithful to Em.

"Oh, something for your mother?" Irene nodded understandingly and, going to another case, she brought out a blue satin bed jacket trimmed in lavish ecru lace. "I'll bet she'll like this; women never get too old to like pretty things. It's a bit more expensive...."

"Oh, that's all right, yes, yes that'll do fine." Ed forced a sickly smile. "Could you wrap it as a gift?" Then he remembered that Emily hated blue but it was too late. He fumbled in his sticky wallet for the bill and passed it to her. Their eyes met and the oldest of communications passed between them. A shiver of anguish swept through both of them. Irene turned away and busied herself wrapping the package. Her fingers got tangled in the ribbon and tissue paper, and she could feel the perspiration trickle down between her breasts.

Suddenly she felt extremely irritated; there was something both fascinating and exasperating about this customer. She could feel his eyes on her back. As a matter of fact, Ed had only dared steal a furtive look at the fine curve of her neck, her back and gently undulating hip-line, hating himself for the foolish, boyish embarrassment that he felt. He thrust his hands into his pockets and tried to assume the air of nonchalance befitting a seasoned traveling salesman, but it only made him more aware of his gawkishness. He passed his hand over his chin and realized that his beard stubble was out, his shirt crumpled and there were large, dark perspiration stains under his arms. Oh, God, for a cold shower!

Irene turned and handed him the package. "Thank you very much and do come in again," she said mechanically, avoiding his eyes. Ed grabbed the package almost rudely and fled from the store.

CଌଃB

On the sizzling hot side walk Ed stood clutching the box with its blue bow, feeling as though he had emerged into a completely strange world. The need for a cool shower and quiet room became so overwhelming that he decided he didn't want to see George Hansen at all—would probably blow the deal anyway. George would likely be as hot and tired as he this time of the afternoon at the end of the week. If he could get a room in the hotel and rest up a little, he might be able to make some sense of what had just happened to him. He went back to the hardware office and, since George had not returned, left a message and strode to his car. Tossing the package inside he headed for the sun-baked stucco building down the street that advertised itself as The Merritsville Hotel though it was more a boarding house. He could drive on to Salt Lake early in the morning when it was cooler. He'd call Emily from the pay phone in the lobby.

Stretched out in one of the stuffy little rooms, smelling of stale cigarette smoke, and Lysol, feeling clean and relaxed in his underclothes in spite of the suffocating evening heat that pushed through the ragged blind, he went back over the scene in the store, detail by detail, word by word, while odd little shocks kept spreading over him like fine showers of sharp glass. An hour or so later when the hot dusk had filled the room, he sat upright and pounded the seersucker bedspread. "God!" he whispered, "My good God!" Swinging his legs to the floor, he sat running his hands through his damp hair. Then he looked at his watch, nearly eight o'clock and he hadn't had any supper. The one little eating place in town would be closed, so he would have to drive back out on the highway to a hamburger stand. He arose and leaned over the dresser until he was very close to his own flushed face. "Man, are you goin' crazy?" he asked himself.

Dressing in his pants and shirt but leaving off tie and coat, Ed went out to the deserted street, still sweltering in the twilight. As he drove to the Night Owl on the fringe of town, he knew quite clearly that he had needed to stay in Merritsville so that in some way he could find out about that woman. Just how he was going to accomplish it he hadn't figured out, but she filled his mind– every word, every movement, the smell of her... tormented him. As he drove back into town, he passed the Merritsville dance hall. The lights were on and it occurred to him that he might spend some time there; maybe dance with someone who knew who she was. Anyway he didn't know what else to do; he was too upset to go back to the suffocating hotel room.

It was 5:30 when Irene glanced at the big clock with the Roman numerals as the disturbing man disappeared from the store. For a moment she was confused; since she had waited on him a few minutes ago, time had seemed to split. This did not seem to be the same day that she had begun that hot morning. Something out of the ordinary had happened to her. She had been very guarded with men all these years, expect with Clinton, with whom she felt safe, but this man had dragged something up to her consciousness that filled her with nervous apprehension. The way he had looked at her? He didn't seem forward or even trying to flirt with her, but it was as though they knew each other in some way.

She began wearily to shift the dresses along the racks, looking for loose belts and pins. How ugly they were, she thought. For the first time since she had started work she was depressed–no, oppressed–by the atmosphere of that decaying, dingy store where the effigies of decaying, dingy women hung limply on wire hangers. Suddenly she could see herself filling that size 38 gray crepe with its sagging surplice bodice and ample skirt, hobbling arthritically around the yellowed glass cases, on and on and on. She stopped, clutched her bosom and stared with distress at herself in the three-way mirror. She was standing there as Clint came out of the stock room, his shirt open at the collar and his hair mussed. Irene almost never saw him other than impeccably neat. She turned and looked at him, her eyes filling with tears.

"The heat's about got you, too?" he asked gently. "Why don't you go on home; there's nobody going to do anymore shopping in this damn heat. We should have closed up a day like this anyway."

Gratefully Irene began to gather up her things. "Oh, by the way, I sold that bed jacket we've had around so long... you know the one you ordered for Sister Washburn and she didn't like it, to some strange man."

"Oh, yes. I think that was the Fancher guy, the one from Salt Lake. Well, I'm glad of that. I was going to have to mark it down; too expensive for anybody around here."

"I'll come in early Monday and straighten," Irene said as she left.

"Don't worry about it." Clinton patted her gently on the shoulder. "Just try to keep cool if you can and get some rest."

Women's bad days, he thought, but in the back of his mind a new pity for Irene stirred faintly. He had deliberately schooled himself not to think of her as a woman, not to think of what she needed that he could not give her even if he were single. He had tried to trim away that animal magnetism, that warm glowing heat of woman, conceal it with clothes and manners that would protect her from the needs of her nature and the lecherous dreams of the country men. In the winter he almost succeeded, but summer clothes were too thin, too revealing. He sighed as he watched her hips sway under the tissuey folds of the voile dress as she retreated down the aisle. He wondered if he was doing the best thing for her after all.

Irene did not go straight home. She had promised to meet Bessie to have a soda or malt at the drugstore where they would make plans for the Saturday evening. As she crossed the hot side street and turned into the J.C. Penney store, she felt so miserable that she decided to tell Bessie she could not go to the dance. Bessie had started her going to the Saturday night dances at the Pandora that summer; it was something to look forward to all week.

Bessie waved gaily to her as she came into the seedy store. She was straightening a pile of pink rayon bloomers; she held up a pair of size 48's, waving them jauntily as Irene came up the aisle.

"Hey, how'd you like to have a behind that'd fill these?" she said loudly.

Irene blushed and laughed in spite of herself. "Have to keep a few of these for old Birdie Thayer and the like," Bessie whispered behind her hand, "How come you're off early? It's only a quarter of."

"Clinton said to go on home, it's so hot." Irene shook the top of her dress to let some air onto her burning skin.

"Boy, I wish this old skinflint'd dare give us two minutes off. You'd think the Penney Company'd go bust if we had an extra minute. If you dropped dead one minute before six o'clock they'd take it out of your pay check." She slapped the stack of bloomers not lowering her voice even though she knew the manager might be listening. Irene shivered for her. Jobs were so hard to find, she didn't see how Bessie dare make such cracks.

Bessie was like that. She was unmarried but "old Maid" was hardly the kind of label that would stick to her with any appropriateness. She was loud, good-natured, rough talking and knew more dirty jokes than anybody in town. She could knock the breath out of many a hardened trucker or sheepherder, but nobody minded it except the nervous, fidgety new manager recently transferred from Provo. In fact, if there was one person in Merritsville that everybody liked and trusted it was Bessie Benson. Her squarish homely face around which the orangish hair fuzzed out like frayed yarn on a rag doll was a comfortable landmark. She had been at the Penney store ten years now and the manager had soon learned that she was indispensable. She and Irene had not been close friends until this last year when their circumstances of being unattached women and salesladies threw them together into what was a warm, enlivening relationship for Irene. They were exact opposites. Bessie's happy-go-lucky, uninhibited attitude helped draw Irene out of herself and gave her a new perspective on the world outside her narrow life.

Directly the hands of the clock moved to six, Mr. Schmidt, the manager, went to the front of the store, pulled down the long brown blind and locked the door. Bessie grabbed her purse. "Goodnight, Smitty," she yelled and she and Irene left by the back door.

Over cold drinks in the drugstore, Irene said she guessed she would not go to the dance tonight; she felt as though one of her headaches was coming on. She wanted urgently to tell Bessie about the man who had come into the store that afternoon but, as she reflected on it, there was nothing really to tell. He hadn't said or done anything out of the ordinary. Though he had struck her as being nice looking, he wasn't remarkable–average height, blondish-brown wavy hair, a well shaped mouth and good teeth–certainly not romantic looking and he wore rimless glasses. It had been something in his face, very kind, lonely; she had felt her own was mirrored in it. But how to tell anyone else about the disturbing feeling.

"Something the matter?" Bessie inquired, "You look kinda peaked.

"The heat, I guess," Irene sighed. "It might be one of these headaches coming on. Maybe I better not go tonight."

"Aw, come on." Bessie patted her hand. "You go on home and lay down, Honey. Put a cold wash cloth on your head and take some aspern. Soon's it cools off, you'll feel better. I'll whistle about nine."

As Bessie had said, after she had lain in the bedroom with a wash cloth across her temples until the silver-blue evening had filtered through the trees outside, and the noise of evening birds had gradually subsided into cricket song, Irene felt a surge of strange restlessness. She could not get that man out of her mind. She supposed she would not likely see him again, but she couldn't stop thinking about him so better she get out somewhere. She got up quickly and began to get ready for the dance. Ellen wandered in as she was slipping a white georgette blouse with a flowing bertha collar over her had and helped her smooth it down.

"Thought you were already over at Grandma's." Irene turned and patted her cheek. Ellen could feel a strange excited glow about her mother.

"Oh, we just got through the rehearsal for Mutual and I wanted to get my Sunday dress," Ellen said. As she moved away, she had the sensation that she had only seen that glowing look on her mother's face once a long time ago but she couldn't remember when.

When Bessie and Irene got to the Pandora, the music was blasting out through the open windows. Inside the floor was filled with laughing, sweating couples, some trying out new dances, the Big Apple, Black Jack. Others were just shuffling around in their own version of gaiety. The crepe paper streamers were swaying and trembling; nobody, looking on, would guess that the country was in the depths of the worst depression the modern world had ever known.

At the door Irene was overcome with a sudden sense of panic. I shouldn't have come, she thought, and could not imagine why she felt so light-headed, giddy. It was as though the music, noise, the thick, warm, multi-colored air were sucking her into an evil and intoxicating world. But before she could think about it, Joe Beck, one of the old steadies of the stag line, had swept her onto the floor. The spring suspended floor jiggled under them as they swept round and round adding to her giddiness.

Ed decided he'd better go back to the hotel for his tie and park the car there. It was only a couple of blocks to the dance hall and the walk would do him good. He was still not sure that he wanted to go dancing tonight, but the thought of spending the evening in that stuffy hotel room trying to untangle his snarled emotions filled him with despair. Out on the street again he glanced at the big four-sided clock on the bank corner; it was only nine-thirty. A few Saturday drunks laughed and lurched along the side walk. He could hear the noise from the pool hall but over and above it all, coaxing, sighing, offering balm to his troubled mind was music from the dance hall. By ten o'clock he found himself shoving the quarter through the mesh of the ticket office, and he lounged uncertainly into the foyer. There he leaned against the wall in the shadows, half-hypnotized by the gyrating figures.

It was a little while before his eyes becoming accustomed to the dim light that he saw her. She had stopped near the edge of the floor and was laughing at something her partner had said, a little man with a prominent Adam's apple and a red face topped by thin sandy hair. Ed jerked away from the wall with acute shock.

As he started forward, Irene turned, saw him, gasped and put her hand to her throat. Poor Joe thought he had said something wrong. Irene looked as though she were going to faint.

"You all right?" Joe asked anxiously "Lemme getcha a drink?"

"Oh, no," she murmured moving away from him, not knowing whether to advance toward the man or flee. "Thanks, I'll be alright...." She looked up into the eyes of Ed Barker who held out his hand to her.

Great, tragic love affairs don't begin in a crepe-paper decorated dance hall with a hoarse saxophone blurting "The Object of my affection can change my complexion from white to rosy red." They begin in great, polished ball rooms hung with glinting crystal chandeliers and a Viennese orchestra dressed in tuxedos playing Strauss waltzes. Everybody knows that from novels and the movies. Except Irene and Ed who moved into each other's arms as though the whole world had conspired to put them there.

Hours later as he walked her home under the deep blue sky filled with summer stars, listening to the rustle of a lazy night wind in the trees, the gurgle of irrigation ditches, the faint noises of cars speeding along the distant highway, they had begun to know the feelings of intense ecstasy and sorrow that come with late love and harsh obstacles–a love which comes when the heart is finally mature enough to accept it, yet when patterns of life are so irrevocably set that it is all but impossible to change them. Ed knew that he ought to get in his Buick that very hour and drive hell-bent for Salt Lake City and, in the future, find a route that would take him safely around Merritsville. Irene knew that she ought to close that little warped gate at her front yard between them and never think of him again.

They stood for a while on the front porch not saying much. Ed was so shaken by his feeling for her that he only took her very gently in his arms and pressed her close for a quick, dry kiss. "Can I see you again soon?" he whispered. She nodded, brushing her cheek against his shoulder. Pressing her hand, he leaped off the porch. "Next week, I'll try...."

Irene stood listening to his rapid footsteps retreating down the graveled path and sidewalk. Then she shivered violently from head to foot in spite of the fact that the night was still warm.

She had never spent such a night in her life. When she went into the warm, dark little house, it seemed lonelier than it had been since Laurence's death. Ellen was staying at Addie's as she always did nights Irene went out: the silence was thick and heavy both with presences and absences. It seemed an alien place, a dream through which she was groping her way carefully and slowly toward something which she had known would always be there. She did not turn on the lights, but undressed in the dark of her bedroom and lay down on the smooth clean sheet.

For a short while she felt very peaceful and drowsy, her body suffused with the pleasurable memory of Ed; she had almost dropped off to sleep when suddenly she was filled with such a flush of fever that she sat bolt upright and put both her hands to her face. In that twilight between sleeping and waking a shocking image had come to her mind of something so long forgotten that she winced with shame–those last nights with Laurence.... It passed and she lay back down feeling very near tears. She was perspiring and the rayon garments which she never removed day or night stuck to her with a malignant tenacity. She plucked them away from her legs and breasts and turned and twisted. Her breasts and thighs throbbed and she became conscious of a swelling in her genitals. Perhaps she had come sick early. Wearily she got up, went out to the bathroom and discovered that she had not. It was only the viscous liquid of desire so long quenched.

She slipped off her garments and began to sponge herself with cold water, wiping vigorously between her legs. As she picked up the sacred garments to put them back on she was seized with a fit of shaking so that she could hardly get them on. Then she caught sight of herself in the dim tilted mirror above the wash basin. In spite of herself she saw how beautiful her naked body was. She was half tempted not to put the garments back on, but then panic swept over her. How could she be so wicked? Slowly, almost contritely, she drew the unshapely garments on but, as she buttoned them up, she could still see the warm, glowing pink flesh, the tips of her nipples, the firm, smooth curve of her belly, through the sheerness. The horror of it almost caused her to faint. She could not, she absolutely could not want another man. She had been betrothed, promised, sealed to Laurence and only to Laurence for time and eternity. Especially she could not want a man who was married. Ed had told her that he was. The thought of him again filled her with an intolerable surge of desire, loneliness, anguish. She leaned over the basin, splashing water on her face and crying at the same time; sobs shook her whole body. She could not remember feeling such violent, mixed emotion in her whole life, not even when Laurence had died. There had been a protective numbness then, a slow, unreal seeping of sorrow into all the cracks of her being but this, this was the ultimate pain of life. Life had completely returned to her this night; she wanted it, how terribly she wanted it.

She wandered back to bed, torn between such exhaustion and exhilaration that she felt she must surely die of it. She thrashed about the bed, stretching her aching legs, wadding and pounding the pillows, tossing them onto the floor, retrieving them, sitting up, lying down, sobbing, then lying very still listening to the little, sad sounds of night and early morning. Through the hot surges of emotion, she had occasional fragments of lucid thought; it struck her to as absurd to imagine that this had happened in so short a time. It had not been quite twelve hours since she had met Ed Barker! How silly it all was. Scalding tears of self-pity and re-crimination ran down both sides of her face into her hair.

At last, as daylight was seeping into the room, resolving never to see him again, she got up, pulled the blinds and fell asleep. Later in the morning she regained consciousness slowly and painfully and was aware that she was in the clutches of one of her deadly migraine headaches. Groping out to the bathroom again, she swallowed some aspirin and went back to bed. The memory of the night was consumed in the abyss of merciful pain.

When Ellen came home after church, she knew that Irene had one of her headaches, so she was very quiet and careful and kept the radio down low as she crouched before it, listening to the Sunday broadcast of the New York Philharmonic.

Toward evening Irene awoke with a feeling of extreme peace, almost happiness. It was cooler, the green light was soft and soothing, her body was rested and life seemed altogether fuller and richer. For a moment she could not remember why; then the face of Ed Barker, his touch, the fine male smell of him came back to her. She must see him again, just to talk to, dance with. There would be nothing beyond that, Dear God, she promised–just friendship, companionship. Couldn't she have just that? She got out of bed, put on a light robe and shaking her hair about her shoulders, went out to the kitchen where Ellen was eating a sandwich and reading a book as usual. She was startled and puzzled by the look of intense rapture on Irene's face; it was as if she had learned an amusing and delightful secret. Irene came over and put her arm around Ellen's shoulder.

"What are you reading?" she asked. She felt a deep, almost overwhelming affection for her daughter. Poor child, they must come closer. She must do something about Ellen's hair. How straight and unbecoming it was, maybe get Lily Marsh to give her a permanent. She brushed it back thoughtfully and noted with a slight shock that the little girl had unmistakable signs of the woman about her. The front of her plain cotton dress had a suspicious roundness; the features of her quizzical face were losing their childish proportions. A sense of grief and panic swept over Irene. No mother is ever prepared for the fact that her daughter has to become a woman, like herself beset with the secret shame and sorrow as well as the glories of womanhood.

⚃

Ed slept as poorly as Irene, struggling with the apprehension and guilt that accompanied his intense physical desire for her and the knowledge that he would have to go home to Emily filled with a new passion that excluded his wife of many years. He now dimly realized that it had been a very long time since she had had any but the most conventional place in his consciousness. Quietly, sadly she had slipped away from him; she was the shadow of his duty and his place in society; the mother of his children and, he thought wryly–although bitterness was not in Ed's nature–the means of his livelihood. The frail picture that he had loved and cherished of her was now so faded like an old photograph that he could hardly make it out. He was not even sure that he had loved her in that way. But he knew he still loved her, felt bound to her in other ways.

At the crack of dawn Ed got up, dressed and started for Salt Lake. It was a radiant morning, a bit too hot for September; the summer seemed reluctant to go. Driving along the almost deserted highway through the rolling farm lands and small settlements, Ed felt a euphoria that he not experienced in many years even though at the back of his mind the memory of Irene's face, the sound of her voice, the fragrance of her lingered in a disturbing way.

Arriving home, he let himself into the house where preparation for Emily's birthday party was already underway in the kitchen. Several people noticed the unusual vigor and cheerfulness in him, most poignantly Emily. After shaving and showering, he strode into her room, laid the tissue wrapped box on her bed and kissed her affectionately. "Beautiful morning, Em," he said a bit too loudly."Beautiful day for a birthday. How're you feeling?" He pulled one of the satin-cushioned chairs up to the side of the bed and sat down astride of it backwards the way he had once done in his mother's kitchen.

Emily looked at him curiously and smiled faintly; her fine, pale oval face was overlaid with the shadow of illness, but she still had an appealing prettiness. "Better this week, I think," she said reaching for the package with a thin hand on which the blue veins stood out heavily like etchings of rivers on a map. It had been some time since Ed had inquired so energetically about her health. He usually tiptoed into the room after asking permission and sat uneasily on the edge of a chair with a sad, uncomfortable expression as though he could scarcely wait to get away.

"Can I open it now, before the party?" she asked coyly.

"Sure, sure hope you like it." Ed leaped up to help her with the ribbon.

"Sorry I couldn't get you anything better, Em. I stopped over to Washburn's yesterday while I was waiting for Hansen. It's the only nice store in town, but being Saturday and all... I know you don't like blue," he apologized as she shook the bed jacket out of the tissue. "It was about the only thing they had that I thought you might be able to use. Happy Birthday, Dear."

He leaned over, kissing her again and pressing her hand. He was flooded with a tender compassion for her that he had not known for years.

Emily tried to conceal a wry smile as she noted the size "40" on the label; a "32" would have been too ample for her thin shoulders. "Thank you, Dear," she patted his hand still resting on her arm. "It's quite lovely. I'm sure I'll enjoy wearing it."

"Come to think of it, I don't know why I got you a bed thing." Ed jumped off the bed and went to the window where he threw open the heavy brocade curtains and let the light filter through stiff lace curtains. "We're gonna get you up and outa here, Em. It's gonna be a beautiful fall. You just need to get out in the fresh air, get some exercise. Start to live again."

He came back to the bed, his hands thrust in his pockets and his shoulders thrown back. He looked younger than he had for years.

"You must have had a good week on the road," Emily said gently.

"Oh fair, fair to middlin' but things are gonna pick up, Em. They got to. I have a feelin' things are gonna change for the better. This depression has got to end soon; people wont stand for it much longer."

"Well, I'm glad to hear that. Bill and Fred don't seem to feel so optimistic. They say they're still a lot of men out of work. They say we may have to let some more go if business doesn't pick up."

Ed looked at her strangely. She wasn't generally interested in the business except as it affected her welfare. "Ought not to worry you with things like that," he murmured.

At that moment Mrs. Hales, the nurse, came in to give Emily her morning bath and medicine. Ed found that, as usual, he was relieved to get out of the sick room. He dodged out, promising to look in again later, wondering why he had burst in there so exuberant and feeling that once again he had been thrust outside Emily's guarded existence.

"Well, well, how's the birthday girl?" Mrs. Hales asked in the high-pitched falsetto that she used with her invalid patients thinking that she was bolstering their spirits. She bustled about efficiently, turning back the covers on Emily's thin, yellow legs, setting our her equipment.

"Oh, my, isn't this pretty?" she clucked, holding up the bed jacket. "From Mr. Barker?"

"Size forty," Emily said wryly. "He expects me to grow, I guess."

Mrs. Hales looked slightly distressed at Emily's sarcasm. "Oh, he probably didn't notice. Men don't know much about women's sizes and you know those sales girls, take advantage of a man every time just to make a sale. They don't care. No sirreee they don't care, just so they get a man's money. We can probably exchange it."

She wrung out her cloth and carefully began to wash Emily's withered leg; efficient, gentle as she was, Em could barely endure her extravagant sentimentality, the way she insisted on treating her as a feeble minded child. "Birthday girl", indeed, she thought.

As she watched Mrs. Hales bathe her emaciated body she reflected on the bitterness of her life. Ed's unexpected vigorousness had stirred something in her, some of the memories of her early happiness with him. For a long time, especially since the crash, he seemed to be losing his good wholesome spirits, the healthfulness and vitality that had attracted her to him, and given her strength and hope. Now she could no longer respond to him or partake of his high energies. She wondered what had brought on this outburst of youthfulness.

Like most invalids she had retreated to a world made up of strictly timed rituals: 8 o'clock, breakfast, 9 o'clock, bath and medication, 10 until noon, such household matters as she could take care of from her bed, decisions about the boys, 12 o'clock luncheon and medication, afternoon rest and frequently the doctor's visit, 5 o'clock dinner and a little reading or embroidery in the evening though her hands were becoming too stiff to do much of that anymore.

Sometimes she listened to the radio although she never liked it as it was so hard to depend on the quality of the broadcasts. Invariably by nine o'clock she would take her medicine and prepare for bed. Sometimes the boys or Ed, when he was home, would come in, being careful not to tire her. Her friends and sisters-in-law dropped in some afternoons and chatted in quiet, soothing tones, assuring her that she was looking ever so much better. Her brothers came punctually at three on Sunday between church meetings and stayed not later than four o'clock, fidgeting nervously on their chairs, looking at their watches and talking mostly to each other.

It had seemed exactly right to Emily, given her affliction. She had arranged her life in the best possible order; any deviation from it caused her extreme agitation as an unfortunate blob of color or smudged line irritated an artist. Hers was the consummate artistry of the weak, the sickly, the physically handicapped. She worked in the extremely malleable material of human guilt and pity. She had, until this strange morning of her fortieth birthday, been satisfied with her creation but now, after Ed's disturbing intrusion and the reminder of another year dwindling away, she felt as though she had awakened inside her coffin. The long rose-brocade draperies over thick ecru curtains, the muted and faded colors of the flowered carpet, the fat over-stuffed chairs and her big bed with its heavy satin old-rose coverlet all seemed to mute life into a kind of rose-colored shadow. The fresh fall roses that had been placed on a heavy legged mahogany table only an hour ago looked as though they were dying already.

Mrs. Hales had gathered up her paraphernalia and pushed her way through the polished gumwood door with her broad white behind, her taffeta petticoat rustling cheerfully and her high falsetto drifting away on bright words of cheer. Emily was alone and the room was just as it had been for almost twenty years; only the chair that Ed had straddled was out of place. Noting it she was filled with a flush of emotion that made her teeth chatter. She wadded up the blue bed jacket and wept into it bitterly.

But she did not weep long. It was the motif of her design that she would present to the world the picture of beautiful and noble suffering. Her whole patiently and painfully woven tapestry could not be destroyed by an unfortunate blue bed jacket. She looked at the tear stains which would surely arouse curiosity or comment, then carefully spread it where, if she knocked over the water glass, which she shortly intended to do, it would be drenched.

"Oh dear me, I'm so clumsy sometimes," she wailed pitiably as Mrs. Hales came at her summons to mop up the water and take the dripping garment away.

"Never you mind, Dearie, I'm sure it'll dry and press out as good as new so you might wear it this afternoon," she soothed, bursting with congenial maternalism.

"I'm feeling a little nervous this morning," Emily pleaded. Couldn't I have just a teeny bit more medicine?"

Mrs. Hales measured out some sedative and Emily drank it gratefully. As the warm liquid twilight filled her body, she sank back into the soft pillows, the dull rose light of the room casting a becoming flush over her pale cheek. Her big eyes closed into their violet shadows. She was wholly the picture of womanly suffering. Poor, brave dear, thought Mrs. Hales as she closed the door gently, the wet bed jacket over her arm. It was exactly the response Emily wished to evoke.

During the afternoon the heat which had lain like a heavy wet wool blanket on the city for almost a week grew even more suffocating. Big thick blue-black clouds rolled up and little darts of lightning kept licking the horizon.

The air in Emily's bedroom where the family had gathered for her birthday party was all but unendurable. A faintly nauseating medicinal smell of the sick room was mixed with the musty odor of clothes half soaked with perspiration and assorted perfumes. The men kept running their forefingers around the inside of their stiff collars and mopping their brows. The women fanned themselves with handkerchiefs or purses and shook the tops of their dresses. But there was a determined effort to keep up the festive atmosphere required at Emily's party.

She was seated in a bedside chair, wearing a pink satin robe the lace trimming of which framed her face becomingly. Ed thought she looked rested but still so fragile. Ice clinked in tall glasses of lemonade and there was a general buzz of conversation punctuated by "oohs" and "aahs" and gasps as Emily opened one after the other of the expensive, useless gifts. Her thin bluish hands trembled as she picked at the ribbons, and she usually ended by handing the gifts to Ed who competently stripped them of their tissue casings. Mrs. Hales stood nearby fanning her patient from time to time and exclaiming loudly over the gifts as one does with a child.

In spite of the heat, Emily was unusually animated and made a great deal of charming fuss about each of the gifts, replicas of which she had received every year for at least twenty years–handkerchiefs and sachet cases, bits of jewelry, nightgowns, trinkets. Having opened them all at last she explained in a demure and self-castigating manner about Ed's gift. He blushed furiously and was grateful that she had managed to get it out of the way, fearing that it would look more unsuitable and cheaper to the family than it was. He resolved hotly to be more conscientious after this, get one of his sisters-in-law to pick out something at Z.C.M.I. well in advance that would be more appropriate. He had always acquiesced in the family rituals and customs.

That is until this odd moment, when, after she had finished explaining about Ed's gift and her own unforgivable carelessness she reached out and took his hand. Her hand was cold as ice in this hot room. Shocked he glanced at her sideways and saw out of the corner of his eye that she was not perspiring or flushed but looked like one of those china dolls with their smooth pink faces and wide glassy eyes. She was completely unreal to him; as he glanced uneasily about the room, everything else, everyone else seemed equally unrecognizable. The light in the room was that odd, greenish-gold that filters through storm clouds: every small detail was chiseled out with sharp hard lines like the figures in the old-fashioned stereoscope on the library table. He knew he had never belonged here. He had always been the enchanted viewer with his eyes pressed into the dark hood that shielded the magic vision. This people had never been his people nor their ways his.

How stiff and false they all seemed. It was almost as though he had been stricken with double vision and could see the shells that looked like people sitting about this smothering room in a forced tableaux. The substance of them had fled the ordeal of pretense that surrounded Emily–Emily the little sick sister who must never be exposed to life because it would destroy her. They had all, including himself, participated in the deadly conspiracy of pity and duty which had prevented Emily from either living or dying decently. Even his sons. Ed looked at them, dressed up and sweating dutifully, vitiated sons of an invalid woman. They were pretty boys, Ed thought, pretty city boys who had been trained to pussy-foot around on carpets and gear all their activities so as not to disturb Mother. They had grown up with a reverent, unhealthy and even tragic ideal of Woman that would cripple them emotionally, maybe physically, as he had been.

He became intensely aware of the cold, bony little hand gripping his and how rigidly he was stuck to the uncomfortable satin chair. Emily's low, satiny voice was going on with a monologue that he realized with a start was about him "... blessed with the best of husbands, eighteen years this last January and never a cross word to each other, have we?"

He turned and met Emily's dark eyes–their unnatural glitter almost frightened him. "No, no, never one," he agreed somewhat lamely, patting her hand which she gently removed, smiling at him tenderly.

A great crash of thunder rolled across the rocky faces of the mountains and a sudden wind, smelling of mud and salt from the lake whipped the lace curtains and lashed the bowl of roses onto the floor. Tissue paper flew madly around the room and the women leaped up catching their hair and dresses. There was a flurry of excuses about open windows and children in the park and Emily's birthday party was over. Ed slammed the windows down and re-arranged the curtains and, in the dusk of the storm, he and Mrs. Hales picked up the papers, roses and scattered gifts and put the room in its usual sedate order.

Emily turned her now feverish face to the pillow and listened with a deep and strange sense of satisfaction to the sound of the thunder. She almost wished that the storm had come in and swept everything away, that everything had ended suddenly, grandly, dramatically, instead of the way she knew it now must–old rose petals falling away into rancid dust among yellowed laces. She would just dwindle and dwindle....

She closed her eyes and pretended to be asleep when Ed finally tiptoed over to the bed. As he stood looking at her in the twilight, he was struck with how very young, yet how old and ill she looked. He leaned over and kissed her forehead. She stirred, smiled and reached out a hand for him which he took reluctantly and tucked it under the covers. "Now you rest a bit, Em. This storm'll be over soon and you'll be better... the air'll be cleared out a bit and we'll...." But something choked him. He couldn't say what he thought the future would be for them. A great wave of sadness swept over him, violent as the cloudburst as he thought of Irene.

Like most mountain thunderstorms, the clouds turned inside out and emptied everything on the valley floor at once. It was over in an hour and the sun was slanting richly across the lake.

Ed had to get out of the dark house in which the heat was still imprisoned. The Avenues of Salt Lake City are on the steep north-eastern rise of the valley and the Fancher house had been built high up on them where it stood alone against the yellow-green hills. But now the narrow streets were canopied thickly over with trees, shading handsome homes with rocked-up lawns and elaborate rose gardens that had driven out the sagebrush and cheat grass. Ed climbed briskly up the wet streets under dripping trees, intent on getting above the rows and rows of solid, square-porched brick houses to where the scrub oak and sagebrush and rocks had not yet been disturbed. He found a huge rock, brushed the water out of a hollow and sat down, looking out over the valley.

He had never felt natural beauty more acutely. Not even the hours and days he had spent hunting and fishing in the mountains when he had been young and full of life. The deep blues and purples of the mountain blended into the floating cloud mists of the sky joining the hazy blues and opalescent mauves of the far lake. The city was a serene stretch of freshly washed greens and yellow-greens with deep blue shadows threaded together by the shining strips of wet concrete and asphalt. The great rocky faces of the mountains had a fine, dull gold sheen. He could not remember ever having seen the world quite like this before. It almost hurt. He ached with sorrow and desire, the face of Irene floated before him in the bluish mist and merged with the image of Emily. Both women were strangely fused. He needed them both; both needed him. Why hadn't he taken Emily out of that great tomb of a house festering with the dead past. He could have built a sunny, sturdy bungalow over there on the eastern slope of the hills south of the University where all the young upcoming people had built. She could have gotten well and strong. He had a feeling of intense despair that it was his fault that she was ailing, near death. And Irene? There was something desperate in her eyes too as though she needed rescuing.

The euphoria Ed had felt during this short hour diminished. It was 1934, the middle of the depression, and Ed Barker was a middle aged man who, in spite of a tantalizing glimpse of a new life, was trapped in circumstances he could not change. As he wandered back toward the house under the wet trees he reached up and picked a leaf. A shower of raindrops fell on him; the cold water felt like sparkling crystals pelting his warm face and neck. He had an impulse to take off his shoes and stockings and wade in the swiftly running gutter as he had once done in the irrigation ditches on the ranch. Not quite ready to admit that he had fallen in love, Ed dropped the leaf gently, with an air of reverence in the rushing water of the gutter. He would try to get Emily out more into the fresh air and beauty of nature, salvage something of their life but somehow, he would find his way back to Merritsville.

CB

Tongues began to wag in Merritsville about the third week that Ed Barker showed up at the Pandora and claimed most of Irene's dances. And the way she danced with him, like a woman in a dream! Some of the local dandies who had put an extra press in their J.C. Penney suits and an extra dash of brilliantine on their hair in delicious anticipation of getting their arms around Irene's waist had their noses cut off. There was muttering at intermission about gangin' up on them damn city slickers who came corruptin' our women and girls with their high falutin' city ways. For although Ed still felt himself something of a gawk in the city, he had taken on a lot more polish than he suspected. Emily had always insisted that his suits be tailored and she had his shirts and ties sent up from Auerbach's or Z.C.'s for her own personal selection. Besides which he was a good dancer. Irene was conscious and proud of the impression he was making.

The animosity toward him, however, got only so far as letting all the air out of his tires one night. After that he parked the Buick at Irene's which was only a couple of blocks from the Pandora, and they walked to the dance with Bessie. Irene had heard the rumors that were beginning to circulate, "Irene Kent's got a beau, some guy from out of town," so she insisted that Bessie accompany them both to and from the dance as far as Irene's gate. But the town was not fooled. Sister Bates got up at 2 a.m. with her cough and saw the car still parked in front of Irene's house and two shadowy figures pressed together on the porch. Sister Davis knew they didn't come in until three o'clock one morning. She heard the car pulling up just as her mantle clock struck three.

That was the night Ed had coaxed Irene to let him take her to dinner in Provo after the dance because there were no decent eating places closer. He was only a little annoyed when she insisted they take Bessie and Bessie accepted.

Reputation in a small town is worth more than a man's (or woman's) purse and often costs a great deal more to keep up.

Gradually the sweet syrup of pity and sentiment that the town held for Irene began to turn to the vinegar of suspicion, envy and moral indignation. But Irene had more things to worry about than putting up an appearance of virtue which was, in fact, genuine. As much in love as they were, as deeply and passionately aroused as she found herself, Irene could not face the ultimate surrender. She held tenaciously to her vision of herself as a "good woman," one who had taken eternal vows of chastity. Ed was patient, desiring her to the point of agony but afraid of forcing her too fast, himself bound by older ideas of love and lust.

Then there was Ellen to think of. Ellen knew about Ed. Generally she avoided meeting him by being at Grandma's when he came around, but one Saturday night she was home when he came early for Irene. She opened the front door, and they stood looking at each other in embarrassment until Irene dashed out of the bedroom, sweeping her hair over her shoulders and flushed with excitement, to introduce them. Irene pushed Ellen nervously toward Ed who was holding out his hand self consciously. Ellen took it reluctantly, wishing her mother would get over her bad habit of pushing her like she was a baby. She noticed that he was very red in the face, and his hand was warm and sticky; she thought he wasn't very good looking nor nearly so young looking as her mother. Irene had talked him up as though he were something special. She dropped her hand as soon as she could and turned away from him.

"Now you two just set down and get acquainted," Irene urged cheerfully, "while I finish getting ready. I won't take but a minute." Ellen could hear the false, nervous note, her store voice, only with a tremor in it. Ed sat down in the old rocking chair by the stove, and Ellen took the chair on the other side, deliberately half out of his sight so that if he talked to her, he was obligated to peer around the stove.

He asked her questions like did she like school and what did she like to do most? She answered him in short, curt monosyllables so that pretty soon she had him running his finger around under his collar and rubbing his hands together. She set her mouth derisively and arched her eyebrows; she was not going to make it too easy for him. When she said that she liked to read more than anything, he brightened a little and said he liked to read too–if he had more time.

Ed looked uneasily around the small room. The faded carpet on the floor was covered with heavy braided rugs on the worn spots. Besides the settee, a stiff squarish piece of furniture with wooden arms and decorated with hand-crochet doilies, there was an assortment of odd chairs, each with ruffles, cushions and doilies. The piano filled most of one wall and there was large radio between the doors that led into the kitchen and hall. A huge fern stand made of gilded sticks woven round like a basket filled one corner, and there were plants in all the deep window sills. The plants all looked healthy and cared for.

The room was very clean and the piano actually gleamed. On top of it was a forest of photographs in gilt frames; the largest was of a young man with a fine, sad face. Ed knew that it was Laurence Kent and was filled with envy and sadness. He liked this room, felt at home here.

He looked affectionately at the short, plump legs of the little girl in their square brown Oxfords and short stockings sticking out on the other side of the stove and the top of the shining brown head bent forward so that he could not see the stubborn little face which had shown him frank distrust. He had the fleeting impression that it was very like that young face in the photograph. Perhaps in time she would come to like him, forgive him his feeling about her mother. At last he ventured, "Do you play the piano?"

Ellen got up self-consciously and went over to the piano where she stood in front of it defensively. "No," she said, "not much but my mother does. My father used to play the violin and they used to play and sing together all the time."

Out of the side of her eyes she could see that she had made Ed wince: it gave her a great sense of self-satisfaction at the same time she was aware of her meanness. She wondered why she felt so mean about him. She could hear her mother humming the tune of one of the popular songs as she finished dressing for the dance;

it irritated her that she could be happy about this stranger in their life.

Irene came out of the bedroom, her face radiant and twirled around in front of them to show off her new dress. Why did she have to act like that? Just like Lorraine did around that old Ted Mullin. And right there with her father sitting on top of the piano, just like she had forgotten he ever was, and she was happy to be going out with some strange man to the dance. When she put her arm around Ellen, Ellen pulled away stiffly.

Irene understood and for a moment was frightened. She had been trying to think of a way of telling her about Ed, of explaining how she felt about Laurence and him. But truth was, she didn't really know herself. That day when she had been dusting the piano, she almost moved the photo of Laurence into her bedroom but thought better of it. Ellen and Addie would be sure to notice and think she was forgetting him.

"You're late getting over to Grandma's. She'll be worried," she said nervously as she fussed with her hair.

"I'm not going," Ellen announced archly; "I told her last week, I'm old enough to stay by myself, besides I want to hear the Hit Parade. Grandma's radio don't work very well."

Irene paused in distress, then shrugged. Ellen was getting very snippy lately; she had always had the stronger will of the two, so without saying more, Irene shrugged into the wrap that Ed was holding for her.

"Be sure to lock all the doors, then." Irene pecked her on the forehead.

Ellen threw herself on the couch and peeked out of the lace curtain, annoyed at the way the man had his arm half around her mother's waist as they went down the walk and the way he helped her into the car, so fancy like, you'd think she'd break. But he had a swell car anyway. Maybe he would take her for a ride in it someday and make the other kids jealous. Maybe he was rich and would take them away from Merritsville and buy them a big house. Elaborate dreams swelled her head, and she saw herself on a fine, big carpeted stairway like the ones Bette Davis was always running up or down in the movies about the South. She would have a floaty, green chiffon dress and high heels and a maid to fix her hair all the time–but a cold thought struck her. Irene would have to marry him if all that happened and then he'd be her step-father! Step-fathers and mothers were apt to be cruel though Ed didn't act like a mean man, but you could never tell.

Marriage was still a mysterious, repelling idea all mixed up with what she read in books, saw in movies or heard the other girls talking about. The thought of it gave her shudders and goose pimples. It was a beautiful, white wedding dress and a handsome man, silver bells and white satin bows and a dance in the recreation hall–and mysterious things that went on in the Temple at Salt Lake. But the thought of her mother marrying that *old* man was just plain nasty.

Dejected she got off the couch and switched on the radio. As the crackling noises began to issue from the round speaker cabinet, Ellen had a curious desire to look inside the upper part as she remembered doing a long time ago when her father had shown it to her. She moved the doily and bowl of paper flowers that Irene kept on top of it and opened the lid. The tubes were all glowing bright, yellow-orange and, as she turned the dials, rows of semicircular plates meshed sinuously. It reminded her of a miniature city of the future with strange shaped house in which she imagined tiny people running about among lighted towers producing the music and voices that burst out of the speaker in a confusion of sounds. She felt big and powerful, a creature from another world who had this one in her power. She amused herself by blending all the odd bits of sound that came from the stations as she twisted the dial–music, advertisements, news, bits of an early evening drama–a crazy muddle of nonsense. She could switch them on or off, the people in the box and they were helpless. She felt like God!

She had begun to think a great deal about God this past year and was always trying to find new ways of understanding what He was up to. The things she heard in church didn't make her like Him very much. He seemed to switch people and things on and off just like she was doing without good reason. When she tried to ask her mother or grandmother questions about "why," they looked solemn and said "there were things we weren't supposed to understand." But Ellen thought that if God gave you a mind that was supposed to help you know and understand, why were there questions that you weren't supposed to ask? The

Church said that the "Glory of God was Intelligence." Ellen thought she was intelligent; she was good in school and could find out things in books. The church books only confused her.

She sighed and closed the lid of the radio, turning to the station that broadcasted the Hit Parade. Bringing her notebook and pencil, she sat down on the rug, close to the speaker and prepared to write down all the songs in the order of their popularity that week. It was one of the sacred rituals of the crowd of girls of which Ellen was a half-hearted member. But she liked music and thought how she would like to dance someday like her mother and Ed.

In time, as Ellen became accustomed to Ed, she lost much of her resentment of him, but her feelings were always precariously balanced. She was not long in sensing how much he meant to Irene. Although she was glad for her mother's happiness, she was still a little jealous that someone else, someone not at all connected with the family could have intruded in their lives. She felt a flush of anger if she ever happened on them "necking" as she coldly put it, and when Ed tried to pat her affectionately she shrugged him off so icily that he didn't try it anymore. On the other hand, she found him comfortable and congenial. Sometimes he and Irene included her on their long Sunday drives or took her to dinner in a real restaurant. And she knew that Ed gave her mother money and things to help out occasionally. Once in a while he brought her a present, usually a book, but he was never silly or pally with her. She noticed that he had nicer manners than most men around Merritsville and was spiffier looking. She took a little cautious pride in the fact that her mother had a "classy" boyfriend who drove a big car.

As the relationship began to take on a regularity that seemed more natural than not, she didn't worry about it too much. Sometimes the kids made sly remarks about her mother's "guy" and asked if she was going to have a new Dad. The thought did trouble her and she flinched at the idea of someone trying to fit into the place her father had held. She didn't know until much later that Ed was not able to marry her mother because he was already married; Irene had not been able to tell her. It would come as a shock, which like God and so many other adult things, she found baffling.

CB

In spite of their great and growing desire for each other, of which they were aware with the slightest touch, Ed and Irene had put off their final intimacy. They struggled through long hours of frustration, but Ed's feelings were becoming more urgent. He found himself looking for places where it might happen. It had to be some place better than the dingy motels struggling for survival along the highways. He could never take Irene into one of those sour cramped rooms with sagging lumpy beds, faded chipped linoleum that smelled of poor plumbing where he spent some of his nights on the road. He dare not suggest that they go to one of the Salt Lake hotels, not only because of the possibility of exposure, but because he had had an encounter or two with *bad* women on some out of state conferences in big posh hotels. They symbolized dens of iniquity to him.

As he retraced this side of his life, its barrenness became increasingly apparent. He had been a virgin when he married Emily, if you didn't count a few unsuccessful experiments that had filled him with terror. Since he had carried into the elegant bedroom of the Fancher house, along with Emily, the vision of "pure" womanhood, he was not greatly disturbed by the moderate sense of incompleteness that he experienced there on his wedding night and after. He accepted that it was as old Bill Fancher had said— man had to live with a certain element of bestiality in his nature and only a good woman could keep it in check by denying its existence. There had been another woman for Bill, Ed suspected, one discreetly hinted at, but Emily often mentioned that she was proud of the fact that her father could never let another woman take her mother's place.

Ed was plagued in a moderate measure with the ambivalence about sex that is the heritage of the Western male between seeing the woman as the object of a forbidden lust and the incarnation of a holy ideal. Irene had aroused depths of both physical and emotional desire that he had never dreamed existed in himself. He was no uninitiated rube; the very nature of his work had resulted in a loss of innocence. As a "traveling salesman" he had been exposed often enough to the seamy side of life and the double standard frequently practiced by a lot of the brethren. He soon learned that it was sound business to look the other way and live and let live. He took an occasional drink and tried to smoke an occasional cigar to put the men with whom he had to associate at ease. He had seldom been tempted by the women he met on the road; basically shy with women and wary both by nature and training, there were a number of things about his own sexuality that he had never had to confront until now. There were times that he was over excited to the point of agony and had to let it go, much to his chagrin, by leaving hastily for the restroom or jumping out of the car.

He sensed the conflict in Irene, too. For fear that if he tried to take possession of her before she had worked things out in her own mind, he would lose her, he held back. The thought of losing her was too painful. Part of his mind was often occupied with visualizing some place, some time, some way that would make *it* different from all that he had had before–wouldn't cheapen it. A beautiful natural place, a mountain grotto, in deep shadows of secretive pines where nature would make right what society and man had spoiled. Could there could be a pure, sweet mating without the marriage bond that tied a man and woman to such bitter and torturing realities? Not that he wouldn't marry her in a minute! In truth he hoped that *something* would make it possible someday, Emily's health...? The thought was too frightening. Actually, when he was home, he was more tender and solicitous of Em than he had been before. It was all a tormenting, hopeless affair that drove him sometimes to the edge of despair.

Irene was tormented in a different way. The definition of goodness that ruled her life was that of the church. For woman it was spotless chastity and religious duty. Any other qualities besides being an immaculate housekeeper and mother which qualities were inherent in the above were almost irrelevant. Irene had fulfilled all the ideals. Her life had made it easier to do so until she met Ed Barker. Her marriage to Laurence had been the idyllic marriage of a young girl and boy, an Adam and Eve in a western Eden. They found in each other's arms the shelter and joy of two loving children. Even the birth of her child had not brought to Irene the full awareness of the pain which love inflicts upon man and woman when they merge into oneness both physically and spiritually. She did not know this until their last weeks together.

That last trip home from the herd Laurence had shown an almost desperate hunger in his love making, an intensity of desire and passion that had exhilarated, but frightened, her.

He made her aware of her body in a different way, of its power over a man, stirred depths of pleasure that frightened but attracted her. And then had so cruelly been taken from her. The shock of his death and the birth of her poor dead little son had made her even more frightened of the consequences of a brush with sin. Even in marriage such lust must be wrong. How much worse outside of it with a married man!

That first agonizing night that she met Ed had awakened those feelings and fears. A dark, feverish symphony, the first bars of which Laurence had created, began to throb and sing in her mind and body. Clinton had made her aware of the value of her body as giving pleasure although in a remote way. She knew men liked to look at her; she was a decoration in the store like the mannequins. When he smoothed and arranged clothes on her, fastened a necklace around her throat or patted her affectionately she felt not the slightest tremor of desire in either of them. She understood that the look of pleasure in Clinton's eyes came from having created a vision like those in the fashion magazines, of woman as a commercial object. But Ed. When his hands touched her, she tingled all over. It was though he were molding her too, only in a different way, for a different reason, just for himself. She felt the full softness of her breasts, the curve in her back where his hand rested lightly just above the swelling of her buttocks as they danced. Although he was never "fresh," she could feel the burning desire in his hands to smooth downward, to caress her thighs. Sometimes when they lingered fondling, or "necking" as Ellen put it scornfully, she thought that she had become another woman, a new woman. The roundness of her throat and shoulders had never been so real until Ed stroked and kissed them. Even her lips seemed to take on a new fullness and fineness when he kissed them as though he would like to eat her. Never before Ed Barker had she had impure thoughts. She could feel the hot blush rising to her cheeks and a flush of fear when once or twice Ed's hand strayed to her crotch and she pushed him away abruptly. He almost always left her hot and sticky down there, much to her embarrassment.

Whatever her desires and needs, the laws of Irene's life were quite clear and uncompromising. No good woman did *that* outside of marriage and the possibilities that Ed could marry her as she so well knew, were slim. He couldn't divorce an invalid woman; no telling how long Emily would live. Irene never dared think about that. As for her, the Temple ritual had sealed both her body and soul to one man *forever*. The sacred garments stood between her and her desires like a sheath of iron. Sometimes when she was overcome with shame at the thoughts that crept into her mind and the sensations that swept over her when she was in his arms or even remembered some warm moment, she was tempted to believe that Ed Barker had been sent by the Devil to destroy her.

So far in almost the year of their acquaintance Ed had made no demands on her. Whenever he sensed her fear and reluctance, he had been the perfect gentleman, backing off and soothing her. Of course their meetings were not too frequent and were almost all public and chaperoned by the ubiquitous Bessie, but she knew, as he knew, that they would have to come to a time of decision. Toward that time she prepared a little speech, rehearsing it over in her mind from time to time. It was to be a noble, simple speech about how she had to live up to her ideals and her vows to Laurence. She was sure he would despise her if she did not. They would be "just friends" with good memories. Irene was never very good with words; the speech did not please her, but she intended to rely on some tender gestures to keep things on a high plane.

But she hoped to put off the delivery of this farewell address as long as possible. She dare not, in fact, face it. She could not imagine life without him. The vision of herself on Bertha's stool, growing old, withered, shaky, dispensing garments from behind Washburn's counter for the rest of her life with no man to love and no one to love her shook her deeply.

It was summer and Saturday night again. Ed had managed to make it to Merritsville and he and Irene were dancing somewhat limply at the Pandora where, even with windows open and crepe paper swaying in a sultry breeze, the heat was overwhelming. Irene had thought about the dance all day in the suffocating heat of the store, half not wanting to go, but wanting to see Ed. Ed had thought about it all day as he pounded down the hot highway. But now they were here, in each other's arms it was somewhat less than they had anticipated. It was certainly too hot to dance close and Irene, although she had bathed late in cool water and applied a lot of talcum powder, felt sticky and untidy. Ed seemed to guide her around the floor mechanically, and he kept looking over her head as though searching for something or someone else. He even answered her questions with listless monosyllables as though his mind were somewhere else. Once he left her for almost two dances and while she was dancing with Piggy Peterson, she was seized with panic. What if he were tired of her? Would he leave her to drop back into the old, weary, empty life? She was flooded with such fear that she could hardly endure the struggle around the floor with the sweating Piggy. She wanted to break and run after Ed, to cling to him, never let him go. She would give up her job and ride with him on his travels anywhere, do anything, except to go back to the death she had known before he had come. When she sighted him threading back through the crowd, mopping his forehead with his handkerchief, obviously looking for her, she could have cried with relief.

Leaving Piggy almost rudely, she grasped Ed's arm. "Let's get out of here, it's too hot to dance. I'm suffocating," she whispered breathlessly. He looked at her in pleased surprise and squeezed her hand.

"I was thinking of that. I'm about cooked. It's a lot cooler outside."

They found Bessie and told her that Irene had a headache; indeed Irene had that intense feeling of strain and excitement which usually preceded one of her crushing headaches. A thick mist was rising up between her and all the realities of her life.

They got into the car and drove away from the dance hall, away from the sleepy, suffocating little town toward the lake. Ed eased the car over the rough road that he was not familiar with, but he had an urgent need to get away from all the things that they knew. Presently they came to a grove of trees that had once surrounded an old lake-side resort. The lake had receded and the resort had been deserted a number of years ago. Only the cement foundations of the buildings and the big, crumbling hole of the pool remained. The cracks were filled with vines and weeds and the grass grew high under tall, lacy topped walnut trees whose limbs interwove to form a canopy over a small picnic area. There was a slender moon caught in them.

Ed got out of the car without speaking and spread a blanket he always carried in the thick grass; silently but trembling and very close to nervous tears Irene followed and they lay down on the blanket. Looking up through the trees they could see the moon and pale distant stars of the silent summer night. The tenderest little breeze stroked the grasses and all the leaves sighed softly. With a flush of overwhelming pain, relief, sorrow, ecstasy, they went into each other's arms. Ed's dreaming came into sharp and clear realization and Irene's farewell speech was pressed back on her eager, anguished, hungry lips. As he entered her, the hot joy swelled her whole body; she knew they were bound for whatever life lay ahead.

At last they lay back quiet, at peace and so full of each other that everything seemed exactly right–the stars were in their exact places, the trees were exactly the right height and shape, exquisitely graceful, the breeze was exactly the right temperature. The shrilling sound of crickets and somewhere in a warm muddy pool a frog croaking, were exactly the sounds that should fill a summer night–the world was what it should be and should have always been.

Ed thought it was the closest that he could come to a truly religious experience–gratitude and awe for the goodness and rightness of all things. Why had he been taught or led somewhat vaguely to believe that this intense fusing of two souls through physical union was wrong, outside the sanction of the churches? True he knew the words–holy bonds of matrimony–but in what he had experienced and gathered from other men, it seldom ever happened in that circumstance. It had certainly not happened in this way in his marriage.

But he was too content at the moment to quibble. To hell with all that, he thought, feeling a great sense of joy and well-being at the touch of the woman at his side. Oh, if only he could reach out and feel her there every night–think of the sterile years, those long cold-sheet, empty-bed years he had spent!

He gave her a gentle squeeze. She had been lying so quietly, warm and fragrant against him that he was shocked when he leaned over to kiss her again to find that her face was wet with tears. As he kissed her and smoothed her hair which had come loose, she shook with convulsive sobs. When after he had held her, soothing her with some gentle words of love, she had quietened, she whispered with deep anguish, "Oh, we shouldn't have, Ed, darling. I've done a terrible thing. I've sinned so terribly."

"No, no, no," he protested, absorbing some of her misery and beginning to feel guilty. "Don't say that. It seemed so right. Didn't it seem right to you?" She nodded in affirmation against his chest. "I've thought and thought and tried to figure out something else, some way. But I've wanted you so much, so long. You seemed like you wanted me, didn't you...?" he asked anxiously.

"Oh, yes, oh yes, my dearest," Irene murmured in a tear thickened voice. "But why couldn't it have been different?"

She sat up and began putting on her dress. Her body still glowed until she felt that there must be a halo of light around her. She had the sensation that if she were touched she would crumble like those brittle mantles on the old-fashioned gas lanterns.

"You weren't married in the Temple, you said?" she stammered, feeling a surge of pain and fear. "You can't realize what I've done, Ed. I'm to blame, not you. You don't have as much to answer for as I do."

She turned away from him, the shadows of the trees obscuring her. Ed was afraid to touch her; she seemed almost angry. "Perhaps I have more, my Darling, more. I should have been stronger. I do know what... you're up against and we're together in this. I never, never felt more together with anybody in my life. I have to feel what you do, I have to suffer what you suffer... I," he began to feel the words clogging in his throat. "I should have waited until I could have asked you honorably to be my wife but I... don't know when...." He reached out to touch her shoulder. Tears had come to his own eyes. He fumbled for his handkerchief; it was wet and sticky. He had used it after their love making. He flung it into the grass.

"Look, Irene, I'll stay away, I'll not see you again if that's what you want. I don't want to hurt you for anything in the world."

She turned to him in panic; putting her hands on his face, she

felt the tears and tried to brush them away. "No! no!" Her voice
was almost harsh. "No, it's done. It can't be changed. I can't stand
to be without you, to be alone anymore. God must be punishing
me for something I did wrong but if I have to suffer, I'd rather
suffer this way than that. Do you know what it is like to be alive
and not feel anything, not anything for years? To feel like you're
walking around dead?

He clutched her tightly, burying his head in her shoulder. "Yes,"
he whispered, "Oh, God, yes."

The choice Irene made that summer night of 1935 was made
from the old instinct of woman. When Ed had left her so long and
unaccountably on the dance floor that night, she knew she had to
do anything to hold him, even surrendering herself and her high
ideals. So began a long period of torment, punctuated by hours of
ecstasy and deep fulfillment and paid for with hours of fear, humiliation and self doubt. Surely Merritsville would soon guess
that she was a sinful woman.

She didn't know which was worse–the fear that she was going
to be found out and shamed or her own struggle with her teachings and conscience. All her life she had heard those phrases and
words–"living in sin," "adultery," "fallen woman." They were
mentioned in church frequently: she had heard them all said of
others whose unspeakable conduct had horrified her in the past.
Could she be one of those fallen scarlet women? Then there was
the fear that what she felt for Ed was wrong and not real. She had
loved two men deeply and genuinely, she thought. But if she were
to be with one man only for all of eternity, how could both loves
be true? Sometimes she was a ashamed of the consuming physical hunger she felt for Ed, the secret passion that made her body
flame and prickle and ache day and night. There was the remote
but nevertheless present fear of eternal damnation for her sins.
The conflict was strong enough to impel her to one courageous
act–she stopped wearing her Temple garments.

Clinton had quickly noticed the change in Irene and her fluc-
tuating moods. He suspected that she had consummated her affair when he observed she was not wearing her garments. Although he was elated because they had always caused a problem
with fashionable clothes, he was surprised to find himself seized
by a rather sharp pang of jealously. He reprimanded himself. He

could never have made her a satisfactory lover because it was not what she was that he could have loved. It was what he could have made of her, given the chance. How he would have displayed her in all the big cities where he would have been a fashion buyer had the Depression not set him down here. But then he would never have known her, anyway. Clinton sighed as he checked orders in the stock room and looked for another dress she might wear to a good advantage.

This love affair with this hick salesman into which she had fallen was likely not only to ruin his creation but take Irene out of Merritsville, he thought with irritation and a tinge of disgust for all the accidents of life that interfere with Art. But the generosity of Clinton's nature squelched his disappointment, and he began to try to help her even more to acquire those skills and a smooth professional shell that would protect her from the nastiness of the world when she finally had to confront it.

He began to hint that he knew something of her emotional turmoil and to offer little bits of advise and comfort in the way of sophisticated knowledge that he hoped would put her wise.

"You know, Irene," he mentioned one afternoon, leaning on the counter where she was arranging some jewelry, "I wish I could take you to New York or San Francisco or even Denver and let you see what the world is like. You belong somewhere else than this poky town."

Irene looked up and smiled. She had begun to understand his sympathy and trust his good sense.

"Oh, I don't know, I like it well enough here."

"Yeah, I know, but there's a lot more to the world than this. A woman with your looks and talent could go a long way in the retail or wholesale fashion business. You've got a fine sense of style, color... I'll tell you, I'm getting out of here first chance I get, soon's this mess is over. I never thought the Depression would last this long." He straightened up and loosened his collar. The summer, the Depression, the whole ordeal seemed interminable and now he had this to worry about. He knew it wouldn't be long before the town would turn on Irene, and she would have to find some way out. How he wished he might take her away himself, get her a place where she would be safe from more hurt. But that was out of the question.

"Come look at some of these fabric samples, when you get time," he mentioned, patting her hand. Time might fix things somehow.

CR

On the surface Irene's life continued much the same but underneath she sensed that it had changed irreversibly. Sometimes she was seized with fears so overwhelming that she could scarcely contain them; she could see everyone in the town pointing a finger at her for her dreadful sins; could see it written in huge, red letters posted on the main street IRENE KENT HAS COMMITTED ADULTERY. She had read *The Scarlet Letter* in high school. At that time she could never have understood such a thing, but now she imagined herself a Hester Prynne, wearing a visible badge of shame. Yet nothing was as powerful as the intense longing to be with Ed, the sheer physical need to feel his hands on her breasts, his mouth on her, her legs wrapped around his and the hot feverish motions that filled her body with little glowing bubbles of ecstasy. But that was not all.

They had discovered that their tastes and needs were very much alike in addition to the physical attraction. Both enjoyed dancing and movies. Neither drank nor smoked so they would have been ill at ease in night clubs of which there weren't many anyway. Irene loved dining out in style and, although it was risky, Ed occasionally took her to the nicer restaurants in Salt Lake, even to the dining room of Hotel Utah. They both liked long drives in which they sat close together, not talking, just happy with each other. One of the things they enjoyed most was picnicking in good weather in the many surrounding hills and canyons. Ed had loved the out of doors when he was younger, and now that he had met Irene, the pleasure he felt in the open among trees, plants, rocks and streams was renewed and doubled.

Irene, though she generally avoided physical discomfort or strenuous activity, liked fixing picnics and spending long, lazy afternoons in the canyons or on the warm hillsides where they could find the privacy they needed. There were so few other places they could go.

It was more than a year since Irene and Ed had become lovers–early fall. It had been a ravishingly beautiful day as only autumn days in Utah can be. They had been dancing the night before at a new place in Summerville–a sort of semi-night club where chicken dinners were served and there was a small dance floor and juke box. Although they got home late, they decided to picnic the next day. Ed had a room at the hotel; neither would have dared stay together in town.

Just after noon Ed picked Irene up. She had gone to Sunday School where she still played the organ. Ellen had gone on down to Addie's after church since she knew Ed was coming. Although used to his seeing her mother, she was still a little put out that he spent so much time with her.

Irene had the food ready and was dressed in a dusty pink blouse and new navy blue slacks. Clinton had persuaded her to try them in hopes of getting the towns women to start wearing them. Although Ed was not accustomed to seeing women in pants, he was pleasantly disturbed by the way their smooth lines revealed her gently rounded buttocks and thighs. He gave her a sly, gentle pat on the bottom as they headed for the car and she protested mildly.

Driving up the canyon to one of their favorite spots where the aspen were vibrant splotches of light against heavy, dark pines, they spread an overall quilt among drying grasses, ate leisurely and then made love. Their passion had been growing steadily and today seemed to have mounted to a fine feverish pitch tempered only by the depth of their feelings for each other. As they explored each other's bodies joyously the exquisite delights of all senses bloomed with unusual vibrancy. He brought her up slowly twice, quivering with joy at the pleasure he could both give to and take from her. Irene abandoned her total being to him, responding with every fiber to his tender but urgent demands. How right, complete, fulfilled she felt in his arms. How profoundly their lives fused into harmony with each other and the mysteries of the world around them.

It was a particularly beautiful spot where they lay very close, desire quieted, with part of the quilt pulled over them. They had spread it in a cluster of aspen trees that stood against a semi-circle of tall, thick pines. The thin, bright yellow leaves of the aspen caught the sunlight with such extravagance that they formed a filigree of gold lace against the far, smooth blue of the September sky. The somber darkness of the pines, so dark they seemed to contain a thousand nights in each of their branches, only made the fragile light of the aspens more poignant. The sweet melancholy of the fall air bestowed a mysterious aura on their union, heightening both its eternal and ephemeral nature. Young love cannot have this extra dimension of beauty added by the shadows of sadness and loss.

Irene grew drowsy and, after she had rearranged her clothes, she turned away and fell asleep. Ed found he was too exhilarated to sleep so he got up carefully so as not to disturb her and tucked the quilt around her shoulders. Wandering down the slope, he came to where the trees opened out on a flat; he could see far across the misty valley. The crispness in the air stung him with a sense of new life. In these past two years he had accepted the limitations of his life, not dwelling too much on what might have been or what he would like it to be, but now something was stirring in him. He sensed change, whether for good or ill, he could not tell.

He sat down with his back against a warm tree and picked up a fallen branch from which he thoughtfully picked the bark. His mind drifted back to the years when he had had dreams, when he had spent a lot of his time out in the beautiful country that surrounded the small towns and cities. Maybe he would have been better off never to have left the ranch, the country life. It had been wrong for him to try to be a city man. His life with Emily appeared to him to have been something like a badly written play in which he had had a clumsy, bit part.

At first it seemed that he could bridge the two lives. Old Bill Fancher had. Ed thought of the times he had hunted with Old Bill in just such places. The old man had been a genuine, old time sportsman. They would camp for a week at a time, hunting leisurely, enjoying the scenery, the rough simplified camp life and the feeling of freedom. A man felt like a man at those times. He missed the old man with whom he had grown closer than his own father, but then it startled him to think what he might do or think if he knew about this. He would never have stood for his daughter being cheated on. Ed sighed and whipped the grass with the stick.

But things were all different. After the old man died, Ed was delegated occasionally to take some of the out-of-town clients on hunting trips since neither of the brothers-in-law liked to hunt. It was part of promoting one of Fancher's most substantial lines—guns. Ed thought of his fine ones at home in Salt Lake in the fancy mahogany case that Emily had had built for them. He smiled wryly. He hadn't used any of them the past few years. The last bunch of drinking, foul-mouthed, trigger-happy louts he had taken out had soured hunting for him, and then he had seized wanting or needing to kill.

As though materializing from his thoughts, the bushes crackled and a small doe came out on the far edge of the flat. She stood nervously surveying the landscape, aware that she was not alone. Ed remained very still enjoying the sight of her with a peculiarly tender emotion. He thought of the last time he had shot a deer and how, when he had stooped over the still warm, still twitching, carcass, a wave of revulsion and futility had swept over him. The memory of the warm, slick blood on his hands as he dressed out the carcass came back vividly to his mind, so vividly that he looked at them involuntarily, half expecting to see stains still there. What was it in man that urged him to death, that made him feel more manly when he could cause it? Was it vengeance for the knowledge that a greater power could slay him as easily? He could not pursue the thought, but he suspected that he still went pheasant hunting with his brothers on the ranch out of the fear that, if he didn't, he would lose something of his manliness in their eyes. He hoped they didn't notice that he deliberately missed as often as he hit and gave the birds he did hit, in their magnificent bloody plumage, to them. Well, he didn't think he would go this fall in spite of that.

Well, maybe he was getting soft, sissy. Maybe city life had ruined him but he knew he wanted something else now. He still loved the out of doors, the splendors of this starkly beautiful mountain country and never more than today with Irene here. He had found a reunion, reconciliation with nature and now in the right love of a woman, he felt he could be at last in harmony with it all. Sitting there in the warm sunlight that made him a little drowsy, perhaps a little light-headed, he even dared to dream. Perhaps there would be a way of straightening out his life and starting over with her. They could get a little place somewhere, have some animals, maybe even a child. They weren't too old, were they? Oddly enough, he had never felt that he had been a part of the creation of his sons, although he claimed to love them. He had been using precautions with Irene, those damn things he disliked but he could hope that in time she might....

He roused himself, a flush of hope surging through him. His movement startled the deer and she crashed into the bushes. A chipmunk scurried across his foot; a bird ruffled out of a tree and some golden leaves drifted languidly down. How beautiful and tranquil it was. He felt, after so many long years of estrangement, welcomed back into the stream of life. All because of this woman. He wondered if Irene were still sleeping and went to see.

She lay as he had left her sleeping soundly, the corner of the quilt pulled over her shoulders but her lower half uncovered. The sunlight struck the curves of her thighs and legs clad in the smooth dark fabric at just the right angle to display their perfect symmetry. Her body was half turned, one breasts lifting the soft pink material of her blouse so that its contour was both revealed and concealed in the most tantalizing way. It moved faintly with her even breathing. The sunlight picked red and gold lights out of her dark, loose hair that fell partly across her serenely beautiful face.

Ed knelt to awaken her but as he did so, a flush of hot physical desire flooded his loins with such violence that it obliterated the glowing emotion with which he had climbed the slope. My God, he wanted her more fiercely than he had an hour or so ago. He was almost ashamed and shrunk back as though his lust, for so he thought of it, might destroy something precious. Irene stirred but didn't waken. She must have been tired from last night. Ed rose and wandered aimlessly over to a big aspen part of which had broken from some violent assault and lay trailing its leaves along the ground. The crotch made a good seat, so he rested there waiting for the erection to subside, feeling confused. Looking at the flesh of the aspen trunk pocked with initials of others who had been here, he was disturbed. They had swelled like infected scabs, marring the powdery, tender-looking skin of the tree in a particularly repulsive way. One set that annoyed him most about midway up the tree enclosed initials in a clumsy heart, probably gouged by some school kid. Others had been here, doing the same thing as he and Irene! The thought startled him, smirched the beauty of the afternoon, made him feel sheepish, cheap.

Then, struck by a wry mood, he got out his pocket knife and standing on the bent limb so he could reach above the other inscriptions to a smooth untouched portion of the trunk, he began laboriously to carve "IK & EB." He had nearly finished drawing a heart around them when Irene awakened and came, shaking sleep out of her eyes, to where he was working.

"What are you doing?" she asked, laughing.

"You know, I never did that for another girl. Always thought it was silly and bad for the tree. Used to make me mad like today when I noticed all those initials and stuff and thought others had been here, maybe making love like us." He put his arm around her and kissed her gaily.

"Then I decided, 'what the heck?' Others have a right, too. Maybe it's good there are a lot of lovers in the world, eh? Are you feeling rested?"

"Yes, I had a good sleep. Must've been tired from last night. It makes me feel kinda young to have you do that, like we're just kids," she murmured, her head tilted back to study the new raw carving. She didn't tell him that Laurence had done the same thing many years ago.

"How I wish we had been," he said wistfully. "I wish we could have started out together and had our life just right all the way, had some kids together and a home...."

Irene nodded but didn't answer. The thought troubled her faintly; she couldn't tell why. Ed looked up at the sky. "It's too early to go back yet. I don't want to go back until we have to, do you?" he asked.

Irene stretched luxuriously, "No, not yet, but I ought to get back to fix something for Ellen if she's back for evening meeting."

"Well, it only takes a half hour to drive down. Let's take a little walk," Ed suggested. "I hate for this day to end."

Irene touched his face in tender agreement and they started off up a trail that wound into the pines, staggering around through the trees and bushes like a drunken miner, until it ended about a quarter of a mile beyond at a small, deserted log cabin. Ed was delighted. He circled the desolate dwelling like a little boy happening on a new cave, inspecting the chinking in the logs and kicking at the foundations. He tried to peer into the small, cob-webby windows.

"Some old homesteader or prospector," he guessed, completely captured by the building while Irene stood at a distance, not shar-ing his interest or enthusiasm. It just looked like a dirty old cabin in which there was undoubtedly spiders and mice.

Not being able to see in the windows, Ed went to the door and lifting the iron latch, pushed the heavy, warped boards inward. A musty, earthy smell rushed out. He stepped in cautiously. Even in the dimness it was evident that it had been without human occu-pancy for a long time and numerous small creatures had taken over. Most of the cabin's furnishings were still there–a rusting stove, a bed in one corner made from stakes driven into the dirt floor and supporting a rusty set of springs covered with crum-bling reddish pine boughs. There were a couple of crude benches and a table thick with dust and animal droppings. The rough cup-boards still held a few dishes and cans. Strewn about the floor were a number of articles including what looked like clothing–old boots and a hat. He had seen such cabins when they were new; his uncle had homesteaded in the northern Utah mountains, and he had spent a summer there. He remembered the charm of these little huts.

"Irene," he called, "C'm 'ere."

She came warily through the door holding her hands in front of her face to brush away cobwebs which she loathed touching her.

"Look at this!" Ed was jubilant. "Bear traps." He pointed to some heavy rusted iron objects hanging from the rafters. "and this–just like home!" he joked. "We could've had a bed all to ourselves today," Going to the bed he pressed the springs. They creaked spookily and a shower of needles fell through to the floor. Irene smiled but backed away covering her mouth and nose from the flurry of dust.

"I'd sure like to have a little place like this where we could get away all by ourselves; fix it up just for us." Ed was peering hap-pily into the cupboards. "Say look at this, an old can of coffee, half full. Somebody must have just walked off or been carried out one day, didn't bother...."

Something scurried across the rafters and there was a shower of dust. A big black spider swung out of the cupboard. Irene shrieked and started for the door. Ed followed her anxiously. Outside she was brushing her hair frantically; he helped her shake it, reassuring that there was nothing in it and then put his arms around her laughing. To his surprise she was trembling violently and had begun to sob.

"There, there, Honey." He tried to sooth her, feeling that there was something more bothering her than just the fright of a spider. "What scared you so?"

The cabin was like the one that she had shared many summers with Laurence in the early days of their marriage. This was almost like opening a grave but she couldn't tell Ed. She got hold of herself after a minute or two.

"I don't know, I just guess I can't stand creepy things like mice and snakes and spiders. It's so dirty and spooky...."

Ed looked back at the cabin. "It could be cleaned out real easy and fixed up," he mused. "It would be nice to have a little place where we could come in the summer and be all by ourselves away from people, the city... wonder who owns it?"

"I don't know that I would like it all that much," Irene murmured, trying to pin her hair up. "I spent a lot of summers in the mountains. It gets tiresome... why do you want to get away?"

It was the first time she had disagreed with him. He looked at her, a little puzzled. "I don't know," he admitted. "I hadn't thought about it until lately and then today, while you were sleeping, I thought how much I'd like to get away from the city and the highways, the grind, get back out where things seem real, natural."

"I wouldn't like it here all the time," Irene said flatly. "It's lonely and scary." She wrapped her arms around her breasts and shivered. A wind had come up in the pines; the sad, lonely sound reminded her of something that she didn't want to remember. It had grown darker suddenly; the light was slanting way down through the pines and lit the small cabin eerily. The dirty windows reflected an orangish glow almost as though there were a ghost fire within. Ed had gone over to close the door and although they were only a few yards apart, she wanted to rush to him, he seemed so far away. The fear of losing him swept over her again. He had revealed a side of him today that she hadn't suspected. What if he changed? What if he wanted something else that she didn't want?

But he was coming back and there was that sweet look of tenderness and concern for her on his face. He held her arm firmly as they picked their way down the darkening path.

Somehow when he pulled the door of the cabin to and slipped the latch, Ed realized that he had shut into that decaying past the fragile dream that had been reborn that afternoon. He had become aware for the first time that they, he and she, man and woman couldn't and wouldn't understand each other all the time even though love was as deep and encompassing as theirs.

Whatever other ideas he harbored, he would go her way just as he had gone Emily's. There was that in him. Maybe he was weak; maybe men were losing their old strengths that had been bred in the early west, becoming city men.

As he felt her warm flesh under his hand, he thought that she would be enough if only they could find a way to be together without fear. As they emerged from the trail, the sun was obscured by some dark clouds that had appeared in the west.

"Look's like we might have some rain," he observed, as they gathered up the picnic. "Sure do need some, it's been a dry fall."

СЗ

Love had restored Irene's vitality and beauty; a lot of the townsfolk noticed how well she was looking–some with sincerity, others with malice. For her the worst of the Depression, if not completely over, had certainly be alleviated. This was not the general case. Economic disaster that most people had thought could not last more than a couple of years and would surely end with the election of Roosevelt was in its fifth year. Like an uninvited poor relation who had just dropped in and whom everyone expected would move on shortly, it had not only settled in indefinitely but brought the rest of the family–hunger, despair, confusion and, for many, hopelessness. Some of the programs initiated so enthusiastically in the first one hundred days were working haphazardly; some had expired. There was still a feeling of confidence that somehow F.D.R. would pull them through. But the effects in Merritsville were not too noticeable.

The Mormons were not wholeheartedly in favor of the new

gover'ment policies although most of them had given up on the old Republican philosophy of free, unrestricted enterprise. They were hanging together by the doctrines on which the church had been founded–stick together, care for and share with each other and obey the teachings of the church. Although few people were starving, not many were well nourished or well clothed and the atmosphere of dejection was growing more palpable.

Although Irene was no longer one of them, there were still a number of unfortunates standing in lines to receive erratic relief supplies. Mrs. Hamilton was not among them either; she had died and the rest of the family had moved over to one of the small mining towns west of Merritsville.

The NRA had fizzled out–ruled unconstitutional–and by the time Irene had settled into her job, the stores had gone back to their nine to six Monday through Saturday hours. They were long and sometimes she was very tired, but she was still grateful to have work and the $30.00 a month salary including a discount at the store. Since Washburn's had a grocery department, this helped immensely.

WPA projects had started in Merritsville; these were less ambitious than the earlier PWA projects and were more humiliating to the men who had been out of work so long they had begun to lose energy. As she walked to work one bright morning, Irene had to pass a dozen or so men who had been put to work improving the rough streets of the town. One of the features of early Utah towns like Merritsville was the rows of Lombardy poplar trees imported by Brigham Young for wind breaks. Many of these trees were now dying, having lived out their relatively short life span; they looked like slatternly old women with uncombed hair, too grimly representative of the depressed mood of the country. It was decided that removal of them would provide a useful occupation for the unemployed. The men were hacking and chopping at them without much enthusiasm. Abe Clark, one of hers and Laurence's school mates, chipped away with dogged sluggishness on a stump as she passed. He looked up at her and greeted her with an wry smile.

Knowing that she was well dressed and fresh looking, she was a little embarrassed about her obvious good fortune. She stopped to inquire about Maude, his wife, who was a friend. She had heard that she was having her sixth baby. Irene sometimes wondered why they kept on having them under the circumstances, but of course, the church encouraged it.

"Well, she's poorly," Abe replied, removing his sweaty, old brown hat and leaning his axe against the tree. "She ain't pickin' up at all this time. Time we was quittin', I guess."

"Oh, I'm sorry," Irene murmured. She must remember to take something over to Maude for the baby.

"You're lookin' fine, Irene," Abe said. "It's good to know some of us are gettin' by one way'r another."

Irene was not sure whether there was a barb in Abe's remark or not.

"Yes, I'm lucky I was able to find a job. It's hard without Laurence. I surely wouldn't be much good at this." She stooped and picked up a chip, examining it a little too minutely. "It sure does look like hard work."

"It ain't the work I mind," Abe burst out. "It's so damn humiliatin'. You know us Clarks never had to take charity from nobody and we never wanted to. It's just make-work, down right degradin' to a man who's still young and got his strength. It ain't real man's work... there's nothin' to look forward to, nothin' to plan for. Just put in yer six 'r eight hours, go home, get up and start over. That's what's depressin'."

He stopped, mopping his face with a soiled bandanna. Irene was very disturbed at the bitterness in his voice. Clinton had told her that the WPA workers got only about forty dollars a month; she felt a surge of guilt that she was making almost as much as that for just her and Ellen although she did buy things for Dosey and her family and Addie.

"Don't give a man no incentive. That's what a man needs. Hard work don't bother him none. I'd say Laurence done well to get out of it when he did...." His voice trailed off as he realized his blunder.

Irene was disturbed, not only by his words, but by the desperate look in his face. He had been such a good-looking, happy-go-lucky fellow. In spite of her own discomfort, she wanted to help him.

"But this is going to improve the town a lot. These old trees have needed taking out for a long time and fixing up the streets will be a big improvement, won't it?"

"Yeah," Abe took up his axe and swung it at the stump. "Yeah, maybe that's the way to look at it. Sorry I got steamed up there; didn't mean what I said...." He gave her an apologetic grin.

She moved on, wishing she could avoid passing the men working along the street. She knew that some of them would make remarks about her as she passed.

Irene was right; the men did make remarks. In the worst of times, even as in the best, all men everywhere are excited and cheered by the sight of a beautiful woman. They greeted her congenially, even tipping their worn hats, but when he thought she was out of sight, Heber Price gave a low whistle and muttered to Pete Peterson, "Sure could stand a little of that–say, you heard anything about her and that city feller, you know the one that takes her to dances up at the Pandora?"

"Naw," Pete was always nervous when Heb got started on women. "Heard he was married, just out to get a bit on the side. Pity a woman like Irene has to git taken in by a slicker."

"Sure is too damn bad we have to let a looker like that git away," Heber pursued. "Wish I wuz free. What's the matter with all us shit heels?"

"Aw," Pete shrugged. "She alwuz wuz a stuck up one, anyway. Nobody could git close to her in school 'cept old Laurence Kent. He glommed on to her and she give ever'body the cold shoulder even after he died. Too high and mighty fer me. Y'know, I often wonder what happened out there. It sure was a peculiar thing the way he died."

Heber nodded as he watched her swing out of sight, the pretty summer dress floating around her legs and hips. "All the same I shoulda tried harder."

Word had got around about Irene and Ed. It bothered her some, if she let herself think about it. She knew what kinds of things were said about people in her situation, and more and more she lived in a world split between her work at the store and the times she could be with Ed. They weren't, of course, as much as either of them wanted. Although she was happy in many ways, there were nagging anxieties to which she could not put a name. She kept up with her Sunday meetings but she had had to give up the womens' activities that took place during the day time in the week like Relief Society where, she knew, most of the news of the town circulated.

And there was Ellen. Ellen was getting to be a woman; her thirteen-going-on-fourteen year old body was beginning to take on a suspicious plumpness. She was good to help Irene around the house and caused her no trouble like having boys hanging around. She was spending more time with her studies and books. One thing that worried Irene was the habit she had got into of going to Everett Gordon's to borrow books. Addie had been responsible for that, sending her over there with food and things for Everett. Irene had always been nervous about Everett, disliking his early hold on Laurence, but there didn't seem to be any special harm that she could put her finger on. Common sense told her that most things, if let alone, would work out.

Her work in the store was absorbing and satisfying. Clinton's dreams for her had materialized more than even he had expected. Her instincts for order and harmony suited the retail dry-goods business perfectly. She was not a high-pressure sales lady but seemed to have a sure sense about people. Clinton knew she was a real asset to the store, and he had made sure that the Washburn brothers knew it too. He was pleased with the fine shell of sophistication that had begun to envelope her hoping it would sustain her when she had to face the bitter truth about her relationship with Ed.

As she went about her work, the triple mirrors in the Ready-to-Wear department reassured Irene that she presented a very fine figure. While not overly vain about herself, Aunt Delia had trained her too austerely for that, she could hardly be unaffected by her own beauty.

One warm, summer Saturday afternoon she was studying herself obliquely in the new green voile dress that Clinton had ordered especially for her now that she could wear lower necklines, when she noticed, with a guilty start, that Dosey had come into the store. Dosey looked very tired and frowzy. She was untidily dressed in an old blue rayon polka-dot dress the misshapen seams of which were split out in several places. She was trailing the twins and Joey who were wearing clean but faded and patched, misfitted overalls. She pretended not to see Irene for a few moments, hovering nervously from counter to counter. She had three dollars in her shabby, white flat purse and the whole family needed clothes. Ordinarily she shopped at Penney's where the prices were a little lower, but she couldn't find the pink anklets that Louise needed to be in the Primary pageant over there. At length she found a pair and took them over resolutely to where Irene, after a self-conscious greeting, had turned to straightening merchandise.

Dosey couldn't help but notice how the pretty soft green dress cast cool shadows on her sister-in-law's smooth, fair skin; how her gleaming hair, which she had finally cut and always kept marcelled in deep waves, framed her face and how, when she bent over to make out the sales slip, her firm, white round breasts gleamed in the dusky light. She could see they were supported by one of those fancy new brassieres with a dainty lace slip over that. Then with profound shock, Dosey realized that Irene was not wearing her garments! A wave of disbelief and anger swept over her.

As Irene raised up, her eyes met Dosey's, and she saw the hostility in them. Neither was able to speak. Turning away, she pretended to wrap the little package with extra care, making strained conversation with the twins who had crowded behind the counter. At last she handed it to Dosey, who almost snatched it and, with averted eyes and a few sharp words to her brood, left the store swiftly. Irene wanted to call after her but could find no words that would suffice to express the misery that she felt.

For a moment Dosey stood on the sidewalk in the cruel, hot, sunshine feeling exceedingly ugly, worn and old. Her discovery so stunned her that she could not recall the rest of her errands that afternoon. Dosey had known that the dreary years and the bitter fight with poverty were telling on her, but she had not, until seeing the cool, serene beauty of Irene this afternoon, been made so devastatingly aware of it. Once a pretty, vivacious woman, her figure was now slipping to the middle. In the last year she had lost all her teeth and wore a pair of ill-fitting dentures whose glossy pink gums were far too conspicuous when she smiled or talked. Her dark hair, streaked with gray, straggled from an untidy bun. There was never any money for clothes for her—the children had to have it all, especially the growing girls. She had worn the old polka-dot dress with the sagging hem and stained underarms so long that she felt she must have been born in it. Her spirits, which had once been so buoyant, had been stretched as far as they would go and were now as limp and worn out as the tired, gray girdle which held up thick, orangish rayon stockings streaked with runs.

As she caught a glimpse of her reflection in Washburn's plate glass windows, she felt ready to burst into hot, searing tears. The total impact of the depression had finally reached her; she might have been its living symbol, a product of the insidious erosion that it had made on the lives and persons of millions of Americans. She felt suddenly detached from meaning and reality, but Joey tugging at her skirts and the twins pushing each other against the store window jerked her back to the moment.

"You kids go on home," she said sharply. "If Dad comes, tell him I'm down at Grandma's."

She felt completely unable to go home to the hot, messy kitchen in which she had been canning fruit all morning and where a stack of ironing and mending awaited her, not to mention the problem of making the next meal from an almost empty cupboard.

"I wanna go to Granma's, too," bawled Joey.

"No, you go on home," Dosey said with an unusual firmness that made the children stare at her. She seldom went anywhere without at least one of them, but now she had an almost desperate desire to be alone, to run away somewhere, although in her present condition there was really no place to run except to her mother's. Joey took the twins' hands and went obediently down the street.

By the time she had reached her mother's house in the hot sun, she was exhausted. Addie was hacking away at the trumpet vine when she heard the gate creak and looked up to see the dejected figure of her daughter. She knew there was something drastically wrong for Dosey to be calling on her at this time without a single child. She could hardly remember seeing Dosey without a baby in her arms and several little ones clinging to her skirts. She was relieved in a way that Dosey's childbearing years seemed over, although she believed that they should welcome as many little spirits into the world as the Lord saw fit to send. After Joey, Dosey had had a miscarriage, but nothing had happened since. She hoped it was nothing like that.

"Pestiferous thing," she scolded, thrashing at the Trumpet vine that had all but taken over the one side of the lawn, twining itself about the fence, the trees and suckering up through the grass. Now it had attacked the porch. Addie kept a corn sickle close by and in odd moments, hacked away at it in hopes of preventing it from eventually covering the whole house like a thick green plague with its orange trumpet-shaped flowers. It was something of an outlet in times of frustration when she couldn't get at the real source of the world's troubles. She was using it now to stall off Dosey's.

"Sorry Sister Randall ever gave me a start of the thing. Just can't keep ahead of it." Addie drew off her ragged gloves, which she wore more from long habit than the fact that they offered any protection for her gnarled hands.

"My land, you look like sour apples, Doris. What's the matter?"

Dosey sank down on the front steps in the shade and Addie sat down beside her.

"I'm so tired, Ma, so awful tired of it all, I could just die."

Addie Kent was not prepared for the grating, bitter despondency in her daughter's voice. Dosey had always been such a brick, nobody ever thought of her giving up. Addie, who was seldom at a loss with any kind of trouble concerning people, felt a wave of helplessness and fear. It is so hard for a mother to do the right thing for a daughter, a grown, married daughter.

"I just can't stand much more of it." Dosey's voice trailed off into a deep sob.

"Anymore of what?" Addie was genuinely puzzled.

"Oh, everything, poverty, work, kids, myself." Dosey could not define the exact parts of her despair. They had accumulated like the odds and ends in a junk drawer.

"It seems so useless to go on strugglin' year after year. It's goin' on six years now since Aaron's had a decent job and we had somethin' we could count on. We're down to the last three dollars, two-seventy-five now, and it's two weeks before he can go back on WPA. All the kids need clothes–the twins're out on the ground again and Louise had to have socks for that Primary thing."

Addie shook her head in acute sympathy.

"And what makes me mad, Ma." Dosey's voice began to quiver. "I was in Washburn's today, they didn't have pink anklets over at Penney's, and Irene has another new dress and beads and her hair all done up at the beauty parlor. I looked just like a hag, I feel like a hag!" She twisted her red, rough hands and tears ran down her cheeks.

Tears welled into Addie's eyes, too, and she patted Dosey's shoulder awkwardly. "Now, now, Doris, you come on in the house and I'll fix you a cool drink. You're all upset and tired. A little lemonade with an egg in it will give you some strength. You must be run down these days. I've never known you to give into self-pity and jealousy. It ain't like you. I know times is bad, but they ain't a tenth as hard as I seen 'em yet."

"Oh, Ma," Dosey said in irritation, wiping her face on the handkerchief Addie held out to her, "don't go telling me about the pioneers and having to dig sego roots again. Sometimes I think that's what we're gonna have to do."

She got up from the porch and followed her mother into the house. It was warm but quiet and neat in the kitchen, and Addie beat up an egg with some cream of tartar and lemon into one of her favorite summer drinks. The signs of overwork and undernourishment added to despair in Dosey's face upset her, but she knew she mustn't let it show. She busied herself about the kitchen while her daughter sipped the drink in silence for a few minutes, but then burst out nervously, "I guess you know about Irene?"

"What about Irene?" Addie asked carefully.

"She's took her garments off, I noticed today and I've heard that she's goin' around with this married man...."

Addie Kent didn't reply for a long moment, then she came over and sat down wearily by the table.

"Yes, I noticed she took them off a while ago," she said quietly. "I guess I don't hear all the gossip. Ellen tells me about Ed, says he's good to them. After what Irene went through you're not willin' to judge her, are you?"

"I don't know, Ma, in a way, yes. It just don't seem right to me that she had a chance to go to the Temple and I never got to yet, and then that she don't care no more about the memory of Laurence than that. It don't seem fair," she cried harshly. "I don't know what she went through is any worse than what I been through and am goin' through. She ain't got six kids, half starvin', no clothes, a stubborn man...."

"Dosey!" Addie rapped the table sharply. "I know you're in a bad state right now and lecturin' you ain't gonna do no good, but you gotta stop this right here, right now. You'll end up a sick woman if you don't. Ain't I give you no more faith, no more trainin' than that you want to destroy yourself and ever'body you love with hate and bitterness. In truth you got more than Irene has or ever will have. You got troubles but you got the character and strength to bear 'em. Irene was always weak. I knew it. I prayed she'd get through it somehow without trouble like this but she's the kind of woman ain't got no life, no strength without a man. I wished it could've been some other way though, maybe he's a good man in his way. Anyway we can't judge her. We ain't put here to judge each other but to love and help. No matter what she does, Irene is one of our family. We can't turn against her and leave her alone because it'd make it harder for her to do right when she sees how."

Dosey looked up surprised at the strange note in her mother's voice. She saw that she was trembling with emotion; no doubt she had heard and been thinking about Irene for quite a while.

"But, Ma, we're taught that to break the Temple covenant is an awful sin. That's our religion, ain't it?"

"I know that, but it's God's business to make the final judgment, Doris. It ain't our religion to abandon our own when they've stumbled and fallen down—it ain't gonna get us in any better with God to make it harder on each other than it already is. Irene's not happy with that man and she ain't never gonna be. Don't you be fooled by outward appearances. I dare say she's gone through all sorts of torments, she's scared of losin' him like she lost Laurence, only in worse ways."

Addie's vehemence came partly from the fact that she, too, had been hearing rumors about Irene. She knew how vicious the town could be and was saddened by the shadow that it cast on her family. She had been chopping on the vine as a way of settling her mind about Irene when Dosey arrived.

"She's got to think about Ellen," said Dosey petulantly.

"Some women can't live for their children alone, they're too much like children themselves. I'm glad Irene took the garments off. It means she still believes in what they stand for, don't you see?"

Dosey was somewhat calmer, a little ashamed and yet not entirely convinced that Irene didn't have the better of it by far. She was still resentful.

"Irene's got lots of trouble ahead, Dosey. It won't always show in the way yours does nor be easy to handle. But it won't lessen yours none to add to hers, will it?" Addie asked. Reaching over she patted Dosey's hand. Her Scottish ancestry made it hard to demonstrate her affections, but when Dosey looked into her tear filled eyes behind the small gold-rimmed glasses, she knew how deeply her mother cared about her and all her family. She felt a little ashamed and arose to go.

"Guess I better be gettin' home, it's nearly supper time again. Laws, it seems like meal times come around so fast every day. Wonder why we couldn't be made so's to eat just once a week or somethin'?" She tried to smile as cheerfully as she could.

"You got plenty of bread?" Addie was already wrapping a couple of fat loaves in brown paper, knowing Dosey could always use extra. "And here, take a jar of this jam."

Dosey trudged home, the warm bread under her arm. Sometimes her mother's stubborn, blind faith and charity exasperated her. It seemed almost simple minded and yet she always clinched her arguments with something like that. It wouldn't do no good to make trouble for Irene and Irene *was* one of their family for all eternity. The warmth of her good nature began to seep back and, before she reached home, she decided that she must take a little time and do something about herself. It was partly her own fault that she had let go. She wouldn't trade her kids for Irene's lonely beauty, not one of them. If only Hal weren't becoming such a handful....

Irene understood Dosey that afternoon in the way that women have of understanding each other's gestures and actions far more than their words. She had seen plainly in Dosey's face the thing she had been dreading ever since the beginning of her romance with Ed. She had known that the town would talk about her; little snatches of gossip had reached her ears but the misty film of rumor can swirl around one for a long time without having a real impact. It was like a fog that concealed the truth until one ran hard against the rough concrete wall hidden by it. Dosey's shocked disapproval cut right into the fiber of Irene's being, reminded her of her dependence upon the love and support of the only family she had ever known. Her guilt at breaking the sacred vows to Laurence seared the very depths of her.

After Dosey left, Irene stood looking at herself in the long mirrors as though they might provide her the answer to the tormenting questions that swirled in her mind. Why, oh why, had she fallen into this horrid predicament? Why couldn't she have met Ed under other circumstances when he wasn't married and could have married her decently? Why couldn't she break it off and go back to living the way she had been taught?

Tears were gathering hotly at the back of her eyes; she felt as though iron pincers were clamped on the back of her neck. Touching her hair lightly, she saw her hand was shaking. How vulnerable she was and, for all the confidence that her good looks gave her, how little pride and sustaining strength she had. But she could make no choice. Her love and needs bound her in every direction; her woman's spirit, caught as it had been between the extremes of male idealism–the old world shining goddess that Laurence had loved and the new world sophisticated artwork that Clinton favored–had had no time to form any solidity of its own. What did Ed love and want in her? A little of both? Perhaps something altogether different that she didn't understand. Sometimes she thought that neither of them really knew what they wanted of love and life. They just clung together like people on a raft not knowing where they were going or why. They couldn't go back to the old wrecked dreams, and they had none to go forward to, but that seemed only to make their need of each other more desperate.

Choking down tears of sheer frustration and bewilderment, Irene went to the stock room where Clinton was perspiring over a pile of orders and said that she thought she had a headache coming on. He told her kindly to go on home and let him know if she didn't feel better the next day. He stared after her with apprehension as she left, knowing that a crisis was imminent.

In her darkened room Irene tossed and turned, crying in little spurts most of the night. There was no position on the pillow where her throbbing head was comfortable. Thinking of how worn and tacky Dosey had looked and how hard her life must be, reminded her bitterly of how selfishly she had been involved in her own problems these past few years. In their earlier years Dosey had been such a good friend and sister to her and such a pillar of strength during the worst months after Lawrence's death. Dosey, in fact, had been closer to her than any other woman. They had been friends even before she started going with Laurence, and afterward Dosey had helped them both through the rough spots. In their early married life they had done almost everything together, sewing, cooking, shopping, planning for holidays. How could they have become such strangers that Dosey could look at her as though she hated her?

Of course, Irene really understood very deep within the betrayal of the family. If they only knew how she needed Ed. If they only knew how kind and decent and right he was for her. But how could she defend him, defend herself knowing that what she was doing was dead wrong in the eyes of the church and God. She knew some might think she went around with him for his money, that because of the car he drove and the company he was associated with and the nice clothes he wore that he was a lot richer than he was. She knew some women might even be jealous of her, but that was not the problem. She would never have a chance to justify herself to the town anyway. It was her own family, her beliefs, at stake. She couldn't, she didn't want to give him up now or ever and yet there was the reality of her ties both earthly and eternally. She always had to come back to that no matter how hard she tried to avoid it. Even if they could be married legally and openly that didn't solve the ultimate problem. She was still married to Laurence for time and eternity in a sacred vow that she had broken, risking not only her own salvation but that of her child and the whole family! Even though she had taken off her garments, symbol of that vow, she found that she still *believed* in what they stood for!

She beat her fists helplessly on the pillow. Maybe there was some way of bringing them all together in one big loving family– Ed's wife, his children, Laurence, Ellen, the whole family. There must be some provision for feelings that struck so deep. Irene had never been able to question the ways of God or the Church. In her mind she could not even examine the structure that was the backdrop of her agony. It was as though she stood before the calm, shining facade of the great Temple whose doors had calmly and implacably closed on her forever. Speech, thought, desire, need, nothing availed before its impassive and formidable bulwark. Eventually everyone she knew or loved would be safe behind that door but herself and perhaps Ed, although men were admitted by special dispensation when women weren't. Laurence could have more than one woman sealed to him but she could have only one celestial husband. It didn't seem fair.

In the smothering darkness of the summer night she moaned and threw off the sheet angrily. Her body was soaked with perspiration, and she got up to take another aspirin. Crawling back to bed in her misery, the vast unassailable abstractions faded and Irene wished only that Ed were there. The simple, sweet natural comfort of his arms; nothing mattered more than that, but no sooner had she conjured up the dearness of his presence, his gentle fine face, his tender lips, than a wave of hurt and anger swept over her. How could he have dared make her love him when he knew very well that he could not marry her? Some of the ugly old imprecations about the selfish male beast that she had heard from other women all her life floated into her mind.

Women seldom talked straight out about such things but she guessed from what they hinted that for most of them marriage and love had not been all they expected. There was the notion that it was a woman's duty to "put up with it" to keep a man from straying though that didn't always seem to work. The older women expressed, in veiled words, that they were glad to be done with "that." Irene had never felt that way either with Laurence or Ed. Their desires seemed as fine as hers. Ed was never rough or demanding, always considerate of her moods, her feelings even during her periods. Once Dosey had told her that Aaron acted like he could hardly stand her when she was that way. It was all too confusing.

In the smothering darkness of the summer night she moaned and threw off the sheet. She sat up on the hot rumpled bed and sobbed bitterly until she was exhausted and fell finally into a few troubled hours of sleep before dawn.

❃

Irene managed to go to work the next day, but she was miserable and Clinton was worried. There was nothing he could do or say until she had made up her mind but he knew the time was growing short when she could stay in Merritsville.

Ellen knew there was something wrong when her mother came

home looking haggard and barely spoke to her. "Thank goodness it's Saturday," she sighed as she began changing clothes. " I couldn't stand another hour in that hot store."

Irene went to her clothes closet and began throwing dresses on the bed. Ellen stood in the doorway bewildered. She could tell her mother was upset but didn't dare ask why.

"I want you to take these things over to Aunt Dosey's after church tomorrow. I can't find a thing in this darned closet anymore," she said crossly. Ellen noticed that some of the things were quite new. "This new dress, too?" she asked holding up the voile that Irene had worn the day before. She tried it against herself. "Maybe you could fix it for me."

"No," Irene said sharply, "The neck is too low."

"Well, Aunt Dosey can't wear it then," persisted Ellen, "Can't I have it? I can fix it or Grandma will."

"I said, No!" Irene turned and looked at Ellen is such a strange way that she let the dress slide to the floor. She hardly recognized her mother, this woman with dark, feverish, sad eyes.

"Well, why don't you take 'em over yourself," Ellen replied stubbornly. "You don't have to be so cross."

Irene sat down on the bed and burst into tears. "I'm sorry," she choked. "I don't know why you can't do anything for me without arguing. You know I'm tired and don't feel well, Ellen. I've had such a bad day."

Ellen was sorry and ashamed. She put her arm around her mother's shoulder. "I'm sorry, Mama. I'll take them over for you. Can I fix some supper?"

It did seem that her mother was changing; they were drifting farther and farther apart. They seldom had time to talk or do anything together. Irene had started nagging Ellen about her appearance and habits, about acting like a "lady" which word Ellen was beginning to hate because it meant acting prissy and not doing anything that was fun. Ellen in turn was annoyed with Irene's preoccupation with that man. In spite of her knowing how happy he made her mother and how much she needed him, she resented Ed, wondering why he didn't marry Irene or leave her alone. It was embarrassing that her mother could be going around to dances and on dates just like a high school girl and with that crazy Bessie Benson. Some of the kids even made sly remarks. Yet she was not sure she would like it if Irene did marry Ed. She could not imagine him living with them really. It was all so tangled and confusing. In Everett Gordon's library she had been reading a book called *Anna Karenina*. It was a long, sad book but she had been fascinated by it; when she tried to picture the face of Anna, it always resembled her mother, beautiful with that same faintly tormented expression. She had a hard time, however fitting the stocky figure of Ed Barker with the dashing Vronsky. If only her mother had met someone really romantic, rich, handsome who could have swept them up and away from this dull little town for so she was beginning to think about Merritsville.

The next afternoon Ellen took the bundle of clothes her mother had laid out over to Aunt Dosey's. Irene had excused herself from church and stayed in bed. Ellen decided she would stay and play with the Walkers so the house would be quiet.

At first Dosey was shocked about the clothes but she said nothing to Ellen. When she found the green dress, she almost burst into angry tears. What on earth was the matter with Irene? Was this some kind of insult? She couldn't believe Irene capable of doing anything so mean. She had half a notion to send it right back or tear it up but the material was so nice.

"Are you sure your Ma meant to send this?" she asked Ellen.

"Yes," Ellen replied with unconcern. "She said she didn't like the neck, it was too low. She said maybe you could fix it or make it over for Lorraine."

"Well," Dosey pondered. "I guess I can put a piece of lace or something in it." The big soft collar would come down over her arms far enough to hide her garments if she tucked them up a bit. I would be a nice change from the polka-dot. She began to smooth her hair in the mirror and her face softened. No matter what you said about Irene, she had a good heart.

Rumors about Irene and Ed grew steadily. They were the chief nugget of gossip of many of the womens' gatherings.

"Well, I don't think it's a proper way for a woman to act who's been raised like she has." Mildred Hanson, whose husband ran the delivery service department for Washburn's, licked the thread and guided it through the eye of a quilting needle.

"And gone through the Temple, too," added Ardella McDaniel,

"Pass me them scissors, will you, Sister Hanson?"

Most of the women gathered around the quilting frames nodded in agreement.

"I heard the man's married and has a family, been carryin' on like this for years. He's a travelin' salesman, you know," Birdie Thayer said grunting a little as she tried to shift her ungainly bulk closer to the quilt.

"Oh, them travelin' men are all alike. It's a shame for one of 'em to make a fool of a nice girl like Irene," Sister Bates clucked through her false teeth.

"George says he ain't such a bad sort." Maddie Swenson, whose husband worked in Washburn's hardware department and knew Ed spoke up. "His wife's been an invalid for years. Maybe you can't blame a man too much and Irene's been a widow now goin' on six years."

"Well, *I* can blame a man," Mildred snapped through tightened lips. "I don't hold with no double standards. Men ought to be just as chaste and clean as women. His wife bein' an invalid don't excuse him at all. He ought to be all the more decent."

"Excuse or not, men ain't made that way," Birdie Thayer put in dryly, jabbing her needle in and out of the bright patch quilt.

"They ought to be and if they ain't, women should have better sense than to encourage them." Mildred's voice was growing chill. The others were becoming a little uneasy since most of them had heard rumors that George was mixed up with a wild widow from Linton.

Sister Marston, a tall, thin gentle woman noted for her tact and peacemaking propensities spoke up, "Sisters, I don't think we ought to condemn Irene offhand until we know what it's like to be in her shoes. She's always been a good woman."

The other women looked at Sister Marston with some annoyance. She was always spoiling a good gossip with her pious little sermons.

"All I can say," Birdie Thayer sighed from the mounds of her flesh, " is that Irene had better watch her step. Joe says that Spencer Washburn knows what's goin' on. She could lose her job there."

Sister Bates raised her eyebrows significantly and nudged Birdie. Addie Kent was coming up the sidewalk; they couldn't discuss Irene in front of her.

Although Ed and Irene's affair had been going on for two years now, nobody had any direct evidence that Irene and Ed were living in sin, but there was plenty of suspicions. Almost everybody had collected a little data. They had stopped going to dances at the Pandora very often, but various people had seen them other places, in Provo, Salt Lake and driving up the canyon. Ed never stayed in Merritsville anymore, and they tried to be careful, but secrecy is a virulent stimulus to the imagination. Many of the women began to envy Irene her beauty, freedom, pretty clothes and her job in the store in these trying times. They felt her calm, gracious demeanor was an arrogant defiance of their moral standards. The news that she no longer wore her Temple garments circulated rapidly.

Bessie Benson was the only one who knew what was going on, and she wouldn't talk about Irene to anybody else. She was troubled about her friend; Irene did seem so oblivious to the storm that was gathering around her. One day Bessie was working down behind the counter in Penney's taking inventory when two good towns women came in. She recognized the high nasal tones of Mildred Hanson and the quieter voice of Josey Anderson. Mildred was saying: "I could've bought a prettier one over at Washburn's with our discount, but I can't stand to let that woman wait on me. I can't think why Washburn's keep her on with all the talk. I think that Clinton Maxwell ain't as lily-white as he ought to be either. George was telling me the other day he thinks Clinton buys half them pretty clothes she wears or marks 'em down just so...."

Bessie was seething. She reared up over the counter.

"Can George produce the evidence of that?" she demanded fiercely.

Mildred stepped back, flustered.

"Well, everybody knows how she's been carryin' on with a married man and how she's broke all her vows ...," she spluttered.

"And everybody else in this town is perfect and behaves decently?" Bessie asked sarcastically, leaning menacingly over the counter until her flushed, homely face was only a few inches away from the startled woman. Mildred backed off fumbling with her pocketbook.

"Well, I never!" She drew in her stomach as well as she could and tried to beat a haughty retreat, but Bessie, thoroughly roused, caught her between the piece goods and hosiery counter.

"Listen to me," she hissed in a low voice, "whatever she's done, she's as good as nine-tenths of the mealy-mouthed, married whores in this town and there's damn few women who have a right to throw mud on her!"

Mildred's face was as red as the bolt of percale she was leaning against. Josey was nervously edging her way down the aisle.

"It's her that should turn up her nose at waiting on jealous old gossips like you whose husbands...." Suddenly Bessie was aware that she had said too much. Mildred's worn face crumpled with anguish. Bessie stepped aside and turned her back. She did not see the manager who had been spying on the scene from the notions counter and who intercepted the two angry customers anxiously. He couldn't make much sense out of what they were saying but it was pretty clear that Bessie had insulted them outrageously.

He had wanted to get rid of that woman for a long time and now, by God.... He stepped lightly, almost gleefully back to where Bessie was nervously straightening the dress racks. Rubbing his hands together and clearing his throat, he began, "Miss Benson, I've just had a complaint...."

"I know." Bessie looked up scornfully and interrupted him. "And whatever else you're going to say, Smitty, just hold it because I'm quitting."

The manager's jaw dropped; he felt distinctly cheated in not being able to deliver the dismissal speech he had prepared many times over in his mind. At the same time he knew it would be hard to replace Bessie.

"Uh, ah, when will you be leaving?" he asked at length.

"Just as soon as I can pick up my pay check and clear out, old dear," she retorted, feeling delightfully lightheaded. She realized she had been fed up with J.C. Penney's and Merritsville a long time.

Although Mr. Smith had been hoping for Bessie's departure, he put on his best Penney manner and demanded, "You should stay until the end of the week until I can get someone satisfactory to take your place, you owe that...."

She broke in again, confronting him squarely, "The way I have it figured, Smitty, I don't owe you or the Penney Company a damn thing. You've had your nickel's worth out of my hide. As a matter of fact how much notice were *you* planning to give me?"

"Well, the usual two weeks, I guess. We can't figure the bonus until the end of the month." he stuttered.

"Ha," Bessie shouted. "Two more weeks of this grind. Thanks, let's just call it even. You take my bonus and go buy yourself a big night out. Get that pinched cash-register look from around your nose and that scared look out of your eyes as though you're afraid the inspectors were going to pop in any minute and find that old merchandise you haven't inventoried."

Seeing that she had hit her mark in the nervous look that came over the manager's face, Bessie turned and from force of habit, checked her cash, totaled her sales book and, taking the ugly black pocket in which she kept it from around her waist, threw it in the trash box. Grabbing her purse, she stalked out of the store. "I'll be back tomorrow for my check," she called as she swung the door closed on fifteen years of her life.

She went directly to Washburn's. "Guess what?" she said gaily to Irene, who looked up in surprise to find her there in the middle of the afternoon. "I've quit my job."

"You what?" Irene's eyes widened in disbelief.

"Walked out, quit my job, left the dear old J.C. Penney company for good and all."

"But what're you going to do?" Irene asked incredulously.

"Right now, a few errands and after that I'm gonna meet you at the drugstore when you get off and after that, I don't know. For the first time in my miserable life, I don't know what I'm going to do tomorrow and it's a wonderful feeling. See ya at six."

She waved joyously as she capered down the aisle and out of the store.

Clinton Maxwell was just emerging from the shadows of his private domain behind the somber walnut paneling.

"What's the matter with her?" he asked grimacing. Bessie's rough homeliness always repelled him.

"She just quit her job," Irene replied, still shocked. "I don't know how she could do it in times like these."

Clinton shook his head but a thought crossed his mind of which he was immediately ashamed. He wished Irene could quit. Mr.

Washburn had been dropping hints to him lately and he, coward that he was, could not bear to tell her that she was in danger of being dismissed. Helen, his wife, was becoming a bit touchy about her too. He was filled with a vast, cold helplessness, a sense of his own inadequacies, when he thought of Irene. She was so helpless in the world, so damnably manageable, malleable, in fact all those who came in contact with her felt obligated to carry her burden, to make her decisions. She responded by being entirely pliant. In his hands she had yielded like clay to his design; she was one of his finest creations, perhaps his only one, since had not succeeded very well with other women, especially not his own wife.

But like clay, Irene wasn't finished; she needed firing in a harder kiln to acquire that final polished sheath that would set her elegance into its permanent mold. It could not be accomplished in Merritsville. If he could only help her get a job in a store like Schubachers in Salt Lake City, at least. Contemplating the long graceful curve of her back and arms as she moved the dresses on the rack, he was sorry he couldn't have loved her. If he had had the capacity to love women instead of their physical ideal, he most surely would have loved her. He would miss her very much when she had to go; there was no question that she would have to go. How to accomplish it with the least hurt and awkwardness? Clinton hated awkwardness. He bit his lip reflectively and went back into his office to lay some plans, not aware that other forces in Merritsville were conspiring to help him.

Besse and Irene sat in the drugstore at one of the small, round marble-topped tables sipping sodas. The sweetish, stale apothecary smell and the greenish dusk contrasted with Bessie's excitement. She was vibrating with triumph. "You shoulda seen his face," she gloated. "Honestly, it was worth twice the bonus. And you know, to think I might've got to look just like that if I'd stayed there much longer."

"But what will you do?" Irene asked with frank admiration.

"Anything, anything at all. I'm going to Salt Lake and I'll do anything for a while–wait tables, jerk sodas, run errands, curl hair, make beds–anything but work for the Penney company."

She took a long exultant draft of the strawberry soda and then looked serious.

"Say, you know the worst thing about this damn depression is that it's got us all so scared, so scared of moving or doing anything, right down scared of living. We think if we leave this stinkin' little town, we'll starve to death. Maybe I will, but it will be better to find out than cringe here for the rest of my life waiting for the blow. What's that the President said, 'The worst thing we have to fear is fear itself,' or something like that?"

Irene nodded, still shaken. There was a space of silence between them, then Bessie said cautiously, "Say, Irene, whyn't you quit Washburn's and come with me?"

Bessie had been careful not to tell Irene about the incident that had precipitated her dramatic severance from the J.C. Penney Company.

"Oh, I couldn't," Irene said quickly, almost recoiling from Bessie's intent gaze.

"Why not? What's to stop you here? I know you could get a job easily with your looks and training, and you could be with Ed a lot more, I bet."

Irene blushed and looked miserable. Bessie knew she had said the wrong thing again.

"Well, there's Ellen for one thing...."

"Yeah, I forgot," Bessie agreed soberly. "But listen, she might get along better in the city–she's a smart kid, really too smart for this town."

Irene shook her head. "I don't know. She's only got two more years of high school and she's doing really good, you know. She's going to be editor of the school paper next year and she got on the debate team. It would probably take her a while to get noticed in big city schools."

Bessie didn't have any argument for that, although she didn't think it would take Ellen long to get noticed anywhere she had a mind to. She was a peculiarly independent minded and stubborn little girl, and she often looked at you as though she knew a whole lot more about you than you did yourself. But there was something a little sad, a little lost about her, Bessie thought as though she didn't really fit in Merritsville.

"Why couldn't Ellen stay here with Addie, then?" Bessie persisted. She wanted to get Irene out of Merritsville before she got hurt too badly.

Irene's lovely face clouded. Her imagination moved slowly

and ponderously. It had never occurred to her in all her thirty-five years that she could live anywhere else but here. She had never even wanted to. All her roots were intertwined with the trunk roots of those people who had given her her identity, mainly the family of her husband. This place held all that she had ever known or dreamed of in life.

Bessie was staring anxiously at the froth in the bottom of her glass. Some of her exuberance, like that of the soda, was now evaporating and her real concern for her friend obscured her own problems. Something in Irene always produced this desire to keep her from facing her own weakness. Bessie debated swiftly in her mind. If she didn't put her next to the truth of the matter, somebody more brutal was likely to.

"Irene," she blurted at last, "you're going to have to make up your mind sooner or later, whether you like it or not. You're going to have to choose between Ed Barker and Merritsville. The talk's already going around hot and heavy."

Irene looked as though someone had thrust a spoonful of some nasty medicine down her throat while she was only toying with the idea of taking it.

"I don't see...."

"I know you don't." Bessie was trying to be gentle. "If you had seen, you wouldn't have been able to stand it this long. You're really too damn innocent, Irene."

Irene shivered, thinking of all the worry and humiliation she had endured, the fear of getting caught and talked about, all the resolutions she had made to give up Ed. How could she make Bessie understand?

"I'm sorry." Bessie patted her hand which was icy cold and not alone from handling the frosty glass.

"I had to tell you."

"I know it's wrong, Bessie. I'm ashamed, but I tell you honestly, I have tried to give him up, but I can't. He's the only real thing since Laurence." Irene's eyes filled with tears, the old sore in her chest ached and throbbed so hard she thought she must faint. "I know you can't understand."

"Maybe I don't understand. No man's ever got under my skin like that for a long time, thank God," Bessie choked. "But I do know this town wont try to understand. I think you'll be a lot better off to go away from here where you wont have to give him up. Merritsville can't give you what he does. I do know that."

The whirring of the big fan above them and the clink of glasses at the fountain seemed very loud and clear in the deep, miserable silence into which the two women had fallen.

Irene wiped her eyes and powdered her nose, trying to smile at Bessie who pressed her hand. They got up wearily, paid for the sodas and went out into the streets of the seedy town sunk in its six-thirty, mid-summer, mid-depression lethargy.

"I'll see you before I go." Bessie waved and went west on Main Street. Irene nodded wanly, sick at heart to think of Bessie leaving and went east toward home.

Ↄ

Bessie took the Interurban to Salt Lake the following week and two weeks later wrote Irene that she had a room and a job in a chain drugstore. She urged Irene to get Ed to bring her up on a Sunday.

Irene told Clinton the news cautiously, sensing his recent interest in Bessie's welfare. "Quite a gal," he said carefully. "I wish I had her nerve."

"Me too." Irene went on unfolding and marking some new lingerie shipments.

Clinton sighed. "I sure would like to get out of this town. If I were as free as you, Irene, I wouldn't stay here another day. There's really nothing holding you and, truth is, you belong in the city." He came over and grasped her by the upper arms, holding her away from him and scrutinizing her with the fondest admiration. He was more openly emotional with her than he had ever dared be. Shaking his head slowly as he studied her face, he murmured, "You ought not to have been made so beautiful and stuck in a place like this. I can just see you working in a big beautiful department store like Schubachers. I'd miss you awfully, of course."

Irene blushed and laughed with nervous embarrassment. "But I'm not going anywhere, Clinton. I've got my home and family here. I'm happy here, I really am. I've always liked Merritsville. I'm really a small town girl."

Clinton dropped his arms in vexation. He meant what he said sincerely, but he had been trying to maneuver her around to the subject of leaving tactfully. Washburn had told him that morning in so many words that something was going to have to be done, there were too many rumors circulating.

Spencer Washburn was genuinely concerned about Irene. This summer morning he pondered her fate in his office on the balcony overlooking Main Street. He had been approached by several indignant women and even some of the men had commented on Irene's "conduct." Joe Thayer had stopped him the other day on the bank corner with some veiled tattle about Irene.

He had in mind that a good talking to would help her see the light, and he intended to catch Ed Barker on his next trip through although he squirmed a little when he tried to imagine how he would approach the subject. It struck him that maybe Brother Thayer might be able to help. Spence recalled that he was Irene's ward teacher. Deep down Washburn despised Joe Thayer; given his choice he would sometimes prefer going to Hell with the worst crook than a sanctimonious bore like Thayer, but when it came to getting business done, he didn't quibble about personal likes. He was going to see him that night at the meeting about the Church Welfare Plan that was being organized to help combat the depression. Dropping a word to Irene might do it if Thayer could manage to appeal to her religious convictions in the right way. He couldn't be sure, Joe was such an ass at times but it was worth a try.

He didn't really want to lose Irene; she had been a real asset to the store and besides that, she had given him some personal satisfaction. There were times when he had stood on the balcony where he could watch Irene without being observed. The sight of her gave him pleasures he would not have confessed even for the promise of revived prosperity. By God, she was a beauty. Now if polygamy were still permitted, he could have taken her into his own care after Laurence died, given her a good home, respectability and a lot of love and affection. Considering a man's nature, polygamy hadn't been altogether a bad thing. His own wife was ailing, unable to take care of his needs now. Some of the apostles still practiced it, he had heard. But that was all useless daydreaming. The problem was here today.

By rights it was Clinton's responsibility, he thought irritably; he had brought her into the store. Crafty eye for women, that Clinton, for all that he was a disappointment as a son-in-law. But business was business, and if women like Mildred Hanson got started and threatened to boycott his store, he would have to fire the Virgin Mary. Come to think of it, he had been hearing a few shady rumors about George Hanson and a woman over in Linton's. He'd have to caution him about that; hoped it wasn't going on, on company time when George made deliveries. If folks could only keep their personal lives in order and not let them interfere with business. Well, he'd talk it over with Joe Thayer and see what could be done about putting Irene wise before it was too late.

Late on a summer evening Brother Joseph Thayer, who worked in the bank, had forced himself back into a white shirt and tie in spite of the heat. He was a tall, thin, nervous man with a handsome face and a disturbing lustre in his deepset, dark eyes under bristling black brows. He was in his late forties but looked older than he was and not quite well as though something were burning him constantly from within. Tonight the flame glowed like an acetylene torch, almost a roaring heat in his ears, as he thought of the task before him. Spence Washburn had spoken to him after the meeting of the Welfare Board about Irene Kent, and he had fasted and prayed for several days. He was sure that he had been called to save the soul of that poor, tender woman. For a long time he had been aware of the attractive widow in church and had looked forward to the visits that he made to her home. He had been especially solicitous of her welfare and felt it a privilege and joy to counsel her. Although she had a general indifference to him, she had not repulsed his well-meant ministrations.

There was almost a lilt in his walk as he went across the porch where his three-hundred pound wife was sitting, perspiring apathetically with good natured resignation. He patted her fondly on the shoulder; although the sight of her jarred him, he went off humming a snatch of "When there's Love at Home." He met Brother Schofield on the corner, a small, sandy-haired man with a prominent Adam's apple and a speech difficulty. Joseph Thayer was glad that he had chosen Perry Schofield as his partner since Perry left things pretty much up to him. He felt this was a very choice mission, one that he alone could handle. He explained briefly to Perry that they wouldn't be going their usual rounds tonight since this was a special visit in which they had been charged to rescue the soul of a woman who had fallen into error. Perry had looked distressed when Joe asked him if he had heard about Irene and nodded his head but made no comment.

"Well, now this must be handled delicately," he admonished Perry as they walked toward Irene's house. "Brother Washburn feels that she must be warned that the town is getting upset about her relations with a certain man from Salt Lake. He don't want to disturb her, but if she keeps on he's afraid he might have to let her go. But that's not the main thing. Her soul is in great jeopardy, and we must try to see if we can save her."

Perry Schofield had nodded and wished he could get out of it; he never liked mixing in other folks affairs, but it was his obligation as a holder of the Priesthood to do his duty.

Irene opened the screen door for them with nervous embarrassment. She hadn't expected them until later in the month and was wearing a thin, white satin-striped housecoat that was a bit too transparent. She felt Brother Thayer's eyes on her as she invited them to sit down; he always made her feel uncomfortable. She clutched the housecoat around her and tried to decide where she could sit to be the least conspicuous.

"Ellen," she called, since it was necessary for all the family to be present when the teachers called. Ellen came out of her bedroom where she had been reading, looking a little annoyed.

Brother Schofield glanced uneasily at Brother Thayer. After a silence Brother Thayer cleared his throat.

"We have something to say to you, Sister Kent, that might be better if your daughter–uh–was–uh–not present," he muttered. His bony hands were stroking the knees of his shabby pants and his collar felt unbearably tight and hot.

Irene looked at them and then at Ellen in surprise and Ellen arose, puzzled. Slightly irritated–she never did like old Brother Thayer who was always patting her in Sunday School and telling her how smart she was–she left the room reluctantly. She was about to close the door of her room when a stubborn impulse seized her. Something about those men made her suspicious, curious about what it was she wasn't supposed to hear. The hall was very short and by standing close to the door, she could catch most of what was going on. She could hear Brother Thayer stammering a little but his voice soon took on that churchy tone, as though he were about to deliver a sermon.

"Sister Kent, there has–uh–we've heard–uh–something to the effect, that is, it has come to our attention from a reliable source that you may have fallen away from the teachings of the gospel in the last few years."

Irene looked at him in terror, then lowered her eyes and began to fumble with the buttons on her housecoat. Brother Thayer plunged on although no longer quite so confident of the success of his mission.

"Now we know that you are a good and true woman, and we know that you have had great trials and tribulations during these past few years. We have tried to sustain you in these hours of need, have we not, Sister?"

Irene nodded miserably, without looking up.

"Now we know, Sister, that there are great laws brought forth in these latter days for our good and true guidance into the Kingdom of the Lord, but we know also that the Devil is at work on the weaker vessels. Those who have fallen into his clutches can only be wrested from him by the power of prayer, faith and repentance." He had leaned forward and gained strength in his delivery. Irene felt as though a white-hot light had been focused on her. She could feel the perspiration trickling down between her breasts and under her arms but she could not move.

"And we know, Sister Kent, that the Lord always accepts true repentance and is exceedingly glad for the return of a lost soul. We have come here tonight to pray with you and deliver you from the power of the Devil." He lowered his voice to a low, vibrating key. "And, Sister Kent, I have fasted and prayed for you myself these past days since I have learned of your sorrowful transgressions."

Irene looked up, her face white with shock and her eyes filling with tears. Brother Thayer was momentarily distracted by her extravagant beauty although he saw complete submission to his accusations in her distraught face. He moved closer and picked up one of her hands, remaining in a kneeling position before her.

"Dear Sister," he said hoarsely, trembling from head to foot himself. "I can see that the spirit has moved you. I can see that the Dove of the Holy Ghost has lighted upon your forehead and that you are ready to yield up your sinful ways and return to His fold. You are ready to give up *that man* and confess your sins unto the Lord and...."

Suddenly Irene jerked her hand away and gave a shriek of agony. The cry startled Ellen who had been listening, biting her knuckles, in the dark doorway, not sure what Brother Thayer was getting at until she heard that cry of fear and anguish from the very bottom of her mother's soul. Suddenly she knew it was about Ed and her mother. She rushed into the room.

"You leave my mother alone," she screamed. "You nasty old man, you get out of here. She's not done anything wrong and Ed Barker has been good to us, a darn sight better than lots of you."

Irene gasped, staring at her in fascinated horror.

Brother Thayer had jumped up and the two men backed toward the door. Ellen pressed on them like a small whirlwind of fury.

"You don't have any right to come around here accusing my mother and telling her what to do. It's none of your business what my mother does; she's as good as any of you."

"Ellen!" Irene managed to gasp weakly, "Ellen, stop! You don't understand."

In her heart Irene had acquiesced completely that it was the Church's business; she had been dreading for so long the painful moment of reckoning. But coming this way had caught her off guard. She had thought many times how much she wanted someone to wrest her from the force of the Devil; help her to do what she could not seem to do for herself, give up Ed. Why had her stubborn, lost spirit recoiled like this? She hung her head unable to do anything about the storm that was raging around her, terrified by what her willing sinfulness had now done to her daughter who was insulting the Ward Teachers.

"Now you get out," Ellen repeated stamping her foot. "And don't you ever come and say or think those things about my mother anymore."

Irene had arisen and grabbed Ellen by the arm, trying to restrain her.

"Well," Joseph Thayer mumbled. "Satan truly has a strong-hold in this house." He pushed Brother Schofield, whose mouth had dropped open, out the screen door and off the porch, shaking with anger.

The two men tramped down the rough sidewalk in silence for a while. Thayer was seething with rage and frustration, but he knew he must not show his discomposure before his companion. He must turn this to a good account for all his wounded pride. "Now this shows us clearly the power of Evil, Brother Schofield," he said unctuously. "It can even possess the soul of a child who has come in its sphere of influence as we have witnessed this evening."

"Umh," murmured Brother Schofield, his Adam's apple work-ing spasmodically, uncertain of what he had really witnessed. "L-l-looks like we might've made a mistake, Brother Thayer, b-b-breakin' in there unexpected."

"Oh, no," Thayer assured him. "Oh, no. The Lord will tri-umph. She has been warned. We must not be discouraged. We must labor long and diligently in the face of great odds for the redemption of even one lost soul. For the time being, we must fast and pray for this poor woman."

"What about the little girl?" Schofield asked. Brother Thayer choked.

They parted company at the corner. Greatly relieved but feel-ing guilty, Brother Schofield vowed he'd take Irene a sack of spuds or some garden produce right away. Joseph Thayer went the few blocks to his home, savoring the bitter taste of his defeat. He knew he had once again bungled a chance to achieve glory. How many times had he reached high and fallen ignobly low? How carefully he had planned and plotted the details of the scene, the salvation of Irene Kent. He re-examined it now to see where he might have gone wrong. He had planned that they would kneel and he would place his hands on her beautiful soft hair and pour out his soul with hers in a mingling of love, grief and sorrow. When they arose, he would be able to touch her fine round arms, the ones he watched as she played the organ in church. He could let his hands linger there to convey the tenderness and sympathy words alone could not express. He had long felt that he under-stood the need of Irene's soul keenly—and, yes, those of her body as well. Of course, he only intended a long, pure association with her as her spiritual advisor in which she would come to lean on him and depend on him for help and guidance she so sorely needed. Oh, with what ecstasy he had planned to lead her back into the way and deliver her to God and the spirit of her rightful husband. He could feel the divine approval of the Almighty shining upon him for the great restraint and purity of his passion for her, for his patience and self-denial as he worked for her ultimate salvation.

Shattered! His dreams shattered by that miserable girl. For a moment he struggled with hatred, plunged on and finally came to rest beside the hot bulk of his wife where he lay suffering until almost dawn. By that time he had almost consoled himself by relinquishing Irene and her daughter to Satan and focusing on a new vision of Glory. He had been appointed director of the Stake Welfare Plan; how diligently he would work to take care of the poor and needy, how he would sacrifice, working his fingers to the very bone to see that the Lord's chosen people were nourished and cared for. Birdie snored loudly and turned over, crushing him almost out of the bed. He arose wearily and sat with his head in his hands by the window where another summer day was dawning.

After the Teachers had gone, Ellen put her arms around her mother.

"You shouldn't have done that, Ellen," Irene said weakly.

Ellen looked stubborn; "Well, they shouldn't have come here and upset you like that. You haven't done anything wrong like they think."

Irene folded and unfolded her hands miserably.

"But I have, Ellen," she whispered. "I can't explain it to you, Ed and I love each other...."

"Why don't you go away and get married, then," Ellen said in a low anguished voice.

Irene had never been able to tell Ellen the truth about Ed. Ellen had heard hints about him and in her youthful way, shrugged them off. She knew about gossip and how people made up things when they didn't really know the truth.

"We can't," Irene said at last with great difficulty. "He's already married. His wife is sick and he doesn't stay home with her very much. But he can't get divorced."

"Oh," said Ellen dropping her arms but not moving away. The fact didn't quite register. In her stubborn innocence she did not imagine that Irene and Ed did anymore than go out on dates together.

"Well, then why don't you just break up?" she asked petulantly.

Irene got up sighing as though she were ill and stood with her back to Ellen, fidgeting with the wedding ring on her finger that she had never been able to remove.

"I don't suppose you will understand for a long time and I–I– can't really explain how it is. I guess I will go away, Ellen, somewhere where I won't hurt you so much and you won't be ashamed."

"I'm not ashamed, I'm not ashamed." Ellen threw her arms around her mother, choking with tears. "I love you, I do love you, don't go away." Terror filled her at the opening of a big, dark chasm between her and her mother, one which had been widening ever since the death of her father.

Irene tried to console her although she, too, could see the chasm.

"Well, I'll probably only be going as far as Salt Lake, and you can come just as soon as I can find a place. Bessie'll help me. You'll probably like it better in the city. We'll always be close together, won't we?" She raised and kissed the bewildered tear-stained face, but she could plainly see that they wouldn't always be together. Ellen's world was already different from hers and Ellen would be a different kind of woman. She would never rely on a man as much as she had.

Irene knew now that she had no choice. Haggard from a sleepless night, she told Clinton the next day, not all that had transpired, but enough that he got the gist of it.

"The old hypocrite!" he swore fervently. "You know, that's what I've always noticed about these 'good' people. They've got to humiliate you good and proper or you can't be saved. You've got to see it their way, be like they are or you're nothing."

He guessed that Spence had put old Joe Thayer up to it. That was his round-about, cowardly way of handling things. "Seems like they can't handle anything in a straight forward way, these Mormons. Always sneaking around behind your back."

Irene couldn't quite get the drift of his reflections. There was that sarcastic note in his voice that made her uncomfortable.

"But I know I've been wrong, Clint," she said dejectedly. "And the worst thing about it is that deep down I can't find that I'm truly sorry, truly repentant–about Ed."

"I don't think we can ever be sorry for having loved genuinely and been loved," Clint said gently, patting her shoulder. She was sitting on a stool behind the counter picking nervously at her fingernails. How almost plain she looked, tired and upset, just the way Merritsville would like her to look. "Contrite" was the word he guessed and plain. Yes plainness and goodness had to go together in a woman. He had been wrong, he guessed in building up Irene's physical charms–opening her in a way to the disaster that had taken place. How were you to know when you were doing right or wrong?

"Ellen scared them off, I guess," Irene smiled wanly as she told Clinton about her daughter's tirade. "I don't know what to make of her sometimes." Clinton laughed heartily, envisioning the Teachers being driven out by an outraged kid. It cheered Irene a little but she fixed her deep, shadowed eyes on him in that hopelessly appealing way. "But what will I do now?"

"Well, I knew it was coming, Irene," Clinton began carefully. "So I've been thinking of taking you to Salt Lake. I know several of the managers of the big stores–Fred Zimmerman of Schubacher's for one. Maybe Bessie can help you find your way around. I don't think you'll have much trouble finding a job now. Things are picking up a little, I hear. I'll fix it to get off one morning next week. I have some business in the city anyway. By the way, there's a new black dress in the last shipment from Kortners. The salesladies have to wear black dresses most of the year in the big city stores and you look stunning in black with pearls."

Clinton was right; Irene had no trouble finding a job. When he introduced her to Fred Zimmerman, he was almost jealous of the glint in Fred's eye. Zimmerman was in confusion for a moment; he hadn't expected anything quite this stunning from the country. Not that he considered her perfection. Egoist and artist that he was, like Clinton he felt that he could improve on both nature and

Clinton Maxwell's work. In his mind he was rapidly sketching the blueprints for his projects. The luxuriant hair must be trimmed a little more stylishly, the bosom lifted a little, the hip trimmed ever so slightly and the foot shod in a more elegant shoe. Maybe the hemline could be lifted a little to show off her superb legs although they'd be behind counters most of the time. The hands must be trained not to fumble with the necklace or other objects and make up could be applied more expertly. Make up! That was it! Although there was really no immediate opening in the sales staff, a new line of cosmetics was coming in. They had been looking for a demonstrator. Perfect. The company would pay half her salary so that he could justify taking her on. He could keep her there until a better place opened up then who knew what the possibilities might be?

As Fred leaned attentively toward Irene, outlining the position, Clinton felt a sharp pain in his chest. He had to go to the window and draw in several sharp breaths of air before he could compose himself to the idea that she would be gone–finally, irrevocably gone. Curse that snide little town. He must get out of it as soon as he could, but he would resign himself for Irene's sake. This would be better for her and solve a lot of problems for everybody.

Late in October Irene left Merritsville. She had found renters for her house, moved most of her valuable furniture including the radio, to Addie's and arranged for Ellen to stay there until satisfactory arrangements could be made for her in Salt Lake.

She had spent a difficult hour with Addie. For all of Addie's kindness to her, she was a reproach to Irene who saw in her mother-in-law the kind of woman she ought to be and could not be. Hadn't Addie lost her husband and built a solid new life around her church, family and community? She was a living example of strength and goodness, and she had been far from stinting of it with Irene.

It was a chilly day and Irene had come dressed in her best because she was going directly from there to the Interurban. Aaron had taken her clothes and what things she needed to Bessie's where she would stay until she could get settled in a place of her own. She was wearing a new coat that Clinton had made a special price on as a sort of going away present, not telling her that he had paid for the rest out of his own pocket. It had a luxurious fox fur collar that framed her face elegantly.

"My, that coat sure is pretty," Addie stroked the fur with genuine pleasure and no trace of disapproval. "You're gettin' prettier every day, my Dear."

Irene blushed, wishing she hadn't worn it, conscious of the contrast between her and the frail, aging woman in her faded percale house dress and baggy sweater. Her hair had grown very gray and thinner and her face had deeper lines. As she shuffled about the kitchen, insisting on making Irene something warm to drink, Irene wondered how she managed to keep the ragged carpet slippers on her feet. But she couldn't feel sorry for Addie; something radiated from her that protected her from pity as well as scorn.

Glancing around the homey but shabby room, Irene wondered how on earth she had done it, how she managed to stay so cheerful, so kindly and infinitely understanding for so many years of widowhood. For all its warmth and congenial atmosphere, the clutter disturbed her–the scroungy old cat asleep on the woodbox–Irene could never stand animals in the house–rag rugs covering holes in the Congoleum, the corners of the table poking through worn, faded oilcloth and piles of sewing, books, odds and ends everywhere. How had Addie contented herself all these years? She sighed unhappily; there was just no use trying to figure it all out. In spite of her distaste for the untidiness of the place, the late morning sun streaming through the plants in the windows, the purr of the kettle, the smell of baking bread gave her a sense of infinite comfort.

Irene had noticed it first when she had started coming here with Laurence. Her Aunt's home had been ever so much finer and neater, but always a trifle chilly, always as though it had not been made for living but for arranging and looking at. And that was the way she had always tried to keep her house. No wonder Ellen often preferred it here. She wished she could stay, too, it seemed so safe, and yet she already felt separated, removed, lost from all of them. For a moment it seemed to her that everyone was making it so easy for her to leave, thrusting her out almost. Even Addie's kindness and failure to reprove her seemed that way. Tears welled up in her eyes as she set the cup of cocoa back in the saucer.

The tears came to Addie's eyes, too, and she fumbled for the piece of rag that she kept in her apron pocket. She wiped her eyes and nose then reached across the table for Irene's cold hand.

"Now, now," Addie soothed. "It ain't that bad. You really ain't goin' so far away as all that and remember this, you belong to us for always no matter what."

This distressed Irene even more. "I wish I had died when Laurence did," she blurted out. "I feel like I did that time I got lost in the pines when we were up on the summer range that summer. You remember the time I started out to meet Laurence and got turned around and wandered around for hours. I couldn't see anything. It was so dark and bristling and even when I called, my voice got lost in all those trees. I've never liked pine trees since then. It was awful. I feel like that now, Ma."

"But we found you, didn't we?" Addie said calmly. "You wasn't lost to us as long as we was lookin' for you and you for us."

Irene wiped her eyes and subsided into silence, still vaguely troubled that this wasn't quite the same.

Addie walked to the gate with her. The sun had grown stronger and light dazzled off muddy puddles left by the recent cold rain. The frost was defeated for another day, though the flowers had drooped under its rough fingers. The leaves of the Trumpet vine were still shining where the sun had not reached them and they covered the fence and light pole with a soft, lacy mantle.

"There's something comfortin' about fall and winter comin'," she mused. "You can get a bit of rest from all the hard work it takes to keep livin'. Now you cheer up, Irene, things'll turn out all right. Don't you worry a minute about Ellen. She'll be fine and you let us know how you are as often as you can." She kissed Irene who held her tightly for a moment then choking, picked her way carefully among the puddles toward the station.

Addie leaned on the gate watching her until she turned the corner, then sighing, went back to the house. She must not give in to the sadness of Irene departing under a cloud of bitterness; there were things to do to keep her spirits up for Ellen and, my goodness, she could smell her bread burning.

PART THREE

CB

Ellen had been moved in with her grandmother nearly two months by Christmas, 1936. Except for a troublesome and persistent sense of loss, life had gone on. She learned not to go by the house where she had lived so many years and not to think back too much. It had been six years since she had lost her father and now, in a way, she had lost her mother. Most of the time people were tactful about Irene, but Ellen knew why they avoided talking about her when she, Ellen, was present. She resented the air of superior virtue which she knew a lot of them felt about Irene. She had heard Aunt Dosey saying how "sorry" she felt for poor Irene. If anyone needed feeling sorry for it was Aunt Dosey; she looked so run down and worried and shabby.

Ellen had been reading in the papers about another love affair that was capturing everyone's interest over the depression and gangster news–the romance of the King of England and an American woman who had been *divorced*. Divorce was still held in the same kind of horror in Merritsville as it was in England. There were almost as few cases of it in these little towns as of homicide, and it was viewed with about as much tolerance. Since most of the marriages were Temple-sealed for time and eternity, it took a brave or foolish person to even contemplate it.

But Ellen, like many of her generation whose consciousness had been stretched beyond the mountains by magazines, newspapers, books and the radio, had a secret admiration for Wallis Simpson and her royal lover, who had set themselves against the established world of custom and thought. Irene had moved the RCA Superheterodyne radio down to Addie's and on December 10th, Ellen listened with little chills of awe to the broadcast from England announcing the abdication of Edward VIII for his love of Mrs. Simpson because he could not "discharge his duties as king without her." It was wonderful that this kind of gallantry and romance could happen in times when everything seemed so dreary, when everyone was so worried about food, shelter, clothes, the bare necessities of life.

Pictures in the papers and magazines didn't make the King out to look like the Great Lover of which most girls dreamed; in fact he resembled Mr. Cameron, the nervous little man who ran the shoe department in Washburn's. But he was a "King." Awe of royalty was still strong in the blood of most English converts and their descendants. To give up a throne for love! It was the epitome of every woman's dreams, a wonderful light note though tinged with sadness, in the grim depression atmosphere.

Unhappily, it made Ellen think of Irene and Ed who had no kingdoms to renounce and no French villas to flee to. They had just had to go along being ordinary human beings, somewhat frowned upon, partially banished, loving each other in the dingy circumstances of their lives. Ellen wondered what the difference in these two loves might be. She thought a deal about love and marriage. Remotely, like the royal romance, it had a shivery, sweet attraction; in reality it seemed dangerous, sometimes silly, sometimes scary. Most of the girls, including Lorraine, were always "falling in love." They would have an awful case on a boy one month and then on another one the next month. They were sure that the one they currently adored was the one and only with whom they would live happily ever after. Sometimes something awful happened like Elma Bates having to quit school and have a baby. The father was a fellow from Draper and didn't want to marry her. Ellen decided she would never find anybody worth that much trouble. He would have to be smart, rich and better looking than the King of England to attract her.

They talked about the King and Mrs. Simpson at Christmas dinner which was held as usual at the Walker's. Uncle Albert and Aunt Bertha and the two well-dressed "city-cousins" had come down from Salt Lake in their new, green four-door Dodge Sedan which properly impressed the country relatives. Aaron, Hal and Albert spent a lot of time hovering around it, Albert explaining all the advanced features. You could see Hal's almost greedy admiration for it. Cars were rapidly replacing the horse as the symbol of masculine prestige even in the country towns. Albert explained the long-term credit deal that he had got in order to buy it; although he had kept his job, they still had to scrape to get by, he assured them.

Irene had come with them to spend Christmas at home because Ed still had to spend it with his family. She brought an armload of expensive gifts from Schubacher's which she distributed self consciously. Ellen noticed that for all that her mother looked and smelled just as beautiful, she seemed a little sad and lost. She noted with surprise that she was wearing the pearls her father had given her so many Christmases ago. They looked nice with the smooth-fitting navy blue crepe dress. She helped with the dinner, but didn't say much. When asked, she said she liked the job and Salt Lake. She and Bessie had found a larger, nicer place and as soon as school was out, Ellen could come stay with them.

The dinner was plentiful and delicious in spite of the deepening depression but it was not an especially happy occasion. Something of the dissension of the world had found its way into the gathering; for all of Uncle Albert's long, solemn blessing on everyone and everything that was immediately blessable, a nervous gloom hung over the table. It burst into open flame in an argument between Albert, who had remained a staunch Republican and Aaron, who had become a fanatic Democrat. Roosevelt had been reelected in the November election. There had been a mild surge of optimism following his re-nomination and his pronouncement at the nominating convention of a renewal of the programs of the New Deal, ending with the portentous statement that "This generation has a rendezvous with destiny." Few had any notion of just what that destiny might be.

Uncle Albert said that Roosevelt was a dictator, a war-monger and a traitor, that his program was ruining the American spirit of self-reliance. It was creating a nation of leaners, bums and beggars who would look to the government for their support and would destroy the whole system of private enterprise and individual initiative.

Uncle Aaron, who didn't know so many big words as Uncle Albert, swore several times in his defense of Roosevelt and his program that was to put those "rich buggers" (economic royalists the President had called them) that had run the country to disaster in their place and give the poor man a chance for a change. His face got very red and blue veins swelled his forehead. It was the first time Ellen could remember an argument at a family dinner.

Aunt Dosey and Grandma kept looking at each other in alarm and finally Dosey admonished Aaron to "be quiet" since it was Christmas and a time of peace. There was an interval of strained silence before someone mentioned the no-longer King of England and "that woman." Uncle Albert, whose spleen had been frustrated on the other issue, rose at once to the topic, delivering his unequivocal opinion of a woman who was three times *divorced*!

"Twice," corrected his daughter Darlene who had become a very knowledgeable and sophisticated young lady and who filled Ellen with despair at her own lack of polish.

Her father glared at her and sputtered, one again emphasizing *divorced*. "Well, once would be a disgrace and now they're held up to the young people through the agencies of all our news media as an example to lead them further astray in these wicked times. Destroying the sanctity of marriage vows in their flaunting of all the standards of decency—destroying all the values we have been at such pains to instill in our young. Their behavior for people in high places is inexcusable."

"Oh, Papa," said Eileen, the quieter of the two girls. "Lots of people do what they did only we don't know about it."

"I think they were very noble and honest," Darlene said archly." They could have just gone on having an affair and covering up like a lot of the nobility used to."

"Young ladies!" Albert exploded, half rising from the table and looking as though his collar was going to choke him. "Don't you ever let me hear you speak with such vulgarity again. Is this what comes of our modern educational system? You see exactly what I mean?" He appealed around the table. "You see how this iniquity has worked on the minds of our young. It is told in the scriptures that there shall be wickedness and corruption in the last days and a falling away of the children from the teaching of the fathers." He settled back in his chair, wiping his mouth with an air of the vindication of prophecy.

There was a deep, troubled silence in which the clinking of silverware and dishes was extremely loud. Ellen, who was sitting beside her mother, noticed Irene's hand trembling as she pushed the food around on the plate, keeping her eyes downcast. She glanced over at her cousin Hal directly opposite. He had got to be big and good-looking but with a sullen, defiant expression. There was a sardonic grimace on his face as he continued to stare at Albert; more than anyone at the table he seemed to regard him as a stuffy old fool, someone so outdated as to be incomprehensible, but all he said in a flat drawl was, "When we gonna get the dessert, Ma, I gotta be back at the service station by three?"

It was a fortunate remark as the dinner was all but spoiled. Darlene had shrugged into exasperated silence; Albert ran his finger around the edge of his collar and applied himself, like most of the others, to the food on his plate. Ellen got up to help her grandma serve the plum pudding thinking what a strange and unhappy time had come upon all of them.

℞

"Our Father in Heaven...." Ellen had been taught to begin her prayers which she said every night, usually when she had got into bed. She never liked kneeling on the cold floor. "Father in Heaven," prayed her grandma over their simple meals. "Oh God the Eternal Father...." began the formal prayers in church. But Ellen's world was fatherless. A long time ago she had prayed through the vision of her *real* father, but what seemed an equally long time ago, he had disappeared into cloudy regions beyond her grasp. Afterward when she tried picturing God in many ways and with many faces, she could never get Him into focus. She could not find a face that fitted among the men in her small world; certainly not Ed Barker, kindly though he was. It seemed so unsatisfying to try to talk to a cloudy, misty presence with an "angry voice" like the Bible said. Why should he be angry, she wondered. He had made things the way they were. Perhaps he was disappointed like she was when something didn't turn out as she had planned and hoped.

When she thought of this kind of God and the way he was described in Sunday School stories from the Old Testament, she invariably thought of Arthur Hamilton. His gaunt, bearded, not unhandsome visage resembled some illustrations she had seen. He had a mysterious frightening quality about him—wild, fierce, subtly angry and secretive. She recalled with a twinge of envy how Simone could always, in a popular phrase, "twist him around her little finger." There were times though when even Simone seemed a little afraid of him. Ellen thought her mind must be possessed of the Devil to think of God and Arthur Hamilton at the same time. Anyway, she didn't like to think about the Hamilton's either. They had moved to Ophir and out of her life, she hoped, although she saw and heard of Simone occasionally. Simone had quit school and was reputed to be running wild, whatever that meant.

In spite of her careful reasoning, Ellen went on searching for a face that would provide her with a picture of God. She tried the face of the President of the Church, Heber J. Grant. whose picture hung above the stand in the ward. It was a long dark, foreign looking face with a beard–God had to have a beard she supposed– a good face but with a remoteness and austerity that chilled her. She even tried the face of Franklin Delano Roosevelt, which filled the newspapers and magazines and was everywhere posted in its radiant good humor. But he smoked a cigarette in a long holder and looked too glamorous, too human. The face of the man to whom she was closest during these last few years she was to live in Merritsville–Everett Gordon–was too ravaged, too sad and powerless before the ruthless mysteries of life. It began to be more and more apparent to her as she grew and observed men that they were unequal to the burdens which they had to bear, to the ideals, dreams, schemes that they built and which came tumbling down on them. It may have seemed more so because of Everett.

Ellen had not seen much of him after that first visit with her father for several years. She never learned why Irene disliked him so and could never find out just what he had done with or for her father. She remembered how fond they seemed of each other that wintry morning she had spent with them and she knew that he was high on her grandma's list of those unfortunate and unhappy people for whom she had assumed a special concern.

As a matter of fact, Addie did have a particular affection for Everett. As a young girl she had worked, as was the general custom of young girls in the poorer families, as a hired girl in the Gordon home, remaining there until her marriage. The Gordon family and home represented to her the ultimate of refinement and grace; it was the nearest to an aristocratic family that

Merritsville could experience. Being not too far removed from her English-Scottish ancestry, Addie cherished a reverence for class distinctions and held Sister Gordon up to herself and later, her daughters, as the model of a Great Lady.

Addie, going to work there when she was only fourteen, had been both house and nurse maid. The children gravitated to her because she loved them and had a great deal of patience as well as a high sense of fun. The two older girls were only slightly younger than she. The little boy Everett was her favorite. He had been an adorable, spoiled child for whom she had a special sympathy. She knew that he was not like other boys and would never fit into the tough western country life. He was exceptionally talented; his mother taught him to play the piano when he was scarcely five years old. Addie cherished the memory of the small, curly haired child who would meet her at the door every morning insisting on playing his songs just for her.

She had never ceased caring about him and his distressing failures still worried her; she looked in on him frequently when he was in town, taking a loaf of bread, a pot of jam or some other food. She knew he neglected his diet, especially when he was drinking too much. That part hurt her so bad.

Although Everett was a special case, he was only one of the many unfortunate persons and families on Addie's constant rounds of charitable visits. When Ellen had been younger, she had enjoyed going about with her grandmother to visit the poor, sick, crippled and afflicted people. She had particularly liked to go with her to Everett's house where there were piles of magazines, books and newspapers littering his back porch. While Grandma and he were visiting, she could leaf through them, discovering strange things about the world of high society, music, theater. He paid attention to her, too, as she remembered he had when she had first visited him, acting almost like a movie star with his fancy manners.

As she grew older, however, Ellen had become embarrassed with her grandmother's concern for people whom she, Ellen, thought were just plain trashy, if not disgusting, like the Lewises with all their dirty children. What was worse, Addie had taken to dispatching her on some of these missions of mercy. When she would hear Grandma muttering as she worked, "Now Sister

Bennett would enjoy a little bit of this apricot jam," or "I bet Matilda Benson would sure like a loaf of this warm bread; she's been laid up with her rheumatism all week," or "We've got more milk than we need today, Ellen. I know them Lewis kids don't get enough," Ellen would try to disappear or make up an excuse. One day she protested outrightly. "But, Grandma, why do you have to take care of all these poor people? The Church and the Relief gives them all kinds of things and I know lots of them like the Lewises just waste things."

"Well, yes," Addie admitted, thoughtfully. "I know the Church and the Government Relief take care of lots of them, gives them the necessities and things, but they don't give with a warm hand and warm heart. They don't make people feel like anybody really cares about them. You have to stay close to people to help 'em, make 'em feel like human beings and that you want to share the good things that you have with them. Them government charities and even the Church makes people feel small and ashamed when they have to accept help. A lot of church people can't give anything without a sermon to go with it and the government don't give you nothin' but the hard goods. You have to give with love or the givin' ain't no good for either the receiver or the giver."

Ellen was annoyed at how right her grandmother was about things and set her stubborn little face against her. "But how can you love all those trashy, dirty Lewises?" she asked irritably. There was a large brood of kids, one for nearly every year, who swarmed about the filthy old house in the north part of town. Marjorie Lewis was her age and none of the girls could stand to be near her, she smelled like dirty underwear.

Grandma sighed, "I do wish poor Hattie could do better. She was one of the prettiest girls you ever want to see and that house was one of the finest in town. Belonged to her folks. Her mother was a Young, you know, and her father gave her and Orson that house as a wedding present all outfitted with everything you could want. Had one of the first bathrooms in Merritsville and satin flocked wall-paper on the parlor. But Hattie never learned to manage. They had girls to help all the time she was growin' up and when Orson couldn't keep up to her style, she just let go. She's got a kind disposition, though, never complains."

Ellen couldn't see any virtue in not complaining when you

had so much to complain about. This "Lord would provide" plan that so many people had a pack of kids on didn't appeal to her sympathies. She was always getting these little bits of history about people in answer to her questions as though they somehow excused everything. Grandma was just too soft-hearted; she never seemed to feel that she had about as little as anyone. Other people did bring her things, though, and sometimes helped her out on her farm.

She couldn't dispute her grandma so she secretly decided to avoid going on as many errands except to Everett Gordon's.

The times that Ellen had gone with her grandmother to visit Everett, they had only been in the small back room where he spent most of his time. It was not until one day that Addie sent her over with some fresh eggs in a lard bucket for him that she saw the rest of the magnificent old ruin of a house.

She was unaccountably nervous about going alone. By now she knew that the stories she had heard about him being crazy and a dangerous drunk weren't true, but her heart beat queerly as she went cautiously up the weedy driveway. Everything was still and dark under the arching trees and in the tangled ruins of the garden. Peering through thorny shrubs that had once been a neatly clipped hedge bordering the drive, she could see broken statuary and a silent rusted fountain. It was the end of summer 1935 and the long matted grass was beginning to turn yellow–there were some ragged blooms on the huge half-dead rose bushes and remnants of other blossoms which thrived in spite of neglect. Even if Everett had been so inclined and spent more time there, it would have been more than he could have managed to keep it up.

Under a large, unkept arbor, half of which had sagged so that its veil of vines partially concealed a stone bench, Ellen saw or sensed a movement. She stood quite still watching the spot where the vines trembled with that curious feeling she had had long ago of entering a new and different world. At length Everett Gordon came out into the spot of sunlight that fell between the huge Locust tree and three immense pines. He stood there smoking for a moment with his face turned up to the warmth, and it struck Ellen that she had never quite seen him before.

She thought that he must have been very good looking at one time; yet there was something in his face that disturbed her. The word "sardonic" was not yet in her vocabulary, but she sensed the presence of something both fascinating and repelling. His face was an unhealthy, ruddy color tinged with fine purple veins. The eyes were set deep under graying bushy brows and the wavy hair, which began far back on the high forehead, was still dark but silvering where the sun struck it. Everett was dressed in baggy riding breeches, a dingy white shirt open at the throat and dark sweater which hung loosely on his thin shoulders. He was not an old man but looked battered by indeterminate years.

At last he moved toward the house, stamping out his cigarette. Ellen had an impulse to run, but as she moved, the eggs rattled in the bucket and Everett was close enough to hear. He came toward the bushes, parted them and stared at her for a moment as though he didn't recognize her. The glare of the sun was still in his eyes; it wasn't until Ellen spoke, holding out the bucket awkwardly, that he recognized her.

"Grandma sent these," she stammered.

"Grandma? Oh yes, Addie, it's Ellen, isn't it?" He stepped through the bushes and taking the bucket from her, put his arms around her shoulders. It made Ellen extremely uncomfortable, but she allowed herself to be guided gently up the driveway. "You must come in and I'll empty the bucket. It's so good of you to come out on such a hot day. I hope your grandmother is well."

Ellen nodded, conscious of the smell of the man–mustiness of the old, unclean fabric of his clothes, the stale tobacco and a kind of faint fragrance like perfume. Not having a father or a man about, she could not identify an after-shave cologne that Everett always used. At the same time it gave her a slight sense of nausea, she wanted to breathe deeply, get it into her very system.

As they approached the packed dirt yard back of the house, Ellen began to feel more hot and irritable and to wish that her Grandma would do her own errands. There was something about being here alone with Everett that frightened her and yet, he seemed to want to put her at ease. He too was ill at ease and noticed with embarrassment the dismal yard, littered with cans, bottles, papers and assorted trash. There was a strong smell of donkey manure and Brahms, stomping about in a litter of catalpa pods and blossoms under the tree to which he was tied, snorted and brayed derisively.

Everett Gordon stopped, dropped his arm and struck his forehead with a gesture of extreme self-disgust. "What a place to receive a lady." He shook his head in mock dismay and then turning to her with the most ingratiating smile she had ever seen on a man, bowed. "Now, Miss Kent, you just pretend that you never saw this back here. You go around the house," he pointed, "and up those big front steps and push that button by the door. I'll have my butler answer the door."

Ellen laughed, charmed in spite of her misgivings. She wondered if he were drunk. Maybe she ought to excuse herself and get away instead of entering the dark, old house. Maybe he was dangerous like some people said and her mother seemed to feel by her chilly attitude toward him. She hesitated, looking up at the heavily curtained windows of the upstairs. Thick vines had grown all over the house and various evidences of decay gave it a kind of haunted look. She went slowly by way of the crumbling walk that joined the driveway and up the steps. As she pressed the button, she could study her reflection in the oval pane of the door with its border of frosted designs and frame of elaborate carvings. Although it was dirty and stained, there were still little flecks of rainbows in the glass that fascinated her. After what seemed a long time, Everett came to the door. He had tucked his shirttail in neatly and brushed the ashes off his sweater; with a deep bow he ushered her into the large front hall, the elegance of which was still visible through dust, cobwebs and the veil of neglect that hung over it. To the left was the parlor, and directly in front was a broad curving stairway with its finely carved banister that led to the upper floor. Everett motioned her into the parlor and indicated a small elegant chair, the satin upholstery of which had faded and split so that as Ellen sat down on it gingerly, the horse hair stuffing scratched the back of her bare legs. There was a thick greenish gloom in the room.

He took a seat opposite her and since he was facing the dingy light from the heavily draped windows, she could see his face closer. His eyes were a misty amber color and his mouth was finely shaped almost like a woman's. There were wrinkles around his chin and neck but none at all on the rest of his face. Again Ellen thought the he must have been very handsome, although there was such sadness in his face that it hurt her to look at it. She felt as though someone was digging a hole in her with a rusty spoon to find things she thought buried.

Everett put his hands on his knees and leaned toward her. Ellen, suddenly aware the she had been staring at him almost rudely, looked fixedly at his hands. They had long slender fingers and, like his mouth, were almost feminine in their graceful shape. He wore a ring with a dark red stone on the third finger of his right hand.

"Well, Miss Kent, I can't tell you how happy I am to see you. I've been waiting for you a very long time, you know."

Ellen thought he was making fun of her, and then she noted the intense seriousness in his eyes. A little chill went over her and she wondered if she were in some kind of danger; the kind her mother hinted at where men were concerned. He was probably a little drunk and play-acting which seemed strange, but Ellen had always enjoyed play acting so she arose to the occasion even adding an artificial inflection to her speech as though she were reciting in a school play.

"I'm very sorry that I couldn't get here sooner. You see, I've been away in Europe this summer."

Her reply delighted Everett.

"Oh my, and how was Paris? I haven't been there in many years but the last time ... " a little smile hovered around his lips and Ellen laughed.

"I knew you had an imagination," Everett chuckled, "You wouldn't be your father's daughter without one. I hoped I'd get to know you someday like I did him. You know, I loved your father very much. Now you must tell me all about yourself. Do you play your father's violin?"

Ellen squirmed and the horsehair scratched her unpleasantly. She shook her head. "No, I play the piano a little bit. My mother taught me."

"Ah yes, your mother, Irene. How is she? I haven't seen her in quite some time. I think she didn't like me very well. A beautiful woman, your mother."

Ellen nodded. "She's fine, she works in Washburn's store."

There was an uncomfortable silence. Everett was studying her face. "You look more like your father, you know."

"Everybody says so," Ellen agreed, sorry that he had dropped the drama they had started and got back to the ordinary subjects of what parent you looked like and what grade you were in, all that childish stuff.

"It's his expression," Everett mused, "as though he didn't quite trust the world. He loved it but didn't quite trust it. That comes of being an idealist. So you don't play his violin? What became of it?"

Ellen shook her head, growing annoyed and wishing she could be gone. "It's in the closet at home. I'm not very good at music," she apologized, trying to get her dress to cover more of her legs. She wished she looked like her mother and were more dressed up. The room, although dusty and in a state of neglect, seemed to demand it. There was an obscured elegance and grace about it that she had never experienced before; the kind of room she had seen in movies and magazines that was the setting for beautiful, gracious women. Everett noticed her eyes wandering about.

"You like this room?" He fumbled for his cigarettes and lit one nervously.

"It, it's so different," Ellen managed. "I never saw anything just like it except in movies. It makes me feel...."

"Yes, like that." He smiled at her kindly. "It was a beautiful house, magnificent ... out of place here in this town. It does belong to the past, like a museum. That's why I don't like to live here very much, dangerous to spend too much time in the past. In these times we can't sell it; too big and in the wrong place. Somebody has to be around part of the time. Would you like to see the rest of it?"

"Oh, yes," She leaped up eagerly. It had begun to enchant her as though she had stepped into a dream. There were twelve rooms in the main part of the house not counting the pantry and kitchen where Everett spent most of his time. The parlor and drawing room occupying the whole southwest side of the house seemed to Ellen almost as big as the meeting house. Everett lead her up the stairs to where there had been five bedroom, a nursery and two bathrooms. He didn't show her all of them because, as he apologized, they had not been cleaned for a long time. As she peered into the quiet, dim rooms, she felt as though she were looking into all the romantic books she had read. Ghosts of persons who must have lived a much more glamorous and exciting life than the people she knew now floated in the dusty light. Outside of books and movies she had never seen heavy velvet drapes, poster beds, crystal chandeliers, deep flowered carpets and elegant furniture.

She hesitated when they came back to the head of the wide, sweeping staircase and conjured a vision of herself in one of those old-fashioned, full-skirted dresses that she had seen Bette Davis wearing as she descended into the arms of a dashing lover.

"Oh, it's just like in a movie," she breathed in wonder.

Everett smiled. "Yes, isn't it? A Civil War saga or Gothic horror, I dare say," he murmured. Ellen wondered what he meant; he was a funny man.

"But come, my Dear, what I most want to show you, your father's favorite place, I saved until last. The library, here." He indicated a door at the end of the hall on the first floor.

The room was dark because of the closed moldering drapes. At first, Ellen could not see shelves filled with books covering most of the walls. Everett pulled the drapes. The low western sun thrust a ramp of sunlight into the room down which the dust motes swarmed. Ellen walked around the room, overwhelmed at the presence of so many books in any one place except the public library. She was filled with an intense hunger to know what was stored up in all those volumes. Awestruck she walked round and round the room, her hands folded behind her back, afraid to reach out and touch anything lest she was enchanted and it would all disappear. Everett, after watching her quizzically for a few, long breathless moments, took down a small volume. The gold edge leaves were stiff and yellow and the book creaked as he opened it at a marked place. In a low vibrant voice he read:

By a lone wall a lonelier column rears
A gray and grief worn aspect of old days
'Tis the last remnant of the wreck of years,
And looks as with a wild-bewildered gaze
Of one to stone converted by amaze
Yet still with consciousness ...

He broke off with a self-conscious laugh, "Ah, poor Byron."

A chill ran up and down Ellen's spine as Everett read. The sound of his voice with its soft, yet husky, intimate quality had penetrated very deep in her nervous consciousness. It created an unbearable excitement in her.

"I write poems sometimes," she burst out and immediately thought it sounded so childish.

"You do?" Everett put down the book and crossed over to her. He took her hands in his. His voice was very low and trembled. "I knew you must have your father's music in you in some way. Ellen, I want you to come over here often if you can and read as much as you like. You may even take the books home if you want to. That way you will learn how to write your poetry best. You must sing your own music in your own way of course, but you must be conscious of the legacy of the world. That was your father's misfortune, he hadn't had time to learn...."

Ellen couldn't understand what he was talking about and, though she didn't mind his holding her hands so long and tightly, she had begun to wish that he would let go and not talk in that strange way. She averted her head slightly, whispering shyly but fervently, "I will, Oh, I will come often. I love books."

He dropped her hands and there was a taut silence between them.

"Well as a starter, why don't you take this small volume of Elizabeth Barrett Browning. She has good rhythms and she can't do a young lady any real harm." He handed her *Sonnets from the Portuguese*, then accompanied her to the door.

It was growing evening as Ellen bounded down the step, waving to Everett who was standing in the shadows of the porch and promising to come again soon. She was filled with an intense excitement and went skipping down the weedy paths, leaping across the irrigation ditches and jumping up to catch leaves off the trees. Once she stopped to read a few lines of a poem where there was a faded satin ribbon marker which began, "How Do I Love Thee?" She stood reading it aloud to a shaggy old fence post, thrills of joy suffusing her.

After he had watched Ellen disappear down the road, Everett went back through the front door of the house. He badly wanted a drink, but he had been trying this summer to get straightened out. The turmoil of emotions that Ellen had stirred in him, memories of her father, the person he had loved in other days as tenderly as any he had ever known had so unsettled him that he was on the verge of tears. He started for the secret cache where he kept a bottle, but as he passed the parlor door where the grand piano stood in its dust and draping, he hesitated and went in. Dusting off the keys with his crumpled, soiled handkerchief, he began to play. His fingers were stiff and the piano was out of tune, but for the first time in such a long time that he could scarcely remember, the need for music was stronger than that for alcohol. He felt the claims of life more than death.

A few people passing the old Gordon place heard melody coming from it quite late in the evening. It was a broken melody stopping, starting over again, faltering, sometimes soaring and sometimes ceasing for an interval then resuming. Some of the townspeople shook their heads sorrowfully and scornfully; others commented on the sin and wastefulness of Everett Gordon's life. Everett, oblivious to them, played on, tears streaming down his face most of the time, dead years rising all around him. The future taunted him in the sweet, smooth face of a young girl that so resembled the face of a young man he had known and loved in other better years. In Byron's words, he had found that he was "yet with consciousness."

❧

Ellen spent a great many hours in the old house after that day. There was a deep window seat in the library, and there she curled up among dusty cushions, buried in the great literary past. Picking the books off the shelves at random, she read without guidance except when Mr. Gillis, her English teacher in high school, mentioned some author or book. Sometimes she talked to him about the library and Everett and he gave her book lists. She found Shakespeare a bit too difficult for the most part, and her attempts to reach the closely packed verse of *Paradise Lost* in a beautifully illustrated volume were futile. She spent most of her time reading novels or the small volumes of poetry by Shelley, Keats, Wordsworth, and others of the romantic and Victorian poets.

In addition to this reading, Everett had piles of magazines that his sisters sent him. She sometimes read these in the kitchen or on the back porch in good weather. He took the *Salt Lake Tri-*

bune by mail and one day Ellen discovered a small supplement in the Sunday issue written entirely by kids around her own age. It was called the *Tribune Junior*; she poured over it eagerly each week until she got up courage to send a couple of her poems to it. When they were printed both she and Everett were ecstatic.

He put a supply of paper, pen and ink at the desk in the library for her and spurred her on constantly. Sometimes sitting at the corner of the cluttered kitchen table with a cup of weak milk tea, she read her things aloud to him. He always praised her warmly. One day she grew impatient and putting her paper down, looked at him sternly. "But you don't help me, Everett, because you don't tell me what's wrong with them."

"They sound all right to me," he said sincerely. "I'm not a very good judge of literature, Ellen, but they sound very good to me for your age. You'll have to keep reading and writing until you find out what you want to say and how you want to say it, then you'll be able to tell yourself whether it's good or not." He patted her head fondly. "Maybe you sound a little too old at times, use too many big words. I don't know. Why don't you ask your teachers?"

She looked at him slyly from under her bangs. "Maybe someday I'll write a story about you," she said and then fired with sudden inspiration, "Why don't you tell me about your life, Everett, and I'll write it all down in a notebook and write a book about you?"

She was surprised at the look of intense pain and sadness that came into his amber eyes. He shook his head. "It would be a sad story, Ellen, one better not told."

Ellen knew she must not push the subject, but from time to time, he did tell her things and Grandma told her others. Gradually she pieced the fragments of his life together in a colorful but imperfect mosaic.

Everett himself never said exactly, although he mentioned things in such a way that it seemed the legends of the town about the Gordon family were more or less true, especially that they had been wealthy and aristocratic. It was not until many years after that Ellen could put it all in perspective, but she did realize that the big house was exceptional in its elegance and grace beyond even the finest houses of which there were a fair number on the west side of town. The library was particularly unusual for in the West, as in much of the rest of pioneer America, wealth and worldly culture did not always go together.

The Gordons had not been true pioneers in the covered wagon sense. They had not come to Utah until the 1880's and they came by train bringing money, education and a fashionable background with them. Everett's mother had been converted to the church mostly through the efforts of a younger brother who became one of the more prominent members of the church. She was by temperament a serious and devoutly religious woman and Mormonism supplied dimensions of religious experience that the Protestant denomination in which she had been raised, did not. She had been a beautiful woman and talented as well. Her picture, an oil painting in a heavy elaborate frame, hung above the fire place in the main parlor. Occasionally Ellen studied it carefully, admiring the incredibly small waist, the elegant tilt of the fine head with its load of heavy dark hair. She could see Everett in that face especially in the shadowed brooding eyes and the fine hands.

His father's picture, also a good oil painting, hung in the library. Ellen had seen a great many portraits like it of the stern, proud Victorian father in a high uncomfortable collar, sitting very stiff and straight and staring out of the picture with piercing eyes. He had side whiskers and his hair was parted in the middle. Ellen was surprised to see that he had the same finely modeled mouth as Everett.

Everett Gordon Senior had allowed himself to get baptized into the Mormon church to please his wife, had performed his duties perfunctorily and had given generous amounts of money to it, but his true faith was in worldly pursuits. He had a keen, retentive, inquisitive mind and was one of those men who made money naturally. He was easily persuaded to come to Utah because he was ready for new fields of endeavor and could see a great potential in the West. He was not disappointed; he did well and contributed a great deal to the development of industry. He had decided to build a home in Merritsville, feeling that Salt Lake was already crowded and too close to the main center of the Church. But he was never a true westerner by either taste or habits.

Everett talked more about his mother, whom he had idolized

but little about his father with whom, Ellen rightly suspected, he hadn't got on so well. There had been five children, three girls and two boys of which Everett was next to the youngest. When Cecil, his younger brother, died of diphtheria at the age of three, Everett who was then five, became the focus of his mother's adoration and his father's ambitions. His mother, who had considerable musical talent and the advantage of dominating him in his earliest and most impressionable years, filled him with music and religion. He took better to the former than the latter. As he grew older his father tried to interest him in business and the pursuit of philosophical knowledge. There was the inevitable confusion. Both parents agreed that Utah schools were inadequate; all the children were sent for varying intervals to eastern schools. Mr. Gordon conceded at length that Everett would never succeed in business and agreed to his pursuing a musical career. He was able to enter a famous conservatory where he did exceptionally well and went on professional concert tours.

Ellen was never able to discover when or why the process of deterioration set in. She knew there had been a woman–Everett had been married in the east and rumor had it that he had a child. He himself never spoke of it to her. He had still been a young man when he came back to Merritsville in a disgraceful condition. His mother had died before this; he was grateful that she hadn't lived to see what he had become. While his father was still alive, he permitted Everett to live in the big house where he seldom spent much time himself; he had moved to a hotel in Salt Lake City and traveled a great deal. When he died he left the house and its furnishings to Everett and a small income strictly administered by a bank. His older sisters assumed a kind of guardianship over him. From time to time they were summoned to place him in care of a sanitarium where he was able to overcome the ravages of alcohol for a while. He would return to Merritsville a little more ravaged each time.

Ellen, in whom the abhorrence of drunkenness had been firmly instilled by her grandmother, mother and the Church, wondered in distress about Everett. She knew that he didn't drink all of the time, but that there were periods when he would succumb to liquor for days or weeks. Once in a while he would not answer her knock or ring. Then she knew that it had got the worst of him, so she would stay away for a time until she thought that he had got himself in hand again. He never talked about it to her, she guessed he was ashamed.

Gradually Ellen learned bits about Everett's association with her father. When Everett had first come back to Merritsville, and even now occasionally, he could be prevailed upon to play in public or help with the presentation of musical events. It was at one of these when Laurence was just past sixteen and already going with Irene, that Everett heard him play his violin and was struck by the skill he displayed. Laurence, who had shown talent at an early age had long been taking lessons from an old German who also mended shoes but whose musical knowledge was sound. Although far from polished, he handled the instrument with great feeling. Everett recognized it at once and offered to give him the benefit of his training and talent. The two became devoted–often to the exclusion and consternation of Irene–and spent all the hours that Laurence could spare working on music and playing together. Everett had a renewed surge of hope and interest; if he couldn't salvage his own talent, perhaps he could still save it through Laurence.

Besides the receptive, sensitive and intelligent young boy filled many needs in Everett's life at the time, and he was the son of his dear Addie Kent. Although, of course, she never ranked in his affections with his mother, it was she who had played with him, laughing, romping, childish games that his mother never could. She had taken him and his sisters out in the fields and hills, show-ing him flowers, birds, trees, insects, animals all the living things that boys ought to know. She had taken him into the warm, homely life of the people around him. How he had loved to go to her house even after she was married just as the fragrant bread was coming out of the oven and get the first steaming piece broken off the loaf, dripping with butter and honey.

After he had been sent away from Merritsville to school, he had lost touch with her for a while, although he could always invoke that warm, sunny feeling associated with the spring smell of blooming alfalfa when he thought of her. He tried to send her little messages and gifts from time to time. She was one of the reasons he had not been entirely reluctant to return to Merritsville; although he was ashamed to have her witness his failure, he knew that she would never judge nor abandon him. Now if he could do something for her, could join their families again in something creative and good, perhaps he might salvage his image in her eyes. Laurence had that good, sweet harmony with the earth that his mother had, something the world was losing, or had lost. There was something in Everett's affection for Laurence that he had to keep carefully guarded. He had discovered in his travels, his experience and his marriage that he was not quite like other men. He had fallen in love with a beautiful woman musician but shortly after their marriage, discovered that there was something lacking, something wrong that he could not define and of which he was ashamed. It had contributed to their unhappiness, separation and his drinking. He knew that Laurence did not suspect, did not reciprocate. He was in love with Irene whom he shortly married, and his affection for Everett, although deep, was secondary to that.

But Everett could not give up the association. It was the one thing that kept him going. He and Laurence had talked about Laurence's musical career, hoping against hope that there would be a way for him to get more training, to perhaps go east. Then the war, his marriage to Irene and the child coming later added to the enticement to get rich quick in the sheep business put an end to Everett's last dream. Because he had come to love Laurence for himself, he helped him keep up the fiction that his training and ambitions might still be realized.

He told Ellen once that he thought that, besides his mother, he had loved Laurence more than anyone he had ever known, but it was through one of those strange, common incidents that no one can plan or foresee that she learned the depth and strength of their bond. It was almost like a message from beyond if one wanted to believe in things like that.

On a bright-blue October day of 1936 Ellen was helping her mother get ready to move. Irene was sorting through the cedar chest, a task which she had put off until the last. In the very bottom under her wedding dress, Ellen's baby clothes, among which was the broken doll and the scrapbook she had made for her father, a collection of towels with crocheted borders, quilts, doilies and other fancy work was a yellowed bundle of music. It was just as Aaron had brought it to them with the rest of Laurence's things that bleak February day almost six years ago.

Ellen noticed that her mother's hand shook as she undid the soiled string and tried to smooth out the curled sheets. Some of it was popular music, including the pieces that Irene had bought Laurence on that last Christmas, but a large part of it was a composition, hand-written, scribbled in Laurence's neat, old-fashioned handwriting. Bending over her mother's shoulder, she tried to make out the fading but vital script. Goose pimples broke out all over her. It was as though they were stumbling on to a secret clue for which they had been searching–the clue that might explain why their lives had broken so tragically apart–only to find that it was in an unreadable language.

Irene was on her knees beside the chest and Ellen knelt beside her, trying to help her press the sheets out flat. Warily they peeled them off one by one but they had been rolled so long that they coiled and sprang out of their hands like live things. When they came to a page that had a strange brownish streak as though something had splashed accidentally across it, Irene gave a choked cry and covered her white face with trembling hands.

"Take 'em out and burn 'em," she cried in a strangled voice and then in a whisper of agony, "No, no, don't do that. Keep them, Ellen, they're yours to remember your father."

Ellen gathered the scattered sheets, her chest full of rocks that rumbled around and ground each other like boulders in a swollen creek bed. As she picked up the pages, she noticed a note at the top of one underlined emphatically, "be sure to show this to Everett." It had a curious urgency, as though written only yesterday. She thought it best not to show it to her mother, who was hastily piling all the things back in the cedar chest as though to keep something from escaping from its fragrant depths, so Ellen put the page on the top of the roll and tied the string around it. She would show it to Everett sometime and maybe he could restore the lost communication between her and her father–the father who was now a blurred legend. She carried it to her room and put it on the pile of "precious" things which she was taking to Grandma's. It rolled over and came to rest beside the doll with a beautiful, broken and imperfectly mended face.

It was several weeks before Ellen got settled at her grandmother's and Irene left for Salt Lake City. In the confusion she had almost forgotten the music which had been stuffed into cardboard boxes with all the other things. The first Sunday in November was cold, gray and the afternoon threatened to be long and dismal. Ellen decided to sort out the boxes and came across several books belonging to Everett that she had long neglected to return. Abandoning the project of putting away her things, which intensified her sense of loss, she started for Everett's. Maybe a new book would help her forget that she no longer had a home in Merritsville. Even though she had always spent a great deal of time at Grandma's, there was always the knowledge that she could go back to where her mother was in the place they had shared so long.

Half way down the road to Everett's she remembered the music and hesitated. Should she really show it to him? Why had her dead father's message seemed so pathetically beseeching, so urgent? She turned back and got the parcel of music that she wrapped in newspaper to protect it from the drizzle of rain.

Everett was slow getting to the door when she knocked. The house was so gloomy and dark when he did let her in that she was almost sorry she had come. Although he seemed pleased to see her, he was somewhat quiet, remote. "Come in, come in," he urged. "It's been quite a while, have you been ill?"

"No," Ellen shook herself out of her coat. "We had to get moved. Mama's got a job in Salt Lake and I have to stay with Grandma to go to school until she finds a place for us."

"Hmm, so Irene is leaving Merritsville. I always thought...." He didn't say what he thought, but turned on the light, a fly specked bulb which hung on a crusty cord from the center of the ceiling. Its sickly yellow glare did nothing to improve the depressing clutter of the room which was very warm and full of the smell that Ellen had come to associate with Everett–coffee, tobacco smoke, old papers, stale food odors. Everett had been eating a small meal on the corner of the table. He pushed some of the clutter back to make a space for her. "Come have a cup of tea; it's so cold and miserable out. I think I'll go down to my sister's place in St. George this winter."

As she had been leaving, her grandmother had thrust a chunk of apple sauce cake in a sack for Everett. She brought it out, and they shared it over the hot drinks with a mild sense of comfort.

"I've got something to show you," she said when they were settled and thrust the parcel of music at him.

"What's this?" He looked at it curiously.

"Something Mama and I found when we were moving, something of Daddy's that had a note in it to you."

Everett looked at her with a frown as he slipped the string off the roll. He was obliged to push some of the stuff off the table in order to find a place to spread out some of the sheets of music. Then he had to get up and adjust the poor light on its round silver pulleys and put on a pair of spidery gold rimmed glasses before he could see what was on the paper.

"It's Daddy's music, we found it in the cedar chest the other day and it had this note in it," she explained, thrusting the page with the notation closer to him. He gave a little choked exclamation of surprise and inspected the sheet closely. Pulling his chair closer and pushing the dishes out of the way, he inspected the manuscript for what seemed to Ellen a long time, mumbling and shaking his head, alternately smiling and frowning. She watched him anxiously. Suddenly he jumped up.

"I must try this on the piano," he murmured and started through the cold, dark house to the parlor. Ellen grabbed her coat and followed him. He opened up the piano and spread the music out as best he could. It was still so curly that Ellen had to stand beside him and hold it out. He opened the heavy draperies, brought a lamp and sitting down, began to feel his way over the cold keys. The melodies awoke in fragments from the pages, filling the room now with sunshine and laughter, now with tears and fear. They didn't fit too well together and it was difficult for Everett to pick them out completely. He studied them with growing anxiety, making those nervous noises with his mouth that sometimes bothered Ellen. His hands were stiff and uncertain; at last they came down on the keyboard with an angry, pitiful crash.

"My God, my God! Why couldn't it have been?" he cried in anguish and put his head down on the piano and sobbed. His shoulders shook beneath the old black sweater and one hand lying on top of the piano was clenched into an agonized fist that kept beating the piano so that the strings vibrated and the music scattered all about them. Ellen was terrified. She had never seen a man so upset and she stood looking at him with fear and a kind of misery that made her want to run but, knowing that it had been her fault by bringing the music, she summoned courage enough to touch him. The rough feel of the sweater surprised her; it was as though she expected to find herself in a dream and that this wasn't happening. Everett grasped her hand so hard that she winced and then pulled her to him. Instinctively, she stiffened and backed away, even more frightened. But then he seemed to get hold of himself, dropped her hand and blew his nose loudly.

"I'm sorry," he mumbled and began gathering up the scattered sheets of music. Silently they went back to the kitchen. Ellen was shivering not only from the cold. Everett poked up the fire and pushed the coffee pot to the front. Then he sat down in the old platform rocker and began looking at the music pensively. After a while he began to talk, almost as though he were talking to himself.

"You know, I had almost convinced myself that it wasn't there, that he didn't have that much of a gift. I had only dreamed or wished it, but, by God, it was there." He smote the sheets of paper with the back of his hand and leaned toward her. "Ellen, *it was there!*"

Ellen didn't know quite what he was talking about; she felt distinctly uneasy, on the verge of tears herself. Jumping up, wide-eyed, she got his coffee cup and filled it carefully while he went on, still mumbling so that she couldn't follow him. Gradually she began to understand.

"You know, Ellen, this is the greatest of all tragedies, to waste a gift or let it be destroyed, even a small one and your father's was not a small one. Neither was mine, but they were incomplete, they were destroyed by this time and place. Mind you, Ellen, it takes three thing to produce great art–natural talent and thorough training and education, and roots in time and place. I had the first two but not the last; your father had the first and last but not the training and education. I think I see it now the way I never saw it before. But what's the good? It's too late...." He stopped on a bitter note and took a sip of the scalding coffee Ellen had handed him. He always drank his coffee very hot, so hot Ellen could hardly believe it. She watched his face anxiously, hoping he wasn't going to cry again.

After a long interval in which he seemed to be gazing off into a very distant time, he resumed, " Yes, I think I see it and maybe that's the important thing to be able to see clearly at some time in your life. It might be good for you, it might just save you." But he lost the train of his thought and lighting a cigarette, sat motionless staring into space. She wondered if she should just slip away but then he roused.

"If only we could have worked together a little longer, if only we had had more means. You see what this time and western country needed was somebody to express it in music as it was. Your father knew these mountains, streams, people in a way I never did. My father never let us really live here or be part of this. He sent me away to the east where music was old. When I got through learning about the rest of the world, I didn't have anything special to say except what had been said. I knew how to say it–oh yes, I was a good musician but I didn't have anything special to say. I was a good concert pianist, did you know that, Ellen?"

"Yes, I heard, Grandma told me. She has clippings," she murmured.

"Now your father, he was part of this world and he felt it and he had something important all his own to say. You could hear a little bit of it when I played, so badly, of course, but," he leaned urgently toward her, "you could hear the high pine-covered mountains, wide deserts, big free skies, couldn't you?" Ellen was not sure what she had heard, but she nodded seriously.

"But he didn't have the means to express it the way he needed, wanted to. He got cut off from the great traditions of music by these mountain barriers and the mountain barriers in the minds of these small-town people. Oh, if we had only had more time. Ellen, there is so little time and yet so much of it when you have wasted it." Tears filled his eyes again and he was obliged to stop and wipe them. His hand shook so that the cup rattled against the arm of the rocker. Ellen took it gently away and went over and looked out the window. It was raining harder, and she had a sense of panic, of being locked in the tragedy of the past. The heat and smells of the room were suffocating her. "I guess I'd better go. Grandma wanted me to come back before church time," she said in a small nervous voice.

Everett got up sighing. "I'm sorry I let myself go like this, Ellen."

He laid his hand gently on her shoulder. "I don't suppose you'll ever know how I felt about your father. Next to my mother, I think I loved him more than any person I ever knew, and I've never been reconciled to his death. You remind me so much of him."

Ellen nodded. "How I wish that you had studied music," he went on. "I think you might have finished what he had begun here." He indicated the sheets of music, now rolled together on the table. "Ah well, you have your own gifts. In a way you can realize his dream if ...ah, "if" is such a futile word. I must be grateful that you have come to me for a little while."

He dropped his hand and sat down in the straight chair by the table. Ellen got into her coat and tied a scarf over her head. She wrapped the roll of music carefully, thinking it might have been better if she and her mother had burned it.

"Did you want to take some more books?" Everett asked as she prepared to leave.

"I'll get some next week when I come to get the paper," she said, anxious to get away, away from Everett's ravaged face, the musty, untidy, dreary house that seemed haunted by so much sadness and regret. She ran all the way home in the rain, the bundle under her coat and was happy to burst into her grandmother's warm, fragrant kitchen where a small supper they ate before going to the evening church meeting was spread out.

In the middle of the next week when she went back to Everett's, the house was dark and there was no smoke coming from the back chimney. Brahms was missing so she knew that he had gone away again. Hal said he had been picked up drunk by the sheriff one night last week, but you couldn't tell about Hal; he was always lying. She didn't know when he would return. Everyone she loved seemed to be leaving her except Grandma; she wondered if life would always be like this.

ᘓ

Ellen missed her mother and Everett but her grandmother, who had always been her anchor through these turbulent years, was still there. They had settled into a comfortable relationship and, while there was a cluster of shadows in the corners of her mind, she was not unhappy. Irene and Ed drove down to see them frequently bringing clothes and gifts and taking them out for rides. Once in a while Ellen went to Salt Lake City on the Interurban and stayed with her mother and Bessie in their apartment. It was those times that seemed strangest; Ellen couldn't yet see her mother separated from the home they had shared in Merritsville. She seemed like a different person. She wondered how Irene managed to put up with Bessie who was noisy and untidy. Most of all she enjoyed going into the big department store where Irene worked. She would stand where she could watch her mother dispense expensive cosmetics from the fragrant, glittering cubicle and try to put her back into the picture of the mother she once knew. Not that she minded so much; she sometimes bragged about her mother working at Schubacher's in Salt Lake.

She kept in touch with Everett, too; his sisters had given Addie a key to the house a long time ago with the understanding that she would keep an eye on Everett when he was there and the house when he wasn't. After Everett's recent departure, Addie and Ellen cleaned up the back rooms as best they could. He had told Ellen that she could have access to the books so sometimes she went there and read or borrowed them, but the big house seemed haunted by his presence. She tried to get her grandmother to talk about the Gordon family; Grandma didn't seem to fully realize that the grandeur of the Gordon house and family was over, meant little to the people of Merritsville, especially in these days of Depression. Everett was simply the town drunk now. The kids thought his house was haunted and everybody made jokes about him and his old donkey. It hurt her to hear them and she felt that she alone knew him, knew what he was like. It struck her as comical when Grandma sometimes referred to him as "that boy." "I hope that boy can get over his trouble for good this time," she said several times as they prowled around through the weeds and debris, checking windows and doors so dismally closed on the world.

Ellen was made especially lonesome by the messy spot where Brahms had been kept–the scattered straw and drying manure and his crude vacant shelter. She had grown fond of the donkey and had learned to talk to him, pet him and laugh at his hideous bray. Once she had asked Everett why he had such a funny pet; he had said that he needed the company of another Jackass and he had discovered that Brahms appreciated music. Sometimes he startled her with an odd sense of humor and fun that didn't fit with what he mostly was. He was so much like a fine gentleman out of the older novels that she read–the way he talked and his gentle, refined manners and intelligence. How could he spend his life as he did here in this decaying, sad place with only a donkey for company or in a sanitarium for drunkards? She had asked her grandmother this question as they walked home one afternoon from their melancholy tour of inspection.

Grandma sighed. "I don't know. I wish I knew. Sometimes I've tried to figure it all out and the nearest I can come, I guess it was because everybody, the girls, his mother, his father–everybody spoiled him but they expected so much of him. All of 'em expected something different. His ma wanted him to be one thing– a musician and faithful to the church. His pa wanted him to be a business man, a money maker. Each sister had a little plan for Everett. Nobody ever seemed to wonder if he had any plans for himself. They spoiled that boy rotten and I guess I did, too, when I was there. My but he was the handsomest little boy, bright and sweet to everybody. You couldn't help but love him and spoil him. His mother, why she doted on that boy, she worshipped the ground he walked on. His father was a lot sterner but you could tell he was proud, my he was proud even though he didn't want Everett to be a musician."

Grandma stopped in the path and looked into the distance as though she was reentering the past. "I used to watch him when I could settin' at the piano with his mother nearby. A fine lookin' pair, just like a picture–him playin' for her and listenin' so careful when she pointed out things to him. Sometimes they'd play duets and then laugh and hug each other like...." Addie's trembling voice trailed off into silence as though she was completely absorbed in the vision that her memories had conjured up. She had evoked a vivid picture for Ellen, who could see the beautiful woman in the portrait sitting at the big polished piano in the fine room, but it was hard to imagine that the man she knew could have been that same boy. He could never have been like the boys she knew–like Hal for instance.

Coming back to the present, Grandma went on in a steadier voice. "He was a prince, we all made him think that, too, and I guess when he got out in the world things was different, harder than he thought they would be. The Prophets warn us about the wickedness of the world. Only the Lord knows what could have happened for him to fall so low; only the Lord can help him now. I did think he was doin' better this time."

Ellen ached now with the thought of the man, the sad, disconcerting but now dear man who was so real to her. A flood of longing to reach back to that beautiful lost boy and help him filled her, help him at the place where his life might have been different, where his talent might have been fulfilled and not just spent on the empty house and the donkey. Yet if he had gone on to be a successful musician, if his life had been different, she wouldn't have known him most likely: anyway he couldn't have been what he now was to her. He couldn't have given her the help, encouragement and stimulation, the precious books that nobody else in the town could have. It was all so peculiar, just as peculiar and unreasonable and absurd as Brahms.

When Everett was away, Brahms was kept by Horace McDaniel in one of the pastures that Addie and Ellen had to pass on the way home. She saw his shaggy, ungainly figure browsing along the near ditchbank and called to him. He raised his head, waved his floppy ears and came loping over to the fence. She patted him fondly and whispered in his ear, "Don't forget him and make him hurry back." Brahms tossed his rough head, curled his thick black lip back over his greenish teeth and gave out with his horrendous, tragic bray.

Ellen's life, however, was largely filled with school, reading, writing and church. Ellen liked school and got along well with most of her teachers with the exception of the gym teacher, Miss McDonald, a solid, square built, no nonsense woman who was determined to build all her young women into fit athletes. They had a constant, but submerged, feud with Ellen getting out of the activities of the gym class as often as she could and Miss McDonald making sarcastic remarks as she wrote "E" in her roll book. "E" meant that you were having a period and once Miss McDonald called Ellen in and told her wryly that perhaps she should see a doctor as hers were abnormally long. It wasn't that Ellen didn't like activity but she hated drill and exercise to music and shuffling round and round the gym in preparation for the "posture parade." She knew she would never be chosen for the track meet no matter what she did. Most especially she hated Volley ball–her hands were thin and delicate and trying to pound that immense, ugly ball back over the net among a bunch of crowding, sweating, giggling girls was a horror to her. The public showers where the girls made remarks about each other's deficiencies, amplitudes or underwear were a humiliation to Ellen whose body seemed so private and personal, so unique that she didn't want it compared with the others. She felt sorry for some of the girls like Marjorie Lewis whose underwear was ragged and dingy and others who were as miserable as she. Finally Miss McDonald gave up and put her in charge of the lockers where she could earn her credit by handing out the gym suits and equipment and where, amid the smells of sweat soaked canvas, drill cloth and rubber, she could get in some extra studying.

Aside from this, it had been wise for Ellen to stay at Merritsville High. Here she had the advantage of being known for her abilities and was given the chance to use them. She was editor of the school paper, on the debate team and in the school play, on the assembly and activities committee and stood a good chance of being representative girl for scholarship. In addition she still wrote for *The Tribune Junior* and had consequently picked up a long list of pen-pals with whom she exchanged frequent long, serious idealistic letters.

Of course she kept on reading voraciously. One of the big events of 1937 was when the Carnegie librarian handed her a crackling new copy of the *Gone With the Wind*. Along with millions of other women, Ellen imagined herself a Scarlett O'Hara as she had once thought of herself as Anne Shirley. Scarlett's heart was the torn and divided one of modern woman–the longing for the old fashioned romantic dreams of the past and the need to survive in a chaotic world that was changing brutally. Nobody wanted to be like the passive, gentle Melanie whose world had been destroyed.

Ellen was not able to understand the need to escape the dreariness of the present for the drama of a fictionalized past, but she succumbed whole heartedly to the charms of Rhett Butler, suffered through the devastation of the burning of Atlanta and cried all one wet spring afternoon over the death of Bonnie Butler. Oddly enough the passage which remained with her the longest and haunted her like a premonition of doom was the one in which Scarlett, married to and enfolded in the arms of the infinitely attractive Rhett, longs for Ashley. It seemed to her the bleakest of all possible fates for a woman–not to be able to love a man to whom she was married. Like a familiar figure in fog that assumes one shape after another, its meaning eluded her. She had never understood her mother's need for Ed, the confusing emotion that made women and men a bit crazy.

Altogether, though, except for occasional spells of depression and purplish melancholy which would strike her and send her on long walks through fields and up over the cemetery hill where she would sometimes sit looking out over the beautiful valley that stretched between blue-purplish hills and high granite peaks far away to the pearlescent lake or, in bad weather, keep her huddled up in the rocking chair by the kitchen window for hours on end, she was content. Life was very strong in her and she enjoyed its nuances, even the darker ones. She could always write poems about her moods. Sometimes she thought she might enjoy her sorrows as much as her joys.

The most troublesome parts of her life still had to do with love and religion. Love, to Ellen, as with all the girls her age, meant the boy-girl-man-woman kind of love. Other kinds of love were pretty well defined but this kind was infinitely varied and confusing even in books. Love of all kinds was intricately linked to religion which meant The Church and, in Utah, Religion with a capital 'R' was the one absolutely unavoidable fact of life. Love was talked about in church a great deal and marriage most explicitly emphasized. At its most elemental level, church was where girls went voluntarily to be near boys and vis-a-versa. Of course, they went to school together, but it was somehow different. There was a heightened sexual consciousness in church because one of the main aims was to get all men and women paired up together for eternity in the Celestial Kingdom.

Ellen, who didn't find most of the boys of Merritsville interesting, went to all the church meetings because she had been accustomed to and living with grandma made it all but impossible not to. Mutual was the worst of all. The Mutual Improvement Association or MIA held meetings on Tuesday nights in the recreation hall. There were a number of activities from dancing to athletics and drama designed to keep the young wholesomely occupied under the watchful eye of the Church. Ellen took part in some of the dramatics, went to her classes and gave readings or talks when called upon. Generally the purpose of Mutual for the young was the pairing off and walking home or taking a ride if somebody could get a car. Few minds could concentrate on the "uplifting lessons " for wondering anxiously whether or not "he" had come and whether, if he hadn't, was he hanging around outside? Some of the boys, frankly bored with the proceedings, loafed about, waiting for the right girl to come out. Ellen knew that none of them waited for her; her mind was busy with other distractions while the well-meaning teacher droned on and on abut the same old things she had heard for an eternity and understood less now than when she had first heard them.

It seemed especially bad tonight. After the preliminaries in which Ellen had participated with a humorous reading, prayers, songs, announcements and inspirational messages, they had filed out to the classes in the basement of the church. The seven girls in the upper "Beehive" class were fidgeting on the hard oak benches in the dull beige-plastered room. In front of them, reading in a breathy voice which had the strained undertones of holy excitement was a large bony woman. She had a handsome face worn with pain and frustration. Several teeth were missing on one side of her mouth which gave her face a lop-sided appearance and her blondish hair streaked with gray was done up in untidy loops fastened with tortoise shell combs and large bone hairpins that kept threatening to drop. She was wearing sparkling earrings, however, in pierced ears and on her long, well-shaped hands were several rings. A cascade of ruffles tumbled down her ample bosom. Sister Hanson was one of the numerous school teachers who had come to Merritsville, taught a few years and married one of the local sons, now delivery man for Washburn's department store. They had a sizable family, struggling to keep body and soul together.

She read the Mutual lesson from a small paper bound manual in a cultivated nasal voice, " ...and all young women must live so that we will be worthy of celestial marriage." Ellen heard fragments of what she was saying now and then through the haze of reverie to which she had retreated. "That is the aim of every Latter-Day-Saint girl and woman, to be chaste and true and to live the gospel so that she may reside in eternal glory with her family eternally. It is the greatest privilege and happiness accorded woman to bring forth the spirits waiting on the other side to help them gain bodies so that they might work for their salvation through the Church...."

The sing-song, sanctimonious cadence of her voice, that "Comecomeyesaints, all is well," voice got on Ellen's nerves. She knew that some of the little spirits that Sister and Brother Hanson had brought into the world were not working very diligently on their salvation. The oldest girl had run away just last year with a tramp musician and was living with him without being married. On top of that there was a lot of talk about George Hanson and another woman, and their youngest son was not quite right in the head. Ellen was feeling truculent, so she raised her hand. Sister Hanson called on her.

"I don't think it's right to bring little spirits into bodies that have to be crippled and things like that," she said.

"Well," Sister Hanson flushed, "even the person who is crippled can learn the ways of the Lord and be saved. He can partake of the blessings of the church and have a pure, clean heart. The Lord loves all His children equally."

"But what if he is feeble minded or crazy or something and can't learn about the ways of the Lord?" Ellen pursued without thinking until she saw the distress on Sister Hanson's face and remembered that Eddie Hanson went around slobbering, with a stupid look on his face. But it seemed like a crucial question because "they" were always saying that intelligence is the Glory of God and things like that. More and more she was discovering discrepancies in her interpretation and that of the Church of what she should learn and what she wanted to know.

"There are some things that the Lord hasn't revealed to us, Ellen," Mildred Hanson said sharply, "some things we are not ready to understand. In his good time they will be revealed. Now do any of the rest of you have questions?"

Ellen felt sorry she had brought the question up without thinking about Marissa Clements who was crippled. More and more she felt frustrated by questions of religion. They were always telling you one thing and meaning another. You were always bumping into solid walls of mystery. Sister Hanson had gone back to her earlier theme, ignoring Ellen. "... it is your duty to remain chaste, clean holy vessels of the spirit."

Elaine Peterson raised her hand. "What does 'chaste' mean?" she asked innocently. Some of the girls tittered and Lorraine poked her, whispering, "I'll tell you when we get out."

"Why, it means to keep your bodies clean and pure and not do those things that you know you shouldn't," stuttered Sister Hanson. "You have all been taught right from wrong."

"Like take baths and things every week," added Marissa Clements, a serious, skinny half-crippled girl on the far end of the bench.

Sister Hanson looked at her startled. "Well, yes." She saw an escape from the thorny problem of chastity. "That's part of it. To keep our bodies clean everyday."

"My ma wont let us bath every day," Celia Burton blurted out. "We don't have a bathroom and it's too hard...."

"Well, you don't have to bathe all of your body every day. You can wash your face and hands in the washbasin and you can get out the mop bucket and wash your feet when they need it." Sister Hanson got carried away with her sudden inspiration regarding cleanliness. Some of the girls tittered, envisioning the Hansons washing their feet in mop buckets each night. Sister Hanson seemed to realized that the session had fizzled out, and she hadn't quite put across the glorious message that she had brought with her from prayer session that evening. Girls this age were such a trial. She fumbled around among her disorganized papers and came up with a glossy magazine picture of a beautiful bride, a silverware ad, and passed it around among the girls.

"Now, in closing, girls, since tonight's lesson was on Celestial marriage, I want you all to find a picture of a pretty bride to put in your Hives of Truth book to represent the ideal of marriage and write your thoughts about what you will do each day to be worthy. Bring it next time."

The piano sounded upstairs, announcing that it was time to reassemble for the closing of the Tuesday night session. Ellen felt depressed and bored by the idea of hunting up a glossy picture and pasting it in a scrapbook to represent the glories of marriage, very little of which she had seen so far. She was glad to burst out of the hall with the rest of the kids.

"Mop-bucket, Milly mop-bucket, you can always wash your feet in the mop-bucket every night, George and all the kids," sang the irrepressible Celia Burton, falling on Lorraine's shoulder as they pranced around in the church yard. They were trying to attract as much attention as they could from the pack of boys milling around in the late chilly spring darkness. Practically everybody had the "one" picked out; it just took a few minutes of enjoyable suspense to get sorted out. Sometimes, to tease and create a little more excitement, the girls would join arms and go skipping down the street so that the boys had to string along, calling insults and laughing uproariously, while they maneuvered to cut the female they wanted out of the exasperating herd.

They usually accomplished this by storming the line and breaking it roughly so that sometimes the girls were pushed into the ditches or fell down in the street squealing and giggling. Ellen detested it and she didn't know how she had come to be caught up tonight, dragged along in the humiliating horseplay, one hand in Celia's, the other in Lorraine's.

When the boys charged and the pairing off was complete, she was left alone as usual and started back in the other direction for home. As she passed the church, she noticed a group of older boys still sitting on the black iron pipe railing that ran along in front. She thought that she had heard Hal's voice among them, but she wasn't sure. He had not been in Mutual tonight that she could recall; he seldom came to church anymore. She walked rapidly past them on the outer edge of the sidewalk and closed her ears to the snickering and ignorant remarks she knew they must be making. She had gone several blocks before she became aware of the footsteps behind her. A chill of fright swept over her. It was an early spring night with just a sliver of a moon and the street lights were very far apart in this lower part of town. There were few things or people to be afraid of in Merritsville, but she was nervous tonight. It was almost half a mile home. She began to walk as fast as she could, then almost to run. So did the feet following her.

Arriving at the street light on Bate's corner, she stopped breathless. The pool of warm yellow light seemed like a haven to her, but the darkness was thicker on all sides and she would have to plunge into it again. She tried to reason with herself. It was probably only one of the boys trying to play a trick on her. None of them had wanted to walk home with her but one of them might have decided to be mean and play a joke on her. She strained her ears. The steps had stopped. There was a thick silence. The light in her eyes prevented her from seeing into the darkness clearly but she sensed there was something hostile there. She had difficulty recognizing Hal for a moment when he stepped quietly into the light and came close to her, grinning maliciously.

"Scared ya, didn't I?" he drawled.

"Hal Walker!" Ellen almost screamed at him, her voice trembling but with considerable relief. This was just like Hal. He had always enjoyed tormenting her. She was indignant, and, tossing her head, started to walk on. He came along a few steps behind her.

"What's the matter, Elly," he teased in a low menacing voice. "None of the boys want to walk home with *you*?"

"Oh, you shut up," she returned furiously. "I don't care. There isn't a boy in this whole town that I want to walk home with."

"Yeah, I know," he mocked. He had caught up with her and was walking very close, almost pushing her against the fences, his hands in his pockets. From time to time he jostled against her so that she had to give him an angry push.

"Trouble with you, Elly, is you're too damn stuck up. Besides you're kinda ugly. Why don't you fix your hair or somethin'?"

"You leave me alone, Hal Walker." Ellen was on the verge of tears. "I hate you, I hate you. You're nothing but a big bum anymore. I don't care what you or any of the dumb boys in this town think!" She started to run but he stepped across the path, his hands still in his pockets. He was very big, almost six feet tall and well built. As Ellen collided with his heavy, strong body, she had a sudden shock of surprise to find so much power, a kind of vibrating, threatening strength. No matter which way she tried to pass him, he put himself in her way with a quick, light movement. At last she stopped and tried to face him down. "Hal Walker, you let me go," she hissed from between clenched teeth. "If you don't...."

He laughed a hateful, sneering laugh. "C'mon, if I don't you'll do what? Tell Grandma?"

Faced with his brutal question that pointed up her sheer lone-liness and helplessness, Ellen realized with a shock there wasn't much she could do. They were on an empty stretch of street near the big cottonwood tree where the Hamilton's had first waylaid her. There were no houses within several blocks, only the silent, half-frozen fields. Ellen's teeth began to chatter. Besides who would believe that her cousin would molest her?

Hall pressed closer, pushing her finally against the wire-mesh fence near a rough cedar post. Suddenly he jerked his hands out of his pockets and grabbed her shoulders, his fingers digging in until they hurt even through her coat.

"Jist too damn stuck-up–that's what's the reason none of the boys like you. Think you're too damn smart, don't ya? Always readin' them books and givin' fancy readin's about lovin' and stuff." Ellen had given a short humorous reading in the prelimi-nary session of Mutual that night, a Hoosier courting scene.

Hall went on to mock her, still holding her tightly against the fence. She could feel the rough bark of the post against her cheek.

"How'd you know, you weren't there?" she challenged.

"I wuz out in the hall, listenin' to ya. Boy did you ever sound cute! Talkin' about 'courtin' and stuff. There's some things you're pretty dumb about, Ellen. Unless you learned somethin' hangin' around old Ev Gordon."

Ellen felt a flush of anger; she had become more and more afraid. There was something so evil and hateful in Hal's voice and the heaviness of his body pressing closer and closer filled her with panic.

"I could learn you things, Elly, jeez, could I learn you things if you'd let me." He put his arms around her roughly and began searching for her mouth. She turned her head away, struggling to get free, but he held her so tight against him that she could hardly breathe. Then he began squirming and working against her, pull-ing up her coat and dress. She could feel a thick, heavy lump swelling his pants. He thrust against her stomach, jabbed again and again into her so that she thought she would faint. He was fumbling to open his pants; his hot breath, coming in gasps, scalded her face. She began to kick and bite his hand as hard as she could, but this seemed to make him even more excited and determined. He laughed insanely, clawing at her clothes. Suddenly she felt so overcome that she went completely limp. Unprepared for this, Hal let her slip from his arms. She slumped into the weeds and knelt there sobbing deeply.

Hal squatted beside her. "I didn't mean to, Elly. I wuz only foolin' Please. Ya know I wouldn't hurt ya, don't ya?" There was a scared, whiny note in his voice. "I wuz only foolin' around, goddammit. Quit it, please."

When she continued to sob, holding her hands over her face so tightly that he couldn't pry them away, he jumped to his feet. "Awright, bawl! Go ahead and bawl! That's all goddam girls can do anyway." After another few moments, he kicked the clumped grass irritably. "Come on, I'll walk you on down to Grandma's," he pleaded.

"No, no!" Ellen gasped. "I hate you, Hal, I wish I never had to see you ever again. Don't you ever come near me again."

"Aw shit!" he said with utmost disgust and strode on down the path.

Ellen remained shivering in the cold, hard weeds until she could no longer hear his footsteps, then got up slowly and stiffly. She was till trembling inwardly and outwardly. It was the time of her monthly period and sharp shooting cramps went through her stomach and legs. The bulky rag that she wore for protection had slipped out of place and the blood was running down her legs. Its hot, sticky warmth filled her with intense fear and disgust. She tried to adjust the rag, but her cold hands were shaking so that she could only hold it awkwardly in place as she hobbled on home, tears streaming down her face and fierce sobs tearing through her.

At first she thought angrily that she would tell Grandma; if it had been any other boy, she would. Holding the gate for support, she tried to get hold of herself. If she told Grandma about Hal, she would have to tell Aunt Dosey and then what would they do? She saw the futility, even the danger. What could they do to Hal that he couldn't do worse to her? She didn't think they could put him in jail for what he had done? When she came right down to it and tried to put it into words, what had he done exactly? She crept slowly into the house. If Grandma asked, she could say that she had fallen down in the dark and that her period had upset her.

Grandma would never talk about it, but it was tacitly understood between them that periods were justification for all sorts of distress.

Ellen went around by the kitchen door and was greatly relieved to find that Grandma had gone to bed, leaving the light on for her. The kitchen fire was still burning. Slowly and with intense revulsion, she set about trying to clean herself. Her body seemed ugly and dirty beyond the natural soil. At last she got herself washed and into a clean, warm nightgown. As she was about to turn out the light, she noticed the bloody rag lying where she had thrown it by the coal bucket. Although they had to save and wash the cloths used for menstruation, she picked it up and stuffed it into the stove with a feeling of such anger and bitterness that she slammed the lid with a clatter and was afraid she had awakened Grandma.

What an absolutely awful, terrible, horrible thing it was to be a woman. Surely it must be, as they hinted in church about Adam and Eve, a curse, a punishment for something. Miserably she crawled into the small, soft cot bed near the window where she often slept during the winter when it was too cold in the back bedroom and lay there watching the flickering circles of light that the dying fire made on the ceiling. Hot tears of self-pity and self-disgust ran down her temples and into her hair but she made no move to wipe or stop them.

There was some truth in what Hal had said tonight about her being stuck up. She suspected that her estrangement from the group exposed her to all sorts of humiliation. The other kids probably did hate her for being so "smart." But she couldn't really help it that she liked books and music and things other than the dumb things they liked. Someday she would show them, she would go away from here and be somebody and show them. The fierce pride and anger in her made her flare back at a world that was becoming ever more hostile.

At last in utter exhaustion, she fell asleep. As she was drifting into troubled dreams, the glossy picture of a bride in white satin and lace wavered in her mind. Ellen jerked out of sleep with a violent spasm when she became aware of a long streak of blood down the beautiful white skirt.

CB

After that Ellen avoided Hal as much as possible, putting the ugly night in the back of her mind along with other dark incidents she knew had had a profound effect upon her life and feelings, but which she could not yet understand. It wasn't difficult to dodge him. She didn't spend as much time at the Walkers as she once had. She and Lorraine were drifting apart since Lorraine had a wild case on Bart McDaniel and could hardly talk about anything else. On top of that, the mess at the Walker's had begun to annoy Ellen although she was still warmly fond of her cousins. Sometimes even Grandma's clutter disturbed her a little, and she longed for the neat, shining house her mother had kept. But that was all in the irretrievable past.

Hal spent little time at home anyway. He hung around with the roughest bunch of boys and men in Merritsville and from neighboring towns. He worked a scanty part time at the service station on the east end of town where they liked to congregate and was frequently seen lounging around with them outside the pool hall. He had begun to smoke and drink. Ellen had smelled it on his breath that night. Dosey complained regularly to Addie about him, but Addie reassured her that he was "sowing his wild oats" and would settle down soon. If only they could find the means to send him on a mission. Addie had always hoped that her oldest grandson would be able to fill a mission; in addition to being a high honor to the family, it would help straighten him out. It didn't seem likely that this would happen; things had not improved with the Walkers as the Depression had stalemated. Besides Hal showed no inclination to want to preach the gospel. Ellen was surprised to see him in church a few weeks later and shocked at what happened in Fast and Testimony meeting that morning.

Fast and Testimony meeting was held on the first Sunday of every month directly after the regular service. On these Sundays everyone was supposed to go without a meal and make a fast offering, then attend both Sunday School and the meeting afterward where they bore their testimonies if the spirit moved them.

Ellen found these meetings extremely tiresome and attended only to please her grandmother. Addie observed the fast strictly, but insisted that Ellen have a glass of milk or piece of bread to tide her through the three hour session. She was still lightheaded and hungry though when they filed back from classes into the chapel this morning. Hal was shuffling along ahead of her; she had managed not to look at him all during Sunday School, although she had noticed him first thing that morning dressed in a new blue suit and wearing a tie. His curly hair glistened with brilliantine, and he looked different although there was that stubborn, uneasy look on his face as though he had been forced to come to church. Ellen, though she thought of him with loathing and tried not to look at him, could not help admitting that he was handsome. Celia Burton had an awful case on him, she knew. She shivered when she remembered their last encounter, but there was a tinge of sadness in her feelings, too. It wasn't as though he were just any boy. They had grown up very close to each other, and he was the nearest to being an older brother that she would ever know. In spite of his roughness and meanness, they had had a lot of good times together. Ellen felt bereaved somehow, cheated of something she felt she had vaguely needed or depended upon. Sometimes a strange thrill went through her when she remembered the impact of his body, the awful truth about men.

It annoyed her when she saw that he was going to bless the sacrament, knowing that he was not worthy. That meant that he sat at the white covered table where the silver trays for bread and small water glasses gleamed, facing the congregation. She could not look at the front of the church without seeing him so she squirmed around sideways in her corner of the bench where she could look out of the window. It was better that way anyway; she could daydream through the whole boring service. It was a pleasant spring morning in April. The cottonwood trees on the ditch bank that ran past the church were a network of lacy bright green against the blue sky glistening as though newly polished. She was scarcely aware when Hal mumbled hastily over the bread; the sacrament was passed and the organ, musing on one of the slow, sad sacrament songs, subsided and the Bishop announced in a solemn voice that "the time was turned over to the congregation to use as they saw fit."

The whole thing about church was becoming more and more irksome to Ellen, especially these meetings when everyone sat in thick silence nervously awaiting the Spirit to move them or hoping that It would pick others until the service was over. As it turned out, it was almost always the same half dozen old people who tottered to their feet and said the same old things in the same old trembling voices. Her grandmother was always among them. She arose as usual today. Ellen was forced to listen with empathetic and embarrassed attention that one gives to people whom one knows and loves intimately. She was sitting across the aisle and slightly in front of her so that turning about to hear, she could see her sharply in the window light. For the first time she saw Grandma as a stranger, a separate person and the merest sensation of pity and shame swept through her at the shabby, aging figure. She was wearing an old purplish hat that looked as though it had been made of a bunch of mashed and faded flowers. Her gray hair stuck out untidily from under it at the back of her neck. She had kept her shabby brown coat on and her mended, grayish gloves. The light reflected off her little round gold rimmed spectacles and the wrinkles under her chin wobbled as she spoke. Her voice, though firmer and clearer than most, quavered with deep emotion. It came to Ellen with a clutch of sharp pain that she was really not different from all the other poor, worn out, old women who helped to fill the rows of hard oak benches every Sunday.

But Grandma did manage to sound a little better than most although she started off with the same tired words–"I know that this is the True Church and I am thankful for my testimony of the Gospel. I know that Joseph Smith was a True Prophet of God and that my Redeemer lives..." Her face shone with a simple radiance that gave unmistakable conviction to her words. But in addition to the standard text, Addie always had a bit of neatly copied out verse or saying from which she made a concise sermon. Today it was a quotation Ellen had brought home from a magazine that she found at Everett's which began, "I know that today will never come again, therefore I will make it the best day in which I ever lived..." There was something touchingly appropriate in it for Addie, for she left eternity to God and concerned herself with the simple and best ordering of each day. Of all the people in Ellen's world, she was the one who was most whole, most genuine, the one who was in private what she appeared in public. Before she had concluded, wiping her eyes and blowing her nose, as she sat down, she had redeemed Ellen's pride and affection. And yet that funny old hat, she must tell her not to wear it ...

As she had listened to her today, Ellen had again that recurring feeling of loss and sadness that was seeping into all her life. She could sense barriers growing slowly, subtly, but irrevocably between all that she knew–even between her and Grandma–for not only was she accumulating experiences which apparently did not exist in Grandma's world, but she was beginning to know that she was alien to the very substance in which she and the rest of these people existed. It appeared to her as a clear, bright liquid of absolute truths in which they were all comfortably and happily immersed while it was drowning her. Whatever else they were or did or thought, they had this vital knowledge about Joseph Smith and the Redeemer and all the rest of it that she had lost somewhere.

She looked up at the benign picture of the Christ hanging on the east wall above the sacrament table. Such a different young man, unreal, girlish, far removed from the problems and realities of the world. Such a curious contrast to the male figures who slouched or dozed under it, especially Hal who sat bent completely forward on the first row of the stand, his head hanging down and his hands clasped between his knees.

Then old Brother Carson struggled to his feet. He was so crippled that when he stood his chin barely reached above the back of the bench. He held forth in his cracked and wavering voice on the sinfulness of the last days and the evils of painted women and short skirts and the iniquities of the young and the direful prophecies of doom so dear to the hearts of most of the elders. But with his chin trembling and the spittle weaving a net of white threads between his withered old lips, he concluded on a rising and tremulous note that he "Thanked God for the blessings of the restored Gospel, and he knew that he was blessed above all men in his firm testimony."

A deep, suspicious irritation filled Ellen. How could he *know* with his simple, dirty old mind? There were all sorts of stories about his *iniquities* when he had been younger; how could all the rest of these people *know* something she could not.

Sister Paul, her head wobbling about on her shoulders and the words coming so laboriously from her afflicted lips; Aunt Dosey, tears running down her long face and her hands picking nervously at one of Irene's old dresses, clumsily remodeled; fat old Birdie Thayer, wheezing and puffing as she heaved her enormous bulk to her protesting feet; senile Bishop Merritt, who pounded everything home with his cane and ranted incoherently until his wife pulling at his coat tails got him to sit down. What gave these frail, ordinary human beings supernatural knowledge?

And more—what difference did their knowing and testimonies make? Ellen knew they went on cheating, lying, stealing, hurting each other and living without grace or love for the most part—just struggling like other people that she read and heard about. What difference did it make after all that Joseph Smith had seen angels—even God The father, His Son and the Holy Ghost as he claimed? How strange these intense superlatives and poetic stories seemed in this poor place, haunted by poverty, despair, ill health, old age, death and yes—sin—that awful sooty, smudged word that was somehow connected with the way Hal had treated her.

These thoughts were oppressing her more than usual today, but they were brought to a poignant focus when, much to hers and a number of other people's surprise, Hal Walker jerked suddenly to his feet. His face was extremely flushed and he looked as though his collar was about to choke him. Even from where she sat, she could see that his hands shook. Addressing the side wall, well above anyone's head, he rushed through the usual testimony and then after an agonized hesitation in which he wrung his hands together nervously, he finished, " ...and I'm sorry for all the wrong things I've done to them I care about, and I hope the Lord will forgive me and help me to do better. These favors and blessings I ask in the name of the Lord Jesus Christ Amen."

Ellen was startled to hear a loud 'Amen' from her grandmother and a murmur throughout the audience. For herself she was stricken by such a feverish emotion that she wanted to run from the church and run and run, never come back. She could not know for sure what Hal meant, if he even thought of her and was sorry for what he had done. Maybe it was smoking and drinking he was sorry about. It didn't seem to her that he had any real conviction about the words he had thrust out hastily, but they had an evil vitality in his mouth. They echoed around her ears as though printed in fire, "I know this is the true church and that Joseph Smith is a true prophet of God and I am grateful for the blessings of the gospel...." Hal had actually said that! Knowing what an agonizing effort it had been for him, Ellen had a feeling of futility. How could Hal, who was not smart at all, who hardly ever read anything but comics and true detective stories, who was mean and did all the things that he had been taught not to, know and say such things? She was utterly seared. The words continued to bounce around in her ears as though she were in a huge dark vault all alone and could not tell where the sound was coming from. She felt cemented off from all around her. Somehow she endured the rest of the meeting, moving her lips mechanically through the closing hymn and then hurried from the chapel. She waited at the far end of the church yard for Grandma to get through with all the handshaking and greetings, her stomach gnawing fiercely. Silent, depressed all the way home, she only murmured something unintelligible when Addie said brightly, "Now wasn't that fine to see Hall get up and bear his testimony? It shows there's lots of good in that boy in spite of all his misdoings. I only hope the Lord will continue to guide him."

A few days later Ellen, who had been more than ordinarily disturbed by Sunday's meeting, was sitting at the kitchen table after school. Something had happened last summer to further threaten Ellen's faith. All her life she had heard about the hardships of the missionaries—how when they were sent out into the world, they would stand on cold street corners preaching the gospel and singing hymns while the wicked, indifferent world ignored or abused them. Doors were slammed in their faces; sometimes they were run out of town, even beaten up. Few people wanted to hear the Truth.

One day two young men had arrived in Merritsville in a battered, old car announcing that they were "missionaries" for some obscure church, Baptists or Methodists or Jehovah Witnesses. They went around town with their Bible and books trying to convert people. Most people wouldn't let them in the house and advised them to leave town as soon as possible. When they came to Grandma's house she let them in and listened politely to what they had to say but told them firmly that she would never consider changing from the True Church. She gave them a loaf of bread and some jam.

They had been allowed to put up their tent in a vacant lot across the street from the ward house where on two Sunday mornings they set up a funny, little portable organ and conducted their services all alone. Ellen watched them through the church window, thin, shabby, pitiful looking in their worn suit coats over dusty denim pants–one pumping away at the organ, both singing their hymns, praying and preaching to the dry cheat grass. It would have been comical if she had not been struck by the realization that this was the way Mormon missionaries must look out in the world. They would be treated as coldly and suspiciously as these had been in Merritsville. What was the difference? Sister Hanson had said that while the Mormon missionaries were preaching the gospel truth, these were spreading lies! But how could you tell? A dark seed of doubt that had been lying dormant in Ellen's heart sprouted into a chilling revelation. The Mormons were just like other people, except in the larger world outside of Utah, they didn't matter any more than these poor fellows did here. They were not the "chosen" people.

She had had a glimpse of the world outside of the mountain-fastness; Everett Gordon had been mostly responsible for that with his talk and books; school had contributed. The Hamiltons had brought their strange, sinister ways into her life, but it wasn't until these pathetic strangers looking so much like any shy, serious young men in town came into her vision that the membrane of her consciousness was fully punctured. She was not able to speak to her grandmother of her doubts, knowing that it would upset her. Grandma's faith was so unshakable anyway. But she had a peculiar dream.

"Grandma," Ellen said abruptly, "I had a dream last night." She was often having dreams that she wanted to tell someone. Her dreams seemed so real to her sometimes that she had difficulty remembering whether an event had actually happened to her or not. Her grandmother was the only one who had the patience to listen to them for Ellen related them in minute detail. She wanted to examine the dream again to discover why it had seemed so real and disturbed her so much as this one had.

Grandma was kneading bread vigorously at the kitchen table, and Ellen was leaning on her elbows on the oilcloth. Supporting her chin in her hands, she could feel the vibrations as Grandma thumped the dough rhythmically.

"It was like I was in Sunday school only someplace a lot bigger. The light was so bright it hurt my eyes. Everybody was there, everybody I ever knew, all sitting in rows and rows that reached way up like the choir only further, maybe like in the Tabernacle in Salt Lake, you know?"

Grandma nodded. "Everybody was dressed in beautiful long white clothes with wings and crowns and though you could tell who they were, they looked just beautiful, full of light and not real. I had a long white dress and wings too and I was sitting in the middle of the front row but not by you or Mama. I don't remember who I was sitting by...." She paused, musing.

Grandma gave the bread a final thump before she began squeezing off chunks for loaves."Well, go on," she said. "You were settin' there in the long dress and wings...."

"I was sitting there in this long dress and these wings," Ellen made winglike motions around her shoulders. "And it was real quiet and then it began to get hot and the wings began to itch. My dress seemed like it was made out of that starchy stuff like the costume I wore in the pageant. My wings kept flopping over to one side; and I couldn't make them stay up and I got hotter and hotter and itchier. Nobody seemed to feel like I did. They just sat there real still, but pretty soon I couldn't stand it any longer so I stood up and yelled right out loud, 'I don't believe Joseph Smith saw angels in the forest.' Well, everybody jumped up mad as could be and they all rushed at me and some pulled me and slapped me and screamed at me."

Grandma was putting the dough balls in a row in black bread pans, but she paused and looked quizically at Ellen. Ellen was talking excitedly now, waving her hands. Her face was flushed.

"I just thought they were going to kill me and then I heard this 'chop, chop, chop,' and all the people began to back away and what do you think it was?"

Grandma shook her head incredulously.

"It was Ferdie Baxter chopping all their wings off!"

Ferdie was the crippled janitor-gardener of the tabernacle and park. One of his shoulder blades protruded like the back bone of some prehistoric creature so that the whole upper part of his body was twisted at an angle of about forty-five degrees from the bottom part of him. He had a voice like sand being stirred in a butter churn. But he was very strong and did almost all the custodian work himself. In the summer he was often in the park or on the tabernacle grounds with his long-bladed pruning shears, chop, chop, chopping about the shrubbery. In Ellen's dream he had been pruning wings off the angels with ferocious glee, and finally their fury turned on him. Ellen was forgotten. She expected that he would chop her wings off, too, even wished for it because they pulled and dragged at her shoulders, but he seemed not to be aware of her at all. The crowd with its shorn wings had drawn away from Ferdie and now he was sweeping up the brittle, bright feathers with immense energy, lurching round and round the huge pile. He was going to make a bonfire of them.

Ellen looked around her. Everything was just like in an ordinary church on an ordinary Sunday. All the people were slumped in their seats, bored, tired, discouraged, bewildered and homely in shabby, ill-fitting, depression-worn clothes. Old Sister Paul's head bobbed continuously with spasms of palsy; old Brother Carson's head kept falling forward onto his chest and Ellen could see the yellow stains on his beard. The Bishop slept with his mouth wide open, spittle forming shining threads like spider webs at the sides of his mouth. Suddenly Ellen was aware that she was sitting by Hal who was grinning at her. "It's all your fault, Ellen, you think you're so smart," he taunted.

Ellen omitted these details and the part about Hal from her telling of the dream to Grandma. She broke off, twisting her hands in anguish. "I don't know what it means...."

Grandma had finished molding the loaves and was washing her hands. "My, my, that was a funny dream. I don't expect it means much of anything. You must've been eatin' green apples again. I told you they wasn't ready."

Ellen smiled in spite of herself and dropped her hands self-consciously into her lap. Grandma went about her work, covering the bread pans with clean dish towels and setting them where it was warm to rise. She was disturbed enough by Ellen's dream that she thought she ought to be careful about what she said. And

Ellen, in telling the dream, had discovered what it was that was troubling her. After a considerable silence, she said hesitantly, " What if I said that in church—what if I said that I didn't believe that Joseph Smith had a vision and saw the angel Moroni?"

Addie sat down, took off her glasses and wiped them carefully on the corner of her apron.

"People have said it in church before and the church went right on," she said calmly. "It don't make so much difference to the church what a person believes as much as it does to themselves. People have got to believe in somethin' and it's better for them to believe in angels and visions and miracles than a lot of things they do believe in ... or in nothin'."

"But it just don't seem possible," Ellen said, her face still screwed up with distress so that Addie wanted to smooth it out and pat the innocence back into it. Ellen was going to have a hard time of it. She had a mind and an eye that saw things so sharply, too clearly as they were set before her, and this was going to blind her to many things that do not have such sharp and clear outlines.

"Well, never you mind," sighed Addie. "I don't suppose there's any way of explainin' it to anybody who don't think it's possible. If I were you I wouldn't worry about it too much. It'll all come to you in time when you're older and see things a little different, maybe. We must trust in the Lord. Now why don't you run out and get me a pan of chips, so I can start the fire for the bread?"

That was Grandma's way of always putting questions off for the immediate concerns; trust in the Lord. Ellen wished she could. She went slowly out to the wood pile with a battered coal bucket and began to gather chips. She couldn't help worrying about all the strange things that were happening to her—the getting to be a woman, the fact that she wasn't like the other girls in the things that she liked and liked to do, not being boystruck like all the other girls and the terrible truth the dream had revealed to her that she didn't even believe in the Church and Joseph Smith anymore. In fact she didn't like to go to church. She would much rather stay home and read a book or listen to the radio, but everybody in Merritsville took it for granted that if you didn't go to church and you didn't believe in Joseph Smith and the Angel there was something dreadfully wrong with you. Only people wicked, fallen people like Everett Gordon didn't go to church. How she wished he were around to talk to, but she remembered that in the past he didn't like to talk about the church and religion very much anyway.

Ellen squatted over the wood pile, putting clean white chips one by one into the bucket. They had a nice smell; she liked the smell of warm wood in the sunshine. She had always like to help Granma saw logs by sitting on one end to hold them steady while Addie scraped the old buck saw back and forth and clean bright sawdust trickled into a pile under the sawhorse. The vibrations had tickled her and she felt excited as she watch the saw bite through. She had to jump off just before the log was cut in two. She was getting so big now that she had to hold it instead of sitting on the log and that was less fun. Well everything was getting to be less fun as you grew-up. Why did people had to grow up at all? In books the adult world was fascinating, full of mysterious, glamorous things and a tantalizing kind of freedom. But in real life it was such a long time getting there, so painful and bewildering along the way. The grown-ups in Merritsville didn't look or act like it was much fun. With a deep sigh, Ellen rose and carried the bucket full of chips back to the house. Anyway, pretty soon there would be hot new bread and jam and milk.

$$\text{CB}$$

Ellen's life continued through the summer of 1937 in the usual way in spite of her growing doubts. The depression was so blended with the slow paced, conservative Mormon ways that it was scarcely noticeable; some of the pious old men even remarked that it was the purpose of the Lord. Didn't the Book of Mormon and the Bible clearly show that prosperity was a device of the Devil for corrupting mankind?

Merritsville heard rumors of violence from far away–from the eastern and midwestern United States where gangsters were robbing banks and killing each other. The glamorous gunmen of the Old West seemed to have moved to Chicago and other cities. Some secretly admired outlaws like Dillinger, Bonnie and Clyde, Ma Barker and her gang who preyed on the banks which were held partially at fault for conditions as they were.

It looked like there might be another war in Europe. Ellen went to the Orpheum to Saturday afternoon movies with the other girls and watched a German with a funny mustache waving and ranting on jerky newsreels. Aaron and other townsmen held a weekly Saturday afternoon council on the bank corner, exchanging solemn opinions and gloomy predictions. Although there was a strong feeling that the United States must stay out of European quarrels, deep in their hearts many of the men, especially those who had not actually fought in the last one, found the thought of war exciting. Almost anything would be better than this dreary stagnation.

Memories of the great World war in which many of them had been involved had faded to a warm glow of comradery and dim heroism. Though few would admit it, war would be a way out of the deadly paralysis that had settled over the country. It would boost the economy for one thing; in spite of the New Deal and all Roosevelt's fine talk, very little had happened to lift the pall of the depression. Hal and his dad argued about it at the breakfast and dinner tables when they chanced to be together. Hal thought it would be a great thing to go over there and "clean up them German bastards." Aaron avowed that he would never sanction young American men being sacrificed for them god damned foreigners. When had they ever done anything for the United States? Dosey shivered and tried to keep peace in her own little domain.

The old men spoke of living in the "last days" and quoted scripture to prove it in sacrament meetings. Even Addie talked of the millennium when the earth would be restored to its "Paradisical Glory." The apocalyptic temper was natural to Mormons, but on summer mornings when the sun had pried its way too early over the high eastern mountains and filled the bowl of the valley with rich, warm light, it was hard to think of the world needing too much improvement.

Most summer mornings Ellen got up before dawn to go picking berries with her cousins and other women and girls. Aaron, unable to find work of any other kind, had finally turned a small tract of land salvaged from the disasters of 1930 into a fruit farm. He figgered that it would tide them over. The land was on the outer edge of town at the lower end of one of the canyons out of which the life-giving streams tumbled from the snows on the high granite mountains. He, Dosey and the children had expanded their patches of strawberries, raspberries and fruit trees. There had been a fairly good sized orchard on the land planted by his father, a spry old man who lived in a little cabin there and watched over things. By 1937 Aaron could keep about twenty girls and women busy in the patches and orchard from the last of May until the end of October. In addition he had become a Stark Nursery representative and, although he was only barely able to scrape along, prices being what they were, there was good food to eat and something to keep busy at.

Between six and seven o'clock Aaron would gather the berry pickers from various corners of town in his old Dodge truck. In addition to Ellen, Lorraine and Louise and ten or twelve girls from ten to eighteen years old, there were older women dressed in striped bib overalls, long sleeved shirts and cheap straw hats whose husbands were out of work or not making enough to keep the family. During raspberry time each one had a couple of lard buckets that she could fasten to a heavy belt with clips. All through July and August they picked cheerfully through the shady, thorny rows making twenty cents a case. A case contained twelve neat wooden cups with green metal edges and had to be filled generously because the berries tended to shrink as the day wore on. Aaron paid an extra bonus of five cents a cup for pickers who worked regularly and stayed the whole season. If he was lucky, he could get a dollar a case at the market in Salt Lake.

Ellen didn't mind the work most of the time; it meant she was earning some money to help buy her school clothes and new rimless glasses that she needed badly. She had become very nearsighted; Grandma said that it was because she read so much that her eyes were bad. Almost all the girls in town picked berries so it wasn't as though it were a hardship. There was lots of gossiping, laughter, teasing and playing of practical jokes but it was hot, sweaty work; she was glad to get home and out of the stiff overalls. The worst thing was the snakes. Blue racers, blow snakes and deadly diamond back rattlers lived on the low hills where the berry patches were located. One day June Healy, who was always tormenting someone, put a blow snake in her bucket and, though she tried to conceal her terror, it gave her nightmares for weeks. She was always nervous as she parted the thick bushes and looked down into their green gloom.

That summer Ellen got to know Elaine Firmage, a big, handsome girl several years older than she who had come to stay in Merritsville with relatives. She picked berries along with the rest of them, and she and Ellen tried to get their rows together. Elaine liked books as well as Ellen and had read even more. At noon, when the pickers gathered around the bridge that crossed the creek running through the farm to eat their lunches, they would stay a little apart from the rest of the crowd and continue their deep, philosophical talks. Lounging under the tall mountain ash and box elder trees that lined the creek, listening to the hypnotic murmuring of the water and watching fat white clouds drift across intense, blue summer skies, Ellen was as happy as she had been in many years. It was the first time that she had had anyone near her age to talk to like that since Everett had gone away. In the evening after they had cleaned up, the two of them would walk to the library or the drug store or park or just sit on the porch while the stars came out exchanging profound ideas on life, love, religion, and the future. They both vowed that they would never marry but would go to college and have careers. Ellen thought she would like to be a writer; Elaine said she wanted to be a scientist, maybe an archeologist and dig up old ruins. They both agreed that men were troublesome bothers, and they didn't want to be bossed around by them. Ellen fell a little in love with Elaine. At the end of the summer they both cried at parting and vowed to write each other and be friends forever.

Only once that halcyon summer did the depression seem as real and dark as it still was over most of the country. Ellen went to the Market in Salt Lake City with her cousins and uncle.

In the cool of the evening the gleaming, fresh wooden crates with their succulent contents were all stacked under the open shed where Aunt Dosey had tallied them. At dusk Uncle Aaron would begin to load them on the big Dodge truck and at about three o'clock in the dewy summer morning, he would drive slowly and carefully the forty-odd miles to Salt Lake City where, if he had good luck, he could sell them. Since he needed some help with the tending of the stalls and unloading, some of the kids usually went along. Hal, who should have been the most help, and his dad didn't get along well anymore. Hal claimed that his job at the service station was more important, and he wasn't interested in farming. He was going to be an auto mechanic. It usually fell to Joey who was nearly ten now–a serious, comical, hard-working boy who sat in the shed during the day tacking up crates, to go along with his dad. The girls began to think they were missing something so they begged for turns to go to Salt Lake City. Aaron yielded and Louise and Lorraine sometimes went with him on the days when there was no picking. Lorraine detested getting up so early so one day Louise proposed that Ellen go with her since Joey was down with the chicken-pox. Ellen, at first reluctant to get up so early when she had a free day, finally decided it might be something interesting to break the monotony.

Somewhat dubious about her decision, she stumbled sleepily into the cab of the truck at three thirty a.m. and she and Louise dozed uncomfortably on each other's shoulders.

The big canvas-covered truck pulled into the streets of west Salt Lake at the sinister hour when only the sickly street lights and a few grimy eating places gave evidence of any kind of human life. Uncle Aaron parked the truck alongside the high wire mesh fence. The girls sat up and looked around dazedly. The dense black shadows of the buildings in the smudgy light of the street lights muddled with dawn reminded Ellen of the pencil drawings of an angry child. She had a cold, depressed, nauseated feeling in her stomach.

"Might as well go back to sleep a bit," Uncle Aaron said, hunching down behind the steering wheel. "It'll be an hour before old Pete opens up." He had to come early because he had not been able to rent one of the stalls for the season and, in order to get a good one near the street end of the market, it was necessary to crowd in with dozens of other farmers as soon as the gate was opened.

Ellen fell back into a thick, uncomfortable doze from which she was startled by a rasping metallic sound of the gates opening ... and unbelievable cacophony. The street was suddenly full of rattling, rumbling, honking, grinding, wheezing trucks of all makes and ages and loud voice with very odd, unfamiliar sounds. Farmers were streaming in, pushing and nudging each other through the high market gates toward a long, cement platform over which a galvanized tin roof was supported by cement columns. The trucks, among which Aaron was one of the lucky first ones, maneuvered their tail gates against the platform and the farmers, swearing and calling good natured insults and greetings to each other, began to unload their fresh produce onto a little square that constituted a stall.

The first hour or two in the cooler part of the morning was like a carnival. Ellen felt wonderfully excited at the sounds of the city, the metallic clanging of streetcars, grinding of delivery trucks and, above all, the different male voices calling vigorously in a fascinating variety of tones, languages and accents. Then there was the profusion of colors and smells from the fresh, glowing heaped-up produce: the lusty orange-yellow of carrots with dark, green feathery plumes, little, fat red radishes, glassy green peppers and paler green, curly lettuce, dark hairy beets and rotund white turnips with purple smudges, pale waxen summer apples or small, pink freckled ones, bumpy ochre squash and big purples globes of eggplant which the neat Japanese farmers displayed so artistically. The sheer, fresh exuberant abundance of it made it hard to believe that this was a time of depression and people everywhere were hungry.

Before the summer sun had hit the market place slantwise like a hot poker, the trading and bargaining had begun. Across the aisle the Greek with his black chin wagging like an accordian hawked sacks of fat gold onions; next to Uncle Aaron's truck two German brothers from north of Salt Lake, one thin, one fat, kept up a perpetual quarrel in German while they fussed over their tender lettuce and radishes like two old maids over sewing baskets. Uncle Aaron examined the crates of raspberries, glistening like caskets of red, translucent jewels where the light fell on them, looking for cups which had shaken down in the ride or had not been generously filled. He would take whole cups from one crate and sprinkle them over the top of another where the green metallic edges of the cups were a little too prominent so that prospective buyers would see that he was giving full measure.

Ellen and Louise hugged each other with delight when he would sell four, five or six crates to a customer and lug them off, leaving them with instructions for handling the next buyer if one should come along while he was gone. Ellen could scarcely contain the bewildering mixture of impressions that assailed her from the friendliness of the neighboring farmer-peddlars who came over to josh with them and offer them things from their own trucks to the rather hostile curiosity with which the stall-boys regarded them–girls–taking meagre jobs that they–males–needed so desperately. Ellen had been shocked when they had popped up first thing between the trucks as though they had come out from under the cement platform, ranging from thin, grubby, half-starved looking kids of seven or eight to twisted old men hoping to earn a dime or two toting the crates and sacks to customers' cars, or in many cases, using this as a pretext to filch something for breakfast. Uncle Aaron didn't like to hire them, not because he was stingy, but because he hated giving them as little as he could only afford to. He thought they ought to have a dollar for a morning's work but that meant his profit from five crates of berries!

Ellen noticed the handsome son of the Greek onion farmer. When his sparkling eyes fell on her and Louise, he came over and talked to them and bought them each a popsicle. His name was Stephen and they wrote their names and addresses on some discarded berry cups promising to write to each other. Mr. Cottington, the manager of the market who looked like a big, congenial frog, stopped by the stall and talked to Uncle Aaron. This flattered him so much that he had to clear his throat and wipe his eyes several times. The wizened old Chinaman who always bought what he could from Uncle Aaron came by. Ellen was fascinated by his funny, brownish, wrinkled face and his high-spirited jabber. He bowed to the girls and gave them each a paper fan. There were Negroes about the platform, too, their black skin shining bluish in the bright light, and their thick, jolly voices distinctive in the babble. Ellen felt nervous when one of them stopped and poked his black finger in a raspberry cup and asked, "How much youall want fer dese, maam?'

Ellen had read about the world in the *National Geographic* and in Grandma's set of Carpenter's geography books as well as other things, but she felt that here, at last, she was seeing the mystery of different nationalities and races as she had never experienced it before. Most Mormon communities were solidly white of British or Scandinavian descent. She was surprised at the harmony of all these people, working together to provide the basic necessities of life. She was so exhilarated with her discovery that the change in atmosphere crept upon her slowly. It seemed as though they had been there for ages when it was only ten o'clock. The stacks of foodstuff and crates and boxes had diminished rapidly; by that time many of the trucks had pulled out leaving lonesome gaps all down the pier. A dejected atmosphere filled the length of the platform, and the early joyousness had evaporated into a kind of depressed anxiety. Those who had not sold out their load began to bargain listlessly with frugal housewives in faded cotton dresses and run-over shoes or with scrummy peddlars who picked their teeth and mauled the produce disdainfully.

Wilted greens littered the ground and platform, fruit and berries were mashed on the cement, imperfect and spoiled vegetables had been tossed deliberately in the dirt and cinders. To her horror, Ellen saw that a hoard of pathetic women and children, even some old men, with ragged shopping bags or gunny sacks were picking around in the mess for food to eat, stuffing even corn husks and carrot tops into their receptacles. When she mentioned this to Uncle Aaron, he shook his head sadly. He was feeling a bit downcast because he still had ten crates of good fat red raspberries and some summer apples that hadn't sold.

"It's a wicked shame," he muttered wiping his eyes again, "people starvin' eatin' dirt and garbage in a country like this."

"Whyn't we give 'em some of our fruit and apples?" Louise, whose tender heart was always so easily moved, asked.

"Can't do it," Uncle Aaron shook his head, "would ruin the market. Stores couldn't sell anything, people'd jist flock around waitin' for a handout when they knew you couldn't sell it. We'd all be out of business in no time."

Ellen tried to avert her eyes from the bitter spectacle and smiled sadly when she saw Louise surreptitiously roll some apples to two skinny Negro kids.

By noon the heat had begun to bear down stewing the remaining stuff, the smell of dust, dirt, sweat, gasoline, grease and rancid produce into a nauseating porridge.

They sold a few more of the crates of raspberries and Uncle Aaron let the last bushel of apples go to a persistent peddlar for a quarter, but they still had five crates of berries left at noon. Ellen was itchy and longing to go home. The bright morning world had turned ugly and brutal. At last, Uncle Aaron, worn out and grumpy, too, reloaded what was left and they started back to Merritsville. Since the berries had wilted too much to take home, he stopped at the bridge that crossed the sluggish Jordan river and dumped them into the stream. Ellen watched the bright red berries floating like an unstrung necklace on the muddy current toward the great Salt Lake. The sight would remain with her as the paradox and symbol of the Great Depression.

Ellen had turned sixteen in March of that year. She had the contours of a young woman like the rest of the girls–small, round breasts, waist and hips. She was neither tall nor short, neither skinny nor fat. The freckles across her nose and cheeks, which she had passionately hated, had faded. Mostly she wore her hair, light brown and glossy, long and straight, although Irene had prevailed upon her to try a permanent once that year. She hated sitting under the weird machines that looked like something out of a torture chamber. Her eyes were her best feature–a curious color that varied from soft gray-green to opaque gray–having thick brown lashes with little gold lights in them. But she had to wear glasses. Although they were the rimless kind with squared off tops, they didn't fit too well so that they obscured the beauty of her eyes. She had a well shaped mouth but her teeth were slightly uneven and had started to cause her trouble. There was only one dentist in town, and Irene had not been able to afford regular dental care. Ellen had suffered with toothache in the past two years and had had to have several of her back teeth extracted. She worried about having to grow up and have false teeth.

If called upon to describe her most of the residents of Merritsville would have said, "Oh, that odd girl of Irene Kent's," or "that smart Kent girl, plain ain't she? Don't have the looks of her ma."

Ellen, herself, could never decide about her face. She studied it in the corner of the mirror of the big old mahogany dresser that Irene had put in the back bedroom at Grandma's where she slept. In the light from the lace curtained window she tried to decide whether she was pretty or not. She knew she would never be beautiful the way her mother was but perhaps some people would find her pretty enough. Although she acted as though she was not interested in boys most of the time, in her secret heart she had visions and dreams of being loved sometime by the right man, by someone very special like the men she read about in books–like Mr. Darcy in *Pride and Prejudice* or Rhett Butler. She hadn't seen enough movies to have a crush on movie stars.

She supposed that her body would be alright eventually.

Once she dared to take off her blouse and underclothing and look at her body as far down as the mirror would permit. Its startling unfamiliar whiteness gleaming in the subdued light disturbed her. She covered her small round breast with little raspberry nipples with her hands and was filled with strange emotions. There was something so private, so vulnerable about the rest of her body that she could not imagine any eyes upon it. Even her own. Sometimes when she squatted in the galvanized tub by the kitchen stove at her Saturday night bath, she was tempted to look at herself, at the mysterious place that had come to exist between her thighs. She never dared and she could only wash there gingerly because when she was little, her mother had repeatedly cautioned her not to play with herself down there. Besides there was Grandma always watching. She missed the privacy of the bathroom they had put in at home; Grandma had not been able to afford one, and she lived beyond where the sewer lines ended.

Bodies were such mysterious things. Why did she have to be afraid of it, ashamed of some of the things it did, like menstruating and breaking wind or a rumbling stomach in public. Worst of all she had learned that her body made her capable of having a baby! It had something to do with getting too close to a man like when Hal had forced himself on her; she was sure she would never let that happen again. She had tried to find out about it in the library and listening to the other girls but it was all very hush-hush. But still there was the longing in her for that other, that boy or man who would enfold her in his arms and give her some kind of delicious feeling that she couldn't define. She could see his face sometimes in her daydreams.

She could not find that face anywhere in Merritsville. Of that she was certain. More and more Ellen had fallen away from the crowd her age. While she continued active in church and school, she never had dates like Lorraine and the other girls.

Something uncomfortable happened to her when she was thrust into the company of boys socially. In other activities like the school paper, she got along reasonably well with them, but when there appeared to be any chance of intimacy, of more than friendliness, she retreated into herself. There was some perversity in her that made her want to protect herself from the perils of the kind of experiences that the other girls were going through. When she listened to Lorraine or Helen or some of the others talking about their boyfriends, she wondered what joys there could be. They were always having fights or pining for someone who didn't like them or fearing that some other girl would take him away.

She did long with part of her to join in the normal activities of high school. She wanted to go to the dances; she liked to dance, liked popular music. You had to have a date to go to the proms and hops but a lot of the girls would go stag to the dances after the ball-games or Mutual. When she did stay to these, she seldom got to dance and not very often with the boys that she really wanted to. She hated sitting on the side benches with Marissa Clements and some of the other girls who never had boyfriends either. Most of the times she preferred to go home, work on her lessons, read her books and dance alone to music on the radio.

Even when she had a chance for a date, it was usually with some of the boys that nobody else would go with. When Carter Cameron, a clumsy, poorly dressed new boy with nice brown eyes asked her to the Senior Hop, she refused him so coldly and abruptly that she was afterwards ashamed.

Occasionally in depressed moods and deepening loneliness, she asked herself why? What was locked up, frozen within her so deep that she could not break away from it. In these moods she hated BOYS! She could not imagine any of the boys in the junior or senior class or anywhere in the vicinity of Merritsville in a romantic relationship with herself. She had discovered that a girl had to put on a false front most of the time to get and keep a boyfriend. Lorraine had told her several times that she would have to stop being at the head of the class and answering all the questions and writing all A papers and winning all the debates and speech prizes if she wanted to be popular. The worst thing you could have in the eyes of a boy was "brains." You couldn't talk about books or ideas or what she considered real, grown-up things. Lorraine said you had to make them believe they were superior even if they weren't. That was simply not in Ellen's nature.

Sometimes she suspected that her judgment was a bit unfair; lumping them all together as mindless monsters didn't quite suit. Leslie Terry who played the trombone in the school orchestra and helped her with geometry problems was nice. David Flinders, the tall, good-looking curly haired president of the student body had smiled at her recently and told her he liked the reading she gave in assembly. Her debate partner, John Bair, and she had a lot of good times on debate trips, but inevitably it all fell back into the old "mating game." In that intricate and involved ritual of intrigue, deceit, subterfuge and what seemed to Ellen like a lot of silliness on the part of the girls, she was totally lost. She turned with greater intensity to her studies, books and writing. When she wanted to dance, she turned on the beloved radio, dancing to the Hit Parade tunes or the big bands that were broadcast from far distant and romantic places and dreamed of a perfect lover holding her in his arms.

It was a warm May night. Ellen and Lorraine had stayed after Mutual to help decorate for the spring festival, and Lorraine had told Louise to tell their mother that she was staying with Ellen at Grandma's. Occasionally she did this and Ellen and she would have long talks about life and love and things.

Even though it was more than an hour before they had finished, Ken Mayne, Lorraine's latest flame, was waiting outside the church for them. Ellen was annoyed but walked on ahead leaving the two, arms about each other, to meander down the weedy path. She reached home quite a bit ahead of them and decided to sit on the front porch–the night was so beautiful–and she was full of a warm, glowing feeling that must be a little like love, she thought. Her body ached for something indefinable and she tried to imagine a boy with whom she might have walked home. Tall, yes, handsome, well not too, kind of nice looking–handsome boys were often too conceited–strong and masculine but not too rough and tough, always showing off like Hal and his bunch. He would, of course, be smart and like books so that he would understand what she loved.

Holding her arms tightly around herself she breathed deeply of the spring night. It was so lovely it hurt her to be alone–the deep blue sky was full of stars like chips of diamonds in a velvet case. The perfume of the lilacs by the gate filled the air and in the soft starlight the apple tree loaded with lacy bloom gleamed like a bride. She ached to be part of it, surely this was like love, this flowing into herself of the stars, the silken night, the apple tree and lilac, scent but she longed also to share it with someone. All the love songs promised that there was that other part of you somewhere in the world, your other half. With him you would know, you would feel complete.

Her ecstatic mood was disturbed by the footsteps of Lorraine and Ken. They stopped in the shadow of the lilac bush. In spite of herself, Ellen strained a little to hear what they were saying, but mostly all she could hear was a low murmur. Lorraine laughed and there was a scuffling then a long silence in which she guessed they were kissing. It made her cross; she knew that Lorraine stayed down at Grandma's with her so she could stand out and neck longer with Ken. Lorraine said that her dad always called out or got up and put his overalls on over his underwear and came out if they stood on the porch too long or parked when Ken had the car. Something else that annoyed Ellen was that Lorraine had a new crush every few months like the other girls, puppy love Grandma called it. They were all so mushy. She was just about to get up and go in the house when she heard Lorraine say "Good night, honey, see ya tomorrow." After a couple more kisses, she came skipping up the path and almost stumbled over Ellen on the step.

"Good grief," she exclaimed in an exasperated voice, "What yo doin' here, eavesdropping on me?"

"Just waiting for you," Ellen said sulkily. "You sure took your time."

"Yeah? It didn't seem very long–it never seems very long when you're in love." Lorraine threw her arms around Ellen and hugged her ecstatically.

Ellen drew away coldly and opened the screen door. Lorraine twirled around the porch several times before skipping lightly after her. As they undressed in the bedroom, she went on oblivious to Ellen's irritation. "I'm really in love this time, just really. We're gonna be married in the Temple as soon as school's out next spring. We talked about it all the way home and oh, Ellen, I can't wait. I just wish he could afford to give me a ring. I could be the first one engaged in our crowd."

"You said you were 'really in love' with Bart Mack last year," Ellen reminded her grumpily getting into her side of the bed and edging over so she wouldn't have to touch Lorraine.

"Did I?" Lorraine seemed unconcerned. "Well that was when I was *younger*. This time I know it's for real. I just feel it deep down. I just tingle all over when he kisses me and when he holds me close like he did tonight, I just want to do it so bad. Sometimes I think we can't wait a whole 'nother year the way we feel, but we got to stay out of trouble or we can't go through the Temple. Our folks wouldn't like that. I hope they don't call him on a mission–his folks want him to go but I couldn't stand to be away from him for two years. I might just give in and try to get him before he gets called if I thought he might. If I got pregnant right off we'd have to get married and he couldn't go away. We could repent and go to the Temple later, I suppose. You remember Belva and Wayne did that?" She seemed to be musing to herself, but Ellen was listening with shock, her eyes wide in the dark.

"Lorraine Walker," she burst out with horror, "you wouldn't really. You wouldn't really ...do that?"

"No, I suppose not," Lorraine admitted drowsily. "I guess I'd wait for him. Most girls don't but I would, he's so sweet. You know it seems kind of silly that you can't do it together before you are married even when you want to so bad then the next day after you're married you have to do it whether you want to or not. Ma acts like it's such a bother, the things she says, just a way to get babies."

"I don't know what you're talking about," Ellen said between clenched teeth. "You sound awful and I don't think you even know what you're talking about either."

"Well, maybe not exactly." Lorraine turned over toward Ellen; she was a trifle put out at Ellen's tone. "But I sure know a lot more than you do, Ellen Kent. I don't know how you can get so many A's in school and still be so dumb."

"Dumb about what?" Ellen curiosity was aroused in spite of her ire.

"Oh, never mind." Lorraine flung herself over and settled down.

"No, tell me, I guess I am." Ellen reached out and jostled her shoulder. "What is it I don't know so much about?"

"Oh, about what boys and girls do together and men and women," Lorraine grumbled. "You probably never even kissed a boy." Ellen had to admit that, except a parties where they played "Post Office," she hadn't and didn't want to.

"What do they do?" She continued to prod Lorraine.

"Well," Lorraine drew a deep breath. "The boy puts his peter in the girl's thing, that's what Helen's married sister told her and they sort of work around together like this...." She grabbed Ellen and went through the elementary motions. Ellen gasped in outrage and thrust her away, remembering the searing scene with Simone so long ago and the brutal encounters with Hal. She recalled fragments of things that she had heard and read and strangely some of the things she recalled about her father and mother that last Christmas they were together. She felt hedged about with dark and ugly shadows both amorphous and insubstantial yet thick and heavy. That wasn't love! It couldn't be!

"Oh, Ellen," said Lorraine, a sort of disgusted despair in her voice. "You are such a funny girl–you know so much and you don't know so much. Sometimes you just make me mad."

She tried to put her arms about Ellen to comfort her, but Ellen's body was so stiff and cold that, finally with a shrug, she turned over murmuring, "Well, you asked me and I tried to tell you." She wadded up her pillow and fell asleep, dreaming of Ken Mayne's warm, sweet young kisses.

But Ellen lay awake staring into the night, her imagination running riot and her body and mind feeling scalded, forlorn, betrayed by a disgusting truth so different from the dream of love she had had earlier that beautiful spring night. Her mother and father, her mother and Ed Barker, all the people in the town who were married and some who weren't doing "that"–how awful.

Ed's wife had died that winter and her mother and Ed had only recently been married. How could she? Her beautiful mother do ugly things like that? She felt like she never wanted to see them again ever. At last she fell into a troubled sleep.

CB

Early in June 1938 Everett Gordon came back to Merritsville. One warm Saturday night Ellen and Addie were sitting on the front porch when Ellen suddenly became aware of a familiar sound–the intermittent strains of a mandolin interspersed with spaces of silence and the occasional braying of a donkey. The sound was faint since it was more than two long blocks between Addie's and Everett's houses. It rose and fell as though part of a dreamy movie sound track. Ellen stopped in the middle of a sentence and put her hand on her grandmother's arm. "Listen!" They both paused and listened intently. "It can't be! Is Everett back?"

"I heard that he was a few days ago," Addie answered quietly.

"Why didn't you tell me?" Ellen jumped up. "Why didn't he tell me or come around or something?" She ran to the corner of the yard and leaned in the direction of the sound for a few moments then, leaping joyfully back through the tall grass, she cried, "Why didn't he come over to see us?"

"Still too proud, I guess," Addie said. "The Gordons never go out to anybody–you have to go to them."

"Well, I will," Ellen announced impulsively. She didn't know why she felt so much elation–she hadn't thought about Everett these past few months. He had been gone such a long time this time; she thought he might not come back at all. Now she knew she had missed him extremely–his face, his fine hands, his rich voice–the talks they had–the memory of him inflamed her mind with a kind of love and longing she didn't remember experiencing before. He was really like nobody else in her world. Only he understood a special part of her.

"I wouldn't go tonight, Ellen," Addie cautioned, putting a restraining hand on Ellen's arm.

"Why not?" Ellen insisted.

"I just wouldn't. It's late and it might upset him. Go tomorrow and take him some bread and things." There was a mysterious note in Grandma's voice that chilled Ellen's enthusiasm. Might there be something wrong with Everett; was he still drinking?

"Oh, all right." Ellen slumped down on the steps again petulantly. The music had grown a little clearer and played steadily through a sentimental old number quavering, melancholy. Ellen strained every nerve to hear–the elusive sound tantalized, beckoned to her. She slept poorly that night, turning and twisting in a curious unhappy dream about Everett that she couldn't recall the moment she wakened from it although the mood of mixed sadness-gladness lingered.

Next afternoon, a bit nervous, her heart beating with anticipation, she went to see him. She found him in the cluttered kitchen very much as she had left him. His face had grown a shade grayer so that it blended with his hair but it was calmer, even rested looking. He held her hands for a long time and gazed at her hungrily. When she saw that there was moisture in his eyes, she dropped hers self-consciously to the base of his wrinkled neck which was revealed by the open white shirt collar. She noticed that he was wearing new clothes and the very clean white shirt gave her a feeling of hope and happiness about him. She knew, even without his telling her over and over again that he had missed her very much.

Gradually their old, comfortable companionship returned as they talked and walked about the house. He didn't say too much about what had happened while he was away except that he thought he was going to be able to stay this time and start doing some more work on his music. He was eager to hear all about Ellen's life and thoughts.

Everett opened the library door. The room was warm and dusty. It was like coming home for Ellen.

"There they are," he nodded, stroking her cheek tenderly, "Waiting for you."

She strolled about touching a book here and there just to make sure they were real, thinking how enchanted this room seemed. How mysterious and wonderful that so much life and thought could be stored this way in all those pages, pressed thinly side by side. Thousands and thousands of words–thoughts, feelings, ideas–all alive, all made permanent. How she longed to leave something of herself like this or at least a part of herself preserved forever in beautiful language.

That summer Ellen spent a lot of time in this room. It was on the north side of the house, cool and quiet. Sometimes Everett sat there with her, reading his paper or dozing; other times he left her alone to read and write. Once in a while they talked about the books and some of the ideas in them; Everett liked her to read out passages and explain them to him or tell him the stories. It had been a long time since he had read them himself, he said.

Sometimes Everett would play the piano for her, and at other times they listened to broadcasts of the New York Philharmonic orchestra together on the small wooden-cabinet radio that stood on his shelves in the kitchen. He would explain things about the composers and the music although at times he seemed to be depressed or upset by it.

It was so good to be near him, sharing parts that she read out of books or bringing him items of news about the town and expressing her own private impressions of them. He gave her such a feeling of pleasure and importance, made her feel as though she were grown-up. With him she was her real self. Nobody, not even Grandma, listened to her as he did. He liked to laugh. She always read him the funny parts she found in her reading and they laughed together. When she read the same things to Grandma or other people they didn't always see the humor in them, especially the humor in play on words like those that Everett showed her in passages of Shakespeare. She was beginning to understand and like Shakespeare a lot more now.

Without their quite knowing how it happened, Everett and Ellen had begun to build a tight little world within a world. For Ellen the hours that she spent there were among the most peaceful and beautiful that she could remember.

Things were not the same for her this summer as they had been the last few. On the surface few things had changed except her own perceptions of them. She went to pick berries with the other girls; Elaine did not come back and there was no one among her age group to talk to. The conversation that went on in the berry patch mostly about dates and local gossip struck her as shallow and boring, there was a lot of childish horseplay in which she didn't take part. All the jokes were about barnyards and backhouses. She frequently took a book with her and read it at lunch time, her back against the rough bark of an apple tree, munching green apples or nibbling at her lunch. After a while the rest of the pickers left her alone, making sly jokes about 'the bookworm.'

Several nights a week, if it wasn't too late when she got home or on the days that there wasn't any picking, she cleaned up and went to Everett's, staying quite late. The summer darkness stole upon her sooner than she realized, buried in a book or talking with him about the things that troubled her. Once Everett told her that he thought maybe she ought to spend more time with others her age.

"But I don't like most of them. All they think about is getting married and going to church. I'm not ever going to get married," she protested vehemently. When Everett didn't answer immediately, she went on. "Nobody I know who is married is very happy and even if you love somebody, you might lose them."

Everett nodded. "That's true, very true, my dear, but you have to love someone even though you might lose them. It isn't natural not to love, is it?"

"What's 'love'?" Ellen persisted. "All these things I read about it seem like it mostly hurts people. All the love stories like "Romeo and Juliet" turn out wrong, don't they?

Everett seemed very ill at ease. He lit a cigarette and blew out a long draught of smoke before he answered. "Yes, I suppose they, do but I don't think most people can help it. They have to love in spite of themselves and all the risks. Besides there are lots of kinds of love besides that between men and women and that's probably what keeps the world going round. Now, think of your Grandma and how much she loves you."

Ellen wanted to ask him if he had ever been in love, something held her back. The subject seemed to distress him and he arose, sighing. "It's getting dark, Ellen, maybe you'd better run along tonight," he said. He seldom suggested that she leave, but there was something sad, even irritable in his voice. Ellen closed her book and said she guessed she would.

The summer darkness had begun to settle down on the valley, but she had never been afraid of going or coming anywhere in Merritsville. It was all so familiar to her. She felt sometimes that she would have been as safe and as happy to lie down and sleep in the fields or on the ditch banks as anywhere inside a house. Besides she loved the summer nights with the crickets keening and the frogs gulping, the creek's rushing-hushing sound in the distance. She liked the silken sounds leaves made when there was a soft warm breeze, the infinite purplish depths of the star-filled summer nights and sometimes Everett playing his mandolin on the back steps after she left. Tonight there was a melancholy silence. She hoped she hadn't upset him. More and more she felt that there was a secret bond between them and that something wonderfully exciting or terrible must happen to her that summer.

One evening later as she was leaving for Everett's, Grandma said casually without looking up from her mending, "Maybe you'd better not stay so late tonight at Everett's."

Ellen was alerted by something out of the ordinary in Grandma's voice.

"Oh, why not?"

"Well," Addie hesitated, not entirely sure of her reasons herself but Isabel Bateman, an old friend of hers who lived in one of the houses on the road that Ellen usually took to Everett's and who was now so crippled that she had to spend most of her time in a wheel chair by the window, had mentioned it to her that afternoon—that it didn't look so good to people to see a young girl like Ellen spending so much time at an older man's house, especially one with a reputation like Everett Gordon's. In spite of Addie's better judgment, it disturbed her. She knew the frightful power of gossip in a small town, and suddenly ugly things, which she only very rarely admitted into her conscious existence, presented themselves forcefully to her. She was absolutely and firmly convinced of the innocence of Ellen and the decency of Everett. Still and all his drinking might ... but the really difficult, the most impossible thing as it turned out was how to tell Ellen.

"Well, it worries me a little you being out alone at night now that you're a young lady. It seems to worry some of the townsfolk that you spend so much time at Everett's and I wouldn't want anything to...." She looked up and was stopped by the angry flush that had come over Ellen's face.

"This dumb town, I hate it!" was all that Ellen could splutter out after a stunned moment.

Addie got up and took her by the shoulders. "Now, now, you know I trust you, Ellen, and I know Everett wouldn't do anything wrong to you, but people are funny and sometimes they think wrong things. I wouldn't want either of you to be hurt by gossip."

"Why do people gossip?" Ellen's eyes filled with tears. "Why do they have to be so nasty and mean?"

Grandma sighed and shook her head. "I guess they don't have any better things to think about. Life is pretty poor for lots of them. Now you go along and take Everett a half dozen of them fresh eggs and don't say anything to him. I guess the truth will prevail over all the wickedness in the world."

She settled back to her sewing with an uneasy feeling, thinking it would be better if Isabel didn't have so much time to look out of the window, but still and all, Ellen had got to a troublesome age. She acted very touchy and moody this summer. She guessed that all she could do was pray for a little extra help from the Lord in guiding her in the paths of righteousness. Still the thought came back to haunt her. Isabel's mind was such a true reflection of the town's, and something in her very tone had smudged the relationship of Ellen and Everett in such a way that Addie felt very blue. Men, she had learned, never got over certain attitudes no matter how old they got. Everett was old enough to be Ellen's father, even grandfather! The thought wrenched the passage of time dramatically into her consciousness. She had to admit that she didn't really know him as a man; memories of the dear little boy overlaid all her sense of him. But she had to trust him with Ellen; she could never bring herself to speak to him of such delicate and outrageous suspicions.

She put her sewing away and got out her church books. She sat there studying the *Pearl of Great Price* and the *Doctrine and Covenants* until Ellen came in just after nine o'clock with several more books under her arm and a happy expression. Together they ate a bowl of bread and milk and went peacefully to bed.

By August the tender beauty of the summer had gone. Day after sweltering day big white clouds like scoops of ice cream moved languidly across the blue enameled sky but gave no moisture or relief from the enervating heat. Occasionally a brief summer storm would rumble across the valley, dumping a refreshing shower, but after a steamy hour or so, the moisture would all be sucked up and the hills and valley would be as hot and dry as before.

The summer activities went on–harvesting of fruits and vegetables, bottling, preserving, haying, endless irrigating, preparing for winter, which seemed lost to memory utterly in the dry, searing temperatures that turned the hills from various shades of green to dull gold. Occasionally there was a respite from the hard, monotonous work. Each small town had a special holiday in addition to the Fourth and Twenty-Fourth. Work would cease for a couple of days to celebrate Onion Days, Cherry Days, Peach Days, Poultry Days, Strawberry Days, Dairy Days, Rodeo Days. Descended from the old European medieval "fairs" and tournaments, they provided a respite from the dreariness of toil and promoted commerce. Parades and contests were held. Booths and concessions were set up: from morning to night the populace reveled each in his own fashion–from congenial sociability to drunken orgies.

In early August there was a flurry of excitement in Merritsville despite the weary heat. The town celebrated "Raspberry Days" since a number of other farmers like Aaron Walker had cultivated acres of the popular berry and had become known for its fine produce.

The morning of the Big Day dawned as clear, hot and bright as the preceding ones. Ellen went to call for Lorraine and Louise with whom she was going to watch the parade. She was wearing a new sheer, satin-striped, white rayon dress that her mother had sent her from the city. She was not particularly comfortable in it; it seemed a little too fussy with a long ruffled collar and a bias skirt that clung to her slip with electric tenacity. Ellen didn't like the way it cupped under her small behind and she kept pulling at it. Louise thought it was very pretty and Lorraine tried to fix the collar so it wouldn't bunch up. When they joined the other girls, Virginia Benson said it looked like a short night-gown and sure did show her shape. Nobody paid much attention to her because she always said the worst things to and about everybody. She was a lot like her Aunt Bessie. All the same, Ellen felt self-conscious and wished she hadn't worn it. The day hadn't got off to a very good start.

The girls swarmed around together all morning consuming cotton candy, popsicles, cold drinks and squandering their berry money happily. For a while Ellen felt like one of them. She threw rings at boards full of pegs, squealed as loud as anyone on the whip, rocked the chairs of the Ferris wheel and bought a fortune from a queer hand that reached out of a velvet sleeve attached to a gilt pole in the middle of a glass case. A scrawny old man dressed in a grubby oriental costume had passed out pieces of paper on the top of which one wrote one's name and date of birth. Then he folded them and gave them to the hand which appeared to be that of a woman with long, red-varnished fingernails. Ellen was fascinated by the serpent-like undulations of the long fingers as they grasped the papers, disappeared for short intervals and then returned them filled with spidery writing in green ink.

Ellen grabbed hers and read avidly: "You are easily hurt and very sensitive. You must learn to protect yourself from life. Although there are signs of disaster in your near future, you must hold firmly to your ideals and courage and you will come through alright. Your love-life will be stormy but will bring you rich rewards. You must rely more on your heart than your head in making big decisions in life...."

The girls read each other's fortunes with intense seriousness, amazed at the uncanny knowledge they displayed, never suspecting that they were selected at random from a large file and quickly copied by a harassed, fat woman with a harsh face and a cigarette dangling from her thick lips in a tent behind the odd case. But real fortune is no less capricious.

Only Virginia made fun of the occult pronouncements. "Ellen's goin' to have stormy love-life," she shrieked waving the paper wildly above her head. "Boy, would I like to see Ellen having any love-life! That would be good." Ellen snatched the paper from her irritably.

"Well, yours isn't so hot," Lorraine put in defense of her cousin.

"So who cares?" Virginia shrugged. "It says in mine that 'my beauty will cause me a great deal of trouble'." A big, homely, red-headed, overweight, freckled girl, she was the first to make fun of herself, so that others could take little offense at the sharp jabs she made at them. They moved away from the fortune teller's booth giggling and jostling each other happily.

At noon the gang broke up with plans to meet later in the day but Ellen knew what was likely to happen. The boys, who had been also traveling in packs all morning, would start singling out the girls for the evening. Some of them already had dates like

Lorraine and Ken. Eventually Ellen would be left with Louise and the little Walkers or Virginia. Although she didn't mind Virginia in the crowd, she didn't like being alone with her so much. The day had already begun to disintegrate. The crowd had thinned and the grounds and street were strewn with candy wrappers, pop-corn boxes, torn paper and ornaments from the floats. The sounds, which only a short time ago seemed happy, joyous, were now nerve-grating, raucous–the jarring, grinding, creaking and thundering of the machines, strident voices of the concession-aires, the crying of hot, hungry children. She was glad to escape except that it wasn't much quieter at the Walker's where she and Grandma were having the noon meal.

Fortunately Hal was not going to be at the dinner table. She had seen him twice that morning, riding in an old green Model A jalopy with four or five other ruffians. It was parked out front when the girls came by, and Hal was bolting out the back door with a sandwich and piece of chocolate cake. He gave them scarcely a glance as he leaped into the car and sputtered off.

Aunt Dosey said he had to mind the service station for the afternoon, and she was glad of that as it gave him something to do and she knew where he was. Ellen detected forced cheerful-ness in her voice with which she tried to hide her worries. Hal was getting a bad reputation.

The three older girls did the dishes and then spent the after-noon lolling around in the back bedroom in their slips. Lorraine got an inspiration to try Ellen's hair a different way and to put make-up on her so that she might be able to catch a date that night. She urged her to go stag to the dance at the Pandora and coached her in some of the ways to catch the boys' attention.

"When a boy looks at you, Ellen, don't stick up your nose like you're so much smarter than he is. Kinda give him a little smile and maybe a wink, kinda stick out your front a bit, like this and act like you're interested. Here, you can open this top button on your dress and show more of your neck. You wanta wear one of my necklaces?"

Ellen shook her head. "There's nobody I want to go with around here," she said.

"You act like the only man you ever liked is that old Mr. Gordon," Lorraine went on. "Lots of boys think that's funny and they might not want to go with you, either. Why do you hang around there so much?"

"Because he's nice and treats me good. I can talk to him and he doesn't act silly and crude like the boys do." Ellen answered hotly. "I guess I better go on home if you're gonna talk like that."

"Oh, c'mon," Lorraine coaxed. "You really are pretty, Ellen, and there'll be some boy you'll like someday. Here, hold still while I fix your hair."

Too hot and bored to resist, Ellen let her do as she pleased with her hair and make-up. As the afternoon wore on she began to long intensely for the cool, quiet library at Everett's house with its soft green light and musty bookish smell, but it was far too hot to walk all that way down there. She had begun to wonder about the things Grandma, and now Lorraine, had said. It made her angry and a little ashamed but she didn't know what she should do. She couldn't give up her friendship with Everett, but she found she had started to look at him in a different light.

Presently it was time to go to the evening parade and program. At Lorraine's and Louise's urging she left her hair in the page-boy curl that they had fixed and kept the mascara and lipstick on. She had to admit that she liked it a little bit.

After the evening parade things happened just as she thought they would. Louise was left in care of the youngest Walker, Lorraine went off with Ken, Celia with Doug, Dot Barker had snagged Joe Hammond and the rest of the girls paired off, prowling for stray males. Ellen and Virginia, who had not failed to make some crude remarks about the change in Ellen's appearance, were left to each other in the sweating crowd.

They drifted aimlessly along in the stream of faces all of which now appeared to Ellen to be stamped with a strange disease, a hysterical passionate greed that frightened her. She had never noticed before how ugly people were in carnival masses when they were supposed to be the happiest. They all seemed to be moved and dragged about senselessly with the awkward, foolish motions of wooden puppets or characters in old silent movies. They made stupid, inhuman noises–grunts, shrieks of shrill laughter, weird exclamations.

As the harsh yellow lights strung above the booths came on, the hideous spectacle was painfully accentuated. Ellen felt her-

self part of a grotesque show in which she had quite forgotten her
part.

Virginia, who seemed supremely at ease with the situation,
indeed very much in her element like the great happy clown that
she was, decided she wanted to play one of the dart games and
pushed into the crowd around that booth. Ellen was crushed
against a fat woman with an oily face and huge breasts over which
a shiny yellow rayon sweater was stretched to bursting. Looking
down she saw that a skinny, half-drunk man with a silly grin on
his face was standing behind the woman and running his hands
languidly over the great yellow breasts while he cheered her
clumsy dart-throwing. Ellen was suddenly nauseated and had
begun to fight her way out of the crowd when she looked up,
startled and dismayed to see Everett Gordon.

He was dressed in a queer old-fashioned suit of clothes that
Ellen had never seen before with a fancy vest and broad printed
tie in spite of the stifling heat. On his head he was wearing a flat
straw hat like she had seen on Fred Astaire in the movies, and he
was carrying a cane and white gloves. He almost looked like something out of a minstrel show. There was an utterly absorbed and
foolish look on his face as he made his way through the crowd
with elaborate flourishes of his cane and gloves. Ellen was so
astonished at first that she stood gaping at him and then, as it
dawned on her that he was quite drunk, she felt panicky. She had
to get away before he saw her–saw that she had seen him, but as
she turned to push away, someone thrust her directly in his path.
For a moment he didn't recognize her; then his face brightened.

"Ellen, my lovely little Ellen," he said. "I've been looking
everywhere for you on this festive occasion. I want to buy you
some happiness, I want to give you the joy you deserve." Although he spoke slowly, deliberately, his words were not slurred.
He gripped her arm and she could feel his hot, whisky-thick breath
on her cheek.

Ellen tried to pull away, burning with humiliation and embarrassment. "Oh, no, I...." She tried to think of some excuse to get
away from him, but he was already propelling her determinedly
through the crowd to the nearest booth where cheap and gaudy
prizes were to be had by throwing balls at pyramids of wooden
pegs. Dying with shame, Ellen watched Everett worry some coins

out of his old-fashioned, long black purse and plunk them osten-
tatiously on the pine-board counter. She tried not to look at him,
tears blurred her eyes and the brightly colored pennants, kewpie
dolls, stuffed animals and glass jewelry all melted together in a
brash dye of agony. She tried to edge away tactfully, but Everett
restrained her. She could feel his hand trembling. "Gonna get
you something beautiful; you deserve something beautiful, my
dear; now don't go away. I'd get you all the jewels in India...."
He took off his coat and handed it and his cane to her. With what
seemed like sheer crazy luck he knocked down the three pyramids of pegs with his six balls. The crowd cheered. He added
considerably to Ellen's distress when he took off his hat and bowed
to them.

Wiping the perspiration from his face, Everett retrieved his
coat and put it on with an elegant flourish, turning to her. "Now,
little lady, you just pick out anything you want." He instructed
the bored attendant, "You give her anything she wants, young
man, the whole wide world if she wants it." Ellen was so miserable she scarcely knew what she was doing. All she could think
of was escaping from this hideous nightmare, of waking up to
find it wasn't true. She pointed numbly to a chalky kewpie with a
wide halo of fuchsia colored feathers edged with tinsel. The attendant got it down and handed it to her with a smirk. She managed to choke out a "thank you" to Everett and was trying to back
away when he did a perfectly shocking thing. He picked up her
left hand and kissed it with an exaggerated bow that nearly upset
him.

"Ah, you're more than welcome, my Princess," he murmured.
Ellen jerked her hand away; a hot, bitter prickling spread over
her, but it turned to a chill of horror as she heard behind her a
familiar, harsh, mocking laugh. She whirled around and stumbled
against Hal who was lounging against the corner of the booth.
The reddish lights from the canopy shining on his face made him
appear diabolical; he was sneering in that knowing way she had
seen so often before. "Lo, Ellen. See ya got your boyfriend." he
drawled in her ear. He grabbed her arm, but she punched him
with her elbow and lunged away from the booth, pushing her
way desperately through the crowd. Some of the kewpie's feathers were torn off, and she heard people making rude remarks as

she pushed them. She could think of nothing but getting out of that awful place. Hot, burning tears were running down her face.

At the far edge of the dusty grounds there was a row of old cottonwood trees against the fence. The lights from the carnival barely reached there. She pressed, trembling into their shadows, clutching the cheap, hard doll to her chest, trying to fight back the sobs. She wished she could die then and there.

CB

Ellen leaned against the heavy wire fence her arm aching from the weight of the hard, silly doll. She had an impulse to dash it to the ground and stomp on it. What was it that prevented her? Numbness? Shock? Or something deeper about Everett–the fact that HE had given it to her and something in his drunken, but not insensible eyes, had touched a fragile nerve of pity and–love? She could not dare to think about that word in connection with him now. He had disgraced her so. How could he have done this to her? Something sinister appeared in the shadowy depths of her mind, but she was far too agitated to get hold of it. Strange words kept flashing through her mind rhythmically–something she had heard in church about those who were unfaithful being "cast into outer darkness where there was a great wailing and gnashing of teeth...."; a region where there was no salvation from one's stubborn wickedness. The words rang with the ultimate of frustration, anger and despair as a livid description of this dark moment. She felt truly cast out cowering here in rancid shadows on the fringe of the gaudy, carnival that was going on completely oblivious to her and her shame. There was no place to go for help or comfort.

The thought of going "home" to Grandma's was unappealing. It would be dark and stuffy, and she would be alone and frightened there. Grandma would be at the stadium with Aunt Dosey where the fireworks and prize drawings would be held. She supposed she could go over there but that, too, seemed out of the question. The other place where she had found a haven, Everett's house, had been brutally closed by the events of this night. From now on it would be a forbidden, alien place; she could never stand to see Everett again. Something had been shattered beyond all repair. She didn't know how long she stood there suffering as she had never remembered–anger, humiliation, self-pity. After what seemed much longer than it really was, she began to regain composure.

She couldn't cringe here in this dusty, noisy darkness much longer full of shame and bitterness. Slowly she started across the carnival grounds, keeping close to the fringes, hoping not to see anyone she knew, but some of the rides were enclosed in the main fence so that she had to go out around them. She was making her way around the Octopus, a contrivance for dislocating all the bones in the body, which was just unloading a group of badly shaken but laughing passengers, when Ellen heard her name called in a high, hilarious and vaguely familiar voice. It was a voice with faint echoes of a sneering drawl and southern accent. "Aehlen!" She looked around nervously, knowing instinctively who it was before she saw the glittering black eyes, the carelessly tossed, extravagantly curling black hair, the full, arrogant red lips of Simone Hamilton. Simone had just staggered off the Octopus and was standing astride Ellen's path, her legs spread wide and her hands on her hips in a brassy movie pose.

Ellen stopped, a peculiar feeling gripped her as though she were being hypnotized. She became acutely conscious of herself–of the sticky, ruffled white dress and the silly doll, the mussed hair and ridiculous traces of make-up. Compared to Simone she felt as though she were an awkward, ignorant, homely little girl clutching that awful doll.

Simone, whom Ellen had seen only a few times in the past several years and of whom she had heard unsavory rumors, appeared wildly beautiful in the carnival lights.

She was a little taller than Ellen with high pointed breasts, the deep crease between which showed above her low-necked, frilly white blouse. She had a very small waist, cinched tightly by a wide leather cowboy belt with a gaudy silver buckle and a full black fringed skirt that swayed as she moved menacingly toward Ellen. She was wearing very high-heeled, sandal-like slippers on her bare feet and her toenails were painted bright red. Ellen saw them because she looked down from the hypnotic eyes and tried to move away as quickly as possible. But she was not quick enough. Simone had grabbed her by the shoulder.

"Ellen Kent, I ain't seen you for a coon's age! Gee, you're lookin' better than you used to." Ellen detected a superior note of sarcasm in Simone's drawl. "Whatcha doin' mostly these days?"

"Oh, nothing much." Ellen was trying to draw away, but Simone's fingers dug unnecessarily hard into her shoulder.

"You all alone?" pursued Simone and when Ellen nodded, she began to urge her toward the entrance to the Octopus ride. "Well, come on and meet some good-lookin' guys and have a little fun!"

Before Ellen could resist, she was surrounded by three men and Simone.

"Ellen Kent, this here's Dod and Med Hallsworth." Simone indicated the two taller figures, then pulling a slightly shorter one from where he had shifted behind, "And this is Ferrin."

The two taller men lifted their big cowboy hats slightly, but the shorter one jerked his off, lurched forward with a strange motion and held out his hand to her. At first she took it warily, thinking he was probably drunk, but she saw in the dim light the face of a young boy not too much older than herself, who seemed almost as confused and miserable. There was an urgent pressure in his sticky hand, too, as he seemed reluctant to let go of hers. She found herself returning his shy smile but drew her hand away cautiously. She had heard vaguely of the Hallsworth brothers; Uncle Aaron had spoken of them in a disparaging way, called them "tough bastards to deal with." Together with their father they owned a large ranch in the western part of the county, the biggest in the area. They were a tough bunch and had earned a reputation for hard dealing and hard living. It was rumored they were worth more than the whole rest of the county put together, but no one knew for sure since they stayed pretty much to themselves, coming over to Merritsville only on business or occasionally to booze and carouse. She knew she ought not to get mixed up with them and especially not if they had taken up with Simone. The unpleasant flavor of her earlier experience remained. But when she looked around for a way to remove herself as quickly as she could, she saw the Simone and the three men had wedged her between the ticket box and the railing that surrounded the Octopus. She had no way of getting by them except to climb over the railing into the concession area which was forbidden anyway.

"If you're alone and not doin' nothin', why dontcha take a ride with us," Simone coaxed. "Gee, that's cute. Where'd you get it?" She snatched the kewpie doll out of Ellen's arm.

Ellen opened her mouth to protest, but caught sight of Ferrin's face in the smudgy carnival light. It was so anxious, almost pleading, and then a strange, wild, completely unexpected impulse seized her. Why not? Who cared anyway whether she went around with the tough Hallsworth guys and Simone? She had no other friends that mattered much. She shrugged her shoulders nonchalantly, almost gaily. "O.K., let's go."

Ferrin stepped forward and took her arm. It was then that she became aware that he was crippled. He had to shift himself forward on one leg, hitch up and drag the other. A feeling of dismay swept over her, but she soon saw that she had been meant to be paired off with him. The other two men were greedily intent on Simone who was having an exhilarating time playing them off against each other. She was waving the doll at them.

"Y'see what Ellen got. Whyn't I got a doll like this? Jist which one of yew is good enough to win me a doll," she teased.

"Aw hell," said one of the men, "Them things is a dime a dozen. We'll buy you a whole crate of 'em if you want later, come on now and ride the Ferris Wheel." He took the doll away from her and handed it back to Ellen.

They all moved toward the Ferris wheel. Ellen and Ferrin got into one chair and the other three in another. As the wheel clanked around, Ellen could see the glow of their three cigarettes. Simone smoked! That was still a very bad thing for a girl to do in Merritsville. Once some of them had tried it on a hike in the hills with some hand rolled smokes. Ellen had nearly choked to death. She would never have dared let her mother or Grandma know. If a girl smoked she was likely to do everything and anything else bad. Ellen was pretty sure Simone lived up to that saying. She listened with growing apprehension to her shrieks of laughter as she could see the seat swaying wildly below them. Simone had not changed, only grown more Simone. After this ride, Ellen knew she must get away from her, but she was still curious.

"Which one of your brothers does Simone go with most?" she ventured to Ferrin who was slumped on the far side of the seat.

"She goes with both of 'em all the time. They wont neither of 'em let the other go out with her alone." He shook a cigarette out of his pack and offered her one. She shook her head; he didn't say anything but lit one for himself.

"But doesn't she like one better than the other?" Ellen pursued.

"Simone don't like nobody but Simone, you can bet your bottom dollar on that," he said calmly as though possessed of vast knowledge about her. "She wouldn't give a snap of her finger for neither of 'em if she couldn't keep 'em all stirred up like this. She lives on it, excitement, thrills, you know."

Ellen was intrigued at the unexpected wisdom and calm assurance of this strange boy. How had he found out Simone so well? She studied his face as sharply as she could in the shifting multi-colored light. It was a fine face, almost handsome except for a rather large nose. She liked his mouth; it was full and nicely shaped and he had pretty teeth. His hair was dark, thick and wavy. But there was such a look of sadness about him. It made him look older, very remote. She had an unaccountable impulse to touch him; she seldom ever wanted to touch people anymore. Maybe it was just curiosity.

"Maybe I will have a cigarette if you'll show me how to smoke," she burst out.

He looked at her with quiet surprise and then got out the pack, smiling. "Sure, sure," he said, shaking one toward her.

Feeling deliciously wicked, she put the white cylinder in her lips. He leaned closer to hold the match and she steadied his hand. There was a nice warm recognition of each other in the touch; it encouraged him to move over and lay his arm across the seat back of her as he instructed her in the art of smoking.

"Now draw in, not too hard, easy now." She had already taken a long nervous drag. The acrid smoke filled her mouth, throat, nose and eyes and she choked violently. When she finally recovered, she handed the cigarette to him, laughing with embarrassment. "I guess I don't really want to learn right now."

"I'm glad, I don't much like to see girls smoke," he said, finishing the cigarette with long, experienced drags.

"But why not, if boys do?" Ellen asked edgily. She had begun to resent the rigid double standard that still bound her life.

"I dunno," admitted Ferrin, flipping the smoke away. "It just seems as though they should be a little more special or somethin'."

There didn't seem to be any point in pursuing the subject, although Ellen was a little ruffled at her clumsy failure. She ought to be able to smoke if she wanted to, yet she agreed with Ferrin a little. Girls were always supposed to be better. She changed the subject.

"How did you hurt your leg?" She hoped he might be only temporarily crippled.

"Yeah, a long time ago," he said shortly and then she knew it wasn't temporary.

"How?" she went on.

"Oh, I got bucked off a horse, hurt my spine." The Ferris wheel had ground to a stop. He hitched himself off quickly, helping Ellen carefully to the platform. She realized at once that it was a painful subject, and she must not let him feel her pity. Of course, she wasn't going to see him again, but she had begun to like and feel comfortable with him.

Simone, Dod and Med, the latter two glowering furtively at each other, were waiting for them.

"I'm sick of this place," Simone said impetuously. "Let's go someplace else."

"Ain't no place else to go," Med growled. "You don't want to go over to the stadium and sit around waitin' for them dumb fireworks, do ya?"

"No, well let's just go for a ride or sumpin'." Simone grabbed him by his leather vest and whirled him around mischievously.

Ellen spoke up hastily. "I have to go now; it was nice seeing you again, Simone...."

"We'll drive you home or where you want to go," Ferrin put in quickly; before she could protest, she was being propelled to the parking lot. The Hallsworth brothers owned a gleaming new black Pontiac sedan with which Ellen, in spite of her discomfort, was impressed. Hardly anybody in Merritsville or even Ed Barker had big new cars like it. Few of the boys even had cars that would run. Ferrin held the front door open for her. Simone and her two partners piled in the back.

"I want sumpin' to drink," demanded Simone as the car pulled out and Ellen was trying to give Ferrin directions to home. She decided that was the best place to go now.

"You heard the dame," Dod drawled sarcastically leaning over the seat, blowing cigarette smoke in Ellen's face. "It's under the front seat, Ferrin, right under yer girl-friend's seat there."

Mumbling something that she couldn't hear, Ferrin fumbled under the seat and passed a bottle back to them.

After they had each taken a long swig from the bottle, Simone's as long as either, she bounced up. "Let's go somewhere to eat, I'm starved."

"I better go now," Ellen said firmly, miserably. "I'm not hungry."

"The hell you do." Med picked her up quickly. "What you wanta go home so early for?"

"Just because I got to," Ellen stammered uneasily.

"You're scared of us, ain't you?" he taunted with a note of pleasure in his raw, rough voice.

"No," Ellen tried to sound casual, "no, I'm not afraid of you, I just think I better go home."

"Oh, Ellen thinks she's just too good for us. Allus was stuck-up," put in Simone wickedly.

"She does, eh?" Dod spoke up. "Well, ain't that jist too bad. Git goin', Ferrin, old man. We'll see who's too nice for who."

Ferrin had been idling the car, waiting for a resolution.

"You wanta go home, I'll take you," he said firmly to Ellen. "But I would like it if you'd come along for a while. They wont hurt you."

She nodded in reluctant agreement, feeling the genuine urgency in his voice although she knew that she should have jumped out of the car then and there. Ferrin gunned the car. He drove fast but expertly, and Ellen was distracted by the exhilaration of tearing along the black highway, the rushing dark shadows and sparse lights flowing by at a speed she had never before experienced. She had never been driving at sixty miles an hour before; Ed had never driven that fast the times she had ridden with him and her mother. She had to admit to a certain exhilaration.

They stopped and ate hamburgers and drank pop at a drive-in, and she began to relax a little. Listening to the banter and laughter that went on in the back seat, she wished that she could join in more easily. Ferrin turned the car off the main highway at Dod's instructions and headed for the canyon. Simone kept up a wild stream of chatter, and there was a lot of tumbling and romping in the back seat. Occasionally there would be oaths and insults between the two fellows as they passed the bottle of liquor back and forth and once in a while pushed it up to Ferrin, who took a short swig but didn't offer any to Ellen. When Dod noticed this, he undertook to right the matter.

"Why the Hell don't ya offer her a swig? Ain't ya got no manners?" he snorted.

"I don't want any," Ellen protested.

"You don't want any," he mocked. "Who the Hell ever heard anybody not wantin' a drink Saturday night? You one of them Goddam strick Mormon girls? Say I hear things about them, they don't smoke and they don't drink but they sure do other things, by damn...."

"Oh shut up, Dod," Simone said suddenly and inexplicably serious. "Ellen don't know nothin' about nothin'. She ain't been around any real men before, you likely to scare her real good and make her bawl."

"But shouhgtahave ju' one lil drink for sociability," insisted Med, who was the drunker of the three. He had the bottle now, and he reached his long arm over the seat and pinned Ellen's head in the crook of his elbow, forcing the bottle to her mouth. As Ellen struggled in panic, the liquor spilled down her chin and neck. Some of the bitter stuff went down her throat and she spat and choked furiously. Ferrin stepped on the brake of the car so hard that it threw Med and the bottle off balance and spilled more of the whisky on Ellen and the seat. Ellen ducked free and tried frantically to open the car door.

Med swore fiercely, "Goddam you, Ferrin, why'd ya do that? Wastin' all the good booze and ain't no place to get anymore this time a night."

"You leave her alone, Med, or I'll wring your bloody neck," Ferrin said grimly.

"Yeah, you and who else, crip?" Med jeered meanly, but Dod had pushed him back in the seat. "Gimme the rest of that likker, Med, fore you spill it all. Cool that damn hot-head of yourn off."

Ferrin had pulled the car off the road into one of the canyon picnic areas and turned off the headlights. Ellen was still hunched in the corner of the car with her back to the windshield. She was trembling so violently that her teeth chattered.

Ferrin lit a cigarette and she could see his hand shaking. Simone, Dod and Med had resumed their wild play in the back seat, wrestling and thrashing around, swearing and saying obscene things that Ellen had never heard uttered before. She crouched miserably in the seat as far away as she could get. At length Simone squealed, "Get off me, you fucking son-of-a-bitch and let me outa here before I piss all over you."

Ellen chilled, she felt she could not endure another minute of the nightmare; she found the handle of the door and opened it stumbling out into the darkness. She ran toward a break in the shadows of the trees beyond which she could hear the rushing of the canyon stream. Uncertain of her footing, she stopped, panting so hard that her chest hurt and her head ached. She heard the uneven drag of Ferrin's feet as he moved toward her as quickly as he could. He came up beside her in the darkness but left a wide space between them. She could almost feel his anguish in the silence.

"I dono what to sssay," he stuttered. "I thought you knew Simone. I didn't know you wasn't good friends...."

"It was a long time ago when they first moved to Merritsville," Ellen said at last in a low strained voice. "I shouldn't have come; it's my fault for coming."

"We forced you, it's really my fault. I knew what they was gonna do most likely but I wanted you to." He moved toward her but when he saw her back away, he stopped helplessly.

"Yeah, we're a rotten mess," he burst out bitterly, "and Simone's like us, but I can see you ain't. I'm damned sorry I drug you into this. I mean, I wouldn't have if I had thought you didn't know." He lit another cigarette, took a couple of deep drags on it, then ground it angrily underfoot. From near the car came the sound of drunken laughter and some liquid splattering onto the ground as though someone were urinating.

Ferrin took hold of Ellen's hand and drew her roughly down the bank of the river to where the distance and rushing water shut out the depraved sounds. He put his arm firmly around her and drew her down on a log beside him; it surprised her and him both that she didn't resist. She was amazed at the strength in his arms and the comfort it gave her to have them around her. It was the first time a boy had put his arms around her that way in firm tenderness. Almost naturally her head fitted the curve of his shoulder, and they sat in silence for a long time, listening to the noise of the water and watching the rough silver gleam of it as it slid and bounced over the rocks. The black lacy fringe of tall trees was silhouetted against the silver-blue star lit sky. After a while Ellen stopped shivering. Ferrin stroked her hair gently and laid his lips against it once, but made no move to do anything more.

"You're a real pretty girl, Ellen," he whispered, "a real pretty one and a nice one. I thought it was funny Simone would have a friend like you, but I won't let 'em hurt you, never you mind."

Ellen had grown uncomfortable from sitting in the same position; she moved gently out of his arm and straightened up. "That's all right, Ferrin. I'm not afraid anymore. It was just that I'm not used to ... just that...."

"All that rotten talk and stuff. Don't pay no attention to it. I guess they'll be pretty drunk goin' back and wont make so much noise. If they don't get in a fight ...," he said with concern as they heard some loud profanity from the direction of the car. "Sometimes I think one of them is gonna kill the other one over that no-good woman." He got up wearily and held out his hand to her.

"Where did they pick up with her?" Ellen asked as they walked slowly back to the car.

"Oh, some tavern or another, I guess," Ferrin said with disgust in his voice. "She was workin' over in that joint in Junction City, I b'lieve."

"Where does she live now? I haven't seen or heard of her folks since they moved away a few years ago. I only knew her when we were little, before her brother died."

"Ma's dead. She don't know where her old man is. Most of the time she stays with us though sometimes she goes off, God knows where, and we can't live with Dod and Med til she comes back." There was a dark bitterness in his voice.

While Ellen stood aside, Ferrin rounded up and got the drunken party into the back seat again. As he had predicted, they were drunk enough to subside in a tangled heap from which only occasional bursts of obscenity, grunts and profanity issued sporadically.

They drove silently down the dark, eery canyon road. Ellen

sat closer to Ferrin and let him hold her hand. He insisted, when they stopped at last in front of her house, on coming as far as the porch with her and stood holding her hand tightly.

"I sure would like to see you again, without these ... that is if you could stand to. If you could forget or if you could just see your way clear...." He was squeezing the words out painfully.

Ellen was so exhausted and anxious for the horrible day to end that she hardly heard him.

"Yes, sometime, thanks." She took the kewpie doll that he had rescued and leaped up the porch steps. Darting through the screen door which was left unlocked for her, she slipped the hook in place with a firm click as though to lock out the night.

"That you, Ellen?" Grandma called from her bedroom.

"Yes, Grandma," Ellen hoped fervently that she wouldn't get up.

"You all right, honey?" Grandma asked sleepily. "thought maybe you was stayin' over with Lorraine?"

"No, I'm fine, see you in the morning." She stumbled into her bedroom, aching with fatigue and disgust and crawled miserably into bed.

C₰

It was a sultry August morning. The heat had lain so long on the earth that it had gone stale and yellowish like rancid butter. Ellen could taste it, bitter, nauseating in her mouth, as she wakened the next morning. The smell of cigarette smoke still clung to her hair and skin, reminding her at once of the nasty night. Bits and pieces of it floated through her mind like the fire they had had last year on the hills above Uncle Aaron's farm. That was like the landscape of her heart—a burned out, burned over, bleak and acrid area into which the stunted green would only slowly return. How she wished she could blot the whole thing out of her memory. She dug her face and fists helplessly into the hot pillow knowing how relentlessly her mind, her heart would torment her with it.

In the greenish-yellow light that filtered through the old green blinds, she could see the doll Everett had won for her standing on the dresser where she had left it last night. What a stupid, babyish face it had with cupid-bow lips and wide, hard, staring eyes–a face of hardened innocence that made her want to slap it. Cheap, chalky so frail that it would crumble almost at the touch, its hideous feathered head dress had been crushed and broken, giving it a kind of vulgar rakishness. Still it fascinated Ellen. As she stared at it, now aware of its reflection in the mirror which showed the little round buttocks with the painted-on short pink costume and its dimpled legs molded into one solid column, it appeared to her to represent something important, the carnival, the illusions of pleasure and love that were so false, so easily broken. She needed someone to talk to about it, and that was the worst of it–the one person who might help her understand was Everett. This silly thing had come between her and him. If he hadn't been drunk he never would have even allowed her to have anything like that! It was he above all who understood the genuine, the real quality things of life, she thought. She wondered how she would ever face him again. Outside the window she could hear the steady chop, chop, chop of a metallic instrument. Grandma chopping at the trumpet vine again even though it was Sunday. She had caught on to the fact that Grandma usually hacked at that old vine when she was upset. She wondered if she guessed anything about last night. There was simply no way of telling Grandma about what had happened; she knew by now that there were things her grandmother would never understand. Once in a while she longed to shake her and say, 'Grandma, there are bad things in the world, there are *bad* people. Hal and Simone are bad, evil and there is no help for it. You can't make them right by going to church and praying.'

She could hear her grandmother saying in that calm determinedly cheerful way, 'But how else can you help people if you don't pray for them. We must be patient with all God's children and learn not to judge; that's the Heavenly Father's privilege.'

To pray for Simone! The idea was preposterous. Simone lived in a world so far beyond prayer in that "Outer Darkness" of which Ellen had been so acutely aware last night and into which she had been dragged irrevocably. This morning she felt that she might be closer to Simone than anyone else, sharing a terrible sense of sin and depravity. But she hoped she would never, never see her again.

Grandma came to the bedroom door and reminded Ellen that it was time to get ready for church. The idea appalled Ellen; she groaned and pretended to be ill. Grandma came apprehensively to the bed and put her hand on her forehead, her favorite way of beginning her diagnosis of all illness.

"You do feel a bit warm, Dear. What's the matter, did you eat something that upset you? You was out a bit too late last night."

"I guess so," feigned Ellen in a weak voice and kept the sheet pulled up around her face so that the white reflection made her look paler.

"Well, I'll bring you an aspirin and you stay in bed this morning," Addie sighed. She had been worried about Ellen last night and had dozed fitfully listening for her to come in. It wasn't like her to stay out late, but she supposed that she had got mixed up with the other girls and boys or decided to stay with Lorraine. She wondered when Ellen hadn't come to the evening program, but then neither had Lorraine and some of the other young people who preferred to go to the dance or show. Now when she detected that stale, bitter odor of cigarette smoke and some other foreign smell as she bent over Ellen, her heart was squeezed with a surge of fear. She was sure that Ellen wouldn't smoke or drink, but if she had been going around with someone who did, what might not happen?

Of course she had been tolerant of others who had fallen in that way like Everett but Everett, in her mind, had some claim to special sympathies. Still it gave her a forlorn feeling. Had she done right to let Ellen spend so much time around him? Maybe Ellen had begun to think drinking and smoking was all right because she had spent so much time with Everett and had become so attached to him. Maybe she, Addie, had been lax in not pointing out that she never approved those things in Everett while she still loved him for himself. Oh how troublesome it all was. She had begun to sense that Ellen was not as open with her as she had once been. Of course, there were things she couldn't talk about, had never even talked about with her own daughters. Ellen's interests seemed to have gone beyond the scope of her world; the young wanted to know about things that she had never even dared think about, let alone talk about!

She went off to meeting with a heavy heart. Addie had never

been one to harp on the degeneration of the young, but she had lately come to fear that they were venturing out into perilous places, places better left unexplored. Sometimes she wished they wouldn't hold those celebrations that encouraged young people to stay out late and get into mischief. She thought she might be too old or not equal to the task of raising a young girl like Ellen, and yet, she supposed, Ellen would be worse off with Irene in the city. She knew it wouldn't do any good to chastise or scold her; Ellen was the kind that suffered ten times over for anything and everything if she thought she had done anything wrong. Sooner or later it would come out. Oh if only the Lord would look after her, maybe send her a fine young man soon. Lately she seemed to be shutting herself away more, brooding.

Ellen swallowed the aspirin, felt better at the presence and touch of her grandmother and drifted back into a hot, troubled slumber from which she didn't awaken until late afternoon.

Just after daylight that hot August morning, Jacob West had been cutting through the Gordon place as he frequently did to reach his lower farmland where he had to take the water. Tromping along in his knee-high gumboots, his shovel over his shoulder, he was startled by the restlessness of Everett's donkey. He was used to the funny creature which, usually dozing with its head lowered and its long ears flopping down listlessly, hardly ever gave him a passing snort. But this morning it was stomping wildly about, rearing its head back against the rope with which it was tied to the catalpa tree and making mournful squeals as though in pain. Partly out of neighborly curiosity and partly out of the feeling there was something wrong, Jacob leaped over the ditch and went to see what was the matter with Brahms. As he came nearer, he saw, blurrily through the bifocals that always rode halfway down the bridge of his nose, a figure stretched out on the hard dirt of the back yard.

It was nothing to be alarmed about, he thought on first glance. Old Ev had probably had one too many again and couldn't make it up the back steps so was just sleeping it off there. The donkey was most likely hungry and thirsty. Jacob came around behind the donkey and reached out toward the agitated animal before he saw that there was something wrong with the prone figure sprawled among the broken bottles and tin cans. Everett lay as though he had fallen very hard or been thrown down, his head in a pool of blood around which the flies were already buzzing.

Jacob leaped to his side and gently, but with the caution of horror and repugnance, turned him over. His face was a mangled pulp of purple bruises and blood was smeared over his fancy vest and coat. His straw hat was crushed into the dirt and his cane, smudged with blood, lay nearby. But he was still breathing with a painful, bubbly sound. Jacob, swearing and muttering with shocked disbelief, eased Everett into a patch of shade and ran into the house. With some cool water and a soiled rag, he mopped some of the blood and dirt off the battered face. It was obvious that it had not been caused by a mere fall. Everett groaned a deep, long anguished groan of almost unbearable pain. Seeing that he could do no more good for him, Jacob leaped to his feet and tore off for help.

They got Everett into the small Merritsville hospital and determined that he was in grave condition. A heavy blow to the skull had resulted in severe concussion, and there were other lacerations and bruises about his frail body. Someone suggested that he might have fallen off the high steps in a drunken stupor, but the nature of the wound indicated that it must have been caused by a deliberate blow, viciously delivered by a heavy hand or instrument. It was not robbery; his heavy old gold watch and chain were still on him and there were a few dollars in his purse. Word went out that he was not likely to live.

Ellen did not hear about it until the next morning. After a long night's rest, she had begun to feel better about the unfortunate holiday, but when Addie told her about how they had found Everett, she went into a state of hysterics, crying, screaming, even laughing, then talking incoherently. First she begged to be allowed to see him, then she was afraid they might let her. She kept repeating over and over, "It's my fault, I know it is my fault. Oh, God, please let him live, please!"

Puzzled, Addie tried to sooth her; she could make no sense of the story about the doll and Everett's funny behavior at the carnival, kissing her hand or something like that, and Hal seeing him do it. Ellen felt sure that Hal had something to do with it when they had determined that it was definitely a brutal beating, but she didn't want to worry Grandma.

The sheriff let it be known that the law was on the trail of the suspects–a bunch of men and boys who had last been seen drinking and carousing with Everett late on the night of the holiday. It was hinted that in the very likely event of Everett's death, the charge would be murder or, at the least, manslaughter. The sheriff let it be known that some leniency would be shown in the case of those who came forth and volunteered information.

Near the end of the week, Willy Pierce, the assistant at the west side service station, appeared in the sheriff's office and, nervously wadding his greasy mechanic's hat into a roll, confessed that five of the gang had picked up Everett that night and offered him a ride home. They had run out of liquor around midnight and suspected that Everett had a supply. They had all been drunk, too drunk, but Everett was even drunker. He had invited them in and insisted that they listen to him play the piano which he couldn't do very well. When they discovered that all he had in the house to drink was half a gallon of wine, they began to get nasty and rough up the house. When he tried to order them out, they laughed and romped all the more but nobody thought of beating him up or doing him any harm until Hal started on him about his cousin Ellen Kent. Hal had accused the old man of bad things with Ellen and taunted him about kissing her hand down at the carnival grounds. The words had so shocked Everett that he had lashed Hal across the face with his cane and then Hal went crazy. If the rest of them hadn't been there, he sure would have killed Everett Gordon right there and then. Willy remembered that Gordon had followed them out to the back porch as they were leaving, shouting something after them. He didn't know that he had fallen down in the yard. All he could think of was getting out of there. He didn't think Hal had hurt the old man that bad, but Hal was crazy like a bull when he got mad. He didn't know whether Hal went back or not.

The sheriff listened to Willy's story intently."None of you went back to see what damage you might have done or apologize?"

Willy shrugged his shoulders and hung his head, still rolling his cap nervously.

"Nope."

"Why not?"

"Guess we wuz too drunk, figgered it wuz best to let wellanough alone," Willy mumbled. "He's jist an old drunk anyway. When drunks get in a brawl, ever'body takes what he gits. We dint know Hal had this big grudge about his cousin. Hal got a pretty nasty cut across his face frum that cane. I don't know as I blame him."

The sheriff recalled that he hadn't seen Hal around the streets or service station the last few day. He was one of the boys that the law had decided to keep an eye on lately.

"What'dya mean?" The sheriff leaned forward and tapped the desk emphatically, "You don't blame him? Everett Gordon has a brain concussion and might not live. Do you know what that means?"

Willy shifted uneasily, an unpleasant, sneaky look came over his face. "In a way. Hal says that ol' man been takin' advantage of that young girl a long time and somebody ought to put a stop to it."

"You fellers think you ought to take the law in your own hands? Does Hal Walker have any evidence to back up that big ugly mouth of his?" The sheriff's face was growing red. "That's a pretty damn serious charge, you know, and he better be mighty sure he knows what he's talkin' about before he goes around shootin' off his trap. You keep your big mouth shut on that score, dya hear me?" He banged the desk and Willy jerked.

"Sure," he said sullenly.

"Meanwhile, stick around close and keep your nose clean."

Willy shuffled dejectedly out of the station feeling that he had been ill treated when he thought he was doing the right thing. The sheriff put his head in his hands wearily. What a tangled, miserable job enforcing the law was. Except for the depression he would quit tomorrow, except for Evvie and the kids, he would ... but what would he do? Like everybody else he had to struggle to keep this as decent a place for them to live as he could; somebody had to, otherwise what was the use of trying to make a living. He was gravely troubled by this affair. He wondered if there could be anything, anything at all, in that story about Everett and the young Kent girl. He'd never had a lot of use for Gordon, but that was not his business.

Sheriff Peck was a big man, over six fee tall, heavy and with a full, red good-natured face. His graying hair showed from beneath his trooper's hat. He stood up now, and picked up his gun from the desk. For a moment he stood looking at the gun; it gleamed blue-black, magnificently efficient and sinister in his fleshy hand. He loved it; he loved the other fine guns that he hunted with; it was a beautiful instrument and he felt a sense of strength with it there at his side that he never knew without it. But for a moment he wondered if guns might not have mastered man, if violence had not won out in the world. Everyday he listened on the radio to the broadcasts about Europe and read in the newspapers about those sons-of-bitches who were taking over over there with their guns and self-made law. Probably push this country into war again. He was a veteran of the last one and didn't want no more of it. But he shrugged, slipping the gun into its tooled-leather holster. What did all this have to do with the beating of an old drunk and a nasty rumor in a little town in the middle of Utah?

Well, he guessed he better go over to the hospital and see how Ev was. He just wished he could scare the shit out of that service station bunch without having to bring all this out in the open, if it could be done.

Everett Gordon lay in a thickly bandaged semi-coma for almost a week and then one day, opened his eyes warily on the dull beige hospital wall. He asked weakly for a drink of water and Mrs. Bartlett gave him some and went to notify the doctor.

"Well, old man," Dr. Carlton said in his gratingly cheerful voice, "so you've decided to live?"

"Don't recall having made any such decision," Everett murmured.

The doctor peered long and intently into his eyes with a small light. "You've had a pretty bad deal. We, your sisters, got a doctor down from Salt Lake, but we decided you were not in good enough shape to move. Not much to do except let nature take its course, but you seem to be pulling out of it alright, going to take a while though". He made the routine pulse check and used his stethoscope here and there, then straightened up. "Heart's still pumpin' away O.K. and that's a good sign. You feel like you could talk to the sheriff?" he asked cautiously.

"Who?" Everett's gray face reflected alarm. "What'd I do now?"

"It's not what you did, it's what was done to you," the doctor pursued, studying Everett closely. "You got a pretty bad beating last week. Willy Pierce, one of the bunch of hoodlums that did it, came in and told the sheriff all about it. For a few days we thought there might be a murder rap against Hal Walker."

Everett started up off the pillow but the pain and weakness forced him back down quickly.

"Looks like we can pull you through and the charges can be reduced, but it's still a pretty nasty business. You might easily have died. You're still not in good enough shape to go to court for a few weeks."

"Court!" echoed Everett.

"Yes, but I guess this is a little out of my department. I'd best call Seth." Dr. Carlton left the room feeling concerned about the fear and unhappiness in Everett's expression.

He was still too ill and weak to recall clearly what had happened to him. It was all one huge, nasty, whirling blur of carnival lights, grotesque crowds, Ellen' face and the face of a young man insanely angry. Hal Walker, Doris and Aaron's boy, Addie's grandson? Yes, that was what was so hideous about it. His mind was cluttered with whirling bits of debris, screening off something that he knew he wanted to avoid but couldn't. But he wasn't prepared to talk to the law, not quite yet.

When Seth Peck arrived, however, half an hour later, and eased his great khaki clad bulk into the flimsy hospital chair, Everett's mind had begun to clear a little.

Seth greeted him with the usual phrases reserved for hospital inmates. Everett tried to smile but was sure that the effort amounted to nothing more than a painful grimace. Seth leaned forward solicitously; his broad, congenial face irked Everett.

"Now don't strain yourself, Ev. I know you probably don't feel up to talkin' much. The doctor says you're not out of the woods yet. I just want you to know that we've got the young bugger that done it. We're gonna need your help to bring charges and straighten out the rest of that bunch. It sure is a good thing for Hal Walker that you're gonna pull through."

He was turning the brim of his trooper's hat around and around in his big plump hands and Everett noticed that his thick hair was quite gray though his face retained a fresh, youthful fleshiness. Seth's face had only two stock expression: a look of stubborn determination and one of self-righteous satisfaction. It was wearing the latter today since law enforcement had the upper hand; his case was about to be wrapped up without too much strain and mess if Gordon could cooperate.

Everett knew he must not speak today. He motioned for a drink and closed his eyes wearily. Sheriff Peck arose, helped him to the water then reassured him. "Now you just take your time. I ain't gonna let them thugs out of my sight. We're gonna need you later on. Soon's you're able, we'll bring around a complaint for you to sign."

A complaint? Everett turned his face away, hoping Seth would leave quickly. The pain of dragging up the past and facing the future was almost worse than the pain of the blow on his head. He simply didn't feel equal to it. Why hadn't he just died?

After the sheriff was gone, he lay staring at the ceiling of the narrow, stuffy hospital room. How like a coffin these close, colorless places are–like lighted coffins, good preparation for the real thing. A lighted coffin would be worse than the darkness, he thought. Being shut up in a box full of everlasting light that you could never turn off would be far worse than being shut up in infinite darkness. The dark was restful; at least you could imagine what you wanted to in it. Crazy thoughts. The blow and sedatives must have affected his mind. He had often thought of death and he was afraid of it, had always been afraid of it until now he had come very close to it. The blessed oblivion of the last few days seemed far and away preferable to all the bleak hell of getting up to live again.

Who wanted to go on being such a fool? That was the worst of it. Once again he had to face the paralyzing fact that he had been a fool–the pawn of his romantic illusions, his excessive emotionalism, his old, tormenting dreams. Does a man never, never get rid of the dreams of his youth; do they always lie in ambush even when he has relinquished everything to protect himself from them? The worst of it was that they not only destroyed you but others, those you love the most. Ellen–when he thought of her he winced with so much pain that he moaned aloud. But the sedatives had so dulled his mind and his energies were so depleted that he could not hold on to any concrete thought for very long. He drifted into a deep, sick sleep again, remembering later that only the nurse kept disturbing him to eat or some other irrelevant thing when all he wanted to do was sleep, or die–mostly to forget.

Everett awakened toward evening not knowing that it was the next day. The effects of the sedatives had worn off, and his mind was in a strangely clear condition. The air was heavy as though a storm were gathering; the ecru lace curtains blew languidly out into the room. Gusts of cool air penetrated the thick antiseptic laden atmosphere and were like the breath of a new life. He felt more sober than he had for years and years and everything both outside and in had a sharp, painful clarity. There was still a dull ache in his head and back; if he moved sharp, shooting pains went through him. He wished desperately for a drink of liquor and then the wish filled him with disgust and self loathing. He had always wished for an easy way of avoiding the clear, cold hard details of life; he had found it for nearly thirty years in alcohol.

Even so he had never been the kind of drunkard who could achieve complete release from reality until he passed out. His acute intelligence and sensitivity was like a recording device that went on outside his will to do anything about it. Although he couldn't always remember things coherently, concrete details, even certain kinds of more elusive things stuck tenaciously in his mind. Now, in spite of himself, the recording device flipped on– that frightful day began to play back to him remorselessly.

He remembered debating about going to the celebration; as a matter of fact, he detested such crude things, but as the hot day wore on, an overpowering sense of frustration and loneliness had come over him. He had heard Ellen say that she was going to be at the festivities, so he didn't have her usual Saturday visit to look forward to. He began drinking in the late afternoon and toward evening had a fine, thick glow on. Certain carefully avoided fancies that had been cropping up lately around Ellen began to tease him. He hadn't wanted to admit how much she had come to mean to him, to fill his empty life. He wasn't quite sure of what it was that he felt about her, but it was something stronger than he liked. It wasn't a fatherly kind of love. he had firmly repudiated that role very early and conclusively. He scarcely ever thought about his son. It certainly wasn't a sentimentally romantic attachment since he had enough of his senses to see how untenable and ridiculous that would be although he had heard of cases.... Well, on that score his conscience was clear; there was no lust for her. It was something he had always had about women, a need to fit them out in a kind of glory–put them on pedestals so to speak. His real carnal desires had been so forbidden that even now he could not admit to them.

When Ellen first came into his life, she had been such a child, and he had mostly indulged her for the warmth and company she brought to the dead old house. But of late she had grown into a lovely young woman who so resembled Laurence that it hurt. He thought that he had arrived at the right relationship–that of an indulgent, but wise and guiding, friend or uncle. The best of all possible relationships, close, warm and yet not overly familiar, none of the agonized posturing of the father, none of the destructive, possessive familiarity of lovers. He could guide, mold and shape and still be lenient. She would respond to and carry on his life and ideas without being burdened by them.

Ah, she belonged to the world he had once known. He had detected in her that avid hunger for life, that instinct for beauty and grace and, above all, the gift of imagination that lifts the purely sensual into the sublime. She was not meant to spend her life in Merritsville; he could prepare her for the wider world. He wished she could have seen him in his better days when he had been someone she would have been proud of.

He had had the looks, manners, taste, talent, even money that would have helped establish her in the right places. *He had had.* There was bitterness in his reflections, but thinking on that hot August afternoon about the vanished past and the dashing figure he had been, his good senses put to sleep by whisky, he was impelled to go to the big, dusty wardrobe in the upstairs bedroom and deck himself in a suit of the fine clothes he had once worn. He recalled having taken a long time to dress in the clothes that fitted him poorly because he had lost weight and his body had changed somewhat, but at last the hall mirror satisfied him that he could still cut a fine figure, outshine all the hicks in Merritsville.

How he wished he still had the diamond stick pin and cuff links he used to wear.

He had flourished his cane and done a few dance steps on the ragged carpet just to test his agility. If only she could see, or could have seen what he had been, what still might be. After all he was only in his early fifties. In the highest mood he had experienced in years, he started towards town, nipping a little now and then from the tarnished silver flask that he used to carry, just enough to give him confidence. He took care to walk straight and with dignity. He was not going to get drunk, he told himself.

After that things were a little blurry. It was about this time of day, dusk, the carnival lights were being turned on; they bleared his eyes as they swung round and round or jiggled up and down on the rides. He remembered exchanging a few words with some old timers, several of whom offered him a drink. He didn't think he had taken any then before he found her. He vaguely remembered thinking that she looked lost and unhappy, but he didn't know what had given him that impression. He did so want her to be happy; he was prepared to give her every kind of happiness within his power. He thought he had won a special prize for her or something, then something had made her dart away ... it must have been connected with what that insane young man had said..."kissed her hand right in public like some goddam sissy Frenchy."

What was wrong with kissing her hand if that was all he had said or done? He had learned to do it in the east and Europe. Of all the gestures toward woman it seemed to him to be the loveliest; the least lustful and degrading of all. He knew there had been nothing in his mind of the horrible things that boy had accused him of.

Now when he reached that part of it, his head began to throb violently and his heart pounded as though he were about to relive the whole ghastly thing. He was about to ring for more sedation but no, this time, just this once he had to look at it squarely, soberly. What was that thing in classical literature that if you looked upon it, it turned you to stone–the Medusa's head, the head of the ugliest creature imaginable whose hair was a mass of writhing snakes. Yes, that was what these memories were like. Well, let it turn him to stone; what better fate for such an unmitigated fool as he?

At last, he had to admit that he loved that girl–that child of a man he had also loved– and that he would never be able to explain that love to anyone, even to himself. He swore vehemently that it was above physical lust; yet if she had only been there when he had been younger and needed her. Now with her youth and intelligence and budding beauty, she could have led him out of the tangled garden in which he lived like a beast cursed.

One thing was clear to him: he must never mention his love for her, never use the word. It was a dirty word in this little town; to most people it meant only one thing and it would condemn her forever. Hal Walker had been right to beat him up. He would swear the boy was jealous, madly jealous; perhaps he loved his cousin and was going insane with the frustrations of it. Love, love, he had inevitably used the same word for both their emotions and they were worlds apart. Or were they? He needed to think they were, that his love was better, finer. It was almost too much for him; he felt as though the already weakened blood vessels in his head must burst, finish him off. But he mustn't die. That would make it too hard on her, on Addie, the two people about whom he genuinely cared in all the world.

He would lie quietly, taking what was coming to him. He had no grudge against the boy; the beating had been his just dues, the means of saving him and Ellen. Hal was only the instrument. This was the just dessert of a fool.

Gradually the anguish subsided and Everett felt very sad but peaceful. He knew what he had to do. First he would see that the matter was cleared up and then he would get out of her life.

CB

When Seth Peck had brought the strong, good-looking Hal Walker into his cramped office behind the fire station, the feeling of frustration and worry that he had had all during the depression was intensified to the breaking point. Here were all these big husky kids growing up with nothing to do, nothing to look forward to. All the make-work projects that just aimed to keep them busy were no good. Young men needed something more, some future to work for, maybe even something to fight for. It was a wonder that there hadn't been more crime than there was; the sobering thought crept into his mind that maybe war wouldn't be such a bad thing. The papers said things were looking pretty black over there–just last week some English bigwig had said that England was ready to go to war if Hitler didn't stay out of Czechoslovakia and if England went to war ... well, in spite of his fervent sympathy with the isolationists, he had seen what happened last time when America had vowed to stay out of foreign quarrels. But it was better for young men to fight than rot and better to fight an "enemy" than his own people or himself.

He shoved a scarred, straight-backed chair toward Hal who slumped uneasily into it. Seth sat for a few tense moments studying his face with the purpose, of course, of making him thoroughly uncomfortable. Hal squirmed, twisting his fingers, occasionally glancing up at the sheriff with a sheepish, guilty expression.

"Guess you've heard that Everett Gordon's in pretty bad shape?" the sheriff said in a low even voice, tapping the palm of one hand with a broken ruler like a school teacher.

Hal nodded, his head slightly bent, partly to conceal the dark, bluish bruise across his face.

"I guess you know that if he don't pull through, somebody's gonna be in bad trouble?"

Hal's head jerked up and his expression changed to one of startled fear mixed with stubborn belligerence. He was cracking the knuckles of his big, grease stained hands.

"You have anything to say about it, Hal?"

"I didn't do it," mumbled Hal.

"Who did then?" Seth picked him up quickly.

"I guess we wuz all shufflin' around, drunk, didn't know what we wuz doin' and I guess he jist got in the way."

"Looks like you got in the way, too, old boy. How come you got that shiner and cut on your face?"

"He hit me first!" Hal flared, his face turning livid.

"Why did he hit you? You claimin' self defense? He's a lot older and smaller than you." Seth's voice had a fine edge of sarcasm.

"Yeah, well, sumpin' like that."

"But what was the fight about?" Seth pursued. "Was it somethin' personal, maybe somethin' you said to insult him?"

"Don't remember." Hal dropped his head sulkily again.

"Was it somethin' you accused Everett of about your cousin Ellen Kent?"

Hal rared partly out of his chair. "Who said so? Anyway he's a dirty old bastard," he lashed out fiercely, his face distorted with hatred.

"What'd he do? What'd you accuse him of?" Seth dug into him relentlessly, disturbed by the look on Hal's face. He remained silent, his face so contorted that Seth couldn't tell whether he was going to cry or do something worse. Finally he shook his hand with its fingers tensely crooked toward the sheriff.

"D'you know what that son-of-a-bitch did right out in public— that dirty old bastard?" He choked and went on, "He kissed her hand, slobbered all over it right there is front of ever'body."

"Ain't you never seen a man kiss a woman's hand before?" Seth asked, trying not to show any reaction to the unreasonably intense display.

"Oh, only some goddam Frenchman in a movie or sumpin'," Hal subsided and slumped back in the chair. The perspiration stood out all over his forehead. He mopped his thick wavy hair back out of his eyes. Seth felt sorry for him; although he couldn't quite put his finger on it, he was just the least little bit in sympathy with the aggravation that Everett had caused the kid. It wasn't exactly the hand kissing, which wasn't done in these parts, but something about Everett Gordon's way, something fancy and foreign that always roused contempt in tough western males. But Seth put his sympathies back; he knew that he must try to act the impartial lawman in this case especially. There was something not quite healthy here, something scary in the boy's burst of excessive passion.

"You think that's good enough reason to beat a man half to death, just because he acts different from you? He didn't, hasn't done anything else to the girl that you know of, has he?"

"I dunno," Hal was still indignant. "She goes there all the time, practically stays there, you can't tell about an old bastard like that if he goes around kissin' her in public. He might do *anything*."

Seth slapped the ruler down on the desk and leaned back in his squeaking swivel chair.

"Just what is *your* main interest in this cousin of yours?"

Hal didn't reply but his nervousness was visible. After a few minutes of silence in which the stuffiness of the room seemed to have trapped them like flies on the amber glue of flypaper, Seth asked gently, "Do *you* like your cousin Ellen?"

"Oh, gaddam," Hal squirmed. "I guess I do. Sometimes I hate her too. She's gettin' like him, sorta stuck up and different. She thinks she's so damn smart."

Seth leaned forward, narrowing his eyes and asked, "Do you think that you done it to hurt her?"

"I dunno, I dunno," Hal shook his head in agony; his voice sounded as though it might break into a sob, but then suddenly he sat back in the chair and his face became an impassive, cold mask. He looked Seth straight in the eye. "I wuz drunk," he said defiantly. "I wuz drunk and so wuz he. I dunno what I done or why I done it. I ain't admittin' to nothin' and I ain't sorry."

"Is that all you can say?" Sheriff Peck pulled himself up at the desk and reached for a pad of paper. "Drunkenness is no excuse for committin' a crime. I can't hold you until we get a complaint from Gordon, but I want you to stick around close and behave yourself. The least little excuse you give me, I've got a cell down there with your name on it. D'you understand?"

Hal made a noise that sounded like a snort or a sob.

"I hate this for your family's sake, Hal. You come from a good family, and it's hard to figger out why you got mixed up with that buncha nogood bums. It's not too late for you to straighten up and I hope for your sake and theirs, you'll think about it real good."

Seth sighed, picked up his hat and motioned to Hal that he could leave. "Yessir," Hal mumbled and backed out.

The heat festered those last few days of August until it broke in a wild thunderstorm that filled the ditches and creek with muddy, swirling water and debris. It came down out of the mountain with an ominous rumble, ripping out trees, bridges, and hurling huge boulders as though they were pebbles. It was terrifying to see the water that was the life-blood of this arid country become an ugly, destructive force and waste itself in such senseless fury. But a week after the flood the creek bed was almost dry again and only the tangle of twigs, boards, cans, brush and miscellaneous trash lodged against the banks amid the ragged limbs of the surviving shrubbery remained of the holocaust.

It seemed almost symbolic to Ellen of the havoc that had happened in her family. It had been a terrible time, first knowing that Everett might die, then finding out that it was Hal who had done it. Hal's summons by the sheriff had been an awful shock, one that affected even Grandma. For the first time in her memory, Ellen saw worry and bewilderment on Addie's face. Aunt Dosey cried and cried, and all the kids went around with a sad, stricken look on their faces, subdued and unusually obedient. Uncle Aaron swore and cursed and spent a long time with the sheriff. Grandma stayed most of the days at the Walker house trying to comfort Aunt Dosey who could not seem to stop crying and asking herself and others what she had done wrong to deserve something like this. When Grandma came home, Ellen noticed her kneeling often by her bed, her gray head bowed over the fine wedding-ring quilt that her hands had so laboriously pieced together into a thing of intricate beauty. Ellen joined in when her grandmother asked her to pray for the family and especially for Hal, but she had a hollow feeling inside. She didn't know what to pray about Hal but all day over and over again, wherever she was, she kept silently praying for Everett, "Please, God, please don't let him die." They wouldn't let her see him. They wouldn't even let Addie in though she went every day to inquire and took fresh flowers from her garden.

The week after the flood the weather had cooled off and there was a faint yellowish promise of fall in the air. It was late on Sunday afternoon and Ellen, filled with a heavy inexpressible sadness, decided to take a walk through the fields toward the creek. She didn't know why she preferred to go that way instead of up toward the hills, but the quiet, melancholy, ravaged creek seemed to match her mood. Anyway she was less likely to run into anyone. Her footsteps echoed brokenly as she slipped and stumbled among the uneven, mud-coated rocks. Overhead the frowzy trees almost locked their yellowing leaves in a high arch through which a stained light filtered quietly and sadly. It was like an abandoned, wrecked church.

She had come, without intention, to the part of the creek where

Robert Lee Hamilton had once brought her. She sat down on a smooth gray log that had been scoured shiny and soft by the waters and, picking up a stick, began scratching on the smooth silt deposit which the water had made below the tree. She wrote her name and the date–Aug. 9th, 1938. There seemed to be something extremely final and ominous about it. What if it were the last day of her life? What if this were the date to be carved on her tombstone? Ellen had often thought romantically about death, had even written poems about it, but today it seemed so close she shivered.

She didn't think she really wanted to die, but what was so wonderful about life when everything was always being wrecked. There seemed to be some malignant, destructive force intent on tearing her life apart. Automatically she traced the initials "E.G." under her own name then realizing what she had done, she leaped to her feet in panic. What had made her do that? That was what kids did who were going together, sweethearts. Was it some kind of message? Was he thinking of her, wanting her? She thought she was not superstitious, but there seemed to be something mysterious guiding her hand as she had traced the initials.... She scratched furiously at the dirt, erasing the writing in the damp sand. Breathing hard she scrambled up the creek bank, startling some dark birds which flew out of the upper foliage and set up a crash of echoes down the silent tunnel of the trees. The sound seemed to be the very answer to her own fright and loneliness.

She tore across the fields, panting furiously as though pursued by some relentless terror, dashing up the backs steps into the kitchen which was quiet and empty. It was a few moments before she saw the note propped against the sugar bowl on the table. It was for her and said simply that Grandma had been called to the hospital and would be back as soon as she could.

Something had happened to Everett! She darted out of the house and was nearly up to the big tree when she remembered how she must look in her old berry-picking overalls and shirt. They probably wouldn't let her in looking like that and she wouldn't want Everett to see her if ... Turning, she ran back to the house, put on a clean dress, her best shoes and ran a comb through her hair. Her heart was beating so wildly as she started out swiftly again that she thought it would leap like a tormented frog right out of her breast. "Please let him be alright," she whispered.

When Everett had awakened that afternoon, he had noticed the big vase of zinnias on the dresser. He knew without asking where they came from and he asked about Addie. When he was told that she had been there that afternoon, he said he would like to see her. Nurse Bartlett got the message to her when she got off shift.

When she came into the room, Everett had a feeling of calm and warmth. She was looking very serious and concerned, but there was that kindness and goodness that had been the constant expression of her face ever since he had known her. She came to the bedside and took his hand.

"I'm so thankful that you're goin' to be alright," Everett," she whispered in a voice full of tears.

Neither of them could speak for a few moments, then Everett managed to say unsteadily, "I don't see how you can be glad, I've brought you so much trouble."

"Don't say that, Everett." Addie had pulled up a chair and was sitting close to the bed. "Seems like we're the ones have caused you the trouble. I can't get to the straights of it yet, but whatever the reason there ain't no excuse for what Hal done."

"Perhaps not an excuse, Addie, but a reason. I don't suppose that reasons make anything any better either."

Addie nodded, so choked up that she was unable to think of anything to say. She took a salt-sack handkerchief out of her bag and wiped the corner of her eyes.

Everett turned his head toward her, his face twisted with pain.

"It's Ellen I'm most concerned about. It's the harm that we might have done to her, that boy and I."

"I don't know what you mean." Addie's face clouded. She had not heard the details of the incident at the carnival, only that Hal had beaten Everett up in a drunken brawl.

Everett struggled on. "But I swear to you, Addie, I have not had any evil intentions toward her, and I would not have embarrassed her publicly if it hadn't been for this damnable drinking." He fumbled nervously for the cigarettes in his pajama pocket. Addie reached over and helped him get them out. The perspiration had broken out on his forehead and his jaw was trembling.

Addie steadied his arm as he lit the cigarette; she was beginning to be alarmed that he might be straining himself in this over-wrought state. After a few puffs, however, he seemed to regain his composure.

"There is one thing," he said after a few agonized moments, not looking directly at her. "There's something unhealthy about that young grandson of yours. I'm not saying this out of any sense of injury; in fact I bear him no grudge. It was as much my fault as his. I shouldn't have been in that condition and I shouldn't have hit him. But he can't really think those things about his own cousin and be quite sane."

Addie had to hold fast to the bed. She had been troubled about Hal for a long time, and she knew that she had averted her eyes from the truth. She had hoped and prayed but there had been something in him that baffled her.

Everett realized that he had touched a bare nerve in the old woman and he wondered again if he were doing right; he had been wrong so much of the time.

"I'm sorry, Addie, I may be wrong. I may be still out of focus because of this. I can't remember too well anyway."

Addie sighed a deep long sigh. "No, I'm afraid you're right. There is something wrong with Hal. Lord knows what it is or why. I've prayed and his mother has, I know, and sometimes he seems to know right from wrong."

"Well, anyway," Everett went on slowly and carefully, "the important thing is to protect Ellen. I think this can be kept quiet if it doesn't get into court, and I don't think they will take it to court if I won't testify against Hal."

"Would that be the right thing to do? Hal ought to take his punishment if he's done wrong," Addie said firmly. "He ought not to be let off. It might lead to him doing a lot worse things. He's strong-headed and he might take it that he can get away with doing wrong things."

Everett shook his head sadly. "No, the kind of punishment they could mete out to him now wouldn't do much good. Now that I'm alive he couldn't get much more than a short prison sentence which would probably turn him into a criminal for good. Maybe parole would help but there's not much use of filing charges. I hit him first, and I ought to have been more responsible, being the older. I don't really hold it against him but when he got mad he didn't have any control. That's what's frightening. I'm still most concerned about Ellen. We would both have to say ugly things in court which would involve her. Everything sounds so much worse in court. I know, I've been there before."

He smoked in silence for a few minutes. Addie got up and went over to the dresser and stood fussing with the flowers.

"As soon as I can get out of here, I'm leaving Merritsville, forever," Everett mused.

"But where'll you go?" queried Addie, her back still to him.

"From one sanitarium to another, I suppose," he answered wryly.

Addie turned on him. "Now you're feeling sorry for yourself, running away, Everett Gordon. You been doin' that all your life and what's it done for you?" She stopped when she saw the look of pain on his face. He was staring at the doorway where Ellen, her face flushed and her chest heaving from having run most of the way stood anxiously. He held out his hand toward her. She darted into the room and clasped both his hands, tears streaming down her face.

"You're, you're ...alright. I was so afraid ... Grandma's note didn't say," she gasped. "I ran all the way. Oh, I'm so glad."

Everett's eyes fill with tears, his head throbbing and his heart pumping painfully, but at that moment he was full of a kind of happiness of which he had never dared dream. He loved and was fully loved and he felt strong enough to bear the consequences. What horrible tricks life played on one to bring so close together two who must remain so far apart, to bring this child-woman, bride-daughter, fulfillment of his dreams at the point of tragedy. But there was a great calm at the center of him, one that he had never expected to experience; for the first time in years he felt that perhaps the total of his life was not wasted, that he had had to live for this one moment of illumination.

Addie pulled Ellen gently away from the bed. "Be careful you might hurt him more, he isn't quite better yet."

Ellen turned and buried her face in her grandmother's shoulder, "I'm sorry, so sorry, I didn't mean...I...."

"There, there, I should have told you in the note that he was alright." Grandma patted her. There was that awkward moment of silence that always takes place when people have over-exposed their hearts, but Grandma picked things up firmly, "Well, we ought to go now, my dear, or we'll give Everett a backset."

Everett made a motion to restrain them but at that moment the pudgy little night nurse came in with a sedative and made to shoo them away.

Ellen turned to the bed and leaned over, brushing Everett's cheek lightly, "I'll come and read to you every day, if you want me to," she said softly. His eyes told her that he did.

Seth couldn't say that he wasn't relieved at the way things turned out. He supposed that maybe he wasn't a very good lawman because he had never been as anxious to see that the letter of the law was carried out as he was to keep things on an even keel and a kind of patched-up peace that prevented drastic scars from disrupting the close family and community life. In a little town where you knew everybody and everybody knew you, you had to take an easier view of people's shortcomings, unless they got too far out of hand or some fanatic like Joe Thayer started preachin' and pushin' at you for justice and the strict enforcement of the "Law." That old bastard stuck his nose into everything, had even took it on himself to mix up in this, something about "for the good of that young girl who was set upon evil ways due to her mother's falling away". That was the one of the bad things about a small town; some people never let things die, never let time smooth things over the way it was meant to, had to keep pickin' the scab off.

The worst problem had been Aaron. He had been pretty shook up by the whole thing. He had come to Seth in such a bad state that Seth had had to force a drink down him to try to calm him down. Seth could see into the trouble–the kid was too much like his old man. Funny all the time they had known each other, been in the service together and all, he hadn't seen this side of Aaron. Aaron had first sworn and cursed his son, declaring that he wanted to see him punished damn good for what he had done then he had turned right around and stuck up for the kid, makin' excuses for him and cussin' old Gordon. Seth had finally been able to get him calmed down and assured that Hal would get what he deserved, yet he would be treated as decent as possible. He knew that things wouldn't be quite the same between him and Aaron after that, because Aaron would be ashamed of himself and there was no way for a friend to change that. These things happened.

It had all depended on Everett Gordon. When he was well enough to talk it over with the sheriff and doctor, he said that he didn't want to make any more of it, that he thought it had been partly his fault. He should have known better and he did strike Hal first. He thought that even if there were a trial and he did testify against Hal, that the boy had a good chance of proving self defense. He, himself, had decided to leave town at least for a while and he thought that things would quiet down. He had said, though, that he thought Hal had a dangerous, ugly streak in his nature and that something ought to be done about it. Seth had to agree with him on that score. Hal ought to get out of town away from the gang he was chasing with and from the family, particularly his dad.

Seth had a lot of respect for old Everett when he left the hospital; he was a real decent old bugger even if he did come from that high'nmighty Gordon bunch and was a drunk. He had a lot of deep good horse sense and he couldn't have been doin' that Kent girl any real harm ... or could he? The shadow of a disturbing thought crossed Seth's mind: he was old enough and had had experience enough with people to know that you can never truly see the insides of another man's mind or heart. Well, what of it? Ev said he was goin' to leave town. He wasn't goin' to be Seth's problem no more.

The flag was whipping in the crisp, fallish breeze above the city-hall-fire-station-court-house-jail, the solid red brick building that served most of Merritsville's civic needs. How serenely beautiful it was against the vibrant blue of the September mountains. In the intoxicating, golden autumn air with the little town going about its business in the usual leisurely rhythm, the middle-aged sheriff of Merritsville was filled with a sense of well being. Fall sure was the best time of the year and things would work out if you just give 'em a chance. This was proved out to him when he went back to the office and found some bulletins about the CCC program on his desk and set to pulling a few strings and talking to a few of the right people and within a week, Hal Walker was on his way to a CCC camp in Montana. Some good hard work under discipline would soon straighten that boy out, he thought, and then the way things looked, there would be the service. There was talk of a draft.

Everett's sisters had taken turns coming down from Salt Lake during his confinement in the hospital. Their sour-sad-how-could-you-do-this-to-us, poorlittlebrother expressions annoyed and depressed him, but he was helpless. And it was his own damn fault; he had never got to be man enough to take care of himself and keep out from under their vigilance, so when the doctor had said that he could be released but would need some kind of care for a little while, they all came together—tall, handsome, elegantly dressed in sober dark colors and stood conferring in low tones around his bed. They reminded him of those three great dark pine trees in the garden at home in which the wind often made mournful sounds as though bemoaning his fate. But at last, with cheerful and firm determination with which they treated him like "baby brother," they decided that he must live among them where they could keep an eye on him for a while. He was packed off in the afternoon without a chance of saying good-bye to Ellen. Addie had chanced into the hospital as he was being wheeled out to the big black car belonging to the elder sister, Hazel, and had promised to tell Ellen that he wanted to say good-bye and he would try to write her. He could say no more but clung to Addie's hand until Hazel had to give him a tug and whisk him away.

When Grandma broke the news of Everett's departure to Ellen, cautiously, not knowing quite what kind of an outburst to expect from her, she was even more disturbed by the quiet, indifferent shrug with which Ellen accepted it. "I guess it's best this way," she said quietly in such a way the subject was closed between them.

The last few times she had been to the hospital there had been a kind of strain between her and Everett. They had talked and she had read to him, but there always seemed to be something they weren't saying to each other, that they should or that they wanted desperately to and didn't know how. It had only been a few days ago that she had learned the truth about the business between Everett and Hal and, although she hadn't spoken to anyone else about it, especially not to Everett, it had so shocked her that she was still in a state of disbelief. It was as though a dark evil stain had spread over everything–nothing would ever be clean and bright again.

It was Lorraine, of course, who had told her what Willy Pierce had told his sister that Hal had said to Everett about him and Ellen. At first Lorraine had tried to tell her in guarded hints but finally she had just had to come right out and tell her in plain language. Ellen just never seemed to understand anything like that. And then she was sorry because she thought Ellen was going to have a fit or die right there in the porch swing.

"You don't really think people would really think that of him, of me?" she had gasped. "Oh, how could they be so ugly, so mean and low-down?" She had begun to sob, tears streaming down her cheeks.

"Oh don't, I'm sorry, Ellen." Lorraine tried to comfort her. "People just have to think that things would be the way they would do them. Most of 'em only think about *that* so they always think a man and woman, boy or girl will always think about only one thing and do it. You're so different, Ellen, and you do stay by yourself. You went there an awful lot this year. It's hard for people to think it was just to read books."

"But it's ugly ...it's ugly," choked Ellen.

"Well, it's really Hal's fault, I guess," Lorraine went on. "I don't know what makes him the way he is. He's been like that ever since he was a little boy. He just thinks about two things, *that* and cars. He just pestered me and Louise all the time when we was littler. But you know, Ellen, I think you're the only one, the only girl he really likes. I think he was just plain jealous of you hangin' around with Everett. Bein' your cousin and all, he's not supposed to like you in that way and that has probably made him just about crazy...."

Ellen was more horrified than ever, and the terrible night she had experienced last spring about which she had never told anyone came back to her with doubled force. She shivered. "I hate him, I hate him," she whispered. She still couldn't talk about it even to Lorraine.

"I think he knows that and that's maybe what made him do what he did," Lorraine went on quietly. They were sitting in the old dilapidated swing in the back yard after school. The thick yellowed grass was full of rotting apples, the sound of silos had started up around the valley and the trees in the yard were all turning from green to yellow and orange. Both girls were in an unhappy, frustrated mood. Lorraine had been quarreling with Ken and Ellen had been under this pall for the last few weeks. How horrid the world was.

"He couldn't stand you hating him." Lorraine kicked a rotten apple aimlessly. The old swing creaked.

"But why didn't he hurt me instead of *him*?" She found she couldn't pronounce Everett's name without quivering.

"Oh, I guess it's mostly because of the way things turned out, the big drunk they was all on. I guess I shouldna told you. I'm sorry Ellen but I thought you ought to know what some people think and some of the kids might say something."

Ellen gave a long wail of despair. "I hate this town," she cried. "I hate it to pieces. I'm leaving as soon as school is out and I hope I never, never come back."

"Yeah, I think I will, too," agreed Lorraine gloomily although at the bottom of her heart, she knew she didn't mean it. She just wanted to marry Ken and settle down here, have some kids and let things be pretty much the way they had been. She was Merritsville. She wasn't like Ellen who just didn't seem to fit here, never had, never would. She was sort of sorry because Ellen was part of her family, and the deeply ingrained Mormon sense of family never let you give up anyone easily, not even the bad ones like Hal. But the world was changing for both of them.

CB

Ellen began her senior year at Merritsville High with grim determination to concentrate strictly on her studies and such activities as those which required only her abilities and talents like debate and the newspaper. She had vowed that the day after school was out in the spring, she would leave Merritsville. She thought she cared about nothing there and nobody but Grandma. Of course, there were some of the teachers she liked especially Mr. Gillis who was also the debate coach, and it was hard to avoid all social activities. But she set her face coldly and went through her days routinely. She was surprised when in the senior assembly, she was nominated to the committee for the Senior Hop. She stood up and firmly declined the nomination, knowing full well that she wouldn't be asked to the dance and didn't want to go anyway. A few days before the event, Mr. Gillis announced that he was excusing his whole senior English class to decorate for it. All the kids whooped happily out of the room, except Ellen who went on calmly writing in her notebook. Mr. Gillis came down the aisle and perched on the desk in front of her, swinging his long, thin leg casually. Ellen, conscious of him, still did not look up. He made that annoying noise in his nose and throat that was caused by his sinus trouble. Finally he spoke up quietly, "Why don't you go on down to the gym and help? You don't need to study any more. You're miles ahead of everybody as it is."

Ellen rubbed her pencil against her cheek, still avoiding his bluish, troubled eyes and said stubbornly, "I don't want to."

"There's something the matter this year, Ellen." He reached out and put his finger under her chin forcing her to look up at him. "Those poems you gave me last week about death and other related subjects–they're pretty melancholy. Oh, I know, I wrote poems like that when I was your age, first year of college mostly. Deep purple in the style of Dowson and Swinburne; you know it's amazing how well prepared the very young are to die and how poorly prepared to live." He sighed. "But, Ellen, you mustn't cut yourself off from everybody your age. It's not healthy."

Ellen shrugged, trying to keep back the tears. She gazed out of the window where the huge maple tree was turning a flaming orange. Death had begun to seem infinitely romantic. At night Ellen lay very straight in her bed with her hands folded over her breasts imagining how pitiful and beautiful she would look in her coffin and how everyone would say that her death was so tragic ... one so young. She had written:

"Walk softly" the sign will say
Here in tendered sleep
Lies a dead dream.
and
It will not be a sad day
When you come bearing death to me
On a fine old silver tray'
You know

That it is the only wine
I have not tasted.

She had brought copies of the poems to Mr. Gillis and now she was sorry.

Mr. Gillis, having removed his finger from under her chin, she dropped her head again. He went on as though he were giving a lecture only with a special kind of intimacy in his voice. Next to Everett she liked him better than any man she had ever known.

"Ellen, you're a bright girl, the brightest in the school and I admire you tremendously. The world needs your gift of intelligence, but not if it destroys the warm human woman in you."

Ellen gave a faint little choke of derision.

"I suppose that was the wrong way to say it." He was becoming uneasy but he was genuinely concerned about her. He took off his glasses and wiped them vigorously.

"Anyway, the thing is you can't live and work without other people. You need them as much as they need you."

"Well, I don't need the people in this town," Ellen burst out bitterly, "And they don't need me."

Mr. Gillis smoothed his thinning hair and tried to choose his words carefully. "People are about the same everywhere, Ellen. Some bad, some good, some neither and both. I know, I've been other places. If you don't learn to cope with them here, it'll be harder somewhere else. Oh, I know they are a bit cloddish, narrow minded for your scope, and they've been cruel to you in some ways but you're doing yourself harm to get so tied up in your bitterness. It'll fester and turn you sour."

"The people in this town are stupid and mean. All they think about is church and dirt and I hate most of them, except you and some others," she said vehemently and slammed her book closed.

"I know you've been hurt." Mr. Gillis stood up and walked away. His shabby suit bagged on his tall, skinny frame and, in spite of herself, Ellen felt sorry for him. How could such a fine intelligent person as he spend his whole life here at Merritsville High?

Suddenly he wheeled on her. His face had changed; it was clouded with anger and annoyance.

"That's the trouble with the young," he said to her, almost

gritting his teeth. "They think they're the only ones who ever get hurt in life. They're so damn selfish and full of self-pity. They think they're the only ones whose dreams have died; they're so busy building precious monuments to their precious sorrows ... My God ...sometimes I think I can't stand anymore of them." He spat the words out so forcefully that Ellen was jarred out of the mood that she realized she had been deliberately cultivating, nursing, wallowing in these past months. Her eyes filled with tears of chagrin; she had never heard him talk like this before.

Immediately he turned gentle again and put his hand on her shoulder.

"But it's really you I care about, Ellen; the world can't afford to lose you. It needs all the intelligence it can get, but intelligence with a good sound heart. I have been afraid that you are developing a crippled heart, one that doesn't know how to love as well as your head knows how to think. I'd give anything not to have that happen."

"But how?" Ellen's throat was so constricted she could hardly speak. "How can I help it? It seems that everything I love gets lost or broken or dirtied up ... by people."

Mr. Gillis shook his head as though he shared her despair and then he smiled at her wanly. "Well, for now, go on down there and string crepe paper around the gym and pretend that you're just an ordinary high school senior and that everybody has faults and secret hurts and 'dead dreams.' It'll keep you from feeling sorry for yourself and I know that helps."

She still eyed him dubiously as though she knew that he had got in a little deeper than he had intended and was feeling his failure. But there was that in his face and wonderful voice that told her he really did care about her. When she hesitated, he said firmly, "That's an assignment for today, Miss Kent, and if you don't want an "F" on the roll, you better hustle about it."

Ellen smiled at him in spite of herself, wiped her eyes and went down to the gym.

Virginia grabbed her immediately and propelled her toward the orchestra stand where she was set to tacking up blue and silver crepe paper and cutting out black silhouettes of musical notes. In a short while she was engrossed in the noise and chaos and high-spirited nonsense. One of the boys even wrapped crepe paper around her neck and tied it in a bow; it almost made her feel as though she were one of them.

She stayed, working furiously with the gang, until nearly eleven o'clock that night. Only five or six of them had remained that late and then, the last festoon of paper in place and the mess cleaned away, they all piled into Arthur Pett's car and went to a drive in. Ellen had been pushed along by Virginia, although at the last minute, she was not sure that she ought to go. She had sent word with Louise to tell Grandma where she was, but still she didn't feel at ease. They drove laughing, singing and cracking utterly stupid jokes to the Foxy Inn on the edge of town.

It was a shabby, patched together affair consisting of an old streetcar to which there was a flimsy frame addition. The board floors were slivery and grease stained, the plastic covered booths worn and split so that the stuffing came out in wads here and there. But it was one of the few places that stayed open late and was decent enough for the young kids to hang around.

They all piled out of the car and stormed in; somebody put a nickel in the juke box and some of the kids danced; others banged on the decrepit pinball machines. Doug Hampstead dragged Ellen out of the booth and began jerking her around the scabby floor. Ellen found herself almost enjoying it. She loved to dance. At first it was hard to follow Doug but when she got the hang of it, she did very well. Dough smiled at her encouragingly and urged, "Atta girl, boy, look at old Ellen go, wouldja?" That made her self-conscious and she stumbled against the juke box. After Doug had caught her and they laughed, she sat down again feeling as though she had just tried out new wings and they were not strong enough, not built quite right for the test.

None of the other boys asked her, and Doug was really interested in Celia Burton so she drank her coke hunched in the corner of the booth and felt very tired. Her old loneliness had crept back. They all began to seem so silly to her, giggling at nothing at all and tumbling each other around like puppies. She had just been born old or she had been around older people so much that she could never be or act young again. For all of Mr. Gillis' encouragement, she couldn't get into this world of the unthinking, carefree young. She felt as though she were watching her companions from a long, cold distance through a screen that distorted their images so they all looked like characters in a bad movie.

She didn't understand their language, sly remarks that she knew must refer to something nasty, slang words they used to mean all sorts of different things. For instance, once that afternoon when she had asked one of the boys to "knock up" a board by the orchestra stand so they could begin putting up the paper around it, he and another one slapped each other and laughed uproariously. She blushed not knowing what she had said that was so funny. It was like that; you needed a special dictionary to know what they were talking about half the time. Although Ellen had scored highest on the state vocabulary test of anyone in high school, she didn't understand the language of her own generation. Having caught on to her innocence, some of the kids like Virginia, addressed cryptic remarks to her and then made fun of her confusion. Mostly they just left her alone like tonight where she yawned miserably in the corner until old Si Peters told them it was time to go home, he had to lock up.

It was no use; she didn't belong. She knew that she would leave Merritsville; she just had to endure the rest of this year.

On the night of the Hop she read *Crime and Punishment*, a book Mr. Gillis had recommended and ate a whole pan of Grandma's delicious fudge curled up on the couch in the kitchen. She wouldn't admit to herself that she would like to have gone; it was the music she missed most.

The week end after the Hop dawned with a cold October rain that fell persistently. That Sunday morning even Grandma had decided to stay home from church; her rheumatism was bothering her so much. She insisted that Ellen go and take her excuse. Addie busied herself about the house and baked an apple-sauce cake, the spicy fragrance of which greeted Ellen when she returned, depressed and bored. All afternoon she worked at her homework or read the book by the Russian that she couldn't pronounce. Mr. Gillis said it was a great book; she wondered exactly why; it seemed so ugly and sad. Were there no happy books in the world anymore like the ones she had loved as she was growing up: *The Wizard of Oz, Anne of Green Gables, Girl of the Limberlost, Rebecca of Sunnybrook Farm?*

The apple-sauce cake made her think of Everett; it was his

favorite kind and Grandma had always sent her with a piece for him. A deep, painful longing for the old house, for him, for the library and the fire he would have made in the fireplace for her on a day like this. She wandered to the window and looked in the direction of the Gordon place. Of course, she couldn't see it, only the road that she had traveled so much to get there. How empty and dreary it must be now; haunted with his presence. It made her shiver with unhappiness.

In the middle of the afternoon, Ellen glanced up from the book. She had gone back to Raskolnikov's bitter story for lack of anything else to do and was just finishing the epilogue. It had grown a bit more cheerful because Sonya had turned out to be such a sweet, kind, loving person and had found something to do with her life. Grandma had built a fire in the front room to take the chill off the house, and Ellen was curled up with the radio playing as she read. She glanced up to see a black car, shining from the wet, that had pulled up alongside the front gate. She stared at it absently, wondering who could be calling in a car like that on Sunday. It wasn't Ed's and Mama's. With a start she recognized the male figure that got out and came up the path with a curious halting motion. It was Ferrin Hallsworth!

She leaped out of the rocking chair and flew to the bedroom before the astonished eyes of her grandmother. What on earth did he want? She had never expected to see him again, hadn't thought much about him since that awful night. She wished she had had time to tell Grandma to say that she wasn't home. But it was too late. Grandma was welcoming him with her exasperating, cheerful way. "Ellen," she called, "there's somebody to see you."

In spite of the fact that she thought she didn't care what he might think of her, she inspected herself in the mirror wishing that she hadn't changed out of her Sunday clothes into this old skirt and blouse and the rain hadn't taken the curl out of her hair. With a grim, unfriendly expression on her face she went out into the living room.

Ferrin was standing self-consciously by the door, a timid smile on his face, so obviously dressed up, tie and suit coat, that he looked foolish, his dark hair shining with Brilliantine. "Hello, Ellen," he said lurching forward. "I guess you're surprised to see me?"

"Yes, I never expected...." she stammered, not making it the least bit easy for him.

"Well, come set down, won't you?" Grandma was fussing around at the davenport, moving some things off it. He hauled himself over to it and sat down. "Sure is a nasty day out," Grandma pursued. "I don't believe I know your name, young man. Ellen ain't told me about all her friends lately."

Ellen stepped forward awkwardly. "This is Ferrin Hallsworth; he's from over at Junction City, Grandma. My grandmother, Ferrin." Ferrin got to his feet and thrust out a hand. Grandma shook it, smiling at him kindly. Ellen sat down in the rocking chair wondering exactly what to do next. Whatever had caused him to turn up on a day like this of all days when she hadn't heard from him in almost two months? He had turned to her from where he had resumed his seat on the edge of the davenport and was saying anxiously, "I sure hope you don't mind me comin' like this, Ellen. I was just drivin' around and I thought I would stop by to see how you was. I thought ... a ...I thought you might like to go for a drive or sumthin."

He had begun to blush and stammer as she stared at him with a frown on her forehead. "I ... a ...it's been such a bad day and it got lonesome so...."

Suddenly the idea appealed to Ellen. Almost anything to get out of the dreariness of the house; besides what would she do with him sitting here? She jumped up, almost too anxiously.

"Yes, I would like that. It is a dreary day and I haven't got anything else to do, I guess, if Grandma don't mind. I'll just change my clothes." If she got him alone away from Grandma, she could let him know that she really didn't want him coming around unexpectedly or otherwise, she mused as she put on her Sunday dress and tied her long hair back with a ribbon.

She heard Grandma giving him the genealogy quiz–who was his father and his grandfather and his aunts, uncles, cousins? She had been working in her precious genealogy books all afternoon. Wouldn't she be upset to know about his family really? She would probably be worried about Ellen going out for a ride with him, but there was no used to upset her. She would get rid of Ferrin Hallsworth pretty shortly.

"You don't mind if I go, do you, Grandma?" she asked rather

too sweetly as she came out of the bedroom.

"Why, no, if you could get back by evening meeting. I thought I might be able to go tonight if the rain lets up a little. Mr. Hallsworth here seems like a nice young man, and I found out I used to know his mother's sister over there in Junction City."

Ellen rolled her eyes at Ferrin and took his proffered arm. He helped her into the car, carefully putting his hand under her elbow like men in the movies did. The car inside was even much nicer than she remembered. Soft gray upholstery and gleaming chrome fittings. It gave one the feeling of being inside an expensive case. There was a strong, thick smell of cigarette smoke that seemed to her remotely glamorous in spite of her distaste for it. It reminded her of the great wide world where she longed to be.

When Ferrin got into the car, the odor of his Brilliantine and shaving lotion added a pleasant man-smell to it that made her feel better than she thought she would. Somehow behind the steering wheel of the car, which he handled with a special loving skill, Ferrin was not at all objectionable. You couldn't tell that he was crippled. From the waist up, he was powerfully built and he had a nice face. She hadn't remembered too much about him that was pleasant, but now he seemed rather attractive. She thought it might have been better if he hadn't worn a suit and tie because it petty well betrayed the fact that he hadn't just been "driving around," that he had planned to come straight to see her. As a matter of fact, he had been thinking about it ever since they had met, agonizing and wondering if she would have anything to do with him.

Out on the highway, in the closed comfort of the car with the windshield wipers swooshing rhythmically and the wet, dark landscape shushing by like a watercolor that was being all smeared over, Ellen had an unexpected flush of pleasure. She had changed her mind; she was glad Ferrin had come that afternoon. At first the conversation went rather stiffly but gradually, they began to find the thread of communication that they had discovered on their first meeting. Ellen began to talk more easily than she thought she would, about the things that had happened since they had last been together on that nightmarish night. She remarked how much she liked the car, and Ferrin replied that he didn't manage to get it very often unless Med and Dod and Simone didn't want it. He said they were all three recuperating from a pretty wild party so he got away without too much trouble.

"Simone is still staying with you, then?" Ellen ventured. She hadn't intended to ask about Simone, but now that the subject had come up, her curiosity was aroused.

"Yeah," Ferrin replied bitterly. "I think she's moved in for good."

"Does your father like it?"

"Oh he don't mind so much, s'long as it don't interfere with work. S'long as Dod and Med don't slack off but there ain't, 'scuse me, isn't so much work this time of year." Ellen noticed that Ferrin was self-conscious about his speech, tried to correct it when he made a slip. She wished he wouldn't; it betrayed his anxiety, and she didn't know how to put him at ease.

"I suppose she helps around the house or something?" Ellen went on, aware that she was prying and was annoyed with herself for being interested in Simone.

"Naw, Simone don't do nothin' but take care of herself," Ferrin spat out, his voice filled with disgust. "She just sits around paintin' her fingernails and toenails or readin' crummy magazines ... them "True Story" things or Dod and Med's detective stories. When they don't go out, they all play cards, Dad with 'em. She's a sharp player and cheats like crazy. Dad gets a kick out of tryin' to catch her at it and when he does, she flies all over him and pounds him with her fists. I never seen, saw, him let anybody else do anything like that to 'im before."

Ellen remembered faintly some other such scene years ago with Simone and her father, but she didn't say anything. In spite of the fact that she didn't want to think about that horrid girl, she found her mind filled with strangely entrancing scenes of Simone in that rough, bleak household of ranchers.

"She's taken to horses just like an old hand. She sometimes helps take care of them and that sets her up with the old man, too." Ferrin went on as though he were puzzling over Simone, too. But then, as if the subject had suddenly become distasteful to him, he dropped it. They were almost to Provo and the rain had stopped. It was growing dark and there was a rich, sepia light in the valley. The street lights had come on and shone greasily in the muddy light. Ellen felt as though she were in a movie, unreal, one-dimensional, a different person. She had suddenly decided that she would not tell Ferrin not to come anymore if he wanted to. He provided a chance to get out, to do something different, and she could act like she had a boyfriend of sorts.

"Wouldja like somethin' to eat?" Ferrin asked slowing the car down as they came to the Provo river bridge. "There's a good little place to eat down there." Ellen saw some pinkish neon lights glowing in the black, wet trees to the left of the bridge.

"Sure, sure," she said gaily. Grandma didn't usually fix much for supper on Sunday nights and Ellen seldom ate in restaurants except when she went to Salt Lake to see her mother. It seemed like a great occasion. Ferrin turned into the parking lot and helped her out. The rain had let up. She felt very self-conscious trying to adjust her steps to the lurch-hobble of Ferrin as they went into the small, over-heated restaurant. It was early and, thank goodness, there were few people. She wasn't ready to be seen out with Ferrin but she told herself, it didn't matter. There wasn't going to be anything serious between them. In a few months she would be gone out of his life and he from hers.

℅

From that time on, Ferrin came frequently, sometimes in the feed store pickup, but as often as he could in the big car because he sensed that Ellen felt better in it–he knew without expressing it either to himself or her that it offset his lameness. Word very quickly got around that Ellen had a "boyfriend," and some of the kids at school teased her about him. A lot of the girls were curious and tried to find out about him, but she didn't want to talk to anyone, not even Lorraine. Part of it was her confusion about her own feelings. There was a bit of a stigma about the Hallsworths, and he was not to her the kind of boyfriend that Ken was. Although she let him put his arm around her and hold her hand and, after a few weeks, even kiss her goodnight, she had none of the feelings, desires or interests about him that Lorraine expressed about Ken. The idea of marrying him was incredible to her. She didn't know what Ferrin thought of that because she wouldn't let him talk about it, but she supposed he thought they were more than just friends.

It wasn't a brother-sister relationship either although she felt a deep kinship with him, a kind of proprietary sympathy as though their lives were knit by the common experience of being outsiders. She missed him when he didn't come as she expected, and frequently she was annoyed when he did come as she expected. Sometimes she felt she needed him very much; other times she was irritated and ashamed when she was in public with him. But Ferrin had certainly expanded her world. He drove her all over the county and to Salt Lake to movies, took her to dinner in swell places that she never would have seen even with other boys.

She introduced him to Irene and Ed, who took to him at once. But her emotions were in constant turmoil, like the night they had taken the long drive around the lake. When they were out driving along the lonely roads, through dark humps of hills with the surface of the lake glowing white, eerily, she felt very close to him, satisfied to have his arm around her and tuck her head into his shoulder. Ferrin liked her to always sit close to him as he drove. His cheerfulness and kindness gave her a sense of security that she had never felt before; it was a kind of maleness she had never experienced. Her relationship with Everett had been altogether different.

She could easily forget his deformity when they were alone. She didn't even mind that he wasn't interested in books and things as she was because he seemed to like to hear her talk about them and had even read some of the things that she suggested. He seemed so anxious to please her, too anxious most of the time, and that sometimes irritated her. But this night, she felt that there might be something more between them. When they came onto the highway on the east side of the lake, however, back among people the mood evaporated, leaving her feeling empty and dismayed. She moved away from him to the other side of the car, watching the lights and the thickening shadows of houses and cars that indicated they were coming into Harnett. Ferrin checked the gas gauge and decided he'd better fill up. He pulled into the oasis of a service station. It was a chill, early winter night and, although not very late, most of the houses in the small town were darkened. They impressed Ellen with the deadly tedium of small town life–getting up, eating, going to church on Sunday, going to bed at nine o'clock over and over again.

The service station attendant, a gnomish old man in greasy coveralls, hopped anxiously out to the car and thrust his wrinkled face at the window. A toothless grin spread over his face. "Well, well, Ferrin Hallsworth, ain't seen you since the ark docked here. Saaay, looks like you got a young lady now. Atsa stuff. What'll y'have, boy?"

"Better fill 'er up, Ike." Ferrin got out of the car and the two of them began to inspect the car intently. Ellen watched through the windshield. She could not hear what they were saying, but Ferrin was nodding and shaking his head with great seriousness as though he set considerable store by the old man's opinions. He had to hobble around and see something that the old man had back of the service station and examine a gun and head of a deer that was mounted and hung inside the station and look at a stack of tires and listen to some long tale about a recent hunt or some other man-thing. Altogether it took more than half an hour to get on the way. Ellen grew restless and then annoyed. By the time Ferrin got back in the car, she was completely out of sorts. She felt down-right hateful toward him; he was so much a part of this hicky, country town, western life to which she didn't want to belong. She hated the silly grin he had on his face as he shook Ike's hand and promised to come again soon.

"Good old guy, used to work for us on the ranch til the work got too hard and a horse threw him and busted his back. I like to spend a little time with him when I get a chance. He's had a rough life. Lost his wife and kids in a terrible fire when he was young. I like to try to cheer him up a bit; he's pretty lonely."

"I guess that's the way you feel about me," Ellen said perversely with tightened lips. "I guess you come over and take me for rides because you feel sorry for me."

Ferrin pulled the car over to the side of the road very sharply and stopped it. He turned his puzzled face toward her. In the light of the dashboard she could see the hurt expression on his face. "What'd you mean?" he asked. "That's not the reason I come to see you at all and you know it. What's the matter, Ellen?"

"Oh, I don't know, I'm so mixed up," Ellen felt herself on the verge of tears. "I guess it's just that I don't like things around here and you do. You seem to belong and I don't. I want to go away, a long way away...." She waved her hand helplessly.

Ferrin moved toward her and put out his hand. When she shrank away, he didn't come closer, but said in a voice tight with emotion, "I'll take you away, if you want to go. I'll do anything in the world for you, Ellen. You know you are the only girl in the world I care for, will ever care about, don't you?"

Ellen shook her head miserably. "Don't say that, Ferrin. Don't pay any attention to me. I'm not worth it. I'm just not feeling well tonight." She was sorry that she had forced words out of him that she didn't want to hear; she was sorry she could listen to them coldly, almost cruelly. She wanted to break up with him, yet she couldn't.

"Just take me home now, will you? I don't know what's the matter, Ferrin. I'll be alright tomorrow." She was getting a headache; it was almost her monthly time and she did feel feverish. She had noticed that she always had these horrid feelings around that time of the month. Her moods swung wildly; she just wanted to crawl away and curl up by herself. She hated just about everything and everybody. Now she was ashamed of herself and sorry for Ferrin so she moved over and touched his arm. "Don't pay any attention to me when I'm like this," she murmured. He put his arm lightly around her and they drove home in silence.

Once in a while Ferrin waited for her outside the high school in the big car, and it would have given her considerable pleasure to get in it and be driven away (it was the fanciest automobile by a full mile that any of the other girls' boyfriends drove) if it hadn't been for the fact that Ferrin always hopped out when he saw her coming, lurched around and held the door open for her. It was not just that his lameness was so conspicuous then, but that none of the other boys did that for the girls except when they went to Hops or Proms in long dresses. Virginia made a good deal of fun out of it, of course, mimicking his fine manners and calling him the "Pontiac Knight from Junction City." Ellen felt like strangling her and was somewhat surprised when Virginia approached her on the sly and wanted her to fix her up with a date with one of the other Hallsworth boys. It gave her a perverse sense of satisfaction to explain that Simone had them both securely in tow. Some of the other girls expressed a grudging admiration for her rich beau.

Ellen soon learned that it was futile to explain to them that he wasn't her "beau," but it was not altogether disagreeable to her to know that the Hallsworths were about the richest family in the mid-section of Utah. She had noticed that Ferrin always had a wallet full of bills and spent money on her freely. Old man Hallsworth and his sons were considered one of the biggest ranching outfits in the state and one of the few solvent ones in these poverty ridden years. They owned practically the whole western part of the county and about half the town of Junction City. When depression had struck, they had been in a position to pick up a lot of land and stock their neighbors lost. Ellen learned in a roundabout way that the less fortunate men like Uncle Aaron hated their guts, especially the old man's. It was said with admiration, if not love, that Willard Hallsworth didn't give a damn about nobody but himself and his outfit. All he looked for was a chance to make a buck. That's what it took to get along in this life–toughness–that's what had won the West and built America. Respect for a man's business sense or brawn always had counted for more than love.

The Hallsworths owned the biggest feed, lumber and hardware store in the area, and it was rumored that they pretty much controlled the Junction City bank. Because Ferrin's legs prevented him from working on the ranch as much as he might have, he was learning the business end of the Hallsworth holdings at the store. He spent a good deal of his time there. He had finished high school, the only one of the three boys who had, was nearly twenty and had studied some bookkeeping by correspondence courses. Ellen went to the store with him several times and saw that he handled the work well and confidently.

It was there she first met his father. He was a small man–about the size of Ferrin, but Ferrin looked like his mother whose picture he kept on his desk. He had softer, more feminine features and her dark eyes. The elder Hallsworth looked like he was made completely out of the toughest, most highly polished saddle leather. Dressed in standard Levis, plain heavy but neat cloth workshirt and faded denim jumper, studded with shiny brass rivets, dull, leather cowboy boots and curled-brim, light-colored Stetson–he was all of one piece. He was so hard and compact that you felt he must have been as indestructible as a cedar post.

There was nothing of the dude about him, but he looked extremely right in his clothes, the sort of man who made the clothes, exuding a kind of power and self-satisfaction that Ellen had never encountered before. She was partly frightened, partly fascinated when Ferrin introduced them. He had only looked at her thirty seconds with eyes that were like steelies under their flat, gray scattered brows but that was enough to appraise her as he would have a horse or a piece of machinery. She saw in that look and in the curt way that he acknowledged the introduction and went crisply back to his business with Ferrin, slapping his leather gloves on his Levi-clad leg, that she wouldn't do, she didn't suit him.

"I don't think your dad likes me," she said as they were driving home in the pickup after Ferrin had closed the store.

"I'm glad," Ferrin said shortly in that grouchy voice that he always used when he talked about his family. "If he did, I wouldn't! With him women don't count anyway. They're like horses—work horses or fancy riding stocks—something to slave for him or give him a big thrill."

Ellen was slightly shocked. Ordinarily Ferrin was very careful not to be coarse or vulgar around her; he appeared now to be addressing some bitterness deep within himself. But the simile had intrigued her. "Simone's like the fancy riding horse, I guess, so she suits him?" she queried, feeling that she might have stumbled on a very important secret.

"Yeah, somethin' like that," he muttered. "But she's trash stock, he oughta be able to see that!" There was such hatred in his voice that Ellen was surprised. Ordinarily he had such pliable good nature. She had discovered that he had a lot of friends in Junction City and was agreeable and efficient in the feed store. This vein of bitter hatred just under such an amiable surface interested her immensely. It was, perhaps the thing that made their relationship endurable. Ellen wanted to probe deeper although something told her that she ought not to.

"Your mother, what was she like to him?"

"Work horse," he said curtly. "I know he killed her anyway."

"You don't mean for really?" Ellen went on. Ferrin hadn't talked much about his mother. She knew that she had been dead quite a while.

"Well, not really, so that you could accuse him of it outright."

Ferrin's voice sounded constricted. "It wasn't exactly so much the hard work that killed her either, think. I was too young to see then but I think now it was just the roughness, the ugliness out there on the ranch. You know," there was a sneer in his voice,"he's the big western he-man type, can't stand anything soft and womanlike, can't stand anything pretty, nice. Weak he calls it. Nothin' that don't fit the rootin-tootin-helluva-shootin cowboy, big rancher type."

Ferrin's chin was actually trembling, he was so emotionally wrought up.

"You sound as though you don't much like that type." Ellen thought maybe she had got on the wrong track, but she was growing more and more curious abut this strange, violent family.

"Hate it!" he spat out. "Course he'd tell you that's because I'm a cripple–weak and can't take it." They had stopped in front of Ellen's gate but she was reluctant to leave him. He wasn't looking at her but at the steering wheel. In his work clothes, Levis and western shirt, he looked younger, like an angry little boy.

"It about killed him after I was sick and turned out to be a weaklin'. He couldn't stand it that a son of HIS could be weak and sickly, couldn't stand up to the tough Hallsworth reputation. I think he'd rather I died. All those years he tried to curse me into walkin' again and maybe that's why I can as much as I can."

"I thought you told me that you were thrown off a horse?" Ellen reminded him, puzzled.

"Did I? Oh yeah, that first time. I always tell that to people I don't know very well ." Ferrin had doubled up his fist and was pounding nervously on the steering wheel. "That's the kind of thing he could have understood. He could have put up with it if it had been an accident, a horse, but to think a son of his could have polio. He was ashamed. *He blamed my mother!*"

Ferrin looked at her, his face blazing. "He blamed my mother for me being weak. The other boys didn't get it or, if they had it, they got over it. He used to look at my legs every day and curse and then she'd cry and he'd try to make me walk. When I couldn't, he'd curse some more."

Ellen realized when he stopped that she must have had a horrified expression on her face. She looked away, not knowing what to say.

"I'm sorry, I shouldna told you, it's just that I guess you should know about me, about us...."

"Oh, I'm glad you did." Ellen tried to sound as kind as she could. "It helps to know since we are together so much anymore. You get around so well, I shouldn't think he'd mind so much anymore."

"Well, I don't give a ... I don't care anymore what he cares or minds. I'm just as tough as he is in some ways. He don't see it but things are changin' in this world. It's gonna take somethin' more to get ahead." His jaw was set so tight that the blue veins stood out on his forehead. He turned and looked straight and hard at her. "You mind me, Ellen, I'm gonna run it all someday. It'll be all mine!" There was a look of dark triumph in his cloudy blue-gray eyes.

Ellen stared back in fascination. It was the first time she had found him attractive, and yet she was repelled–such fierce, exposed determination. She only sensed the strength derived from such intense hatred was bound to consume all else eventually but, like all women, she was attracted to strength, pure, hard, strength in the male. There were she supposed two kinds of men–those who were tough on the outside and soft inside or soft on the outside and tough at the very core.

Dod and Med were the first kind, Ferrin the second; only old man Hallsworth seemed tough all the way through. He was the older kind of man, she supposed, and they must be the hardest kind for a woman to handle. From these revelations she could see that with Ferrin any woman he wanted or loved could have anything she wanted from him if she didn't try to disturb or interfere with the purposes and determination of the inner core. Oh well, she was still keeping herself to herself. For all that Ferrin now appeared more desirable, she had not, could not fall in love with him. He was saying in a husky voice, "And you can share it all with me, Ellen, if you want to."

She let him take her hand and smiled at him in the wintry dusk. "Maybe, someday."

Ellen saw Simone at the feed store on a Saturday afternoon. It was just before Christmas. The snow had been light but it was cold. Simone, Dod and Med were fooling around in the lumber yard, throwing snow on each other and laughing uproariously.

Ellen was waiting quietly in the office where Ferrin was working on some of the accounts. He had picked her up earlier in the day; they had been planning to go to Salt Lake to shop, then to dinner and a show. But when Ferrin had stopped by the office to get some extra money, he had found orders from his dad to get the payroll out early for the men, so there they were. They would probably be too late to do much shopping. Ellen was leafing through some dingy catalogues full of harnesses, saddles, western paraphernalia. She had grown tired and bored; she leaned on her elbow looking out the window of the office at the romping trio. She hoped Simone wouldn't see her; she didn't want to talk to her.

Simone, as usual, was vibrantly beautiful. She was wearing Levis that fit her like skin and a heavy plaid jacket too big for her, probably one of the boys'. How clumsy Ellen would have felt and looked in such an outfit, but not Simone. Her wild, dark hair was flying madly about her face as she leapt about in the snow like some exuberant wild animal. When she threw back her head to shake out the snow that Med had rubbed in it, Ellen thought she must be the happiest, most carefree person in the world. If only Ellen had been able to play like that. But someone, mostly her mother, had always been reminding her to "be a lady." Pants were still only working clothes for the summer, and besides she and most girls never would look like Simone in them. She resembled those glamorous illustrations of girls in the confession or fashion magazines–smooth, every line converging in the right place.

After a while the three of them came up on the loading platform that ran along the side and back of the store. Willard Hallsworth had driven up in the big cattle truck, and he sprang out agilely, striding toward them. As he stood beside Dod and Med on the platform, he was a good head shorter than either, but Ellen could see them bend to attention. They really were handsome men, the two sons, she thought–big, muscular, dark tanned skins, thick waving hair, Dod's a little lighter than Med's, yet beside their father, there was something juvenile little boyish, about them. Ellen couldn't hear what he was saying to them with a good deal of gesturing, but it appeared they were both being commanded to do something at once and in different places. She saw them shift their weight, not immediately removing their hands from the back pockets of their Levis, and exchange hostile looks over Simone's dark hair that was shining in the orangish light of the setting winter sun. Willard Hallsworth saw the hesitation and looks and grabbed Simone. Ellen thought he said something like, "I'll take her back myself." As he looked at Simone there was a strange, mischievous triumph on his leathery face. He jabbed a thumb toward the pickup. Simone went almost obediently and got in while Dod climbed into the cattle truck and Med went off in the opposite direction.

When he burst into the feed store, Willard brought a blast of vigor which was more than cold, crisp air in with him. Ellen could smell the pungent odor of whisky; he was obviously in high spirits, but not drunk. It would have been an unforgivable weakness for him not to be able to hold his liquor well. He never drank on the job, but a few of his clients had invited him for some Christmas cheer that afternoon. The smell reminded Ellen unhappily of Everett. She had a sharp pain in her chest. She hadn't heard a word from him since he had left–been taken away–from Merritsville.

Willard Hallsworth addressed himself briskly and cheerfully to Ferrin after he had given her a perfunctory nod. "Got that payroll out yet, boy?"

"Just about." Ferrin tossed back the lock of hair that always fell forward. He was cross, since he had expected to have the afternoon off. "Well, take an extra twenty, and treat your gal to somethin' special tonight, kid," his dad ordered, slapping the counter with his fringed glove. "It's Christmas," he said almost derisively, "Time of good will, eh?" He turned and nodded to Ellen. "Say, by the way, Med's gone over to get that last load of baled hay from the Scott's, and I sent Dod to help unload that batch of cedar posts came in from Vernal this mornin'."

"Thanks," Ferrin replied without looking up from his ledger. As the door swung behind Willard, the ornaments on the little tree that Ferrin had decorated for the office shivered and tinkled. "That's his idea of Christmas, 'take twenty'," Ferrin said out of the side of his mouth. "I guess it's better than nothin'." Twenty dollars was a lot of money to Ellen. She could never remember having that much all at once.

Ellen smiled and went over and put her chin on his shoulder. "Grandma says to invite you to Christmas dinner if you want to come. It's kinda noisy and messy; we always have it at the Walkers'."

He patted her cheek; the look on his face was so full of tenderness and happiness, she was moved in spite of herself. "I sure would like that. Well, let's go before it gets dark." He closed his ledger, straightened the desk and putting his arm around her kissed her hard. She felt a pleasant warm sensation trickling down her body. Maybe it would come out right for them. She knew she risked leading Ferrin on by inviting him into the family. She was afraid he might begin to think,... that people might begin to think they were getting serious. Oh well, what could you do about what people thought? It would be something special for Ferrin who would otherwise have to spend Christmas day at the ranch probably with Dod, Med and Simone drunk or lying around with hangovers. Ellen, herself was dreading the Christmas dinner that year; it might help to have Ferrin there. He, at least, would be happy; he was so crazy about her that it didn't matter very much what she felt.

❧

As Ellen unpacked the Christmas trimmings from neat newspaper parcels in which Grandma had carefully wrapped them, she was struck by how shabby and dingy they were. Many of the ornaments were tarnished; the tinsel was crushed and had lost its sparkle; the little birds that had glowed on her tree ten years ago were chipped, their once glossy tails bedraggled. Everything about Christmas was worn, threadbare. Ellen felt like crying.

Tears did blur her eyes as she set about trimming the small tree that Ferrin had brought them. He had cut it himself on the western hills; it was like the one Laurence had brought so many Christmases ago.

Grandma was singing snatches of Christmas hymns in the kitchen, "Away in a manger ... Oh, little town of Bethlehem ... we three kings of orient are–a few lines here, a humming and de, dum hum. Ellen wished she would sing the whole thing through.

What was there to sing about? Sometimes she felt older than her grandmother who was bustling about making homemade presents, wrapping them in tissue paper that she had saved and smoothed out, baking and cooking and generally carrying on as though Christmas were a joyous, happy occasion. She worried whether Louise should have the pillow slips with the blue embroidery and crocheting for her trousseau or whether she should have the pink ones and Lorraine the blue ones. She had been especially delighted by the string of electric Christmas lights that Ferrin had brought them.

Ellen draped them around the tree and added them into the socket on the extension cord to which the radio was plugged, wishing only that the whole, sad, farcical time was over with. The old RCA Superheterodyne was playing softly, Christmas carols now and advertisements. On the hour it broadcast the chimes from the Walker Bank Building in Salt Lake. She had heard them on the streets last week with Ferrin; they almost made her believe in Christmas again. The Depression was not so visible if you looked in the glittering windows of the stores still filled with enticing objects and didn't see the ragged people begging on the street corners.

When Ferrin took her to Salt Lake, they always stopped in at the store to see her mother and sometimes went up to the apartment in the Avenues to have dinner with her and Ed. On one such occasion, while Ed and Ferrin played checkers, Irene and Ellen did the dishes together. Ellen was glad that her mother seemed happy here in a cozy apartment, but she did seem to belong to a different world so remote from Merritsville.

It was still difficult for Irene to talk to her daughter intimately but she ventured to say, "I really like your young man, Ellen. Do you think you might get married after school is out?"

The question startled and annoyed Ellen. "No, I don't think so. He hasn't asked me yet."

"I think he takes it pretty much for granted." Irene took off her apron and sat down at the kitchen table. "Oh, my feet hurt tonight. Ed wants me to quit, but I don't think I would like being just cooped up here. He still has to travel sometimes. Well, I was looking at some china on special today in the store that I thought I might get for your trousseau...."

Ellen flushed. It seemed like everyone was trying to push her into marriage. Of course, for her mother and most women it was the only thing.

"I think I want to go to college, if I can." She sat down at the other end of the small table and began to fiddle with the salt and pepper shaker. There were no windows in this city kitchen filled with geraniums; her mother was not like geraniums anymore. She was more like the hothouse roses in a crystal vase in the hallway.

"I don't know if we can manage college," Irene said a hesitantly. "Ferrin is such a nice boy, we like him so much. I think he is going to get ahead and you can see that he thinks the world and all of you."

Ellen traced invisible designs on the neat lace-trimmed cloth. She felt all choked up inside; there were things she thought she ought to be able to tell her mother but just couldn't. "But I don't feel that way about him," she mumbled.

Irene reached out and took her hand, moved by the distress she saw on Ellen's face.

"If you don't love him, Ellen, I wouldn't want you to marry him. I've loved two men very much and it is something I would want for you. I do think marriage would be awful without...." She stopped, seeing the tears glistening in Ellen's eyes. Getting up she gave her a hug. "Never mind, it'll work out alright. Come on in the bedroom and see if you like the new dress I got for Christmas."

On the way back to Merritsville, Ellen sat close to Ferrin the way he liked her to, feeling warm and emotional. Christmas did that to you in spite of all. Ferrin's congeniality and generosity was infectious and they had had a very agreeable evening with Ed and Irene, almost like a family. In some ways marrying him could be right. All her family liked and accepted him; except for his physical handicap he had all the things to be desired in a husband. He was ambitious, hard-working and he did care about her so much. As they drove along in the wintry night, Ferrin handling the handsome car so confidently, the back seat full of presents, Ellen was lulled into a kind of contentment.

It did seem like college was a very remote possibility.

"Your mother sure is a beautiful woman," Ferrin said after a stretch of silence. "Her and Ed seem to love each other a lot."

"Yes," Ellen agreed. "I'm glad they're happy. She was very sad when my father died, and it wasn't too easy when she first met Ed." She didn't know if he knew about the scandal and all, but it wouldn't matter to him anyway.

"I hope we're that happy together when we're that old." Ferrin squeezed her hand tenderly. She was only faintly disturbed by his notion that it was all settled that they would be married. She decided not to say anything about it. She was very nearly happy for a brief while tonight.

Ferrin was so excited about spending Christmas with them. He had asked her about all of them and tried to get her to buy presents for the whole family with his money. She finally talked him into just buying a big box of chocolates for the Walkers and bedroom slippers for Grandma. He asked if he could come over early Christmas morning and help open the gifts. Of course, she couldn't say no. By nine o'clock he had arrived, bearing more packages.

Under the fragrant cedar tree he placed several more boxes, and they set about the happy business of opening the gifts. In addition to perfume, silk stockings, a pretty blouse, and necklace Ferrin had brought a small oblong box which he handed to Ellen, eagerly watching her face as she opened it. It was a beautiful gold wrist watch. For a moment Ellen was stunned. In the tradition of the times, the wrist watch was always followed by the cedar chest and then the engagement ring. But she was truly thrilled to have it; the girls who didn't yet have one would be green with envy. She kept turning it over and over and then Ferrin fastened in on her wrist. "You like it?" he asked his voice trembling.

She nodded, and murmured, "You shouldn't have. Oh, look, Grandma."

"Oh my," Grandma said, admiring it. "My goodness, Ferrin, aren't you spoiling us? Now you must take good care of that. I never seen such a pretty one." Ferrin glowed with pleasure.

Ellen examined the rest of the gifts, the pillow cases that Grandma had done for her in lavender, the clothes her mother had sent, and an elegant bottle of cologne. The homemade gifts from her cousins, Louise's laboriously stitched hot pads, a set of dish-towels from her aunt embroidered with birds doing something on every day of the week, Lorraine's finger nail polish set. Then she noticed a brown wrapped parcel that had been placed at the back of the tree.

"What's this?" she asked. It was addressed to her in care of Grandma. She felt a chill of sadness as she tore off the wrapping to find a small, old-fashioned book with gold lettering *Poems of Christina Rossetti*. Inside on the book plate of the Gordon library was an inscription in a wavering hand, "To Ellen, Merry Christmas, from Everett." As she leafed through the crisp, yellowing pages, a hard lump formed in her chest–she could hardly keep back the tears.

"Well, who's it from?" Grandma peered over her spectacles.

"From Everett, just a book of poetry." She knew she had better not look at it until later, when she was alone. She put it back under the tree and jumped up.

"Well, I've got to get dressed. It's almost time we got over to the Walker's. Thank you, Ferrin, thank you, Grandma, for a wonderful Christmas." She had got Ferrin a nice pair of leather gloves with her mother's help and a tie clasp. He was exclaiming over them as though they were the most wonderful things. She was embarrassed thinking of the gifts he had lavished on her. But he seemed so happy.

The rest of Christmas day, however, was as dismal as she had imagined it would be. Everyone exclaimed over her watch; she could see Ferrin flush with pride as she showed it around. Lorraine had got her cedar chest. Ken had not been able to afford both the watch and the chest, so he had decided the latter would be more practical. Lorraine was ecstatic. She whispered to Ellen. "You'll get one soon, I bet, after that watch."

"Don't want one," Ellen whispered back. Lorraine just smiled and shrugged.

Christmas dinner was subdued. The family had dwindled so much that it hardly seemed the same. Bertha, Albert and the girls from Salt Lake were not there. They had made an excuse that sounded too polite. Irene was so tired from the Christmas rush that she had caught a bad cold and couldn't come. Hal was somewhere in the forests of Montana, but Lorraine had invited Ken and Ellen brought Ferrin. Everybody welcomed Ferrin into the family in spite of his being a Hallsworth. Uncle Aaron was the only one who was a bit chilly, but even he thawed to Ferrin's congeniality. They were ready and willing to fit Ferrin neatly into the family pattern as though he had grown up with them. Ellen thought she detected something in their attitude of relief to have found something to do with her. Like Ken and Lorraine, they would have her and Ferrin married and settled down as soon as she got out of high school.

She smiled a derisive smile to herself. That was fine for Ken and Lorraine, who held hands practically all day, but she had other ideas. She was annoyed that Ferrin fitted himself in so comfortably, joking and playing with the kids, talking with Ken and Uncle Aaron about business and the impending trouble in Europe. He kidded with Aunt Dosey and Grandma as he insisted on limping around the kitchen, wiping dishes after dinner. Grandma adored him. She had started coddling him right from the beginning.

It was only when the family had gathered around the old piano to sing a few Christmas songs with Louise playing that he sat on the fringe of things. Ellen had sung a few songs with them then moved over by the window. Ferrin came to stand by her and slipped his arm around her. "This is the happiest Christmas I've spent since my mother died," he whispered, "maybe the happiest ever. This is what I want, Honey, a big happy family, everybody together."

A chill went through her, but she couldn't bring herself to spoil it for him just then–the vision of a big happy family that just wasn't so. Yet, at the moment, they did look happy and warm, and there was certainly something here that Ferrin had not ever had. Ellen had had the merest glimpse of the vast, bleak coldness of his life the one time he had taken her to the big, isolated ranch house for a few moments.

It was an old Victorian mansion standing out on the rolling, yellow western hills something like a setting in a nightmare. It had once been a grand place, built at the end of the last century to display the prosperity of the stock industry. There were no other houses within several miles; it dominated the landscape like a brooding dowager. Ferrin had taken her into the house when no one was there. She was impressed by the space and fading grandeur, but it was cold and neglected. Most of the living was done in the large kitchen which stuck out in Ellen's minds as being all of one grayish-yellow color with the exception of the red-checked oil cloth covering on the big table.

It was kept neat–Willard Hallsworth had that demand of order that had to be maintained, but there was nothing the least bit homey–no rugs, limp curtains at the long, gaunt windows, no plants, doilies, pretty dishes, cushions, pictures or ornaments–no feminine touch. It was a bachelor's house. Ferrin explained that a woman came in once a week or so and did up the laundry and other chores, but they hadn't been able to keep a cook and house-keeper because of the isolation. The men had learned to do the basic cooking; there was a heavy smell of grease, coffee and to-bacco. No wonder Ferrin seemed reluctant to go back to it when finally, toward dusk, Christmas day 1938 was over.

He suggested that they take in the last movie so, after they had taken Grandma home, she and he, Ken and Lorraine sat through a Bing Crosby film, holding hands. It was late when he took her home; she let him hold her closer than usual and kiss her several times. Ferrin usually kissed her with tight dry lips, but tonight they were moist. He tried to pry hers apart with his tongue. She was slightly repelled responding without much warmth. After all, he had been so good to her, but she was dismayed at how little she felt for him. She was being slowly but surely sucked into something for which she was not ready. Pleading weariness, she wouldn't let him come in and promised that he could come soon again.

All day she had been trying not to think about something, some-one. She turned on the Christmas tree lights; Grandma had gone to bed, but the room was still warm–she must have come home and built up the fire thinking Ferrin and Ellen would want to spend a little time alone there.

Ellen knelt down by the tree and searched for the book from Everett. It was lying next to one of Ferrin's presents, a large gold and white box lined with pleated white satin containing a silver-backed mirror, brush and comb. Dresser sets were a popular gift for young women that year; this was especially beautiful She knew Ferrin had got her mother to help him pick it out. She picked up the mirror and studied her face in the dim light. Did Ferrin see her as the kind of woman who would sit at a dressing table combing her long, lustrous tresses and looking beautiful for him? Yes, of course– Ferrin really didn't see her as she was; there was a side of her totally oblivious to him. This may be the reason she held back from him, the reason she couldn't feel what she ought to or wanted to. She sighed, laying the mirror back in its indented satin space, and picked up the book Everett had sent.

She wondered how he had got the book from the library where she had seen it, even read to him from it. Had he come back and not tried to see her and Grandma? Never mind, she squinted to read the fine spidery print. Some of the lines were underlined, but it appeared they had been marked ages and ages ago. Here and there were some fresher looking marks, and a satin ribbon marker had been inserted in a page where an arrow pointed to some lines: "Better by far you should forget and smile
Than that you should remember and be sad."

He was trying to tell her something; trying to say that he wasn't ever coming back into her life. The hard cold lump in her breast began to dissolve and hot burning tears ran down her cheeks. She undressed for bed, and putting the book under her pillow, fell asleep with tears drying stiffly, coldly on her face.

☙

The late winter, early spring months were cold, dismal and in the harsh winter light, the town of Merritsville in 1939 showed the ravages of ten years of depression the way an aging woman caught in her shabby bathrobe shows the depredations of age. The only new buildings in town, if you could really call them "new buildings," were the basement houses. Ken and Lorraine were planning to build one on the corner of his parents' lot in the northeast corner of town.

Lorraine had her cedar chest already half full of embroidered dishtowels, pillow cases, crocheted doilies and a quilt. Grandma and Dosey had had two quiltings for her. She was bubbling with happiness, wearing Ken's FFA pin until he could make the down payment on a diamond. A lot of other girls were doing the same. Although jobs were still hard to find and money was scarce, the young went on with their stubborn optimism believing in a better world that their love and hope would build.

The clouds over Europe were getting darker; there was an ominous, restless current in the atmosphere. A big plant was being built in west Salt Lake for the processing of ammunition; a lot of men, young and older, were looking forward to jobs there. Something was going to happen. But that spring war still seemed remote. Especially in the west where isolationism was deeply entrenched. One of the high school debate questions was about American involvement–"Resolved that the United States should stay out of all foreign entanglements." Ellen studied the papers a lot and tried to imagine what war would be like.

She had found a part time job in the library. She had spent so much time there that when Mrs. Pratt, the librarian, had become ill and needed help, she thought of Ellen at once. Although Irene faithfully sent her money, and Grandma was always willing to share her small pension, Ellen liked the feeling of earning on her own. She had become determined to live her own life, to be free, but all around she felt a conspiracy to make her conform to the familiar pattern: marriage, babies, domestic chores. None of the other girls understood; they were all like Lorraine.

The two girls were sitting in the drug store one late, dull wintry afternoon over a coke before Ellen had to go to work at the library. Ellen was thinking as she looked at their reflections in the yellowing, splotchy mirror back of the counter how pretty Lorraine was–tall, blond and slender with big eyes, a "turnip nose" as the popular song said and a cupid bow mouth. Her jawline, like Ellen's was a trifle too broad and square–the Kent jaw, but when she fixed her hair a little softer around it, she looked like some of the movie stars whose glossy pictures on the covers of magazines brightened up one corner of the drug store. But in a few years she would probably go all blowzy and saggy with a frizzy permanent twice a year, her one effort to keep up. She would always have a baby in her arms and two or three little kids with runny noses hanging to her shapeless house dress. It happened to most of the women in Merritsville.

At the same time Lorraine was thinking how Ellen could easily get herself another boyfriend if she didn't want Ferrin Hallsworth as she was saying now. She was really pretty, especially her eyes, if it weren't for those awful glasses she had to wear that never seemed to sit straight on her nose. She could fix her hair up a little bit and wear more make up. Lorraine couldn't understand how any girl would not want to get married and have children. She wanted Ellen to share her dreams of happiness.

"Really, Ellen," Lorraine said, making a noise with the straw in the bottom of her glass. "I don't see why you feel the way you do. Is it just that Ferrin's crippled? Really, after you know him, he's so nice you forget it. And your kids won't be crippled because we found out in eugenics class that kids don't inherit those kinds of things. I'll bet he could make you the best husband, if you'd let him."

Ellen sighed and the stubborn, frustrated look settled on her face more deeply. "It's not that, 'Rainy. I don't mind him being crippled either. It's just that I don't want to get married right now. I don't want to have kids and settle down. I want to do things, see things. I want to go to college if I can."

"But all alone?" Lorraine asked incredulously. "I don't want to do anything without Ken. I don't enjoy doing it unless he does. I just don't understand you, Ellen. How can you stand to be so lonely?"

Ellen shrugged. There was no use trying to explain. Maybe she didn't understand herself what it was that impelled her in a direction different from all the girls her age. She had been memorizing a poem for speech class by Amy Lowell, the last line of which was "Christ! What are patterns for?" She felt like the woman in the poem. Patterns, Ellen supposed, were meant to torture those who didn't fit them. Anyway those who fit them had a hard time putting up with those who didn't.

She slid off the stool wearily. It had begun to snow lightly outside in the dirty winter dusk; the blur of Merritsville's main street filled her with extreme dread of spending year after year in this dumpy, tired town. But the pattern was powerful and sinister. You had to fight hard to keep it from closing in.

Tonight after she and Mrs. Pratt had closed the library at nine o'clock, she would find Ferrin waiting. He came over almost every night now. He would take her to get something to eat, and then they would go home and probably play the Monopoly game he had bought her and Grandma. Grandma would play with them most of the nights, enjoying herself immensely as Ferrin instructed her about the rental and hotels. On Saturday nights they would go for a drive or to a movie. Sunday afternoon Ferrin would come over after church. Grandma had invited him to go to church with them, but it was the one thing he seemed reluctant to do. He would eat Sunday dinner with them and then they would play Monopoly. If Ellen had homework, Ferrin would read the papers, waiting for her to go out for a drive. He always seemed so reluctant to leave her; it would take an hour or so to say goodnight. More and more he wanted to neck in the car, and it became harder for Ellen to resist him. Sometimes she almost enjoyed it, but when it got too heavy, she would push him away and say that they had better not go too far.

"I respect you for that, Ellen," he told her one night. "I know if you weren't strong, I couldn't be. I love you so much. I want you but I'm willin' to wait."

She wished she felt the way Lorraine felt about Ken. Lorraine said she would give in any day that Ken wanted her to, but they both wanted to be married in the Temple so they were trying hard not to. The trouble with Ellen was that she really didn't want to do it with Ferrin; he was becoming a problem. She knew clearly what was in his mind and heart although she prevented him from talking about it to her. But, in spite of the dreariness of the pattern into which they had fallen, it would even be more dreary without him. There would be no one to take her anywhere at all. She knew guiltily that she was making use of him, yet, she argued with herself, there was nothing else for him either. He wouldn't easily find another girl.

Life at the ranch was becoming more and more intolerable. Ferrin would like a home of his own. She knew that what Lorraine said was true; Ferrin would make a good husband in the conventional patterning of it. Furthermore, they wouldn't have to live in a basement house to start with. Yet, deep within her, Ellen sensed that life with him would be impossible for her. She had gradually discovered that he held a vision of her as the perfect woman encased in his heart. It was like being under one of those glass bells Grandma had on the sideboard with dried flowers and the picture of her father in it.

When she discovered the power of hatred and disillusion in

Ferrin toward his father and brothers, she had somehow felt she was seeing the real Ferrin, the basic person under a carefully nurtured and cultivated facade of good nature, the "handicap overcome" congeniality that was particularly winning in him. She felt that if she could draw some of that reality to herself, both of them would be ultimately safer. It would be easier to break the ties and dreams that were forming around her like steel cobwebs.

The more patient, loving and forgiving Ferrin became, the more perverse was Ellen's need to break through it. There were times when she burst out at him with rudeness and cruelty that shocked even herself. She despised him for his simple minded worship of her; Lorraine had said it, "He worshipped the ground she walked on." It was supposed to be the ultimate tribute to a woman, but it drove her to the lengths of fury. She sensed, rightly, though she could not have explained it to herself or anyone that it was not she Ferrin loved but the idea, the need he had of her. There was no use trying to talk to Grandma about it; she was completely taken with Ferrin.

She saved, unintentionally perhaps, the worst cruelty for a dull, tedious, almost unbearably boring Sunday afternoon in February. Those ugly, muddy days of late winter were the most horrid time of year in Utah. Long series of slushy, gray, thawing and freezing, snowing and melting; depressing days running one into the other with relentless monotony. School, library, home, homework, Ferrin, church and then starting all over.

They had been playing Monopoly since early afternoon; Ellen was growing desperately bored. Although she was winning, suddenly she swept all the pawns, cards and everything off the board and jumped up. "I'm sick and tired of all this," she sputtered. Grandma looked at her puzzled, then sighed and got up and went into the kitchen. Ferrin got down awkwardly and began picking up the pieces of the game. "Y'wanta go for a ride?" he asked. Ellen had turned on the radio and began to whirl around the room. "No," she said perversely. "I want to dance!" She danced wildly and provocatively over the pieces of the Monopoly set that Ferrin was trying to gather up, once stepping on his fingers. He shook them and laughed up at her then sat back on the rug against the davenport to watch her, amused but troubled.

There was only a small space in the living room, but Ellen

whirled about it like a gypsy. She was wearing a full skirt that flared out, showing her underthings. She knew it and didn't care. When the music stopped and some announcement came on, she threw herself panting down on the rug. "I love to dance," she said passionately, looking defiantly at Ferrin.

"Well, it's Sunday and there's no place to dance today."

"I mean sometime. You can't understand. I want to dance with *someone* and *you'll never be able to*." At the moment Ellen felt herself close to frenzy. It seemed the only thing that she wanted to do, the only thing that would release all the pent up, destructive forces that she had borne so long.

As another light dancing tune started on the radio, she leaped to her feet and went flying around the room. Ferrin struggled to his feet, put the pieces of the Monopoly game on the table and stood uneasily by the table until Ellen came to a standstill.

Her face was flushed, her hair shaken loose from its ribbon all disarranged, she felt exultant and wicked and cruel. For the first time something had been unlocked or she had found a way to unlock it. When she saw the look on Ferrin's face of dismay, hurt, she experienced a shock of pleasure. For the first time, the very first time, she felt like a woman. She had made a man look at her with hopeless pain and longing. And he looked at HER, not at the unreal image he had made of her in the roseate looking glass of his heart. At the moment, for the first time, he didn't know whether he liked her or not.

Ellen went over to the mirror above the sideboard and stooped a little to see herself so that she could smooth out her hair. She was exhilarated by the vision she caught of herself, and, as she straightened up, she could see the image of Ferrin standing at the table fumbling with the table doily. His face was quite white. She turned and leaned temptingly against the sideboard as she had seen women do it in the movies. It made her feel extremely grown up.

"I'll take you dancing if you want to go," he said in a low, strangled voice.

"What good would that do?" Ellen asked acidly. "You couldn't dance with me. I'm sure you'd enjoy sitting and watching all the time. Besides nobody else would dance with me if you couldn't dance with the other girls."

Ferrin winced as though she had struck him. "I could take you up to the Coconut Grove where Dod and Med and Simone go. The girls there just dance with who they want to. I wouldn't mind so much. I want to do anything that will make you happy, Ellen." He looked at her with pleading, whipped-puppy-dog eyes. A feeling of utter despair washed over Ellen. For a moment she thought she was free or going to be. She dropped her eyes and the pose in defeat and, snapping off the radio with its maddening music, she threw herself petulantly on the davenport. "It wouldn't work," she said and then repeated slowly, looking at him darkly and meaning more than just about the dancing. "*It just wouldn't work.* Besides who wants to go where Dod and Med and Simone go?"

There was a horrid silence. Ferrin sat down and was leaning over, aimlessly reaching the little wooden houses and hotels that were still scattered about and throwing them on the table. Grandma came to the door of the living room and looked around uneasily. "You two want a snack or somethin'?" she said nervously wiping her hands on her apron. She had never seen Ellen act like this. Whatever had got in to her?

Ferrin smiled at her sadly, "No, thanks, guess I better be goin'. I got some work to do in the store anyway."

Ellen got his things silently and silently watched him jerk through the door. She wished she could say she was sorry or something, but the words stuck in her throat. He didn't touch her or say that he would be back, nothing, just went.

For the first time in months she saw him stop on the edge of the porch and light a cigarette; he had been trying to quit because he knew Ellen and Grandma didn't like it. As she watched him through the lace curtains lurch along the walk, shaking the ashes off his smoke, she felt ashamed of herself and wanted to run after him, not knowing exactly what had possessed her. Yet she had a sense of release of freedom along with the sadness.

Ferrin did not come back, not the first week nor the second and on into the third week. February turned into the raw, cold, windy month of March. Life for Ellen had slipped back into the worn routine of school, home, church and library. At the end of the first week Ellen had a fit of remorse and fright. She knew she must have hurt him dreadfully, but it would be quite useless to tell him that she hadn't meant to. She knew she had. What she hadn't fully realized was how possible it was to hurt him because he seemed so insulated by his own feelings about her. She had picked on the one thing that she knew would get at him the worst–his lameness. It was downright awful of her; she wondered how she could be so rotten.

She really couldn't say she was sorry because, for the first time, she had made communication with him from the center of her being to the center of his. She was aware of how terrible it must be to be crippled, especially for a young man. Actually, she suffered for him sometimes when she watched him at a distance and admired the strength and courage that it had taken to live with his affliction in a tough western world.

But her pity for him was not *love*. Reflecting on the past months, she hadn't known Ferrin for a year yet, she had come to the knowledge that she deeply wanted to love as he did. It was not enough to be loved as the magazines, movies and songs urged; the other girls talked and dreamed of the abject lover, the one who adored and worshiped them, but she had seen enough to know how fragile this was. What was important was that *you* could love someone whole heartedly. Of all the people she had known, Ferrin needed her love most. It made her ashamed that she could not feel that all-consuming devotion.

Away from him, she thought of the grim picture of his life that she had glimpsed in her contacts with the Hallsworths. She shuddered when she thought of the gaunt house thrusting its barrenness against the wide empty skies of the desert country, the cheerless interior to which he had had to return every night to snatch something to eat from the frying pans on the stove, reading under the dim light on the oil-cloth table, hobbling to bed in a cold bedroom.

Now with Simone and his brothers lounging around, playing their eternally rough, obscene, tormented game or sleeping off sodden drunks, it must be even more than Hell. From time to time he had remarked on their goings-on. Ellen always felt a shiver of disgust and yet an almost greedy interest when he talked about Simone. Her wild life so incredibly outside Ellen's experience; her freedom so unbelievable, yet so strangely intriguing. Ferrin detested her and could seldom be persuaded to talk about her very much.

While Ellen's own life was less than she dreamed or desired, it was certainly not without the warm, good things that nurture the heart, even the mind. She recognized a fineness in Ferrin, a longing for the better things that she had. Why did she resent his thrusting his way into her life as he had? But she had to admit that she missed him.

As the days wore on she schemed of ways to try to reach him. She could go to the drug store pay phone and call him at the feed store. She could try to say she was sorry; she felt that he would be glad but something held her back. If she asked him to come back, she would have to be prepared to accept him on his terms. She would have to deny again something in herself that she was not sure could be denied. She knew that it wouldn't be fair in the long run to lead him on, to let him believe that she cared for him more than she was capable of caring. Why couldn't she love him, feel anything more than just pity and sometimes friendly fondness? It would be a good thing, a noble thing to make him happy, to try to give him all he had missed. He was so pathetically grateful for everything she and Grandma did for him. He acted as though Grandma's poor little house was the most wonderful place he had ever been.

She tried to put him out of her mind, thinking guiltily that if they were really finished, she ought to give back the watch which is what you were supposed to do. But if she contacted him ...? She worked hard on her school work, and spent the hours at the library comforting herself that it would only be a short while and she could leave Merritsville and Ferrin behind.

ॐ

That spring was cold and bleak, the worst since Ellen's father had died. March is a treacherous month. The snows were mostly melted with only patches of smudged white here and there under the trees and in the ditches. The country roads were turned to holes full of dirty water and oozing deep troughs of mud. Perversely, the sun shone steadily for a week or so, and the dry air sucked up all the moisture; the innocent buds and leaves, as anxious for spring as anyone, swelled up much too soon like children getting ready for a party. Then a bitter frost clamped down on everything. Freezing winds howled out of the canyon; the soggy wet snow weighted down all the trees and bushes, breaking some of them off and destroying a large part of the hopes for summer. In March and April the fruit of the summer was frequently killed. Orchards that one day stood full of blossom on the hill sides would on the next be covered with browning, ruined petals.

Ellen caught a very bad cold that kept her out of school and home on the couch in the kitchen for most of a week. Grandma made her wear a flannel rag around her neck, brewed her nasty hot ginger tea and rubbed her chest with a horrible stinging red ointment that she got from the Raleigh man, called most appropriately "Mustard ointment." Ellen had to hold her breath one minute and then blow down her chest the next to endure the frightful burning. She hated the stuff, and only permitted her grandmother to rub it on her because it seemed to make Grandma feel so much better. A substitute for old-fashioned mustard plasters, it was one of those remedies that was bound to cure or kill.

It was a miserable spell and with time to mull over the past few years of her life and probe her sensations, Ellen fell into a thick depression. She hardly even wanted to read, although Grandma had gone to the library and got some new books for her. One afternoon when she was feeling as though she must either get better or get out of the house and take her chances of dying, the Raleigh man's old black Model A wheezed up to the front gate.

Brother Schmidt still wore the same kind of heavy brown corduroy pants and leather cap he had worn when he called on Irene several years ago. Ellen thought he resembled a shaggy owl with his thick glasses that made his eyes eerily large and diffuse as he came lugging his wire basket full of Raleigh goods into the kitchen.

"My goodness, I'm glad to see you, Brother Schmidt," Grandma greeted him, genuinely pleased. It was not only that she did depend on a number of items that he peddled, but he was such a congenial source of the kind of news that seldom reached the newspapers. "I'm almost out of mustard ointment. Ellen here's been sick and I've about used up the last jar on her."

Ellen groaned at the thought of a fresh supply of the wicked medication, but was glad for some little change in the monotony of the day. She listened to the tidbits of gossip that Brother Schmidt tucked in with his sales talk as he showed Grandma the "specials" for the month writing down her order in his gray sales book, licking the stub of a pencil and spelling it out laboriously. Nobody could figure out how he supported a large family of children and his pudgy wife, who lived on a small, poor farm in the bottoms between Merritsville and Junction City, on what he made peddling salves, extracts, pills and lotions all over the county.

Somehow he managed; most people bought a little something from him. He was active in the church, too. He had musical and dramatic talents and directed the pageants, plays and many programs all over the whole stake. He was a most congenial and sympathetic man, able to communicate with all and any in spite of his thick accent. "Yah, Sister Perry, she don't go so good these days. I say to her, 'You ought to get out more and do tings to take your mind off your drubbles.' It's when we get all shut up inside ourselves that ve haf da most drubble, I say ... Yes, by the vay, yunk lady," he addressed himself to Ellen, "don't I see you mit that fine yunk man from Junction City, him vat run da feed store, Yah?"

"Yes," admitted Ellen, leaning forward with interest. "Ferrin Hallsworth."

"Yah, da Hallsworth boy, yah." Brother Schmidt nodded energetically. "Yah, you been so sick you don't see him dese past few days?"

"I haven't seen him for quite a while," Ellen said testily.

"Yah, maybe dats goot, you don't hear?"

Ellen shrugged. "I guess so. He just hasn't come over for a while. Busy I guess. We were just friends."

"Yah, vell, dat's so? It's like I hear dis morning dey got some kind of bad drubble wif the Hallsworth family, someding about da older brudders, maybe. I don't get da straight of it, qvite. I hear it in the drug store, a little, ven I stop dere. Some drubble wif da girl, the vild vun, you know?"

"What did you hear?" Ellen, agitated, moved to the end of the couch where she was closer to Brother Schmidt.

Brother Schmidt took his thick glasses off and wiped them on a grubby handkerchief. How sad his eyes looked, thought Ellen, how different when they were no longer concealed behind the thick magnifying glasses. He shook his head mournfully. "I don't tink I should say. I only hear dings just in liddle bits, so I don't know vat is true. Somebuddy vas shot it seems like. I don't know who, if it vas da girl or da boys or who, somevere like in Nevada, is it?"

"OH, no," Ellen gasped and clapped both her hands to her cheeks. Oh, no!" It couldn't be Ferrin; he wasn't involved with Simone, was he?

"Oh, my gootness," Brother Schmidt was genuinely alarmed. "I shouldn't bring such bad news ven I don't know it truly. I dink you hear it because you are vriends mit da younger boy. I dink maybe to learn from you. Oh my gootness!"

"Oh, it's all right," Ellen pacified him. "Maybe it will be on the radio. The news will come on soon." She leaped off the couch and started for the front room.

"Don't go in there and get chilled." Grandma jumped up in caution. "You might get a backset. Now you wait a bit and I'll build a little fire and then you can hear. Oh my land, that is too bad. Ferrin is such a nice boy. We have missed him comin' around." She looked meaningfully at Ellen who had not talked about it to her. "I do hope he ain't been hurt."

After Brother Schmidt had gathered up his samples in his basket and left, Grandma laid a fire in the front room stove. During the week she seldom made one in there to save fuel. She was going to have to get one of Dosey's boys to come and chop up some more of the old apple stumps in the orchard if it didn't warm up soon.

As soon as the room was warm, she and Ellen turned on the radio, twisting the dial nervously up and down to find a news broadcast. It was late in the afternoon when the calm, impersonal voice of the newscaster gave the sparse details. "Dudley Willard Hallsworth, son of Willard H. Hallsworth of Junction City, Utah, was shot and killed early today in a fight with his brother, Melvin O. Hallsworth at the Shady Haven Motel in Elko, Nevada. Details of the incident are not available at this time. With the victim at the time of the shooting was his bride of a few days, Simone Hamilton Hallsworth. We will have more details later."

Ellen gave a strangled cry. Goose pimples covered her whole

body; she felt cold and frightened. She wished desperately that she could reach Ferrin, do something for him, see how he was taking it. Another part of her was glad that she was this distance from it. In spite of herself, she could not get it out of her mind. Memories kept playing over and over. In the background was the carnival at which she had first met them last summer. She could hear the shrill, harsh, false music and Simone's wild laughter, her wicked taunting pleasure in putting the two strong, hot-blooded men at each other's throats. By why had she chosen Dod over Med? Did she have any real feeling for either of them? Tormented by such questions, she was eager to see Ferrin again. She didn't have long to wait. Toward dusk the pick up truck drew up in front of the gate, and Ferrin shuffled slowly up the path, his head down, a glowing cigarette dangling from his hand.

Ellen saw him from behind the plants and the lace curtain in the front window. She was thrown into a panic. Around her throat was the thick, crumpled flannel rag; her hair was tangled and greasy feeling, and she was wearing a faded, warm old bathrobe of Grandma's that made her look like a moth-eaten rag-bag. She leaped out of the rocker, ran into her bedroom and sent Grandma to the door. When she returned to the room, a little neater looking but nervous, Ferrin was sitting by the stove, a stricken half apologetic look on his face. "I know you didn't want to see me, Ellen, especially not now, but I just...didn't...know where else to go."

Ellen felt a surge of warmth and pity toward him. She held out her hand to him. "I'm glad you came, Ferrin. We, I, did want to see you. I've missed you a lot and we're terribly sorry about ...it."

Grandma had already welcomed him warmly and was fixing him a bite to eat in the kitchen. While he nibbled at the home-made bread and jam and drank the hot cocoa that she had fixed him, he told them, haltingly, what he knew of the fracas. A few days before, Dod and Simone had just disappeared, taking the big car. Med, of course, went into a frenzy. When they did not return for two days and nights, he had jumped into the big cattle truck and started out. How he found out where they were, Ferrin had no idea. He had tracked them into Nevada and learned that Dod and Simone had been married there. He supposed they had just got in a fight and that was that.

Ferrin did not seem surprised that it happened or to feel very sorry. It was as though he were dazed, but there was something of the satisfaction of a prophet in his dark face as he said. "It was bound to happen with that b ... I mean witch there. I expected some kind of mess but not this." He pinched the last crumbs of his bread and jam around the plate grimly.

"But what made her choose Dod? When I saw her and from what you said, she didn't care more for one than the other."

"Only thing I can figger out is that she got bored and wanted to stir up some excitement, or she figgered she could get more money out of us. Last week she said she was sick and tired of sittin' around out there or just goin' into town and doin' the same old things. She and them was quarreling because she threatened to go away alone, said she had some friends in Reno she wanted to see. Dad said that he didn't want the boys to go away right then and leave him with the lambing. He said one of 'em could go for a few days but not both." Ferrin stared at the floor a long time.

"I guess Dod decided since he was the oldest, he'd just take it on himself and take her away. But he shoulda known that Med would go crazy."

Ferrin dropped his head into his hands and sat silently. The dim light from the shaded electric globe spilled a sad yellow light over the waves in his hair. Ellen reached out and touched him tentatively. He looked up at her, tears shining in his eyes.   " I shouldna come, Ellen. You don't wanna be mixed up with a family that has criminals in it as well as cripples." Ellen winced.

"I'm sorry," she whispered. "I'm sorry about last time you were here. I was just feeling mean, I guess. I'm glad you came tonight."

"There ain't, ... isn't nobody else I can talk to," he whispered huskily. "There's only Dad, 'n I don't think he'll be fit to live with now. He needed the boys and was proud of 'em. He had things all planned for 'em and now she's got both of 'em."

Ellen was paralyzed with pity and fear and a whole mixture of emotions so intense and disturbing that she didn't know what to say or do. It was Grandma who came to their rescue.

"It ain't your fault, Ferrin," Grandma spoke up firmly. "You don't need to be afraid that we'll turn our back on you when you need us. We'll let the Lord and the law do the judgin', and we'll stick by them we love."

Ferrin gave her of look of deep gratitude, his face distorted with so much emotion that Ellen could not bear to look at it. She turned her face away. The least little shadow of misgiving flitted across her heart when Grandma said "those *we* love." She was deeply glad that Ferrin had come, glad that they could help and share his suffering, but she feared that her sympathy would be misunderstood. She was not in love with him. She didn't know exactly what it was that she wanted to feel for him other than she did but she knew enough, being woman, that the ultimate feeling wasn't there. There was nothing to do about it. They were bonded deeper by this tragedy.

They sat, holding hands on the davenport until the fire died down in the stove. When Ferrin offered to go get some more coal, Ellen had to explain they didn't have anymore. Very reluctantly and with promise to come the next day or let her know what was taking place, Ferrin left. The next day the coal truck from Hallsworth Feed, Lumber and Hardware store dumped a ton of coal in Grandma's back yard.

ᑕᗷ

Ferrin asked Ellen if she would come with him to the graveside services for Dod. He said he needed her. Since her cold was much better and since the services would be short, Grandma thought that it would be alright if she wrapped up warmly. Later she wished she had never gone.

It was a cloudy, chilly Saturday afternoon. There had been spells of cold sleet, but now these had passed leaving everything sodden. The taupe colored clouds boiled across the sky, letting patches of thick, yellowish light fall on the barren rolling hills where Dod was to be buried. The small family cemetery was at the far edge of the ranch enclosed by an ornate black fence. There were only about a dozen graves, some marked with peaked wooden markers dark gray from the recent moisture, their names and dates fading. One large granite stone reared above the grave of Ferrin's mother. To the right of it were the heaps of raw, sticky clay and between them, on the heavy supporting bands of the undertaking apparatus, stood the pale gray metal coffin. A wreath of stiff-looking red and white flowers lay on the cover.

Ellen's stomach constricted to a hard, gray knot as she walked slowly beside Ferrin to the far side of the grave. It wasn't until they had taken their place that Ellen composed herself and looked warily about. Near the head of the grave on the other side stood Willard Hallsworth wearing an old fashioned black suit that made him look much older but no less formidable. His graying hair was uncovered and his face set grimly; he held his Stetson stiffly in front of him. Clinging to his arm, her face framed by the heavy fur of an elegant black coat, was Simone–the widow–thought Ellen with a shock as though she had not expected to find her here.

How on earth could she fill that solemn role? But what was worse, how could Mr. Hallsworth bear her clinging to him like that? He seemed almost proud, to accept it as though it were perfectly natural. Simone gave Ellen a little wave of her hand with its bright red nails. Ellen noted, as she returned the gesture with a tight smile, that Simone was more beautiful than ever with her long lashed dark eyes sparkling in the wan sunlight, her full scarlet lips and lustrous curling hair. She appeared to have no remorse; her expression was one of defiant triumph. That was something Ellen had never been able to understand about her. She appeared to have no sense of right and wrong, no awareness of the mischief she caused all about her. Ellen's throat constricted with a spasm of hatred and fear; she turned away so she didn't have to look at her directly but, out of the corner of her eye, she saw Simone snuggle a little closer to Willard. The power she had over men awed Ellen.

Ellen's eyes swept around the small crowd–mostly rancher friends and their wives standing in small, uneasy knots, talking in distressed undertones. A heavy man, bareheaded but with his overcoat turned up around his neck, stood near the head of the open grave. He began to speak in a low, firm tone and gradually the murmur of talk subsided. Ellen heard the flow of familiar funeral words, only very greatly abridged for this bitter, tragic occasion. There was so little to say about the tall young man who lay in that gray box. When the man, a Mormon bishop from Junction City, had finished, three sober-faced young men stepped forward and sang a mournful song. Something Ellen had read recently slipped into her mind. Oh yes, it was in the book Everett had sent her for Christmas: "When I am dead my dearest, sing no sad songs for me...." Did it matter?

One of the young men remained standing by the grave after the notes of the song had fallen into the sodden grasses; he lowered his head and said a short prayer, closing the services and dedicating the grave. There was a ripple of "Amens" and a loud sob from a dark clad woman standing behind Willard Hallsworth, an aunt or someone.

Ellen had had extreme difficulty standing still even in that short time and finding a place to look away from the searing scene. Once or twice she glanced at Ferrin. His face was set in a grim mask of anger, sorrow, fear; it was hard to tell which. The muscles of his jaw were twitching nervously. He held her arm as though he would crush it. Finally she looked up into the sky. The ragged clouds were scudding across toward the far eastern mountains; patches of deep blue were showing through. The afternoon light, when it escaped like a sharp blade from the cloud edges, chiseled out every feature, every blade of grass; every detail of the miserable scene was etched sharply on her mind and heart. She wanted to flee. What was she doing here anyway? She wasn't a member of this wretched family.

A feeling of panic swept over her at the idea of her and Simone belonging to the same family, sisters-in-law! They could both be Hallsworths. Eventually both of them could be brought here to lie side by side in this heavy cold earth with no difference between them. Simone was already Mrs. Dudley Willard Hallsworth by Nevada law. If things kept going the way they were she would be Mrs. Ferrin Hallsworth. She was almost overcome by the thought.

The undertakers were busy now lowering the coffin. With an unbearably slow, even motion it sank down out of sight. Ellen could not take her eyes off it much as she wished to. Only a few days ago a strong, healthy young body, pulsing with life now sinking into the clammy yellow clay to lie here forever among gray pebbles and brownish yellow cheat grass, under snow, under rain, under the blistering sun of these bleak, rolling desert hills. She could almost feel the weight of that wet clay on her chest as she heard the thudding of the first shovelful of earth on the coffin top.

She plucked at Ferrin's sleeve. She was shivering all over, afraid that she might be taking sick again. "Let's go, I'm freezing," she whispered miserably. At that moment Ferrin had to disengage his hand from her arm to shake hands with several people. Ellen started away, glancing back only once to see the silhouette of Simone against the sky, the light breeze ruffling the fur on her coat collar and her dark hair. The pale light made a strange aureole of light all about her–a black angel–Ellen thought, guarding the grave of the man she had killed. As Ellen picked her way down the rutted road, she wondered whatever made such a strange thing come into her mind.

She noticed to her surprise that there were number of cars lining the narrow road below. Reporters, she guessed. They were blocked from coming up the short trail to the burial lot by two police cars. Two men with cameras were climbing the hill; they glanced at her shortly as she passed, but apparently decided she was of no interest. She stopped and looked after them feeling angry and sick. Big, black, sticky letters flashed before her eyes: MURDERED MAN BURIED, FAMILY MOURNS, YOUNG WIDOW SAYS... But Simone would love it! All this attention and sensationalism. Another morbid picture flashed into her mind– a small fidgety, dark haired child enjoying the bitter limelight of a funeral–that of her brother Robert Lee so long ago.

Ellen stumbled on down the path, "Why am I here? Get me out of this," she prayed. No matter what she did, Simone was always intruding in her life, always drawing her into a vortex of evil. Was there no way to get away from her? As she reached the car and stood waiting for Ferrin, she looked out over the broad valley, miles and miles across to the blue barrier of the Rocky Mountains where Timpanogos gleamed blue-white. The clouds had rolled away once more, the sun had come out, and a little bird sang somewhere in the fields. There was the fragrance of spring in the air.

"Dear God," thought Ellen in despair. "You confuse me so with all this sudden shifting of light, all these changing shadows and colors. The bleak, irreversible fact of death up here and out there the soft, innocent stirring of life, of spring, new things. How will I ever be able to know what is truth, what is real? How can I have a calm heart and steady faith in such a country, such a climate?" She huddled in the car, watching Ferrin hobble down the hill toward her. "Especially how can I know what I feel about him? A line from a poem that Mr. Gillis had been reading to them drifted through her mind–"Pity me that the heart is slow to learn...."

She had to know what she felt about him soon because Ferrin moved lock, stock and almost barrel into her life in the next few weeks. He picked her up at school or the library and came practically every night, bringing groceries and things he thought they needed. He ate meals with them and helped Grandma around the house and yard. Feeling sorry for him, Ellen had been more affectionate; he thrived on it like a starved, beaten creature. She felt she was being closed in from all sides–at school she enjoyed a kind of perverse glamor from being associated with the most sensational event of the year in the whole county.

As she had expected, the papers were full of pictures of Simone in the "tragic widow" pose. There were ugly pictures of Dod and Med, even Ferrin and the old man. The place of the crime was marked out with circles and arrows. It was called the "Tragic Love Triangle." Love triangle! Ferrin had snorted–it was more a hate triangle. Ferrin reported frequently on the progress of the trial which was fortunately short. Med had put up no defense although his attorney established that there had been a fight in which the shot might have been accidental or self-defense.

When questioned Med had said sullenly that he didn't know whether he had gone after the two with the intent of killing his brother and her or just what. He had been crazy mad at being double-crossed. He didn't think he intended to kill Dod "in cold blood." He had intended to scare him and get things settled between them. When he found they had been settled to the extent of a marriage, he must have lost his mind.

There were certain cross currents of sympathy for Med in the jury and community, especially when they looked at Simone, her beautiful silk-clad legs exposed even though the skirt fashions were longish, her arrogant dark head with those flashing black eyes as seductive as a snake. It was easy to see, some otherwise sober citizens thought secretly, how a young man could go off his head about her. She posed and preened and flirted with all the men. It was noted that her father-in-law, grim of face and tired looking, was always quite near her. Ferrin said he hated them all, thought they were all guilty, even his dad for allowing Simone to hang around there like she did and hoped they'd all get punished. He only wished Simone would get what she deserved. She was the real killer.

They were sitting in the front room after dinner; Grandma was crocheting, Ellen was reviewing her debate cards for an upcoming tournament. Newspapers that Ferrin had brought were scattered about. At the top of one in gruesome black letters was the grim pronunciation: KILLER GETS TEN YEARS TO LIFE. Underneath was the picture of Med between two officers. In the shadowy background could be seen the figures of Simone and Willard Hallsworth. Ferrin was staring at it fixedly with a black look on his face. From time to time he would shake his head as though is bewilderment and despair. It was hard to realize what had happened.

Ellen put her cards in the file. She came over and stared at the picture with him. "What d'you think she'll do now? she asked indicating the shadow with her finger tip.

"I don't know," Ferrin sighed morosely. "It looks like she'll just stick around with us. She's Dod's wife...widow...and entitled to his share of the property the lawyer says. She's already asked for his horses and the car. Dad sure acts funny. He acts like it's all right with him, like she has all those rights. She just seems to take it for granted that it's her home. I'll tell you one thing," he clenched his fists and tightened his lips grimly. "If she stays around there, I won't."

"But she wouldn't stay out there all alone with your father in that lonesome house, I don't think," Ellen reasoned. "She's gotta have crowds and excitement, people to torment."

"Yeah, I know," Ferrin replied, his forehead wrinkling. "But she's funny. Sometimes she acts like a little lost kid. She's gotta have somebody to stick to, somewhere to go like all of us. Nobody knows where her family is. Sometimes I see her looking kinda sad and lonely. Course, she soon gets up and goes off on a tare."

They settled into an unhappy silence and, after a few minutes, Ferrin suggested they go out for a drive and a root beer. When they came back, they sat in the car for a while. Ellen let Ferrin kiss her several times. Each time he did, she prayed fervently, 'Let something happen, let me feel something real.' Although she had never kissed any other boy, she knew there was something not quite right in the way he kissed her with his lips closed, dry and as though he were half afraid. She could sense that he probably wanted to do more, but he held her as though she were something breakable.

She couldn't think what more she wanted him to do. There was an urgent pressure in her breasts and crotch, yet she knew Ferrin would never touch her there likely until after they were married. Of course, she didn't want to go too far, but she had no idea of how far was too far. On the few times they had been double dating with Ken and Lorraine, those two had sat pressed together making disgusting noises and shuffling about in the back seat for long times while she and Ferrin would just sit in the front with their arms about each other, aching.

What was it she wanted? It was certainly something Ferrin couldn't or didn't know how to give her. He treated her with such respect; She supposed that was the right way but it left her feeling so cold, frustrated she could scream. Tonight when he helped her out of the car, she wished she wouldn't see him for a while. She had an impulse to break and run away from him as she measured her steps to his crippled gait up the walk. As he pressed his childish kiss on her lips at the door, she wanted to bite him. All she could do was say, "Good night, Ferrin, see you soon."

As she went into the kitchen, Grandma was laying out the kindling for the morning fire, neatly on the apron of the stove with wadded up newspapers. Her gray hair was hanging in a braid down her back over her old flannel gown and she looked so shrunken, sad and old. She had taken her false teeth, out and her chin almost met the tip of her nose. she looked like a kindly old spirit from a story book performing magic rituals. Ellen wanted to talk to her, to ask her what "Love" was, to try to find out what it was that she felt that she wanted from Ferrin that she couldn't get, why she couldn't feel what she wanted to.

But there seemed to be an unbridgeable gap between them. It was so long since Grandma had thought anything about the kinds of things that bothered Ellen. She was sure that Grandma would think that the way Ferrin treated her was exactly the right way. Ferrin was simply old-fashioned, he was gentlemanly. Once she heard Grandma say that Grandpa had never kissed her until they were engaged. Ellen supposed her mother wouldn't be much more help. She thought she might venture just one question.

"Grandma," she said, slumping into a chair. "How do you know if you're in love?"

Addie looked up in surprise. "Why child, it's different for different people, I guess. Do you think you're in love?

"That's what I can't tell. Aren't there ways...."

Grandma hesitated. "Well, I guess it's the feeling about the person that he's the one you want to live and be with forever. You want to help him, share everything with him, troubles and joys. Your Grandpa and me seldom had a cross word; we had our differences but we always got over them because we wanted to be together for all eternity and I never saw anybody else I wanted to be with that way." She sat down by the table, clasping her hands nervously.

Ellen sighed. "Eternity" stood out in her mind like those monotonous rolling yellow hills where they had buried Dod, going on and on, compounding loneliness so vast that it staggered one. This old talk everybody in the church came up with when she wanted to know something seemed like the cheat grasses on those stretching hills, to cover everything with the same suffocating mantle. The picture of her and Ferrin locked there in that boring wilderness appalled her. "I guess that I don't love Ferrin, then, in that way."

"Sometimes you can learn to love a person who is good and kind and decent," Grandma said. "I shouldn't worry about it. It'll work itself out if you pray about it. If it's meant to be, it'll turn out alright."

"But Ferrin thinks...." Ellen began and then hesitated. She wasn't exactly sure what Ferrin thought. "Well he acts like he's one of the family. He's just moved in and I don't want to hurt him. He's had such a bad life and he is good and kind and decent. But, Grandma, I don't think I can learn to love him the way I want to ."

"Well, don't fret about it, Ellen. Just pray for guidance." Addie was feeling nervous and distressed about Ellen. She had often of late glimpsed her inner turmoil. Like all good parents and grand-parents, she wanted to protect her from hurt but how could she do that? It seemed like everyone had to learn the hard way. She, too, had noticed Ferrin's devotion, his attachment to them and understood how necessary they were to him as he tried to find some anchor in his turbulent world. She was glad to be there for him, but not if he hurt Ellen too much. Prayer was her only re-course. "Sometimes I don't think I understand God very well," Ellen said in a low, tight voice.

"Perhaps none of us do." Grandma sighed, jarred by the stub-born look that settled around Ellen's mouth. "Sometimes we pray for something we're not supposed to have. It's best just to pray for guidance and help with your problems. It seems to me that there's always love to spare if you look for it in the right places. Right now we've got love to spare for Ferrin, ain't we?"

She reached out and patted Ellen's unhappy face. "Let's go to bed now. Things'll look better in the mornin'"

Grandma was always like that–looking on the bright side. Things didn't always look better in the morning; sometimes they look worse. There was no use arguing with her though; they were both tired.

Oddly enough, things did look better the next morning. Spring had been sneaking in and out of Merritsville for several weeks, and by the end of April, had decided to make camp for a while. It was a sparkling blue-green morning with trees breaking into bud and spring flowers embroidering the ditch banks. The lawn was a solid gold mass of dandelions and the wary old crab apple tree had that faint pinkish flush that announced its intention of put-ting out the extravagant white lace of its bloom once again.

Ellen felt like dancing all the way to school, full of the exhila-ration of springtime that filled young veins with dreams, desires, plans, hopes, all the wildly foolish and beautiful things that com-pensate the young for being young. Except for a few tender April showers, the weather stayed beautiful for the next two weeks. How entrancing, absolutely beautiful this mountain country could be.

She was in unusually high spirits those weeks. Ferrin had never seen her so bubbling and happy, and it cheered him to be with her. She, herself, was unable to account for the change of mood after the dark days they had gone through. Maybe it was the knowledge that she was nearing the end of her school days and would soon be able to leave all the troublesome things of these past ten years behind. Whatever it was, the feeling that all was going to be well, that life and love and all the right things would come to her, persisted.

The sour news that Ferrin brought one evening as he picked her up at the library disturbed the climate of her joyousness slightly. He was sitting in his new car, a neat green Dodge, when Ellen came out. He had had to get a new car because Simone had taken over the big one and drove it about the county at maniacal speeds, reveling in her affluent widowhood. It was just coming dusk as Ellen came out and got into the car. Even in the pale spring-greenish light, she could see anger and pain in his face.

"You have to go right home?" he asked in a tight, strained voice.

"No, I guess not, why?" Ellen was puzzled.

"Just feel like drivin' and talkin' if you don't mind." Ferrin started the car and stepped on the gas vehemently, the engine roared and they squealed away from the curb. It wasn't like him at all. There was something very wrong. He drove very fast, taking the road that dipped down through the farmlands toward the lake.

"Hey, what's the matter?" Ellen asked after she had been jolted about for half an hour. "Where are you going anyway?"

"I dunno, I don't much care," he said sullenly, drawing the car into a grassy spot beneath some tall, black walnut trees. It was near an abandoned resort. The grasses and weeds had grown all through the cement foundations and what was left of a once happy play-spot of the twenties. The lake had receded but it could be seen shining far out through the screen of trees.

Ferrin turned in his seat, facing her. She could see a bruise on his cheek. She put out her hand to touch it but drew it back when she saw Ferrin wince and shiver. "Whatever did you do?" she asked. He put his hand to his cheek as though to ward off another blow.

"He hit me," he said fiercely, deep hatred in his voice.

"Who?" Ellen asked, puzzled and nervous.

"Him, my dad," he spat the word out as though it was nasty in his mouth.

"What for?"

Ferrin choked, "I can't, ...I shouldn't tell you. I ...ought to kill them."

"Who's them?"

"Him and her," Ferrin was having the greatest difficulty squeezing the words out. Ellen guessed, rightly, that it was Simone and Ferrin's father.

"Well, what about them?" Ellen was curious.

"I don't know if I can tell you, Ellen; I don't think that awful girl ought to be mentioned in your presence, in the presence of a decent girl. she, she ... you ought not even to be in the same world." Ferrin shook his head in agony.

"Well, if you're not going to tell me..." Ellen spread her hands in exasperation.

There was silence for a moment. Ferrin traced the pattern of the seat upholstery with his fingers; at last he said without looking up, "I've moved out, anyway, but I've decided I'm not givin' in. She's not gonna end up gettin' everything we've worked and slaved for on that ranch. That old bug ... I mean that old man has strapped us right down to that place all our lives, made us work like the devil on it and I'm not givin' it up to no tramp like her."

"What do you mean?" Ellen leaned forward anxiously.

Ferrin made a fist of his hand and pounded the steering wheel fiercely. "If he marries her, I've a notion to shoot him, too."

"If he marries her!" Ellen was aghast. "Whatever makes you think...."

"And if he don't, he ought to, the old...the old...." Ferrin's voice quivered.

Gradually with the soft spring night falling around them, Ellen got the horrid tale out of him in fragments. Simone had got the old man almost under her scarlet enameled thumbnail. She had been getting anything she wanted out of him. Ferrin had been furious but had to admit that legally she did have claim of Dod's share. Ferrin would have been willing to have given her a generous settlement and get rid of her. But it became more and more apparent that Willard Hallsworth didn't want to get rid of her; in fact little hints indicated that that was one of her chief weapons– when all else failed, she threatened to run off.

Ferrin could have put up with all that, but last night when he had come home later than usual, he had caught Willard coming out of Simone's room. Simone had taken one of the large upstairs bedrooms when she moved in with them, and there was his dad coming out of it with only his pants on and them not buttoned up. Ferrin had confronted his father at the foot of the stairs, had called him some bad names. Simone had come running out stark naked except for a man's shirt tossed over her shoulders.

Willard had hit Ferrin across the face and taunted him about being a cripple, said all he had left now was half a man. He said that if his sons had had half the spunk and guts that Simone had they would all be better off. He said he and she would do as they damned well pleased.

When he finished the disconnected, painful account, Ferrin was sobbing, choking, heart-broken sobs. Ellen moved over and put her arms around him, pulling him to her and stroking his hair gently. She felt almost motherly; it was the first time she had seen his total, vulnerable shattered weakness. When he got hold of himself, he straightened up, looking away dejectedly. "I guess I'm not really a man or I wouldn't blubber like this. I wouldn't let 'em get me. I'd go over there and kill both of 'em."

"Don't you think there's been enough killing in the Hallsworth family for one year? Ellen asked gently. "Do you think it solves things?"

"You know, I didn't used to think so. I thought things could be talked out and worked out. I thought if you tried to reason things out and lived as honest as you could that somehow things would come out all right." Ferrin was calmer now but he was holding her hand so tight it hurt.

"But now I see that there is a kind of person you can't deal with that way. It's kill or be killed. I can see that it was men like my father prospered in this country; if you don't play that way you don't count—you're not a man. I can see what he meant about Simone bein' more like the sons he wanted. She takes what she wants when she wants it. She's tough and hard and don't worry about nobody but herself. In a way she don't even worry about that. I've seen her thrown off that horse Dad gave her last fall, get up like a man without sheddin' a tear and get back on determined to get the upper hand. She's the only one I ever seen face Dad down, and she does it just the way I've seen him face the other ranchers and people down when he wanted something. I can't explain it exactly but none of us boys could ever do it. We thought he would have killed us. When he said 'jump,' we asked 'how high?'"

His voice faltered and he stared out of the windshield for a few minutes. His voice was low and hurt. "But, my God, I never thought he wasn't decent. I never thought he was a fool."

That was the worst of it, thought Ellen, the hardest thing for him, because, in spite of everything else, the hatred he felt for his father and brothers, he had been proud of their power, of his dad's granite strength and integrity. Now, like herself, he was fatherless without any supporting vision.

"I'm sorry, Ferrin," she said in a low voice.

"Oh, Ellen," he squeezed her hand even tighter. "I'm sorry I told you all this ... dirty stuff. You are so far above and pure and beautiful I hate to have you mixed up in all this. Ellen, I worship you."

Ellen felt the chill that she had felt so many times before when Ferrin began to expose his feelings for her. She tried to head him off.

"Oh, I'm not all that good," she demurred. "I knew Simone a long time before you did, and I knew some of the bad things about her. I'm not so dumb as all that and, Ferrin, I don't want to be worshipped.! I'm really bad in some ways."

"Oh, no," Ferrin drew her to him roughly. "No, you're the most wonderful girl in the whole world. I don't feel half good enough for you. I feel like I ought not to even touch you when I have been mixed up with so many foul things. Ellen, how could a fellow ask a girl like you to be part of a family like mine?"

Ellen had drawn gently away and was looking out the window. Her heart was beating hard, more from fright than any other emotion. "I guess it wouldn't matter if she loved ... liked you enough for yourself." She knew immediately that she had said the wrong thing, the worst thing she could have possibly said.

છ

Walking to school this radiant spring morning, Ellen thought of Pippa in Browning's poem, "God's in his heaven–All's right

with the world." Wild roses bloomed along the fences and hawthorn and choke cherry bushes were loaded with white lace. At
the bend in the road, she stopped under a Russian Olive tree and
inhaled its sweetish musty perfume, picking a few leaves. The
smell of Russian Olive trees would always mean spring. But all
was not exactly well. There was Ferrin.

She had almost stumbled into saying that she would marry
Ferrin; part of her had begun to have a fatalistic attitude about it.
Maybe she would marry him. What else was there to do? She
sensed that her mother was not going to be able to put her through
college even though she half promised. If she went to the University of Utah she would have to live with Irene and Ed. For some
reason or other she thought that would be impossible. Not that
she disliked Ed; it was just that she didn't seem to fit into their
lives. She didn't want to go to the BYU where a few of the other
kids were planning to go.

Mr. Gillis wanted her to go to college, said he would help get
her a scholarship, but she had been doing some research and found
that there was a great many more expenses than tuition. It was
hard to get a job that paid very much. Suddenly the problems
loomed thick and black. Ferrin might be the best answer; no matter how she figured it, he spelled security with a capital "S."

In spite of Simone, he would be running the Hallsworth outfit
in a few years with Med in prison and Willard having to rely on
him more and more. Ferrin was very very sharp about many things
she had discovered. He and his dad had had a reckoning after that
horrid revelation, and Willard had assured him that he had no
intention of letting Simone take the ranch or any part of it away
from him and his sons. Med would still be a young man when he
got out of prison; with good behavior perhaps he wouldn't have
to serve more than the five or ten years. The ranch must stay in
the Hallsworth name and hands.

Ferrin had moved out of the big house, however, and fixed
himself a neat apartment over the Feed Store. Because of his legs
he would not have to go in the army as it appeared many boys
would have to. There was constant talk of war and a draft. If she
married Ferrin, she would never want for anything as Lorraine
assured her. She would have a full house, not just a basement, a
car and lots of money. It was an attractive prospect in some ways

if only Ellen could block off a very large part of her, deny her yearnings for more education, experience, accomplishments. Perhaps Ferrin would let her do her writing. He always said he only wanted to make her happy, yet she wasn't quite sure that he knew what would make her the happiest. She had held back a great many things from him; things that had to do with her mind more than her heart.

She had begun to see, through her reading, that a woman was often split in the ways that men perceived her. Hal had looked at her only as a body, a physical being that answered his physical needs; Ferrin looked at her as an ideal, a guiding star. No man had seemed to care about her mind unless it was Everett. There was a sharp pain under her heart when she thought of him. She stopped under the big pines in front of Bishop Bodily's house. Where was he? Why hadn't he even written to her? Had he forgotten or was he so lost or sick that he couldn't? She was overcome with such longing for him that she could scarcely walk on. But was it possible for an older man and a young girl to be together? Horrified she thought of Willard Hallsworth and Simone. The idea repelled her but then, Everett was different. She sighed deeply and profoundly. How could one's thoughts get from the bright beauty of wild roses to these tormented ones.

She looked up the street that climbed the hill to the big, old red high school that she would soon be leaving. She thought she had been so confined and unhappy there, but now, at this moment, she wished she could stay forever. How safe and familiar it looked. What a sanctuary from all the disturbing problems that loomed on the horizon.

As she walked on slowly, Virginia and Celia over took her. She was glad of their noisy company. So many things that troubled her never seemed to faze them. The end and all of their being was to get "a man," almost any man would do so they could slip comfortably into the pattern and settle down without thinking about or encountering much outside of life in the Kingdom, in the shadow of these great blue-green-sparkling mountains.

"I wonder who's gonna get to be Valedictorian this year?" Virginia said. "They're gonna decide it today, I heard. Not me for sure." They had struck up a conversation about the approaching graduation.

"Oh probably Ellen," shrugged Celia. "She's the smartest girl in the school, the smartest person."

"Don't you remember, we're not having Valedictorians anymore," Ellen reminded them. "We're having 'Representative Girl and Boy.' I'm not 'representative' because I don't do good in gym, can't play volleyball."

The girls laughed. "Well, anyway, you ought to be something, you're so smart," Celia said generously. "Gee, I wish I had your brains, only boys don't like brains in girls and I like boys too much. The trouble with you, Ellen is either you don't like boys or you don't try to hide your brains from them."

Ellen nodded her head in agreement. "I guess it's a little of both," she admitted.

"Yeah, but she's got Ferrin Hallsworth," Virginia put in. "He don't seem to mind your brains, does he?"

Ellen was suddenly angry. "I don't really care what he minds and I haven't got him and he hasn't got me!"

"Oh, don't be so touchy," Virginia admonished, tossing her carroty hair. "I'd be proud if I had him; I don't care what they say about his family. He's gonna be the richest man in this county by far, and I'm gonna marry for money when I marry. It's the only thing that lasts from what I can tell."

Ellen looked at her companions with despair and disgust. Would they never understand her? Would she never understand them? It gave her such a helpless, hopeless feeling.

The faculty of Merritsville High was meeting to decide–among other things, the student or students who were to perform at the graduation exercises as "representative" boy and girl. It was a difficult task since the term "valedictorian" had been abolished as being too old fashioned and undemocratic. The criterion of distinguished scholarship was no longer the important one–leadership, citizenship, personality, popularity and athletic ability all had to be taken into consideration now.

At this hour of the spring afternoon, the weary teachers, each with a dozen other things pressing on their minds and with no less urgent desire than the kids to be out of the chalky, oily, dusty confines of the classroom into the spring air, brought little enthusiasm to the task.

"Read the list," Miss Wardle, the home economics teacher said to the principal crisply. She was anxious to get home and set out some petunia plants. Five girls and five boys had been selected. Ellen's name was among them.

When Principal Bingham had spluttered out the list, there was a silence in which each of the faculty looked nervously at the others, hoping that some one would relieve them of making a decision. Mr. Gillis snuffled his sinuses loudly and cleared his throat. "My vote for the girl is Ellen Kent. She's got the best scholastic record, the best mind of anybody in the senior class and she's a good, clear speaker."

There were several nods of agreement, but Miss Wardle spoke out in a truculent voice. "Well, that may be so but I don't think Ellen can truly be called a 'representative girl.' She didn't distinguish herself in my area."

There was a slight murmur among the more bored and uncommitted members.

"That's true," boomed Miss McDonald in the same strident military tone that always reached the far corners of the gymnasium. "She's not what you call well-rounded."

Mr. Gillis knew he had made a mistake by leading out with Ellen's name; he should, after all these years of experience with collective school teachers, have let them exhaust their rhetoric on some other unfortunate candidate then pushed the crucial one through at the time when confusion and fatigue made them anxious to be done with it. He thought dejectedly that it was true that Ellen was not representative of Merritsville High or Merritsville. She was not ordinary enough. She refused the patterning of both Miss Wardle and Miss McDonald.

"As a matter of fact, although I know I have already been overruled in the matter, I protest this 'representative' thing again. In an educational institution scholarship should have the highest priority." He smacked the table loudly with the palm of his hand.

"Yes, that's true, Charlie," interposed Principal Bingham, the spittle wobbling nervously on his lips, "but we must remember there are other things in life to be considered as important."

"I agree, I agree." Mr. Gillis knew that he was getting too worked up about this thing again. "But there are other agencies and places for consideration and honoring of these other things.

If we don't honor intellectual achievement above all other things in a school, who else will? God know it has little enough force in our life as it is. This, Ladies and Gentlemen, it what our work all about or should be–the training and expanding of the mind."

He looked around at the group; from the varying expressions on their faces he could see that some were in mild agreement, others unconcerned, some downright hostile but one and all anxious to get on with it. He felt that he was separated from his colleagues by a thick sheet of plate glass through which his words would not penetrate. The trend in education now was to "help the child adjust to life and not develop the mind so that it overwhelmed the rest of the personality." This was what the public wanted–the adjusted person. It had been hard enough to hold a job in the schools these precarious years without bucking the public and the system.

The very thing that was the core and center of his, Charles Gillis' Life–the perpetuation and stimulation of ideas, the transferring to the young of the rich heritage of Western civilization, was negated by everything outside the school and was now being further reduced in importance inside it. A few others, the history, science and math teacher, saw his point.

Mr. Dobbie the science teacher, cleared his throat. "I must say that I agree with Charles on the ...uh...one point, but...the scholarship honors might be separated from the others...." He waved his hands in the air and grew red in the face. "

"Representative honors," interposed Miss Wardle impatiently.

"Yes, uh, yes," he nodded gratefully to her, "yes, the representative honors, now if they could be distinguished apart in some way...now wouldn't that solve...?

Everyone shuddered when Mr. Dobbie got started in a faculty meeting. Mr. Gillis stepped in firmly. "Well, perhaps they needn't be separated but I still think *scholarship* should be emphasized. It isn't that I don't think the fry cook and the garage mechanic are as important to the scheme of things as I am, maybe more so, and the accomplished athlete is surely to be recognized. I'm all for the sound mind in sound body theory, but all this other stuff like popularity, my dear colleagues, aren't we cutting the ground from under our very feet, denigrating our very *raison d'etre*, apologizing for the very thing that most of us have devoted our lives to when we subordinate the disciplining and training of the mind to the cutting of crepe paper, cheer leading, club attending ...?"

"Oh, Chuck," admonished one of the other English teachers, Pauline Bushman, "aren't you making a little too much out of this thing? I don't think we're in any special danger of becoming either more important or less with the great American public. 'Representative,' 'Valedictorian,' What does it matter? They don't know the difference. They're just words after all. All they care is that we keep their kids out of their hair so long as possible, keep 'em off the streets. All these kids on this list have good academic records."

Gillis glared at Pauline and then dropped his hands helplessly on the table. "Well, if it doesn't really matter why don't we just say eeny, meeny, miny, moe and be done with it? The kids know the difference, and it will make a big difference to the ones who are chosen, won't it?" He was thinking that it might help make up to Ellen for the deprivations and humiliations of these past years.

"Let's get on with the business," interrupted Miss Wardle. "I've got work to do." She knew the men could go on wrangling like this until the cows came home.

"As Pauline says, all the students selected have high scholastic records. As a matter of fact, Miss Kent's record isn't all that much better than Marcia Davenport's." She pushed the records belligerently under Mr. Gillis' nose. He noted a dotting of C's among the majority of straight A's on Ellen's transcript, then smiled wryly. They were mostly in sewing, cooking and phys. ed. with one in the first year of typing. Marcia had more B's in the hard subjects. The records, would average out pretty evenly, yet every teacher in the room knew that there was a wide difference in the quality of intelligence of the two girls. Marcia was diligent, capable, amiable and the kind of good conscientious student that forced an A out of a teacher when he or she knew that the subject had scarcely penetrated beyond the outer layer of her consciousness. She would never be able to think deeply or creatively. But wasn't that what was wanted in this society?

"Marcia got the most votes on the student poll, too." put in Miss McDonald. "She's certainly a fine all around student and person."

Looks neat in a gym suit, too, Mr. Gillis thought wickedly.

There was a general murmur of assent. Mr. Gillis sat back, feeling very tired and empty. Perhaps he was wrong. Perhaps the world around him had changed without his being aware. As a matter of fact, Marcia Davenport was likely to get along far better than Ellen in this world. He had been sensitive to the turmoil in her life these past few years, the struggle she had had to balance herself in this particular world of the small Mormon town. She would have a far tougher time of it than Marcia.

While Mr. Gillis was off on his defeated train of thought, Marcia was affirmed as the representative girl. He nodded his weary assent with the others. Paula Bushman spoke up, a little guiltily, since she really did concur with Charles. "I'd like to propose, in view of her talents and abilities, that Ellen Kent be given recognition on the program. Perhaps she could read one of her poems or a short essay or something."

Secretly she wondered if old Chuck might have something for that girl? 'She spends a lot of time with him after school and on those debate trips. Well, he had reasons with that wife of his,' she thought, but of course, she did feel that Ellen deserved some honors. There was a general agreement, almost in relief. As they were leaving the faculty room, Mr. Gillis heard Miss Wardle say to Miss McDonald, "Isn't Ellen Kent mixed up with that Hallsworth bunch, the one that had that nasty trouble this spring?"

"She goes with one of the boys, the crippled one," Miss McDonald replied. "I think it's better she didn't get to be representative girl. I don't think a lot of people would like it...there was her mother, you know, and that other scandal."

Charles Gillis didn't know whether to swear or cry. Knowing that neither would do much good, he went to his empty school room and sat down at his scarred desk. He had spent nearly twenty years in this room trying to stir the hearts and minds of hundreds of young people with the love of literature and language. So few had rewarded him like Ellen. She had been such a joy these past two years. She shared his sense of delight in the beauty and richness of language that he thought had almost died out of the world. Often when he read aloud to the class some of his most cherished lines, he felt that she alone listened, understood, responded fully. He had tried to guide her, give her encouragement with her writing, her poetry, knowing how little value the world at large placed on it. He wondered, had he given her anything that would help her to go forward into what he now knew was a perilous, often harsh life? He sighed. Ah, if he had his own to over again....

He picked up a book of poems that he intended giving her for a graduation present. It was a volume of the poems of Edna St. Vincent Millay. He had marked "Sonnet XXIX" and now he read it with a sense of sadness, "... Pity me that the heart is slow to learn/ What the swift mind beholds at every turn."

"Me, that's me," he said aloud, "and Ellen, yes." He underlined the passage and put an exclamation mark in the margin. As he inscribed the front of the book with her name and best wishes, he felt somehow reconciled. As a matter of fact, Ellen was not a "representative girl," thank God.

 C3

It was one of those exuberant May evenings that are only possible in the mountains in spring. The fine, crystal air was full of fragrance of lew leaves and blossoms, the exhilarating smell of earth renewing Life. On the lawn just outside the window of her bedroom Ellen could see the old crab apple tree loaded with extravagant pinkish-tinged white blossoms, each almost as large as the apples would be later. So many of them crowded on the tree that it was like a huge bridal bouquet. Above it through the coarse lace curtains she could see a corner of the bluish-silver sky.

Standing before the mirror in her slip, she felt a kinship with the tree, as though it alone expressed or understood the exhilarating, almost excessive blooming of life within her. She touched the pinkish-white skin of her throat, her arms, her gently swelling young breasts, burgeoning with life, pale petaled, and trembling with promise. She smelled the intoxicating fragrance of her own freshly washed body. Was it wrong to like the smell of yourself, the sweetness of your own skin, she wondered? She put our her hand to touch the image in the mirror. The hard, cold silver glass surprised her for, at that moment, she had believed in the existence of her own reflection. She had felt that the serene loveliness of the young girl on that gleaming surface was the real one and not the teeming mass of confusions, hopes, dreams, loves, hates, joys, sorrows, ambitions that she knew herself to be. If only one could be what one could make the surface appear, or better still, as simple and graceful as the tree. She saw it shimmeringly reflected in the side of the mirror through the curtains. If only one could be like the tree, accepting life and its seasons; accepting in bitter winter, that the tangle of stark, dead looking twigs would always burst into magnificent bloom in the spring; bearing the fruit of summer, then wearing the bright gypsy gown of colored leaves in the fall before submitting again, without anguish, to the winter. Accepting without so much torment and questioning the purposeful rhythm securely rooted in the earth, in the seasons, in the totality of life.

This was what her poem was about, the one she was going to read on the program at the graduation exercises tonight. She was practicing it in front of the mirror, a little nervous because she knew that it wasn't quite what was expected although Mr. Gillis had approved of it. He had helped her shape it up, encouraging her as he had done these past two years. In their last meeting, she thought he seemed a little sad and wanted to say something to her that he couldn't. Ellen felt guilty that she had not told him about the short dedication that she was going to read: "This poem is dedicated in respect and affection to my friend, Everett Gordon, the person who first helped and inspired me in my writing, with appreciation also to Mr. Charles Gillis, my teacher who has encouraged me a great deal."

How she wished Everett could have been there to hear her speak it clearly, defiantly to that audience, think what they would! She had sent him a graduation announcement and invitation in care of one of the sisters in Salt Lake, but she had no way of knowing whether or not he would receive it. Someday she would send him a copy of the poem if she could find out where he was so that he would know what the hours she had spent with him in the fine old house among his splendid books and what his gentle encouragement and understanding had meant to her in spite of that last ugly thing that had happened to them.

The garish chalk doll still stood on one corner of the dresser, her bland kewpie face smiling stupidly beneath her bedraggled crown of fuschia colored feathers. Ellen picked her up and smiled sadly. It was so different from all that Everett had been, had stood for in her life. She ought to throw it away as being unworthy of her memories of him. Yet there was something compelling about it, as though it held a secret she was yet to learn. Smoothing the doll's feathers, she set it back down. Some of the silver spangles crumbled off onto the dresser and sparkled in the softening light. False and cheap though it was, the brightness stood for something in her feelings for Everett that she had not lost.

Ellen was startled out of her reverie by the sound of an automobile pulling into the driveway. Surely Ferrin hadn't come already. No, it was her mother and Ed. A wave of gladness swept over her. She had so wanted her mother to be there tonight, to help her into the pale aqua blue chiffon dress that Irene had helped her choose at Schubachers. It lay across the bed, its lovely soft skirt spread out gracefully. Ellen caressed it with her eyes as she slipped into her housecoat and started for the door.

Irene and Grandma smoothed, patted and tucked her into the dress. Irene was also helping her rearrange her shining brown hair. Ellen had had a local beautician work on it, it had turned out too stiffly set in finger waves. As her mother was gently combing and fluffing it so that it fell in more becoming waves about her face, Ellen had the strange feeling that time had either evaporated or become fused in the image that she saw of herself and her mother in the mahogany frame of the mirror. The wounds between them had healed, leaving them separate women and yet eternally fused. There was a vaguely disturbing memory of another time that Ellen could not quite focus, another place when she had felt this transcendent bond with her mother.

How astonishingly beautiful her mother still was. She was wearing a beige crepe dress with elegant pleats and drapes and her dark hair was immaculately set. Her natural woman fragrance was subdued by an expensive perfume and her make up was applied with the hand of an artist. On the third finger of her left hand was a glittering set of diamond rings instead of the plain gold one that she had worn so long in Ellen's memory. Something of the softness and vulnerability was gone from her, yet there were violet shadows around her eyes that spoke of the deep pain and suffering she had known. Ellen with her square-cut Kent jaw and ordinary brown hair would never be so beautiful, she knew, but she didn't mind. Her heart was swollen with affection and tenderness, the joy of their nearness tonight. Suddenly her eyes filled with tears and the picture shimmered as though under water. She turned and threw her arms around Irene. Irene's full bosom shook with an unexpected sob. Neither of them could speak for several moments.

Ellen was finally able to say, "Thank you, Mama, I love you so much."

"I love you, too, Ellen," Irene murmured. "I'm so proud of you."

At last when they had moved apart, and Irene had carefully wiped her eyes to keep her mascara from smudging, she took something out of her purse wrapped in tissue paper. It was a string of pearls.

"I want you to have these," she said. "They are the ones your father gave me...that last Christmas. I know he would want you to have them at this time since...he couldn't be here." She fastened them around Ellen's neck. Ellen gave a gasp of delight and fear as she touched them.

"Oh, Ed and I bought you something else." Irene hastened to get over the emotional stress of the moment. "Something from the two of us." It was a cream colored velvet evening wrap.

Ferrin had arrived while Ellen was dressing and was talking to Ed in the front room. When Ellen entered, her mother's fingertips guiding her lightly, almost possessively as when she had been a little girl, both men rose and made appropriate male noises. Ellen was aware of Ferrin's deep and genuine admiration. It shown too transparently on his face, and he advanced with a white florist's box in which was an exquisite corsage of pink roses and white gardenias. Irene fastened it to her dress, and Ed put the wrap about her shoulders. She was so glowingly happy she even threw her arms around Ed and kissed him, leaving a pale lipstick smear on his cheek and making him blush.

"Don't I get one?" Ferrin teased. She reached up and pecked him on the cheek. "Thank you so much," she said, feeling a flush of emotion. He did look so very handsome in a new blue-gray suit so carefully tailored that, until he moved, it was not apparent that there was anything wrong. There was something fine and manly about him; Ellen knew that the love and tenderness that shown in his eyes was a prize not to be taken lightly.

Grandma was standing in the doorway, wiping the tears happily from under the rim of her gold rimmed glasses. Ellen went over to her and hugged her. "I love you, Grandma," she whispered, near tears herself. Grandma couldn't answer, overcome with love and pride, but also with sadness; Ellen would soon be leaving her.

When they arrived at the tabernacle, the nervous graduates, boys in stiff new suits, girls in soft, rainbow hued formals were lining up in the vestibule. The organ struck up the somber tones of "Pomp and Circumstance." In a dazzle of sound and floating sea of faces, Ellen marched, third in the line, down the right aisle to the stand, where, when, rustling, whispering, shuffling and coughing subsided, the graduation exercises for the class of '39, Merritsville High School began.

After the other speeches and before the final musical number, Ellen, with an encouraging wink from Mr. Gillis, stood up and read her poem. She read the dedication loud and clear and thought, but was not sure, that she heard a soft ripple of surprise in the audience but she plunged into the poem and sat down, not knowing, since applause was not permitted, what response it had elicited. She suspected rightly that not many people had heard it; those who did probably did not understand what she was trying to say and didn't care anyway. Oh well, it was all over. Trembling still from the normal exertion of performing, she sat quietly until the strains of the organ announced the presentation of diplomas. She accepted hers and the congratulations of the faculty and moved quickly to where she saw her family and Ferrin waiting for her.

She wasn't sure when, in the milling crowd at the back of the vestibule, she saw his face. She thought she must be dreaming but no, there, looking very well in spite of some apprehension in his face, was Everett. In a finely tailored new gray suit that made the gray in his wavy hair look splendidly distinguished, he moved toward her. With a strangled cry she broke away from Ferrin and her family and pushing through the crowd, almost rudely, tears blinding her eyes, she threw herself into his timidly extended arms. A great sob shook her whole body as she kissed him and put her head against his chest. She could feel his frail body shaking as he held her lightly but longingly.

All she could say was, "Everett, Everett, you're here, did you hear...? He nodded, so choked with emotion that he could not speak at all for a minute or so. "Ellen, my Ellen," he whispered into her hair. There are moments that seem like a whole lifetime; this was one of them even though little more than a minute or two was ticked off by the big, impassive oak framed clock on the back wall of the tabernacle.

Ellen wanted to tell him that she felt as though great, pearl-encrusted doors had swung wide, opening on a new world, as though magnificent gold and white wings were sprouting from her shoulders. For the briefest time, she was never sure how long, she knew she had experienced it–the miracle of love–forever an opening out, a lifting up. She knew this even while she knew and he knew that this was all there ever could be for them. It was not enough, not enough to fill the brief, but bleak, future for Everett; nor to assuage the confusion and longing for Ellen but it had to be. It was a tragic, though wonderful, thing for Everett, one for which he had been living most of his painful adult life. It was one for which Ellen would search through many years ahead to find again.

Ellen slowly became aware that people were staring at them, that her family were waiting uneasily. Irene had come over and touched her gently on the shoulder, only barely acknowledging Everett who turned to go. But Ellen would not let go of him and insisted on pulling him with the rest of them out into the spring night. They all gathered under the catalpa trees heavy with overwhelmingly sweet blooms. A lace of shadows from the street lights fell over them.

Aunt Dosey and Uncle Aaron and all the Walkers in their best clothes took turns congratulating and hugging Ellen. Lorraine, lovely in a white dress that would be her wedding dress shortly, hugged her. They cried a little, knowing how irrevocably their lives were changing. Grandma, Irene and Ed hovered proudly and then Ellen took Ferrin's hand and introduced him to Everett; she stood between them supremely happy, feeling that the world had come right at last. How she wished she could hold on to this moment, hold all the people she loved together in this silvery tinted warm spring night. But reality intervened.

There was some awkward shuffling and apologies. Ed and Irene guessed they would have to get started back to Salt Lake since they both had to work the next day. Lorraine and Ken were going on to the dance at the Pandora. Grandma was talking to Everett who explained that he would be staying a few days at the old house and would try to see them. He had some books and things he wanted to give Ellen. He gave her a friendly pat on the arm and promised to see her soon, but she had a cold, sad feeling as she saw his figure retreating in the shadows.

At last she and Ferrin were alone with Grandma. After they took her home, they made their way to Provo where Ferrin had made reservations at the best restaurant for a fine dinner since he couldn't take her to the graduation dance. They ate there in a strained silence. Ellen knew there was a small square box in Ferrin's coat pocket. She had felt it when she brushed against him. When she thought of it, she was filled with apprehension. It was a relief when the meal was over and they were back in the car.

"Where would you like to go?" Ferrin asked anxiously. "Maybe a show?"

"Not tonight, Ferrin," Ellen replied in a voice as steady as she could command. "I know this sounds strange but I would like to ride out toward your ranch, out over the western hills."

"Why, why there?" Ferrin asked in surprise.

"I'm not quite sure," Ellen hesitated. "I just have this strange feeling that I would like to go out there. Maybe it's because that was where my father was when he died. He was the only one of my family who wasn't with me tonight and then there's something else...I'm not quite sure of."

"All right," Ferrin sighed reluctantly. "It's your party tonight."

Ferrin took the lower road so that they didn't have to pass the Pandora again where the dance was in progress. The moon had come out and the soft, grayish-chiffon light clung to everything like a cobweb. As they passed the deserted sugar factory beyond Junction City, the old waste pond shone like a dark mirror. He reached out his arm, beckoning Ellen to come closer; she moved into the circle of it stiffly. The beautiful mood of the early evening had given way to a threatening storm.

As they drove along in silence, she watched the moon racing beside them like a greyhound. A lean gray cloud had crossed its face, very dark in the center but frayed out to silver on the edge. She shivered slightly, so Ferrin rolled up the window. Except for lonely farm houses, now mostly dark although it wasn't really late, they had left the town and people behind.

They had turned up the road that led toward the ranch house running along parallel with the smooth, swelling hills. How lonely, bleak, menacing they seemed. The last time she had been here was for Dod's funeral.

"There it is, the Hallsworth ranch by moonlight," Ferrin said with a bitter edge to his voice. They had begun to climb the gentle slope on top of which stood the gaunt ranch house surrounded by big, old cottonwood trees and a cluster of smaller buildings and corrals. Against the deep shadow of the undulating hills, the house reminded Ellen of something out of a movie, intentionally and dramatically ugly but strong. Its isolation and strength were made more forcefully grim by the black, angular shadows that the moonlight cast on its sharp gables.

Ferrin did not turn into the gate over which the sign of the ranch could be made out roughly in the eery light, but swung the car around to the southwest where the road led out to the hills. For miles and miles two hard, smooth ruts wound out over the barren swells of land now purplish-gray, deepening into black. The ruts looped back quite close to the house and corral and, as they passed by, Ellen saw a sagging clothesline propped up by a smooth gray pole which reflected the moonlight with a metallic sheen. On the line, carelessly pegged, hung several light colored feminine garments and some men's shirts. The image they evoked of the persons who now lived in the house, Simone and Willard Hallsworth, disturbed Ellen but she said nothing. Suddenly she regretted asking to come here. Why had she felt she must? Was she forcing herself to accept what she suspected she might?

Ferrin had maneuvered the car over the rutted road until the house was out of sight and then turned it around so that they were looking back over the moon-filled dish of the valley toward the towering granite mountains. The few lights in the valley looked comforting. When he had turned out the lights and set the brakes, he pulled her firmly to him. She could feel his breath warm against her face as he sought her mouth. He smelled faintly of shaving lotion, tobacco and new cloth, not unpleasant but she stiffened.

"Ellen," he whispered, hurt, "don't pull away from me. I love you so much, and I have something to want to say to you." He released her slightly and fumbled in his pockets. Turning on the dash lights, he opened a small, black velvet box; there they were, just as she had known they would be–the diamond set, engagement and wedding rings, larger than any that the other girls had or would get.

"I want you to marry me, Ellen." Ferrin rushed into his speech as though he had rehearsed it. "I need you, love you and I'll give you anything and everything you want. I know, I know I'm not as much as some men because of my...legs but they'll never keep me back. I promise you. I'll be running all of this someday and, Ellen," he stammered, his hand tightening on hers, "I'm as good as any man... in every other way. I'll get the doctor to tell you if you want." He stopped. Ellen knew he was suffering with embarrassment even though she couldn't see his face clearly in the dark.

She was stunned even though she had expected it for some time now; she too had rehearsed speeches, even trying one in which she accepted him. Why shouldn't she? After all the highest place in the land was filled by a man with crippled legs who had fought and overcome the same disease and tragedy that Ferrin had. Her mind told her that perhaps never again would she be offered anything better than what she had here and now; everything she knew about him, everything everybody said about him was good. In spite of this, she wanted to push the sparkling box away from her as though the rays were the eyes of a serpent. Ferrin had brought up the very things that were the hardest to confront. She felt so helpless. Try as she might, she was sure she could never convince him that it was not his crippled legs, it was not him; it was herself. She had not known until now what her feelings were, probably would not have if Everett hadn't come there tonight, if just for the briefest moment he hadn't held her in his arms and shown her what love might be. Even then she knew it must be a rare experience and one perhaps that could never endure in the course of ordinary life, but she knew, if only in the vague and troublesome way, that she had to seek further for this thing, a kind of liberating force, a tragic-beautiful, if fleeting meeting with another human soul. But how, how to make Ferrin understand this, that it hadn't happened to her with him.

She started to stammer something when he picked up her left hand and was about to transfer the ring from the box to her finger. She drew back with a sharp cry. "No, no, Ferrin, I can't, I... I don't want to get married yet."

"I know you don't love me, Ellen, the way I love you," he said in a tender, pleading voice, "and I don't care. I love you enough for both of us, forever and ever. You are the only girl I have ever loved. For me there will never be anyone else."

"Please don't say that," she cried. "It isn't fair. it isn't fair for you to do all the loving. I have a right to love to. I want to feel the way you say you do. And I don't. I don't know why. You are a wonderful, good, strong person, Ferrin. I'll always admire you but that's not love. I think you don't love me as much as you love what you think I am.... You know, I've tried to make you see that I'm not perfect."

She drew her hand away and put both her hands to her face in distress.

"Maybe in a year or two, in a little while, do you think you might change your mind? Don't you think you could come to love, like, me a little? I bought a lot in Junction City and we could build just the kind of house you wanted and... here keep these." He thrust the box into her hand. "If ever you feel like you could put them on even if it's ten years, I'll be waiting."

Ellen's hand was too limp to close around the box; it rolled to the floor. Neither of them could move to pick it up. The night had turned cold, black, as lonely as the endless silent hills. Suddenly Ellen noticed a shadow moving and heard the faint sound of hoof beats. Both of them turned to see a dark horse and rider strike out across the hills. As horse and rider sped along the ridge silhouetted against the silvery sky, they could see long hair flying out behind. "Who's that?" Ellen asked although she had already guessed.

"I guess it's Simone," Ferrin replied in a low, cross voice.

"Riding around at night, whatever for?" Ellen was incredulous.

Ferrin shrugged. "Oh she does what she wants to when she wants to do it." He leaned over the seat and peered intently after the dark speeding figure. "She better not have my horse. I told her I'd wring her neck if she touched him," he muttered.

Ellen leaned beside him, peering toward the horizon. How wonderful to be so free, free of time, of ties, of ideas and customs and...yes, if only briefly, free of people. The earlier mood of the evening when the safety and warmth of the family seemed so ultimately desirable had completely vanished. Ellen had an overwhelming urge to break away, violently, quickly. "I wish I could do that," she whispered almost to herself.

"You could have a horse, two or three, if you wanted," Ferrin said moving toward her putting his arm around her. "Fact is I even had a colt picked out for you, a wedding present."

Ellen started, wished he would take his arm away. "Oh, well, it's not exactly... I don't mean that, just ride. I mean be free, like Simone, not worry about anything, about what people wanted you to be or feel or think."

"You *never* want to be like *her*!" Ferrin exploded.

Ellen sighed and turned back around in the seat. As she moved, her foot touched the ring box. She picked it up and handed it to Ferrin. "I know I can't explain what I mean. I don't quite understand myself why I feel so different from everyone here, why I want things different from most girls. I don't know why I change my mind so much. Just this afternoon, I thought for a few minutes that it would be wonderful to be with you, to have a family...but when I saw Everett...."

"You're not in love with him?" Ferrin choked the words out. "He, he's an old man!"

"Of course not, it's not like that, it's that he taught me about how life could be with books and music and things." She wilted, feeling so dreadfully tired, so inexpressibly futile. "Please, Ferrin, don't misunderstand me."

She lapsed into silence. Ferrin sat with his arms crossed on the steering wheel, his head lowered on them. They remained that way for a long time, the moon washing the hills with its sterile light. At last he moved, wearily putting the car in motion and drove Ellen home.

He took her to the door, brushed her face with a light kiss and said mournfully, "If you ever change your mind, Ellen... "

Ellen stood inside the screen door, listening to the jerky rhythm of his crippled leg being dragged through the gravel of the path. In her mind was the image of a dark horse and rider racing across the moonlit western hills.

A week later Ellen and Grandma walked along the streets in sparkling June sunshine. Merritsville, though run-down, looked warm, congenial. Ellen, dressed in a new blue suit, was exhilarated but sad. In her purse was a letter informing her of a scholarship to the University of Utah, due to Mr. Gillis no doubt. Ed and Irene had assured her that she would be welcome to live with them, that they would help her go to college.

They avoided the Gordon house where there was a prominent, "For Sale" sign, but passed the house where Ellen had spent most of her life. It seemed a whole life time away.

Ellen had seen Ferrin once more that week and finally agreed that he could come to Salt Lake to see her.

Wearing a yellow straw hat with a bunch of artificial cherries, Grandma was dressed to do some shopping after she saw Ellen off on the Interurban to Salt Lake. She called cheerfully to folks going briskly about business as usual. Brother Washburn was standing in front of the store, his gold watch chain gleaming across his ample stomach.

"Mornin', Addie," he greeted. "You two off to the city?"

He noted the small case Ellen was carrying. Grandma explained.

"Oh, so this is Irene's girl. My she's grown-up, hardly recognized her. Pretty as her mother and smart I hear."

Ellen felt a flush of annoyance.

"Leavin' us like all the young folks." Brother Washburn teetered on his polished shoes. "That's the way of it. Can't blame 'em, not much here in these times. Well, good luck, Ellen. Be sure to come back and see us when you get famous." They shook hands and crossed the street to wait for the train.

A small ray of light danced along the railroad tracks. The train would be coming from Provo, from the east where the great mountains were in shadow. Addie and Ellen stood in silence, knowing that the long, dark years were ending.

As the train swayed into sight, Ellen threw her arms around her grandmother. "I'll be back, Grandma. I'll always love you."

"I know," Addie comforted her. "It'll all be fine. We'll always be here. Times are gettin' better."

Ellen believed it as she boarded the train for the city and a new life.

ABOUT THE AUTHOR

LaVon B. Carroll is a native of Utah who experienced the 1930's first hand. She has won many awards in Utah and nationally. She received her A.A. from Weber College, B.S. and M.A. from Utah State University, and Ph.D. from the University of Utah. She studied at the University of California at Berkeley.

She traveled widely in Europe and did Post-doctoral work at Oxford University in England, University College Dublin in Ireland, and the University of Edinburgh in Scotland.

Most recently, the author was awarded an Honorary Doctorate of Humanities from Weber State University.

Dr. Carroll taught English and Literature at Weber State for twenty-four years and retired in 1986. She was selected Poet of the Year by the Utah State Poetry Society in 1982, and published *The Shrouded Carousel.*

The League of Utah Writers awarded her first place for her novels in 1989 and 1995.

Dr. Carroll is married and has two children.